Formwork
A guide to good practice

Joint Committee of the Concrete Society
and
The Institution of Structural Engineers

Acknowledgements

The Concrete Society and The Institution of Structural Engineers acknowledge the contribution made by the West Midlands Regional Committee of the Society to the initiation and completion of this work.

The Joint Committee wishes to express its gratitude to all those participating organisations and individuals who have assisted in the preparation of this guide, and in particular to Rapid Metal Developments Ltd., Tarmac Construction Holdings Ltd., GKN-Kwikform Ltd., Alfred McAlpine Construction South Region Ltd., and the University of Birmingham.

The Committee also thank all those who supplied the photographs included in this guide. Many organisations have taken advertising space in Appendix G and The Concrete Society expresses its gratitude for the support given to the guide by the inclusion of these advertisements.

The Data Sheet in Appendix E is reproduced from CIRIA Report 108, *Concrete Pressure on Formwork*, by permission of the Director of CIRIA. It is also available from CIRIA in laminated sheet format as Special Publication 39.

Published by The Concrete Society, Devon House, 12-15 Dartmouth Street, London SW1H 9BL in conjunction with The Institution of Structural Engineers, 11 Upper Belgrave Street, London SW1X 8BH

First Published August 1986

ISBN 0 946691 15 0 (cased)
      0 946691 16 9 (limp)

British Library Cataloguing in Publication Data
Concrete Society
    Formwork: a guide to good practice
    1. Concrete construction — Formwork
    I. Title   II. Concrete Society   III. Institution of Structural Engineers
    624.1'834   TA682.44

    ISBN 0-946691-15-0
    ISBN 0-946691-16-9 Pbk

Designed by Keating Industrial Design, 42 Church Crescent, Muswell Hill, London N10 3NE

Index prepared by Paul Nash, Kirkton Farmhouse, Abernyte, Inchture, Perthshire PH 14 9SS

Typeset and printed by The Chameleon Press Limited, 5-25 Burr Road, Wandsworth, London SW18 4SG

Members of the Joint Committee

Chairman: **P. F. Pallett, BSc, CEng, MICE, MBIM**
Rapid Metal Developments Limited

Secretary: **R. T. Ward**
Tarmac Construction Holdings Limited

Section
Chairman: **D. W. Lovering (Sections Two and Three)**
GKN-Kwikform Limited
P. F. Pallett (Sections Four and Five)
Rapid Metal Developments Limited
P. R. Luckett, CEng, MIMechE (Sections Six and Seven)
Chart Formwork Limited

Members: **J. E. Ash, BSc, PhD, CEng, MICE**
University of Birmingham
D. A. Biddlecombe, CEng, MICE
GKN-Kwikform Limited
J. N. Clarke, BSc(Tech)
The Concrete Society
D. K. Doran, BSc, DIC, CEng, FICE, FIStructE, MSocIS
Private Consultant
A. B. Hall, BSc, FIWSc
Finnish Plywood International
I. R. Hart, TechCEI, MIE, FISM
Consultant to British Solvent Oils Limited
D. J. Irvine, BSc, CEng, FICE
Tarmac Construction Holdings Limited
Rev. M. James, CEng, MIStructE, MICE
Health & Safety Executive
F. Lane
Sir Robert McAlpine & Sons Limited
I. D. G. Lee, BSc, FIWSc
Chipboard Promotion Association
B. H. North, CEng, FICE, FIStructE, FIHT, FWeldI
Kennedy Henderson Limited
J. A. Partridge, CBE, ARA, FRIBA
Howell, Killick, Partridge & Amis
G. W. Richards, BSc, CEng, MICE, MIStructE
Alfred McAlpine Construction Limited South Region
J. G. Richardson, FIIM, MICT
Cement & Concrete Association
H. W. Skeemer
Primeplot Limited
G. F. True, HNC Mech Eng, MICT
Tarmac Construction Holdings Limited
D. A. Warrior, BA(Dunelm)
Pilkington Reinforcements Limited
A. S. White
Scaffolding Great Britain Limited
J. R. White, BA(Oxon)
Cordek Limited
M. A. Williams, BSc, CEng, MICE, MIHT
Health & Safety Executive
C. J. Wilshere, OBE, BA, BAI, CEng, FICE
Laing Design and Construction Services
J. F. Withers, CEng, MIMechE
Timber Research and Development Association

Corresponding
Members: **T. A. Harrison, BSc, PhD, CEng, MICE, MICT**
Cement & Concrete Association
J. Melville, BSc, CEng, MICE
Balfour Beatty Construction (Scotland) Limited
D. Maher
Q. R. Systems Limited
R. F. Roberts, BSc, CEng, MICE
Cement & Concrete Association

Summary

This guide has been prepared to promote good practice in the design, specification, construction and safe use of formwork for both insitu and precast concrete. It contains information for the economic and safe design of wall formwork used in both building and civil engineering construction. When used for the design of soffit formwork the guide is intended to be read in conjunction with BS 5975, *Code of Practice for Falsework*. The guide assumes that formwork will be designed by persons with the relevant design and practical experience. The guide gives information for the building design team, for the contractor as well as for the sub-contractor and supplier. It supercedes Concrete Society Technical Report No. 13, published in 1977.

Wall formwork for a motorway pier at a railway crossing on the M42 motorway

concrete society

Contents

List of Figures

List of Tables

Section One
General

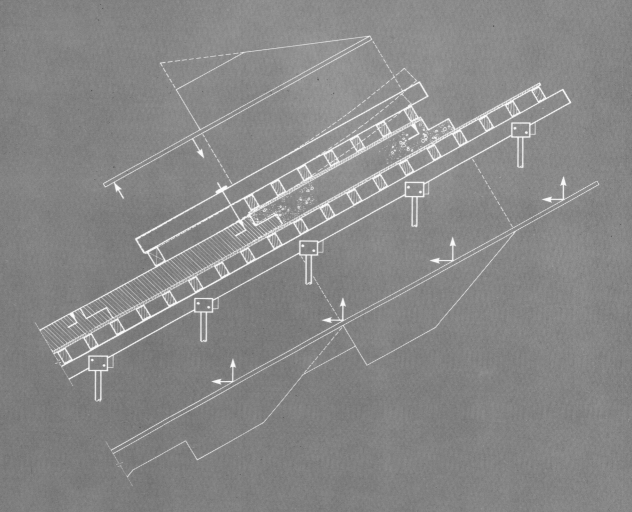

concrete
society

Section One – General

Section 1.1 – Introduction

This guide is a joint report of The Concrete Society and the Institution of Structural Engineers and was approved by both bodies in March 1986. In preparing the guide, The Concrete Society through its Construction and Civil Engineering Steering Group set up a special committee in 1982 with the West Midlands Region of the Society acting as a focus, to review the Concrete Society Technical Report No. 13, *Formwork* – The report of a joint committee of the Society and the Institution of Structural Engineers (Ref. 1) which was published in 1977.

Concrete Society Technical Report No. 13, Formwork. (Ref. 1).

The committee invited assistance from experts in the industry including Contractors, Architects, Consulting Engineers, Educational Establishments, Specialist Suppliers and Trade Associations in the preparation of this revision. In addition advice was sought by correspondence from other experts.

BS 5975 Code of Practice for Falsework (Ref. 2).

BS 5975 *Code of Practice for Falsework* (Ref. 2) was published in 1982 and it was desirable that this guide be written as a complementary document to that code. The code only covered the support of soffit formwork, so for wall formwork the guide would need to be self sufficient. The format selected was similar to BS 5975 with separate sections on materials, loadings and design.

CIRIA Report 108. Concrete Pressure on Formwork. (Ref. 3).

BS 5268 Structural use of timber Part 2: Code of practice for permissible stress design, materials and workmanship. (Ref. 4).

Since publication of TR13 there have been several innovations in formwork. In 1985 CIRIA Report 108 *Concrete Pressure on Formwork* was published (Ref. 3). The introduction of strength classes for timber and details for plywood properties in BS 5268 *Structural use of timber Part 2: Code of practice for permissible stress design, materials and workmanship* in 1984 (Ref. 4) has revised the allowable loads on wood-based products. Aluminium members have increased in use in the industry.

Wherever possible the guide states the acceptable working values for structural properties of members to enable direct use by designers and specifiers. Other changes have been the introduction of improved proprietary formwork systems and the increasing use of permanent formwork to reduce labour content of formwork in use. Many of the systems are described in detail within the guide as their nature and operation are often not fully appreciated. New materials and ideas are given fuller consideration in the document than conventional materials and equipment.

Worked examples in Appendices C and D.

Section 1.6, on economics.

A principal recommendation of the 1977 Report was that design guides and text books to assist the education of personnel at all levels in the Industry should be commissioned. It was considered that this had not been achieved in sufficient detail and that The Concrete Society should provide the necessary guidance and authoritative text for the Industry. This guide has been written to promote good practice and give detailed guidance to both the newcomer and the regular user of formwork. Several sections contain more detail than will normally be necessary for the experienced reader, in particular Section 5 on design, but the result represents a significant contribution to the Industry by identifying the problems and forces associated with formwork and providing for their solution. The worked examples in Appendices C and D will allow the reader to follow the design philosophy of the guide. Section 1.6, on economics, is included to familiarise the inexperienced with the essential factors involved in the design of formwork which affect the final economics of both the temporary and permanent works.

Typical loading cases in Appendix B.

The very practical nature of formwork, its attention to detail and the experience of the persons engaged in its design, based on their own knowledge and judgement, recommend that exhaustive and complex mathematics are rarely justified, and for this reason the guide is deliberately written in an easily understood format. The use of the tabulated typical loading cases in Appendix B will, with engineering judgement, provide safe and economic formwork designs for the majority of applications.

A separate section in the guide on computers and their application was not considered necessary as they analyse the mathematical problem and not the design problem. Whenever a computer is used in formwork design the relevance of the answer should always be related to the accuracy and assumptions of the initial input. For example, in a wall form design the assessment of design concrete pressure will require judgement based on several factors; changing any one factor by a small amount may cause a disproportionate change in the pressure and change the answer, whether calculated by computer, or otherwise. The elasticity of the formwork system will also influence the final outcome on the site, thus rendering an exhaustive analysis unrealistic.

Research Recommendations are listed in Section 8.

Further research and investigation are still needed in some areas and recommendations are listed in Section 8.

This document has taken into consideration the written comments on TR13 received by The Concrete Society prior to January 1983.

In this guide the approximation is made that a mass of 100 kilograms (kg) exerts a vertical force of one kilonewton (kN).

A mass of 100 kilograms (kg) exerts a vertical force of one kilonewton (kN).

The diagrams in the guide are indicative of formwork systems and the concrete pressure diagrams are shown acting in the 'wrong direction'. This method of indicating the pressure is used throughout the guide and is standard practice in the Industry.

Section 1.2 – Scope

This guide covers good practice in the design, construction and safe use of formwork employed in insitu and precast concrete work. The guide is complementary to BS 5975 *Code of Practice for Falsework* (Ref. 2) and is intended primarily for use by the temporary works designer (TWD) and by those involved in supplying, constructing and supervising the work. Additional information is provided to assist the permanent works designer (PWD) to take appropriate account of formwork in designing and specifying the permanent works.

BS 5975 Code of Practice for Falsework (Ref. 2).

Section 1.3 – References

The full titles of standards, publications and articles referred to in the guide are given in Section 9. The number of the reference is included in brackets in the text. In Section 3.3.3 and Section 5.9 several British Standards have been listed for information only and these are not referenced in Section 9. BS 5975 (Ref. 2) is considered to be a complementary document and is not always referenced in the text.

A useful trade index of proprietary equipment suppliers is given in *The Concrete Year Book* published annually (Ref. 5). In addition, advertisements in Appendix G provide further information on specialist suppliers.

Advertisements in Appendix G provide further information on specialist suppliers.

An additional list of publications is given in the bibliography in Section 10. This is not an exhaustive list, neither is it representative of the opinion of the committee; therefore readers will require to make their own assessment of the validity and relevance of the document(s).

Bibliography in Section 10.

Names and addresses of relevant organisations are listed in Appendix F.

Addresses of organisations are listed in Appendix F.

Section 1.4 – Definitions and Abbreviations

The following definitions are used in this guide. They are generally in accordance with BS 5975 *Code of Practice for Falsework* and with BS 4340 *Glossary of Formwork Terms* (Ref. 6) (under revision).

Backpropping   Means by which construction loads are distributed through more than one level of construction.

Bow   Curvature of the length or width of a component expressed as a deviation from a straight line connecting the extremities.

Camber   The intentional upwards curvature of a beam or form, either established initially to compensate for subsequent deflection under load, or produced as a permanent effect for aesthetic reasons.

Component   A part of the formwork system used and identifiable as a distinct unit.

Deviation   The difference between an actual size or position and a specified size or position.

Factor of safety   The ratio of ultimate load to the maximum working load.

Falsework   Any temporary structure used to support a permanent structure while it is not self-supporting.

Formwork   A structure, usually temporary, but in some cases wholly or partly permanent, used to contain poured concrete to mould it to the required dimensions and support it until it is able to support itself. It consists primarily of the face contact material and the bearers that directly support the face contact material.

Face contact material   The material in direct contact with the poured concrete acting as the containment shape. It will normally produce a mirror image on the concrete finish.

Permissible stress   The stress that can be sustained safely by a structural material under the particular condition of service or loading.

Permissible deviation   The specified limit(s) of deviation.

Repropping	A system used during construction operations in which the original supports to a member being cast are removed and replaced in a sequence planned to avoid any damage to the partially cured concrete.
Strength class	A classification of timber based on particular values of grade stress.
Tolerance	The difference between the limits within which a size or position should lie. Tolerance is an absolute value without sign but the dimension or axis to which it applies has to be stated.

The following abbreviations are used in this guide:-

ABS	acrylonitrile butadiene styrene
APA	American Plywood Association
BRE	Building Research Establishment
BS	British Standard
BSI	British Standards Institution
C&CA	Cement and Concrete Association
Cat.	Category
CEGB	Central Electricity Generating Board
CIRIA	Construction Industry Research and Information Association
CITB	Construction Industry Training Board
cm	centimetre
COFI	Council of Forest Industries of British Columbia
CP	Code of Practice
CPA	Chipboard Promotion Association
DTp	Department of Transport
EPS	expanded polystyrene
Fig.	Figure
ggbfs	ground granulated blastfurnace slag
GIS	good one side
GRC	glass fibre reinforced cement
GRCA	Glass Fibre Reinforced Cement Association
GRP	glass fibre reinforced plastic
HMSO	Her Majesty's Stationery Office
HSE	Health and Safety Executive
HT	high tensile
kg	kilogram
kN	kilonewton
LHPBFC	low heat Portland blastfurnace cement
m	metre
mm	millimetre
MS	mild steel
N	newton
NAFC	National Association of Formwork Contractors
NGRDL	National Grading Rules for Dimension Lumber (Canada)
NLGA	National Lumber Grading Association (Canada)
OPC	ordinary Portland cement
PBFC	Portland blastfurnace cement
perp'r	perpendicular
pfa	pulverised-fuel ash
PPFAC	Portland pulverised-fuel ash cement
PSA	Property Services Agency
PVC	polyvinyl chloride
PWD	permanent works designer
Ref.	Reference
RHPC	rapid-hardening Portland cement
SC	strength class
SRPC	sulphate-resisting Portland cement
SWL	safe working load
TE	tempered
TRADA	Timber Research and Development Association
TWD	temporary works designer
UK	United Kingdom
UKWFBS	United Kingdom Water Fittings Byelaws Scheme
WBP	weather and boil-proof
WRC	Water Research Centre

Section 1.5 – Symbols

The following symbols are used in this guide:-

Symbol	Quantity	Unit of Measurement
A	Cross sectional area of member	m²
A_F	Face area of formwork	m²
B	Overall width of beam or section	m
C_1	Coefficient for concrete pressure on shape	–
C_2	Coefficient for concrete pressure on type of mix	–
D	Overall depth of beam or section	m
d	Dimension	m
E	Modulus of elasticity of material	kN/m²
F_c	Compressive force	kN
F_p	Force arising from concrete pressure	kN
F_t	Tensile force	kN
FG	Direction of face grain (in plywood)	–
f	Permissible stress	kN/m² or N/mm²
H	Form height	m
h	Height	m
h_f	Windward height of formwork	m
I	Second moment of area of member (Moment of inertia)	m⁴
K_n etc	Modification factors for timber and plywood	–
k	Coefficient to allow for the continuity of sheet material on multiple spans	–
L	Length of one span of member (measured centre to centre)	m
L_c	Length of cantilever member from its support	m
L_w	Width between vertical forms	m
l_a	Length of lever arm	m
M	Moment of resistance	kNm
P_{max}	Maximum concrete pressure	kN/m²
P	Single vertically applied force or load	kN
q	Average shear stress	kN/m²
R	Rate of rise of concrete in a form	m/h
range	The total of largest positive and negative deflection in a multi-span beam/member	m
S	Shear capacity or permissible shear load	kN
S_s	Shear load for sheet material	kN/metre run
T	Total triangular force on one span or cantilever of a member	kN
t	Thickness of sheet material	m
W	Vertically applied force	kN
W_c	Mass of concrete	kN
W_f	Mass of formwork per face (self-weight)	kN
W_m	Maximum wind force on formwork	kN
W_s	Total load uniformly distributed on one span of sheet material per metre length of support	kN/m
W_w	Working wind force on formwork	kN
Z	Section modulus of member	m³
δ	Deflection in one span, or tip deflection in case of cantilever, measured from the line of supports	m

Section 1.6 – Economics of Formwork and Falsework

Section 1.6.1 – General

See Table 1.

The cost of formwork and its associated falsework is a significant element of the total cost of constructing any concrete structure. In a typical insitu reinforced concrete building the formwork and falsework may amount to nearly 30% of the total cost of the frame (see Table 1). In other types of construction (e.g. insitu concrete bridges) the proportion may rise to 45%; in a particular bridge structure the proportion was 65%.

See also Section 6.1 and Fig. 102.

From Table 1 it can be seen that where reasonable reuse of formwork materials is possible, the cost of labour and plant has the greatest influence on the unit price. It follows that efforts to reduce the cost of making, fixing and striking formwork are likely to yield greater savings than merely seeking the use of cheaper formwork materials. (See also Section 6.1 and Fig. 102). One way of eliminating striking of formwork is to use permanent formwork.

Item	Material Cost	Labour and Plant Cost	% of Total Cost
Concrete	12%	8%	20%
Reinforcement	19%	6%	25%
Formwork	6%	22%	28%
Sundries	18%	9%	27%
Total	55%	45%	100%

Note to Table 1:   *The formwork cost is related to the number of uses. This example assumes several uses of the formwork. See Fig.102.*

Table 1.   *Typical Construction Costs for a Reinforced Concrete Frame*

Section 1.6.2 – Influence of the Permanent Works Designer (PWD)

Table 1.

The permanent works designer (PWD) should be aware of the inter-relationships between the costs of concrete, reinforcement, formwork and other items. Some typical costs are shown in Table 1; but the repetitive use of formwork will reduce the unit costs. Often a small increase in the size of a concrete member will make the placing and satisfactory compaction of the concrete easier and more assured whilst adding little to the overall cost. Thus the PWD's selection of member sizes and arrangements should take into account the effects of these on the formwork and other construction activities.

Other factors which can have an adverse influence on formwork costs are:

(a)   Variations in column centres.
(b)   Variations in slab soffits.
(c)   Variations in wall heights.
(d)   Variations in beam sizes.
(e)   Steps and staggers in walls and slabs.
(f)   Box-outs.
(g)   Inserts, particularly in walls.
(h)   Corbels.
(i)   Special joints.
(j)   Special grades of tolerances for line, level and plane.
(k)   Inappropriate as-cast finishes.
(l)   Restrictions on the use, type and position of ties.
(m)   Restrictions on sequence and timing of construction.

The PWD should have regard for these factors in his design concept and attempt to dissuade other members of the design team from requiring them, unless they are fully appraised of the costs involved.

Section 1.6.3 – Influence of the Temporary Works Designer (TWD)

The shape of the formwork follows from the requirements of the permanent works drawings and specification. However, within these parameters the temporary works designer (TWD) must make a number of decisions which affect the initial cost of the formwork, the cost of its use on site, and the indirect costs associated with other construction activities. The objective is to produce a functional temporary works design. A well engineered formwork and falsework scheme can have an effect on quality and cost well beyond the benefits accruing directly to the concrete work. For economy and good results formwork should be kept simple.

Many of the factors affecting cost will be decided during the preparation of the temporary works design brief (see also Section 2.9). The construction management will call for certain features as a consequence of site or programme restraints. These may include:

See also Section 2.9.

(a)   Time of construction (season) and the need for insulation or solar protection.
(b)   Mix design and concrete grade together with rate of placing concrete (maximum and optimum).
(c)   Crane capacity (weight and height).
(d)   Key dates for all or parts of the structure.
(e)   Limitations imposed by phased construction.
(f)   Site restrictions.
(g)   Availability of key labour.
(h)   Limitations on working hours, noise etc.
(i)   Availability of existing formwork/falsework equipment (plant holding etc).

Other factors will be added to the brief by the TWD including those listed in BS 5975, Clause 41.1 (Ref. 2).

BS 5975, Clause 41.1 (Ref. 2).

It will then be necessary to consider the concept of the temporary works design to conform with the brief and to consider the cost implications of the choices available. These may include:

(a)   Position of construction joints.
(b)   Few large pours or many small pours.
(c)   Inexpensive face material with few uses versus more expensive material with more uses. Alternatively, allow for refacing and/or repairs. (See Fig. 102.)
(d)   Clear span or multiple support.
(e)   Ease of stripping and refixing (cycle time).
(f)   The need for backpropping and repropping.
(g)   Purchase or hire of support materials.

See Fig. 102.

The contract TWD may also consider proposing modifications to the design of the permanent works to permit the use of his preferred methods of construction and available equipment. Such modifications could only be undertaken after the full implications have been assessed and evaluated, and would need the approval of the PWD. When assessing the possible benefits the TWD should allow for the additional time (and costs) which may be expended when seeking such approval and during redesign.

concrete society

Section Two
Preamble to Design

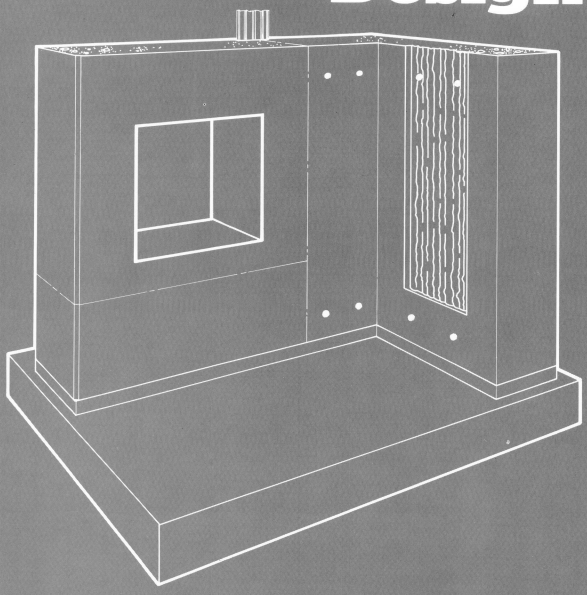

concrete
society

Section Two – Preamble to Design

Section 2.1 – General

Whenever carrying out a formwork design, whether simple or complex, the temporary works designer (TWD) will require to have access to certain detailed information prior to commencing the design. Often the procedure for collating this information is formalised within an organisation. This section of the guide details the collation of that information, commencing with the relationships between the various parties to the design and then outlining the statutory requirements for safety. The comprehensive requirements for the formwork are covered by the formwork specification, the finishes, the tolerances and the permissible deflections of the formwork. Finally all the information is assembled into the TWD's brief before design proper is started.

Formwork designer's brief, Section 2.9.

Responsibility for achieving the specified result always remains with the contractor. Any approval that the PWD may give to formwork proposals does not reduce this responsibility.

Section 2.2 – Parties to the Design

A satisfactory standard of construction requires the cooperation of all the parties concerned in the design. The principal parties usually involved are the permanent works designer (PWD), the contractor, the sub-contractors, and the supplier of specialist or proprietary equipment.

Section 2.2.1 – Permanent Works Designer (PWD)

The permanent works designer (PWD) should:

(a) Have due regard to economy and feasibility of formwork in preparing the design of the structure, by rationalising dimensions and simplifying outlines to allow reuse and to reduce complexity of forms.

(b) Describe adequately the required outlines and finishes by drawings and specification clauses and, if necessary, amplified by other suitable means.

(c) Make available samples of any special surface finish or member to illustrate what is required and indicate where its uses can be seen.

(d) Specify any limits which have to be placed on formwork removal, repropping and support of the completed structure.

(e) Specify any limits on size of pours, position of construction joints and any special sequences of construction required by the design.

(f) State for what work, if any, the contractor will be required to submit details of the formwork for comment before fabrication is commenced.

(g) Describe any trial panels or members which the contractor is required to construct for approval before work is begun.

(h) When considering specifying proprietary equipment, such as waffle or trough moulds or sculptured forms, in order to produce a particular result, he should satisfy himself that the result can be achieved from the equipment in question, for example, by consulting the proprietary supplier or examining examples of finished work.

Section 2.2.2 – Contractor

The contractor undertaking the work should:

(a) Examine the specification, drawings, sample panels etc at tender stage, to ensure that prices are properly formulated.

(b) Raise with the PWD, during tender stage, any point in the contract documents which is considered insufficiently clear to price properly.

(c) Draw to the attention of the PWD any items which require clarification.

(d) State clearly any alternatives to specified methods which may be used. Quoted rates for the work should be for methods as specified, but rates may also be given for alternatives offered.

(e) Design and construct formwork to the appropriate standard to achieve the specified results and to ensure the safety of all parties concerned.

(f) Ensure adequate quality of materials, workmanship and supervision to achieve the specified requirements.

(g) When specified by the PWD, provide details of formwork for comment and/or approval before commencing fabrication.

(h) Construct trial panels or members if specified, and obtain the approval of the PWD before proceeding further with the work.

(i)   Ensure that all proprietary formwork specified complies with the description on which the design of the concrete work has been based.

(j)   Provide any formwork sub-contractor with full information from the documents and details of the work to be carried out.

(k)   Ensure that the terms of appointment of any formwork sub-contractor are clearly set out and agreed, and that the sub-contractors adequately discharge all responsibilities entrusted to them (see Section 5.1.1).

See Section 5.1.1.

Section 2.2.3 – Sub-contractor

It has become very common for contractors to employ specialist sub-contractors to carry out formwork operations. These sub-contractors are almost always of the contractor's own choice. Having appointed a sub-contractor, the main contractor should supervise the design and erection in such a way that operations are carried out in a safe manner and that the specified result is achieved. Only when there are very special requirements for formwork, perhaps involving special decorative finishes or important structural elements, are specialist sub-contractors nominated by the PWD in the main contract.

The range and scope of the sub-contractor's work can vary considerably depending on the nature of the job in question, the contractor's requirements and the sub-contractor's capabilities. It is neither possible nor desirable to make detailed recommendations in this connection. The trade association for formwork sub-contractors is the National Association of Formwork Contractors (NAFC). See Appendix F for address.

National Association of Formwork Contractors. See Appendix F for address.

When a sub-contractor is appointed, the contractor's contractual and statutory responsibilities for quality and safety of work respectively cannot be delegated to them, though at the same time the sub-contractor has duties regarding safety under the Health and Safety at Work, etc Act (Ref. 7). (See also Sections 2.3 and 5.1.1.)

Health and Safety at Work, etc Act (Ref. 7).

See also Sections 2.3 and 5.1.1.

Section 2.2.4 – Supplier of Specialist or Proprietary Equipment

Suppliers are required under the Health and Safety at Work Act (Ref. 7) to ensure that their products are properly designed for safe use and to provide sufficient information for this (see also Section 3.6).

See also Section 3.6.

In addition they may provide a design service to relate the use of their products to specific jobs. Where the contractor intends to make use of such a service he should provide a comprehensive design brief.

Section 2.3 – Safety

The Health and Safety at Work, etc Act 1974 (Ref. 7) has carried over into Statute Law the Common Law concept of a 'duty of care' and covers most work situations in respect of safety and health, not only for employers and employees but also for the self-employed, persons in control of premises and members of the public affected by work activities.

Health and Safety at Work, etc Act (Ref. 7).

Employers now have a statutory duty to ensure that their employees are given adequate information, training, supervision, and that they are provided with a safe and healthy place of work.

The Act places responsibilities for safety on all parties in the construction industry.

A person who designs, manufactures, imports or supplies any article or substance for use at work must ensure, so far as is reasonably practicable, that the article or substance is designed, constructed or manufactured so as to be safe and its use not injurious to health. Also adequate information about the use of the article or substance, with details of any necessary precautions, should be provided.

The Act also enables the Factory Inspectorate to take action by issuing notices:

Improvement Notices give any person who contravenes the law a specified period for the contravention to be remedied and the defective item or system brought up to standard.

Prohibition Notices can become effective immediately or state a time after which the activity will be prohibited unless the required steps are taken.

Particular safety considerations are outlined below:

(a)   The provisions of adequate access and working platforms are covered by the Construction (Working Places) Regulations 1966 (Ref. 8). This is an important consideration in formwork design. Section 7.5.2 gives detailed guidance on access and working platforms.

Construction (Working Places) Regulations 1966 (Ref. 8).

Section 7.5.2.

(b) The mechanical handling of formwork on site is covered by the Construction (Lifting Operations) Regulations 1961 (Ref. 9). Although not strictly formwork, it is a critical operation on site. Section 5.9 of this guide gives references and design information for formwork when mechanised handling is involved.

Section 5.9.

(c) The increasing use of chemicals on site can cause its own hazards. A useful guide is the CIRIA publication *A Guide to Safe Use of Chemicals in Construction* (Ref. 10). Particularly in enclosed environments, toxic fumes can be dangerous. Users of such substances should be made aware of the applications and limitations of each chemical.

A Guide to Safe Use of Chemicals in Construction (Ref. 10).

(d) Particular care is necessary in striking soffit and beam forms. Guidance on suitable striking procedures is given in Section 5.3.6.

Section 5.3.6.

The formwork designer and the site personnel should all be aware of the detailed requirements for safety in the assembly, handling and striking of formwork. Some general items for consideration are given in Section 7.5.

Section 7.5.

Section 2.4 – Formwork Specification

Section 2.4.1 General

A properly conceived and appropriate specification is of paramount importance to all parties involved in the construction process. Unnecessarily exacting specifications which may be difficult to achieve should be avoided.

Department of Transport (Ref. 11).

Property Services Agency (Ref. 12).

Central Electricity Generating Board (Ref. 13).

BS 8110 (Ref. 14).

National Building Specification (Ref. 93).

See Section 8.1, Item 4.

Section 2.5.

Three UK specifying authorities responsible for the majority of concrete construction are the Department of Transport (DTp) (Ref. 11), the Property Services Agency (PSA) (Ref. 12) and the Central Electricity Generating Board (CEGB) (Ref. 13). BS 8110 *Code of Practice for the Structural Use of Concrete* (Ref. 14) and National Building Specification Section E13 (Ref. 93) also specify formwork and concrete finishes. There are differences between the specifications and it is a recommendation of this guide that more standardisation of specifications is needed (see Section 8.1, Item 4). The contractor should, wherever possible, be given the option of proposing alternative means of achieving the outline or surface finish required. Section 2.5 details the classes and likely materials for achieving different concrete surface finishes.

Section 2.4.2 – Specification by Method or Performance

A performance specification is a description of a desired end result, whereas a method specification is a description of how the specifier requires that a result is to be achieved.

Specifications should be written in performance terms as far as possible, so enabling the contractor to optimise his procedures and use equipment and expertise available to him. The contractor should be given all necessary liberty in the manner of the execution of the work because he carries contractual liability for its production. In addition, performance specifications have the advantage of avoiding disputes that arise when the contractor's implementation of a method specification fails to achieve the required result. If the specifier cannot anticipate the end result of his performance specification then he should call for trials.

See Section 2.8, Sample and trial panels.

There may be instances when the nature of the work demands a method statement. Method statements tend to be needed where special surface finishes are required, but may be avoided by providing sample panels or photographs or citing sections of nearby finished work. It is always advisable to allow the contractor to propose alternative methods.

The main difficulty in the use of performance specifications is that the PWD will be aware at tender stage of the required end product but may not be aware of the method the successful contractor will adopt. This can be overcome by specifying that the contractor advises the PWD of the proposed methods prior to commencement of formwork construction, in order that the latter has the opportunity of commenting on the procedure in the light of the requirements for the finished result.

See also Section 7.3 on supervision.

Specification by performance places a greater workload on site supervisory staff. In particular, advice by the resident engineer or clerk of works, that he considers that the formwork will not produce the required result, will not necessarily be accepted by the contractor. Insistence that procedures be modified may result in a variation to the contract, changes in responsibility and increased costs.

Section 2.5 – Finishes

Section 2.5.1 – General

The prime purpose of formwork is to form and contain the concrete. Very frequently, formwork materials which perform this function adequately cannot be relied upon to give a satisfactory finish.

If there is a particular concern about the finish, texture, pattern or appearance of the hardened concrete the requirements should be accurately specified since such finishes are more costly to produce. A set of useful reference documents is given in the Appearance Matters Series published by the Cement and Concrete Association (Ref. 15, 16, 17, 107 and 108). The fundamental aspects of visual concrete are discussed in No.1 *Visual concrete – design and production* (Ref. 15). Blemish-free concrete finishes of uniform colour and texture are very difficult if not impossible to produce consistently. This is discussed in Appearance Matters No. 3 *The Control of Blemishes in Concrete* (Ref. 15).

Appearance Matters Series (Ref. 15, 16, 17, 107 and 108).

Visual Concrete – Design and Production (Ref. 15).

The Control of Blemishes in Concrete (Ref. 15).

Among the basic considerations for exposed concrete finishes are durability, appearance and weathering. Generally speaking an 'open' textured finish may have a better resistance to weathering than a smooth 'closed' finish. The subject of design for weathering, the effect of rain washing dirt down the structure, is very important and deserves separate detailed consideration. See also Appearance Matters No. 6 *The Weathering of Concrete Buildings* (Ref. 16).

The Weathering of Concrete Buildings (Ref. 16).

The importance of the appearance of a concrete finish is relative to the observer. There is no point in specifying a high quality finish unless it is really required. The appearance of concrete should relate to its environment and its proximity to those who have to live with it. Thus before specifying a finish these aspects should be considered and assessed, and specified accordingly. Certain situations will require the addition of paints or renders to the concrete surface as discussed in Appearance Matters No. 2 *External Rendering* (Ref. 17).

External Rendering (Ref. 17).

Whilst the difficulties of producing finishes of uniform colour and texture cannot be over-emphasised, the chances of success can be improved by considering the following factors:

(a)   The right concrete mix.
(b)   Consistency of the concrete and its materials.
(c)   Use of a constant rate of placing.
(d)   Uniformity of compaction.
(e)   Uniformity of face contact material.
(f)   Avoid the direct flow of concrete against the form face by the use of a baffle, raised as concreting proceeds. Similarly, there should never be a surcharge of more than 150 mm above the compacted concrete and placing should be in a steady stream so that vibrators consolidate from the bottom upwards.
(g)   Walls and columns should have a minimum of joints and preferably be poured in one lift. See Section 5.7.
(h)   The correct choice of formwork pretreatment and release agent. See Section 3.10.
(i)   Trial panels, if required, should be made using similar materials, formwork and placing techniques to those planned for the permanent works. See Section 2.8.
(j)   It is difficult to reproduce complicated features on vertical faces since they tend to trap air bubbles, encourage plastic cracking and local honeycombing. Features should be designed to be predominantly vertical, such as ribbing, and permit easy run-off of water and dirt. Horizontal or sloping features will often weather badly.

See Section 5.7.

See Section 3.10.

See Section 2.8.

Section 2.5.2 – Classes of Finish

Finishes should be specified so as to provide the appropriate desired finish. Whilst the quality and complexity of the formwork will vary, all formwork must satisfy the requirements for structural integrity, safe handling, grout-tightness, watertightness and

Department of Transport (DTp)	Property Services Agency	Central Electricity Generating Board	See Section
F1	Basic formed finish	Rough or board form	2.5.3
F2	Plain formed finish	Normal	2.5.4
F4	Fine formed finish	High class	2.5.6
F3 (see Note 2)	Super fine formed finish		2.5.5
Special surface finish			2.5.7

Notes to Table 2:   (1) Note the sequence of the DTp Classification.
(2) The DTp Specification has a class F5 finish normally only to be used for precast pre-tensioned beams. This is similar to the class F4 but of a lower standard.
(3) National Building Specification (Ref. 93) has not been included in this table.

Table 2.   *Comparison of the Major UK Specifications for Concrete Finishes*

Department of Transport (DTp) Specification for Road and Bridge Works, Clause 1708 (Ref. 11).

Property Services Agency General Specification, Concrete Work (CO) Formwork, Sections 3 and 8 (Ref. 12).

Central Electricity Generating Board Specification for Structural Works, Clauses 53 and 64 (Ref. 13).

Fig. 1.
See also Fig. 38.

compliance with the safety regulations.

Typical classes of finish are specified in the Department of Transport (DTp) *Specification for Road and Bridge Works*, Clause 1708 (Ref. 11) and in the Property Services Agency General Specification, Concrete Work (CO) Formwork, Sections 3 and 8 (Ref. 12), and also in the Central Electricity Generating Board Specification for Structural Works, Clauses 53 and 64 (Ref. 13). The specifications are similar in many respects. Table 2 compares the description of the finish in these specifications.

Whilst the DTp Specification is primarily intended for bridge structures, it is often used in other classes of work directly or by reference.

Section 2.5.3 – Class F1, Basic or Rough/Board Form Finish

This class of formwork is the least costly of the classes. It is normally used where appearance is of minimal or no importance, e.g. backs of retaining walls and abutments, foundations, inside faces of voided structures, areas to be subsequently clad, rendered or plastered, in fact, any non-exposed concrete. An example is shown in Fig. 1. A further example of the soffit to a car park is shown in Fig. 38.

Whilst appearance is of minimal or no importance, the formwork should still be structurally adequate, grout-tight and watertight, be safe for handling and comply with the safety regulations. However, the class does permit the use of secondhand face contact materials of mixed type and irregular pattern, which may have had many uses and been repaired. Allowance may have to be made for reduction of strength of secondhand materials, particularly plywood.

Fig. 1 *Example of an F1 finish to a caisson under construction on a floating pontoon.*

Section 2.5.4 – Class F2, Plain and Normal Finish

Fig. 2.
Fig. 3.

This class is more costly than Class F1/Basic/Rough and is confined to exposed areas not normally or easily visible, e.g. inward-facing beam sides, the insides of box beams, deck soffits between beams, walls and undersides of ceiling slabs in plant rooms, etc. An example is shown in Fig. 2 for a wall. An example of this finish to the underside of a bridge soffit is shown in Fig. 3.

Fig. 2 *Example of an F2 finish on a retaining wall using a proprietary panel system.*

Fig. 3   *Example of an F2 finish to the soffit of a bridge with an F3 sloping side and precast parapet.*

It is recommended that plywood-faced or proprietary panel forms be used for this class. Sound, used forms will probably suffice. However, care will be required to prevent grout loss at joints. Some repairs to the face of plywood, boards or other materials can be accepted.

Some clauses of old specifications refer to board forms. The production of consistently good finishes with boards or planks is difficult and expensive and is not recommended for this class. Use of 'sawn board' formwork is covered in Section 2.5.7.

Section 2.5.7.

Imperfections and non-uniformity of colour are normally permitted as is the making good of blowholes, fins and discolorations. Making good of small areas of defects such as honeycombing and grout leakage may sometimes be permitted dependent on their position and extent.

Section 2.5.5 – Class F3, High Class Finish without Ties

Designing and using vertical formwork of any significant height without ties is difficult. Pour heights above 2.5 m are particularly difficult without through ties as the size of strongbacks necessary to control deflection makes the forms very expensive, heavy and difficult to handle. Absence of anchorage points at the top of the previous lift makes good grout-free construction joints very unlikely.

Most clients restrict 'no-tie' areas to the edges of bridge decks and parapets, but even these can present a contractor with problems, such as when insitu sections have to be attached to steel or precast concrete girders. Examples are shown in Figs. 3 and 4. Some specifications permit ties and specify that they shall be evenly spaced, placed in grooves or where their presence can be disguised or hidden. Obviously the use of textured surfaces facilitates this.

Figs. 3 and 4.

The required finish may be obtained using permanent formwork – see Section 3.7.

See Section 3.7.

Fig. 4   *Example of an F3 finish to the edge of a highway bridge.*

Section 2.5.6 – Class F4, Fine/High Class Finish

This class (and particularly F4 in the DTp Specification) is intended for visible surfaces. Typical areas are the sides of bridge superstructures, abutments and retaining walls, and walls of buildings. An example is shown in Fig. 5.

Fig. 5.

Plain, unblemished concrete of uniform colour is extremely difficult to produce with predictable certainty. Many factors affect appearance which are beyond the scope of this guide, but some are given in Section 2.5.1. An example of colour change in concrete from a plain plywood surface after weathering is shown in Fig. 6.

Section 2.5.1.
Fig. 6.

Fig. 5 *Example of an F4 finish to a sample wall cast at the Cement and Concrete Association in 1972 using plywood with a chemical release agent. Photographed in 1976.*

The task of producing this class of finish is a formidable one. Given certain conditions an inexpensive form may produce results equally acceptable to those obtained from expensive purpose made forms. However, the use of expensive forms will not guarantee acceptable results if the quality of workmanship is sub-standard.

Textured and Profiled Concrete Finishes (Ref. 15).

Fig. 5.

See Sections 3.7 and 3.12.

Where a large plain untextured surface is produced there is nothing to draw the eye away from any blemishes which may occur. Thus it is sensible, where appearance is important, to provide significant features, or to make such surfaces patterned or textured using one of the many techniques now available such as form liners or permanent formwork. See Appearance Matters No. 7 *Textured and Profiled Concrete Finishes* (Ref. 15). An example of the use of grooves to divert the eye is shown in Fig. 5. See Sections 3.7 and 3.12.

Fig. 6
Finish obtained from plain unsealed douglas-fir plywood with a chemical release agent after weathering for twelve years.

Section 2.5.7 – Special Surface Finishes

A special surface finish may be either functional or aesthetic. An example of the former is a finish on a spillway or weir channel, and an example of the latter would include the wide range of surface finishes used for decorative effects, or where special quality is required.

See Section 3.1.2.

In view of the difficulties experienced in obtaining visually satisfactory smooth finishes, such as the risk of black markings from any impervious shiny surface (see Section 3.1.2) it is advisable to introduce a pattern or controlled degree of roughness to the face of the concrete where appearance is important. Some of the methods by which this can be achieved are discussed in this section.

Surface roughness can be obtained by the use of textured linings of plywood, rubber or plastic. Rubber linings are made in a large range of patterns and, whilst expensive initially, can have a large number of uses. An example is shown in Fig. 7.

Fig. 7.

Glass fibre reinforced plastic sheets also give excellent results. High density polystyrene in proprietary panels is also used to give textured finishes. Examples of the finishes obtained are shown in Figs. 8 and 9.

Figs. 8 and 9.

Fig. 7 *Finish obtained using a proprietary rubber liner on a wall.*

Fig. 8 *Finish obtained using a GRP form liner with a chemical release agent. (Subway to Gateshead elevated road.)*

Fig. 9
Finish obtained using a proprietary high density polystyrene form liner with factory applied special release coating.

Figs. 10, 11 and 12.

Striated Finish for insitu Concrete Using Timber Formwork (Ref. 18).

Textured and Profiled Concrete Finishes (Ref. 15).

Vertical grooved finishes are an excellent way of breaking up a large surface and they also weather well. The tops of the ribs can be treated in a variety of ways, by bush-hammering, light abrasive blasting, or by controlled hammering off to produce a random roughened effect. Examples of vertical striations are shown in Figs. 10, 11 and 12. Useful C&CA guides are the Advisory Note on *Striated Finish for insitu Concrete Using Timber Formwork* (Ref. 18) and Appearance Matters No. 7 *Textured and Profiled Concrete Finishes* (Ref. 15).

Fig. 10 *Special surface finish to a large wall area with vertical and horizontal profiling; (Carlsberg Brewery Northampton; Commendation in 1980 Concrete Society Awards.)*

Fig. 11 *Finish obtained using vertical grooving with edges subsequently hammered to expose the aggregate.*

Fig. 12 *Finish obtained using vertical grooving with light bush-hammering to ribs.*

Selection of a face contact material to achieve a specified finish may depend more upon its reuse potential than upon the actual finish required, and due account should be taken of this in the selection. This is particularly so in the case of 'sawn board' formwork, where it can be expensive to produce a consistent special finish and maintain the quality. An example is shown in Fig. 13. Detailed guidance on the preparation of material and specification for this finish is given in Section 3.2.2.1.

Fig. 13.
Section 3.2.2.1.

Foamed polyurethane and polyethylene are also produced in a range of patterns, but can normally be used only once. Care is needed during compaction of the concrete to keep vibrators away from these materials. They are also used for sculptured concrete, and an example is shown in Fig. 14 which combines sculptured precast panels and insitu sawn board formwork.

Fig. 14.

Fig. 13 *Finish obtained using 'Rough Sawn' boards with polyurethane sealer and chemical release agent.*

Fig. 14 *Finish obtained from precast sculptured panel (cast face down) with insitu white cement concrete and 'Sawn Board' formwork. (Cathedral Church of SS Peter and Paul, Clifton Winner of 1974 Concrete Society Awards.)*

The general requirements for special surface finishes are the same as for Class F4, Fine/High Class finish. However, forms for special surface finishes are often larger than for normal work and this may impose particular requirements, such as cranage.

A number of the more common form liners and face contact materials are listed and considered in Section 3.12.

Section 3.12.

Surface roughening of cast concrete to alter the appearance of the as-struck face can be achieved either by chemical methods, such as surface retarders to expose the aggregate, or by tooling such as bush-hammering, though these are outside the scope of this guide. Further information is contained in Appearance Matters Nos. 8 and 9 (Ref. 15). A satisfactory tooled finish can however only be achieved from concrete that has been correctly designed, well compacted, cast against uniform formwork, and made to a high standard. An example is shown in Fig. 15. Tooled finishes are labour intensive, very expensive and should only be specified when they are required for architectural reasons and can be seen at close range.

Exposed Aggregate Concrete Finishes

Tooled Concrete Finishes (Ref. 15).

Fig. 15.

Tooling can sometimes be used to improve a plain smooth finish which is discoloured or blemished, but should only be considered as a last resort since it is an expensive remedial method. **Tooling will not remedy bad concrete.** The cover to the reinforcement is reduced by tooling and the designer (PWD) should make the necessary allowances.

Fig. 15 *Finish obtained on insitu wall with a deeply point-tooled finish.*

Section 2.6 – Tolerances

Section 2.6.1 – General

All members of the construction team should be aware of the importance of tolerances and their implications. The aim is to construct a concrete structure which complies with the drawings and specification. Absolute accuracy is impossible, and the level of inaccuracy that can be accepted needs to be considered. The relationship between accuracy and cost is complex, but the smaller the tolerances, the greater will be the cost. Close tolerances should only be specified when the result will make a significant contribution to quality, function, appearance or overall economy.

See also Section 2.6.4.

Code of Practice for Accuracy in Building BS 5606: 1978 (Ref. 19).

When specifying the permissible deviation for a member of a structure that tolerance should be able to be measured and should be within the accuracy range of the measuring equipment. For example, on a member with a permissible deviation of ± 5 mm the tolerance is 10 mm; this could be the product of deviations at the base and top of a column. In this example, a base could be + 5 mm from intended position with head −5 mm measured from the same datum, giving a 10 mm departure from vertical. However, this does not mean that the head or base can deviate from the datum + 10 mm or −10 mm. See also Section 2.6.4. Similarly on a member of permissible deviation + 2 mm, −8 mm, the tolerance is also 10 mm. If it cannot be measured then it is unrealistic to specify it as a target for the site to achieve. The *Code of Practice for Accuracy in Building* BS 5606: 1978 (Ref. 19) records the expected dimensional deviations of buildings from site measurements completed and gives statistical guidance on the accuracy likely to be achieved. This section discusses the likely standards of accuracy in formwork which will, of course, be a contributory factor to the overall accuracy of the structure.

BS 5606, Clause 6.5 (Ref. 19).

The three sources of deviations in the finished structure are inherent deviations, induced deviations and errors. (BS 5606, Clause 6.5 (Ref. 19).)

Section 5.1.3.1.

Inherent deviation. An example of this is elastic deflection of formwork under load. This is covered in more detail in Section 5.1.3.1 which suggests limits. Inherent deviations can also occur from foundations consolidating during concreting, or if changes in form length take place due to thermal effects.

See Section 3.2.2.4.

Induced deviations arise from inaccuracies in the measuring equipment, such as the error in the actual bench mark used. Another induced deviation is the manufacturing tolerance of the components of the formwork. For example, the permitted overall tolerances on the thickness of certain wood-based sheet materials may cause lipping (see Section 3.2.2.4). When specifying straightness the PWD and the TWD should be aware of the straightness tolerance inherent in the materials. For example, the tolerance on straightness of rolled steel sections may be greater than those permitted in the finished concrete structure.

Errors arising from inaccurate setting out or misreading of drawings etc.

The following sections discuss the realistic deviations that can be specified on site for walls, soffits and columns, which may differ from those stated in the contract specification.

Section 2.6.2 – Wall Formwork

The final position of a cast-insitu wall will be affected by several factors: accuracy of the initial setting out; plumbing and starting location of the kicker; means of stabilising the form to resist horizontal forces arising from wind etc. Within the formwork system not only will the face contact material deflect between walings but the walings will also deflect between the soldiers (if fitted). In turn the soldiers will deflect between ties or propping positions. If tie rods are used through double faced forms then elastic lengthening of the tie rods at working loads will occur. These factors will all contribute to the final position and thickness of the wall.

NAFC Data Sheet No. 4 (Ref. 20).

NAFC Data Sheet No. 4 (Ref. 20) recommends that the inherent deviation from elastic deflections need only be considered on the member in which they act, and not cumulatively as the summation of all the deviations on all the members. This ensures that the elastic deviations can sensibly be measured, if required, on the surface of the finished concrete.

Specifying a particular spacing of tie rods in a wall will automatically decide the likely order of deflections in the formwork. Thus the specification of a maximum deflection value can cause significant increase in cost of the formwork.

Typical deviations for nominally vertical formwork for insitu walls are:

Forms 4 m high	± 10 mm
Forms 7 m high	± 15 mm
Forms 10 m high	± 20 mm
Straightness in 5 m length	± 10 mm

BS 5655 (Ref. 99) gives specific tolerances for walls to lift shafts.

BS 5655 (Ref. 99).

The surface finish of the concrete should be considered when selecting the tolerance. For example, a wall used in an apartment formwork system (Section 3.6.5) may be required to be suitable for direct decoration with minimum surface preparation; this will require tight control for straightness and minimum elastic movement to give an acceptable visual appearance, whereas a tall retaining wall with a patterned form liner will not require such a degree of control. Certainly in the latter case the visual straightness of the wall could not be measured over short lengths and the deviations recommended above would be suitable. In contrast, if precast units are to be incorporated in a structure then improved speed of construction may justify a much stricter control of overall dimensions of the insitu walls. It is then important to control the maximum area of bearing surfaces and maximum width of joints to be filled.

Section 3.6.5.

Section 2.6.3 – Soffit Formwork

The final position of an insitu concrete slab is determined by several factors. The falsework, its location and stiffness, will affect the final soffit level. Not only will the falsework shorten elastically under the applied load of fluid concrete but its own supports and foundations will also be subject to settlement. Combining these with the 'take-up' at the joints of falsework items and the induced deviations in the manufacture of the falsework, causes the soffit formwork to settle overall as load is applied, the normal practice being to set the forms about 5 mm high to allow for the expected take-up.

Set soffit forms about 5 mm high.

The TWD should be aware that designs with uniform settlement will reduce differential deflections and give more satisfactory solutions. Some guidance on joint take-up and elastic shortening is given in BS 5975, Clause 43.2 (Ref. 2).

BS 5975, Clause 43.2 (Ref. 2).

The top surface level of the slab is generally set from screeding rails or set out from the soffit form. The final level, with suitable care, should be correct to a tolerance of ± 3 mm in 3 m. However, it should be remembered that on a large slab area the measuring equipment would not realistically set out to ± 5 mm over a 50 m length of construction and the final tolerance should be set with this in mind. The introduction of cambers, either as residual cambers or, on long span members for elastic deflections, will affect the tolerance of the soffit and top of slab levels. See also Section 2.7.

Top slab levels ± 3 mm in 3 m.

See also Section 2.7.

Attention is drawn to the effect of induced deviations on long lengths of structure when considering the reinforcement detailing. For insitu slabs up to 40 m long BS 5606 recognises a dimensional accuracy of ± 35 mm. On a flat slab soffit this presents no problems but on a soffit such as that of a waffle or trough floor the effect of this deviation may cause serious lack of fit of edge reinforcement. This total deviation is generally positive and arises not only from the cumulative tolerances from the moulds but also from manufacturing tolerances in any supporting falsework with its spacing of supports.

BS 5606 Table T.2.4 (Ref. 19).

Section 2.6.4 – Column Formwork

The control of tolerance in column forms requires consideration in three dimensions.

Firstly, the **plan sizes** depend on the arrangement of restraint of the concrete pressures. The higher pressures at low level can give larger local face deflections. Generally, for columns with plan sizes of up to 450 × 450 mm the dimensions can be controlled to ± 3 mm. Larger plan sizes of up to 1.0 m can be generally kept within ±5 mm.

Secondly, the tolerance on the overall **height** of the column should be considered. It is common practice to take the top of the column concrete into the next slab or beam by, say, 10 to 25 mm (to assist when the slab formwork is being fitted around the top of the completed column).

Thirdly, the **verticality** of the column (or alignment in the case of a sloping column) must be controlled. This needs to be considered along two axes mutually at right angles.

Typical deviations for insitu column forms from these axes are:-

Forms 4 m high	± 10 mm
Forms 10 m high	± 25 mm
Forms up to 20 m high	± 40 mm

The final position of the top relative to the intended position depends also on the accuracy of the starting point at the kicker and, for rectangular columns, the squareness at the top. The tendency for the form to 'wind' or rotate torsionally is more prevalent on tall square columns. Provided the form is robust, is carefully handled between uses, and props are fitted to secure points on the form, then this will not generally be a serious problem.

Section 2.7 – Deflection Limits and Cambers

*δ = 1/270 of span
See also Fig. 55.*

The appearance and function of most concrete work is satisfied by limiting the design deflection of individual formwork members to 1/270 of the span. This value can be taken as a guide unless stricter requirements prevail in the specification for the finished work.

Economies may be made by the relaxation of this deflection limit where appearance and practical criteria permit.

Effects such as 'quilting' of face material can be greatly exaggerated by lighting effects and by colour changes in the concrete. Where appearance is critical, special consideration should be given by the PWD to the requirements written into the specification.

See also Section 5.1.3.

On slab or beam soffit formwork where the permanent work consists of long spans, say over 8 m, the specifier may require a residual camber to be incorporated. Where the support involves clear span members, such as adjustable floor centres, there will also be an additional precambering required to allow for the elastic deformation of the members under the imposed loads. See also Section 5.1.3. The position of the soffit will depend on the accuracy of the estimates made in predicting the precamber values; differences between estimated loads and those occurring in practice, together with varying load characteristics for the members of the formwork or falsework, will all contribute to the final camber.

Specifiers should be aware of the increased costs involved when incorporating residual cambers, particularly if a constant slab thickness is also required, as this will necessitate precambering the top of the slab. The value of the specified residual camber should be included in the designer's brief and should be considered with the permitted deviation on the soffit levels. Further, it will require to be within realistic limits of measurement. In general residual cambers should only be specified where visual appearance is critical. If considered necessary, then a generous tolerance on the camber will contribute more to an acceptable appearance than attempting to produce an unrealistically flat soffit to a tight tolerance. Residual cambers alongside fixed items such as existing walls or steel beams are extremely difficult to achieve and should be avoided.

Section 2.8 – Sample and Trial Panels

Fig. 16.

Particular requirements of a job may indicate that a sample or trial panel is necessary. Normally these will incorporate significant features in the design of the structure, particularly where high standards of finish are required. The hypothetical sample or trial panel shown in Fig. 16 is designed to incorporate a number of features that will affect the appearance of a typical job. Panels must be specifically designed to incorporate those features which affect the appearance of the job in question.

Sample panels or sample sections of the work are those prepared to the PWD's instruction in order to demonstrate to tendering contractors the type of finish required. The size of the samples should be consistent with relevant elements of the proposed works and it is essential to retain the formwork for inspection by tenderers. In making sample panels due regard must be paid to the practicability of obtaining the required finish on the site. On occasions it may be possible to designate a section of nearby finished work as indicative of the standard required. Data on the formwork used should be made available.

*See Appendix F
for address.*

The Cement and Concrete Association have a permanent display of sample panels of many types of finish, mix etc erected at their Research Station at Wexham Springs near Slough, west of London.

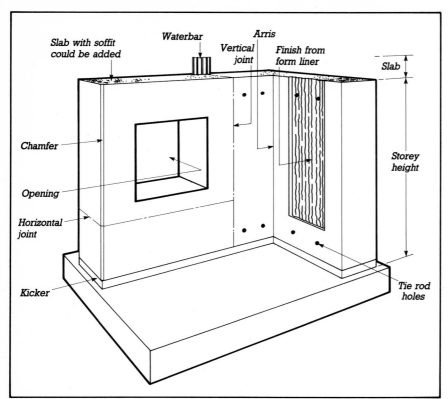

Labels in figure: Slab with soffit could be added; Waterbar; Arris; Vertical joint; Finish from form liner; Slab; Storey height; Chamfer; Opening; Horizontal joint; Kicker; Tie rod holes

The hypothetical panel shown does not indicate any reinforcement projecting from the wall. The width of the wall, together with the position and density of reinforcement, may affect the standard of workmanship on the panel and, if considered significant for the appearance of the work, then similar reinforcement to that specified for the permanent works should be included in the panel. Note that some reinforcement may be needed for the stability of the panel.

Fig. 16 *Composite sample or trial panel (hypothetical).*

Trial panels are those panels or trial sections which are carried out by the contractor, under the contract, in the preliminary stages of the work, as a means of establishing that his proposed method of working will achieve the required results. Such panels, when accepted, may be used as the standard by which the completed work will be judged. There may be advantages in using visually unimportant parts of a structure for trial, e.g. basement retaining walls, in order that realistic site conditions may be simulated, but where the consequences of an unsatisfactory trial need not lead to demolition.

It should be noted that the finish obtained from the first use of formwork on sample or trial panels, may not necessarily be repeated on subsequent casts.

Section 2.9 – Formwork Designer's Brief

The formwork designer's brief is the basic information which may be required by the design office for the purpose of preparing a formwork scheme. The lists below are not exhaustive but do include important details for each type of construction and are representative of the type of information required.

It is the responsibility of the formwork designer to ensure that he has all the information required to complete the design. However, information on all factors affecting a design will not necessarily be available at an early stage. Where assumptions have to be made to complete a design, it is the responsibility of the designer to ensure that the assumptions made are clearly identifiable, so that they can be checked at a later stage and, where necessary, the design can be amended.

Basic Information Required

(a)   All detail and general arrangement drawings, programme and relevant specification clauses including location of the site.
(b)   Types of finish required.
(c)   Whether or not through ties are allowed and, if so, if a particular type is specified.
(d)   Structural dimensions on curves and gradients. Can curved surfaces be formed in facets? If so, state the allowable offset. Details of any residual cambers.

See Fig. 64.

(e)   Method of placing and compaction, e.g. pumping, crane and skip/internal poker vibration/external formwork vibration.
(f)   Type and position of construction joints.
(g)   Striking times.
(h)   Any exceptional requirements to be fulfilled, e.g. Special finishes.
(i)   Site restrictions, e.g. overhead cables, flood water levels etc.
(j)   Rate of placing concrete.
(k)   Sequence of concreting, pour height and length limitations.
(l)   Length of form required and approximate rate of progress.

(m)   Capacity of plant to be used for handling forms.
(n)   Material or equipment available for use.
(o)   Date for submitting schemes for approval.

Design Details Required

The following is a check list of details which the formwork designer (TWD) may be required to convey in the design.

(a)   Material and surface finish of form face or lining.
(b)   Material, size and position of other formwork members, including propping arrangements.
(c)   Arrangements and dimensions of panels and/or forms.
(d)   Description and position of form ties, anchors and spacers.
(e)   Method of sealing the form face.
(f)   Method of sealing panel joints.
(g)   Method of sealing tie holes.
(h)   Method of forming and sealing construction joints.
(j)   Method of forming features such as ribs or patterned surfaces.
(j)   Method of forming holes and openings, indents, drips, chamfers etc.
(k)   Method of securing inserts.
(l)   Method of striking formwork to ensure that completed work is not damaged or overstressed.
(m)   Method of preventing formwork from restraining concrete movement, which could cause cracking.
(n)   In the case of prestressed members, method of ensuring that elastic shortening due to tensioning is not restrained by the formwork.
(o)   Position of air release holes and/or access doors, if required.
(p)   Position and details of clean-out openings.
(q)   Procedure to be adopted to ensure that the specified construction sequences are observed.
(r)   Method of achieving required falls and cambers.
(s)   Types of release agents.
(t)   The area required for the formwork and the associated working spaces etc.

Section Three
Materials and Equipment

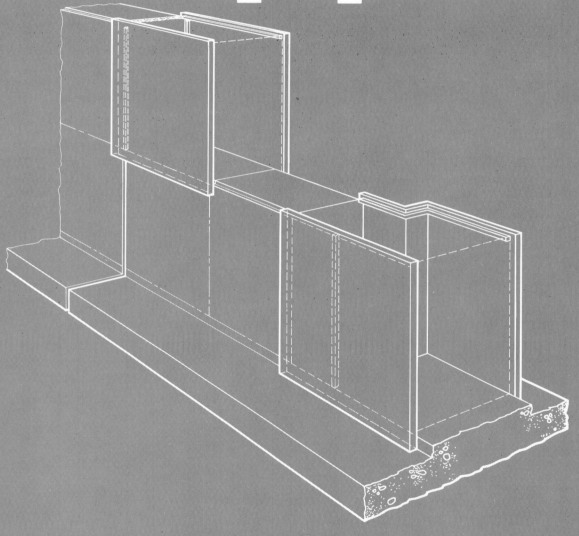

concrete
society

Section Three – Materials and Equipment

Section 3.1 – General

Section 3.1.1 – Permissible Stresses

Permissible stresses in formwork should be selected bearing in mind the properties of the material to be employed, especially its behaviour under short term loading. The importance of this is illustrated by the fact that the properties of timber allow an increase in working stress above that permitted in the design of permanent structures. In contrast, properties of steel are unaffected by load duration so no increase of permissible stress under load is allowable, although some is permitted under maximum wind loading.

BS 5268 (Ref. 4).

As the largest proportion of formwork involves the use of timber and plywood, and as it is difficult to extract the relevant design stresses from BS 5268 (Ref. 4), detailed recommendations are given in this guide. For formwork designed using other materials the relevant BS and other references are stated, from which the design stresses may be readily obtained. Furthermore such formwork design is normally carried out by specialists.

Section 3.6.1.

In addition to the use of basic materials, formwork design involves the application of many different types of proprietary equipment. In preparing the design, the supplier's technical literature should be consulted. Section 3.6.1 gives recommendations on the detailed information which should be available.

Section 3.1.2 – Materials as Form Facing

The choice of material in face contact with the concrete has a significant effect on the resultant finish. Specification of finish, and class of finish are discussed in Sections 2.4 and 2.5. The main features requiring consideration are the hardness, permeability and surface texture.

Hardness will contribute to long life and consistency of performance.

Permeability has an effect on the resulting colour. Generally, absorbent forms give a dark finish whereas impermeable forms give a light finish. The permeability of the face reduces with use as the cement paste fills the pores, hence the quality of finish changes. Where the surface is impermeable and vertical, the air does not escape easily during compaction and blow holes are formed on the concrete face.

See also Section 3.3.1 on steel formwork.

Surface textures range from highly glossed, through matt, to deliberately textured. High gloss or even glass-like surfaces can occur in new forms made of impervious materials and, despite the generally light colour expected, can give rise to blackening of the concrete. See also Section 3.3.1 on steel formwork. It is thought that this effect is caused by the effects of vibration where the smooth surface allows the movement of water and fine particles of sand and cement.

Highly glossed surfaces which are repeated on the cast face of the concrete frequently show crazing of the concrete and exaggerate the effect of blowholes. The crazing may only be very shallow cracks and the effects will fade as the concrete carbonates, but the gloss imparted to the concrete is reflective and exaggerates the visual effects. As a result there is an unnatural marbled effect.

Highly polished faces of formwork only remain polished for one or two uses before being abraded to a matt texture. Where necessary the gloss can be reduced by 'pre-ageing' or by light abrading before use. A matt surface avoids the worst aspects of the results from glossy forms. Alternatively a deliberately textured surface may produce light and shadow effects which are more noticeable than, and divert attention from, the colour variations and blemishes from other causes.

The concrete pressure developed in a wall will also have an effect on appearance. The pressures at the bottom of a form cause greater effects than at the top. Other pressure variations due to varying rates of rise, changes in day to day conditions such as temperature, can also affect the concrete colour produced from porous forms.

Although the effect is not fully understood, the positions of stiffeners on an impermeable form can sometimes be seen repeated on the concrete face. This seems to indicate a secondary effect of pressure and form face deflection, in the migration of water in the concrete during setting.

To achieve consistent quality of finish in the concrete it follows that variations in mix, materials etc should be reduced as much as possible. See also Section 2.5.1. Selection and use of the correct pretreatment and release agent is an essential prerequisite for maintaining quality of finish.

See also Section 2.5.1.

Sections 3.2 to 3.7 give the descriptions, illustrations, working stresses etc for the majority of materials commonly used in formwork. Many are used in applications where they are not in direct contact with the concrete, and Section 3.12 considers the particular characteristics of these materials when used as form liners.

Formliners. See also Section 3.12.

Section 3.2 – Timber and Wood-based Materials

Section 3.2 1 – Timber

Section 3.2.1.1 – General

Timber, both home grown and imported, is used for a wide variety of purposes other than for formwork and falsework. In formwork, timber is used structurally and its use is governed by the *Code of Practice for structural use of timber* BS 5268: Part 2: 1984 (Ref. 4). This Code introduces strength classes for timber and it is recommended that Strength Class SC3 should be the minimum quality for use in formwork. Timber that is graded to appropriate standards of other countries may be used together with ungraded timbers provided account is taken of the appropriate stresses.

BS 5268: Part 2: 1984 (Ref. 4).

Strength Class SC3 should be the minimum quality for use in formwork.

Guidance on selecting a timber that will comply with the above strength classes for different species, equivalent grades and species by origin, is given in BS 5975 (Ref. 2) and in BS 5268 (Ref. 4).

BS 5975 (Ref. 2).
BS 5268 (Ref. 4).

Formwork timber will generally be used either as a waling or a bearer and reuse will be expected. Examples are shown in Figs. 24, 41, 42, 43 and 66. A more complex timber form is shown in Fig. 17. Care should be taken to ensure that the strength class of a timber is clearly marked. Timber which is stress graded to BS 4978 (Ref. 21) will be marked and protection of the mark by clear varnish is recommended. Whenever timber is re-used it should be inspected to ensure that it has not deteriorated due to environmental conditions and is not damaged in excess of the permissable defects for its grade. The TRADA booklet *Simplified rules for the inspection of secondhand timber for load bearing use* (Ref. 22) is a helpful guide for the visual stress grading of SC3 timber.

BS 4978 (Ref. 21).

Simplified rules for the inspection of secondhand timber for load bearing use (Ref. 22).

Section 3.2.1.2 – Permissible Stresses for Solid Timber

The permissible working stresses in timber for temporary works applications are greater than for permanent structural use because of the shorter duration of load in temporary works. This behaviour under short term loading is a property of timber. When in use on a soffit form the timber will remain stressed until striking takes place, possibly up to one week after casting. In comparison, on wall formwork the same timber will be stressed for a shorter time period from time of casting to time of striking, probably only one or two days. (Note that even after the concrete has stiffened the timber will remain stressed and in its deflected state until the form is struck.) The permissible stress for the same piece of reusable timber used in a wall and then in a soffit will vary because of the different duration of load factors that can be applied to the stresses. The two conditions are stated to allow the designer to make the economic choice for a particular form. On any given site, with both walls and soffit forms, it may be decided to use only one condition, i.e. the more conservative general formwork condition. Unless the appropriate grade of timber is used, the lower general formwork stresses for Strength Class SC3 should be adopted.

Table 3 gives recommended working stresses for general formwork and also for vertical wall formwork. The stresses stated are for the wet exposure condition to be found on site (i.e. moisture greater than 18%). The wet condition is evaluated from the dry stresses by multiplying by a modification factor, K_2. To assist the reader when referring to BS 5268 (Ref. 4) the relevant modification factors used are shown at the foot of Table 3.

BS 5268 (Ref. 4).

Fig. 17 *Complex timber formwork for the spiral volute of a power station turbine block (photographed during the trial erection).*

Condition	Strength Class	Bending Stress Parallel to grain (N/mm²)	Tensile Stress Parallel to grain (N/mm²)	Compressive Stress Perpendicular to grain (N/mm²)	Shear Stress Perpendicular to grain (N/mm²)	Modulus of Elasticity 'E' (N/mm²)	
						mean	minimum
General Formwork	SC3	6.29	3.73	2.63	1.32	7603	5011
	SC4	8.90	5.24	2.87	1.40	8554	5702
	SC5	11.87	6.99	3.35	1.97	9245	6134
Vertical Wall Formwork	SC3	6.74	3.99	2.82	1.41	7603	5011
	SC4	9.54	5.62	3.07	1.50	8554	5702
	SC5	12.72	7.49	3.58	2.11	9245	6134
Modification factors from BS 5268		$K_1 K_2 K_3$	$K_1 K_2 K_3$	$K_1 K_2 K_3 K_4$ and 1.2 See Note (g)	$K_1 K_2 K_3$ and 1.5 See Note (h)	$K_1 K_2$	$K_1 K_2$

Table 3. *Permissible Stresses and Moduli of Elasticity for Formwork Timber in the Wet Exposure Condition*

In using stress values in Table 3 the designer should be aware that the following conditions apply:

(a)   The timber has been accepted as appropriate to the class concerned, has not been reduced in cross section and is still in good condition.

(b)   In calculations the dry sizes of members are used. (Factor K_1 modifies the dry stress values accordingly.)

(c)   The wet exposure condition is assumed (Factor K_2 allows for the change in stresses and moduli). Note: It is only in countries of much lower humidity than the UK that the dry condition will be appropriate.

Load duration factors:
Wall forms $K_3 = 1.5$
Soffit and general forms $K_3 = 1.4$

(d)   The load duration factors for K_3 have been taken as 1.4 and 1.5 for the general and vertical wall formwork values respectively.

(e)   The bearing length does not exceed 75 mm and there is at least 75 mm of timber each side of the bearing and take-up is not critical. (Factor K_4 allows for this condition.)

(f)   The depth factor K_7 is taken as 1.0 for depth of timber 300 mm. For depths 72 mm to 300 mm the value is amended using the formula from BS 5268, Clause 14.6 (Ref. 4):

BS 5268, Clause 14.6 (Ref. 4).

Depth factor K_7

$$K_7 = \left(\frac{300}{\text{depth}} \right)^{0.11}$$

BS 5975, Clause 18.2.5 (Ref. 2).

(g)   Values for compressive stress perpendicular to the grain have been increased by a factor of 1.2 for formwork in agreement with BS 5975, Clause 18.2.5 (Ref. 2).

BS 5975, Clause 18.2.8 (Ref. 2).

(h)   Maximum permitted shear stress values have been increased by a factor of 1.5 in agreement with BS 5975, Clause 18.2.8.

(i)   The depth to breadth ratios of BS 5975, Table 7, have not been exceeded.

(j)   There is no wane at any point of bearing.

(k)   The grade stresses relate to individual members and no account is taken of load sharing.

The value of permissible shear stress stated is the maximum permitted. To clarify the relationship between the average and maximum shear stress for a rectangular section, see Fig. 18 which shows a parabolic shear distribution. When the cross section is not rectangular the distribution is not parabolic and reference should be made to structural design handbooks for evaluation of the maximum stress.

See Fig. 18.

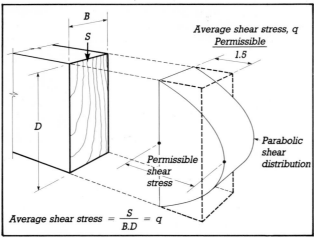

Fig. 18 *Shear stress diagram for a rectangular solid section.*

Section 3.2.1.3 – Structural Properties for Solid Timber

To assist the designer to evaluate the structural properties of solid timber members Tables 4, 5 and 6 list the permissible moment of resistance (**M**), permissible bending stiffness (**EI**), maximum shear load and bearing stress value for five sections commonly used in formwork. The tables are for softwood constructional timber which is planed all round. The geometric properties of the sections are listed in Table 7.

Tables are for softwood constructional timber.

The structural properties are derived from the permissible stresses and moduli of elasticity listed in Table 3 and modified by applying factors for the depth of section selected, and under certain conditions for its load sharing application.

Wherever four or more timbers, each one spaced not further apart than 610 mm, and which have provision for lateral distribution of loads (for example with plywood face contact material), then the stresses in Table 3 can be increased by 10% and the mean modulus of elasticity used when calculating deflections from concrete pressures etc. See BS 5268, Clause 13.0 (Ref. 4). The load sharing modification factor K_8 is 1.1.

See BS 5268, Clause 13.0 (Ref. 4).

	Strength Class	Basic Sizes (mm)					
		50 × 100	75 × 100	50 × 150	75 × 150	75 × 225	
Bending Stiffness EI (kNm²)	SC3	17.89	27.46	59.63	91.70	315.69	
	SC4	20.36	31.25	67.85	104.35	359.23	
	SC5	21.90	33.61	73.00	112.25	386.44	
Moment of Resistance $fZ\,K_7\,K_8$ (kNm)	SC3	0.523	0.802	1.120	1.711	3.740	
	SC4	0.740	1.135	1.585	2.421	5.293	
	SC5	0.987	1.513	2.114	3.228	7.057	
Shear Load qA (kN)	SC3	4.00	6.13	5.98	9.17	13.84	
	SC4	4.24	6.50	6.34	9.72	14.68	
	SC5	5.98	9.15	8.93	13.68	20.67	
Bearing Stress *Note (2)* (kN/m²)	SC3		2630	(2030)			
	SC4		2870	(2270)			
	SC5		3350	(2870)			

Notes to Table 4: (1) Assumes no load sharing i.e. $K_8 = 1.0$
(2) In bearing stress considerations where wane is permitted in grading, use the values in brackets.

Table 4. *Structural Properties of Individually Loaded Timbers General Formwork Applications*

BS 5268 (Ref. 4).
BS 4978 (Ref. 21).
BS 5756 (Ref. 23).
NLGA and NGRDL Joist
and Plank Rules
(Ref. 24).

Generally, timber used in wall and soffit formwork, as either walings or bearers, will be behind face contact materials which will allow load sharing to be considered. In soffits the primary timbers may be classified as falsework or formwork; load sharing will not be appropriate and the permissible stresses in Table 3 will apply.

The stress values from Table 3 are used with a depth of section factor K_7 incorporated, the assumption being in all cases that the timber is used in the stronger direction. The geometric properties and K_7 factors are given in Table 7. The depth factor from BS 5268 (Ref. 4) applies to solid timber beams assigned to a strength class or graded to BS 4978 (Ref. 21), BS 5756 (Ref. 23) or NLGA and NGRDL Joist and Plank Rules (Ref. 24). The use of the depth factor for all stress graded or strength classified timber used in formwork applications is recommended and the structural properties in Tables 4, 5 and 6 include the factor. When timber is used in tension the depth factor can also be used to modify the stress values from Table 3.

See BS 5268, Clause 14.9 (Ref. 4).

Allowance for holes and notches has to be made when calculating the bending strength; see also BS 5268, Clause 14.9 (Ref. 4). Such holes and notches will have little effect on the deflection unless they are of some length, say, with notches exceeding 12% of depth and holes on the centreline with diameters greater than 25% of the depth.

Centres up to 610 mm

Values assume four or more timbers

	Strength Class	Basic Sizes (mm)				
		50 × 100	75 × 100	50 × 150	75 × 150	75 × 225
Bending Stiffness EI (kNm²)	SC3	27.14	41.66	90.48	139.14	478.99
	SC4	30.54	46.88	101.79	156.54	538.90
	SC5	33.01	50.66	110.02	169.18	582.44
Moment of Resistance fZ K_7 K_8 (kNm)	SC3	0.575	0.882	1.232	1.882	4.114
	SC4	0.814	1.248	1.744	2.663	5.822
	SC5	1.086	1.665	2.325	3.551	7.763
Shear Load qA K_8 (kN)	SC3	4.40	6.75	6.58	10.08	15.23
	SC4	4.67	7.15	6.98	10.69	16.14
	SC5	6.57	10.07	9.83	15.05	22.73
Bearing Stress *Note (2)* (kN/m²)	SC3	2890	(2230)			
	SC4	3150	(2490)			
	SC5	3680	(3150)			

Table 5. *Structural Properties of Load Sharing Timbers General Formwork and Soffit Applications. See Note (1)*

	Strength Class	Basic Sizes (mm)				
		50 × 100	75 × 100	50 × 150	75 × 150	75 × 225
Bending Stiffness EI (kNm²)	SC3	27.14	41.66	90.48	139.14	478.99
	SC4	30.54	46.88	101.79	156.54	538.90
	SC5	33.01	50.66	110.02	169.18	582.44
Moment of Resistance fZ K_7 K_8 (kNm)	SC3	0.617	0.945	1.320	2.017	4.408
	SC4	0.872	1.338	1.868	2.853	6.238
	SC5	1.163	1.783	2.491	3.805	8.317
Shear Load qA K_8 (kN)	SC3	4.72	7.23	7.05	10.80	16.32
	SC4	5.00	7.66	7.47	11.45	17.29
	SC5	7.04	10.79	10.53	16.12	24.35
Bearing Stress *Note (2)* (kN/m²)	SC3	3100	(2390)			
	SC4	3370	(2670)			
	SC5	3930	(3370)			

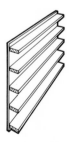

Centres up to 610 mm

Values assume four or more timbers

Table 6. *Structural Properties of Load Sharing Timbers Wall Formwork Applications. See Note (1)*

Notes to Tables 5 and 6:

(1) Tables assume load sharing ($K_8 = 1.1$) and that the face contact material will laterally distribute the applied loads.

(2) In bearing stress considerations where wane is permitted in grading, use the values in brackets.

Basic Sizes (mm) (B × D)	50 × 100	75 × 100	50 × 150	75 × 150	75 × 225
Finished size (mm)	47 × 97	72 × 97	47 × 145	72 × 145	72 × 219
Area (mm²)	4559	6984	6815	10440	15768
Section Modulus Z (mm³)	73.7×10^3	113×10^3	165×10^3	252×10^3	576×10^3
Moment of Inertia I (mm⁴)	3.57×10^6	5.48×10^6	11.9×10^6	18.3×10^6	63.0×10^6
Depth Factor K_7	1.128	1.128	1.079	1.079	1.032

Geometric properties from BS 5268, Appendix D, Table 99 (Ref. 4).

Table 7.   *Geometric Properties and Depth Factor (K_7) for Basic Sizes of Solid Timber*

Section 3.2.2 – Wood-based Face Contact Materials

Timber is used either for direct face contact in the shape of boards or as sheets of wood-based materials. The former is generally known as 'sawn board' formwork when it is specified as a finish, and is considered separately.

Section 3.2.2.1 – Sawn Board Formwork

Finish and Specification: A wide range of finishes may be obtained from sawn board formwork, varying from smooth to deeply grained markings with expressed joints. Sawmarks are often used as the main feature. It is also possible to sculpt timber to form an even bolder relief. The joints between boards/forms will form part of the final appearance and should be designed. See Figs. 13 and 14 for examples of 'sawn board' finish.

See Figs. 13 and 14.

All common softwoods can be used, but hardwoods are occasionally adopted for multi-use forms, and are usual for features, striking pieces and wedges. Timber should not be too dry, or it will swell with absorbed moisture and make removal difficult. 'Green' timber distorts in hot weather, making alignment awkward. Moisture content, variations in absorbency and any natural resins, salts, or wood sugars may affect the colour of the finished concrete. The selection of pretreatment and release agent is covered in Section 3.10.

Section 3.10.

Some timbers, such as keruing and merante, are known to create serious problems due to their interaction with the concrete, causing retardation of the surface, severe discoloration, or adhesion of the timber to the concrete. Advice should be sought from TRADA if there is any doubt about the suitability of a particular species. (Appendix F lists addresses.)

Appendix F lists addresses.

Surface Preparation and Reuse: Timber may be prepared either with a smooth finish or to emphasise its natural grain. The grain can be enhanced by soaking in water or weak (1.3%) ammonium hydroxide solution. In cutting the timber, marks may form part of the feature. However, even with smooth timber it is inevitable that some grain marks will be transferred to the concrete face. Jointing may be butt, tongued and grooved, or sealed with a plastic foam strip.

Additional texture to the concrete surface can be obtained by using either radial or tangentially sawn boards. A deeply exposed grain appearance may be achieved by grit blasting the boards. Rough sawn timber with a hairy or splintery surface should be avoided, especially for large panels, due to difficulties in striking. Boardmarked features will be emphasised by using boards of varying thickness. Unless a random finish is required, consistency of timber supply is essential. Form joints should be watertight.

Untreated timber boarded formwork can normally be re-used between 1 and 10 times depending on the care taken in striking and handling, and the quality of final finish required.

Considerably more uses may be obtained if care is taken to maintain the forms. The life of beading fixed to the surface of the form is more limited.

Carefully selected timber should be used. Unless it is to be sealed with either a barrier paint or a proprietary wax, the form should be treated initially with two or three applications of release agent to seal the surface and to create

concrete society

initial swelling which will close up joints between boards. This, however, will not prevent water migration from the initial cast into the boards, with ensuing discoloration of the concrete. Subsequent casts, however, will be less affected.

Boards must be sufficiently well fixed to the frame to prevent separation during striking. If for any reason a board has to be replaced it should be brought to the same condition as the existing boards to prevent very distinctive colour variations on the concrete surface in subsequent casts.

Painting of forms after the application of a release agent is virtually impossible, although wax treatments can be successfully applied.

Use stresses from Table 3.

Permissible Stresses: It is recommended that the stresses in Table 3 are used in the design of timber as face contact material. The relevant section properties and depth factors may need determining separately from BS 5268 (Ref. 4) if the timber is used structurally in the 'weaker' direction as planks. When used as a lining the material will be non-structural.

Economics: The cost of sawn board formwork will vary widely depending on the class of finish required but for high class work the cost is usually very high. This expense is derived not only from the construction of the form and cost of materials used, but also from the cost involved in selection of materials and maintenance and repair of the form. It is advisable to make allowance in design for repair of the facing boards.

Section 3.2.2.2 – Plywood and other Sheet Materials

(a)   Type and Specification

Comparative testing of wood-based formwork linings. (Ref. 25).

No single sheet material has all the attributes required as a face contact material for all formwork. Where there is little information known about a particular sheet material a useful guide is the TRADA publication *Comparative testing of wood-based formwork linings.* (Ref. 25). Often the manufacturing process provides a sheet with a low moisture content which ideally should be allowed to reach moisture equilibrium in the same atmosphere as other timber for formwork to reduce moisture 'pick up' which could result in distortion. Wood-based sheet materials used for formwork may be classified as plywood, particle board and fibre building board:

BS 5268 (Ref. 4).

Plywood, its manufacture and uses (Ref. 26).

Plywood consists of cross-laminated veneers of wood, bonded with synthetic resin adhesives. Coniferous (softwood) species are used extensively for formwork. Hardwood species, principally birch and tropical hardwoods, generally provide a finer surface and give increased strength, but are initially more costly. Structural plywoods are included in BS 5268 (Ref. 4). An example of the finish obtained from one plywood is shown in Fig. 6. Readers unfamiliar with this material should refer to TRADA publication *Plywood, its manufacture and uses* (Ref. 26).

Particle Board (wood chipboard) consists of graded wood chips, flakes or strands bonded with synthetic resin adhesives. Like plywood, the material can be layered to ensure that surfaces are dense and fine-textured. The normal manufacturing process gives a board with uniform properties in two directions but longer strands can be orientated in manufacture to influence strength. Particle board is susceptible to moisture movement, including change of thickness, and differential movement within that thickness either from absorption or from the environment, and it is recommended that improved moisture resistant Type III or Type II/III to BS 5669 (Ref. 27) should be used for formwork. Some guidance on the behaviour of the material is given in an ISE/TRADA state of the art report (Ref. 112), which although written for its application in flooring does provide useful information on the material including moisture movement. Its use as a structural lining is covered by Concrete Society Current Practice Sheets Nos. 72a and 72b (Ref. 116).

BS 5669 (Ref. 27).

ISE/TRADA state of the art report (Ref. 112).

Concrete Society Current Practice Sheets Nos. 72a and 72b (Ref. 116).

BS 1142: Part 2 (Ref. 28). See Section 3.12.

Fibre Building Boards are high, medium or low density boards. High density boards include standard and tempered hardboards. They are specified in BS 1142: Part 2 (Ref. 28) and are mainly used as linings. See Section 3.12.

When in use as structural board the TE grade of tempered hardboard is usually used. Properties of this grade are given in BS 5268 (Ref. 4).

BS 5268 (Ref. 4).

(b)   **Bonding**

Adhesives used to bond veneers or laminations of plywood must be sufficiently moisture resistant, heatproof and weatherproof to meet the requirements of wet forming operations. Plywoods with a WBP adhesive bond as classified in BS 6566: Part 8 (Ref. 29) are generally suitable and are usually bonded with a phenol formaldehyde adhesive.

BS 6566: Part 8 (Ref. 29).

Particle board (chipboard) bonded with melamine-urea resin adhesives (Type III and II/III) have increased moisture resistance and are appropriate for formwork. Boards marked V 313 normally meet this requirement.

(c)   **Surface Treatment and Reuse**

Untreated surfaces have a limited life (typically 1 to 10 reuses). An advantage is their slight absorbency in early life. However, it is not homogeneous and may be patchy and can mark the concrete with a grain pattern.

Untreated timber exposed to ultraviolet light can suffer degradation and formation of hemicelluloses (wood sugars) which will retard the concrete. Treatment is covered in Section 3.10.1.

Section 3.10.1.

Resin-coating (paints/varnishes) can extend the board life (typically 5 to 20 reuses). These are best applied under factory conditions as they will only adhere properly to dry surfaces. They can increase the susceptibility of boards splitting due to moisture movement.

Resin impregnation is a manufacturing process which seals and stabilises the face veneer of plywood. A slight texture in the form of a weave pattern (similar to the reverse side of hardboard) can be impressed on the surface. This retains release agents more effectively. It also helps to disguise colour variations on the concrete surface by reducing light reflection.

Resin-film Overlays: Both plywood and chipboard factory treated with a continuous resin-impregnated film fused to the surface have proved durable for multiple reuse. Care in handling is important. The lower porosity of the overlay can create problems with dark densified patches appearing on the concrete.

GRP Coatings: Heavy duty overlays of glass fibre impregnated with polyester or phenol resins greatly prolong the life of form panels (estimated 100 reuses) but at a considerably greater initial cost. Surfaces may be plain or patterned. They give a good surface finish but require care when concreting to avoid damage by vibration which can cause 'star' shaped cracking on the overlay.

Section 3.2.2.3 – Structural Properties of Sheet Materials

There are many different types of wood-based sheet materials listed in BS 5268 (Ref. 4) and BS 5669 (Ref. 27). In formwork only a few are in common use and structural properties of seven common materials are given in Tables 8 and 9. The designer using other materials should consult either the supplier or the relevant British Standard for design information. The Tables list the bending stiffness, moment of resistance and shear load for a 1 m width of loaded material, assuming two conditions for duration of load, i.e. wall forms and general formwork/soffit forms applications using the duration factors of 1.5 and 1.4 respectively. The wet exposure condition is allowed using factor K_{36} from BS 5268 (Ref. 4) for a moisture content exceeding 18%.

BS 5268 (Ref. 4).
BS 5669 (Ref. 27).

Load duration factors:
Wall forms $K_3 = 1.5$
Soffit and general forms $K_3 = 1.4$

In plywood the timber species, veneer thickness and grain direction principally influence strength and stiffness. Because plywood is generally more rigid along its face grain, the plywood should span walings and supporting frames in this direction (see Fig. 19). The value of bending stiffness, permissible moment and shear load for the two directions are stated in the tables. The site should be aware of the implications of placing a plywood sheet material the 'wrong way round'.

See Fig. 19.

	Face Grain relative to span *Note (1)*	Plywood					Particle Board (chipboard)	
		Canadian 19 mm COFI Douglas Fir GIS	GIS	Finnish 18 mm (13 Ply)		American 19 mm (APA) B-C Grade: Group 1	Type III or II/III to BS 5669 18 mm	22 mm
		6 Ply	7 Ply	Birch-faced	Birch	(5 or 6 Ply)		
Bending Stiffness EI (kNm²/m)	Parallel	3.14	3.40	3.02	3.23	2.99	1.12	2.08
	Perp'r	1.54	1.54	1.58	2.23	2.99	1.12	2.08
Moment of Resistance fZ (kNm/m)	Parallel	0.367	0.398	0.611	0.778	0.395	0.202	0.267
	Perp'r	0.227	0.228	0.465	0.578	0.488	0.202	0.267
Shear Load qA (kN/m)	Parallel	7.141	5.774	9.832	14.465	9.472	4.334	5.324
	Perp'r	4.710	4.862	5.899	12.782	6.263	4.334	5.324

Notes to Table 8:
(1) The face grain relative to its span indicates the disposition of the plywood face grain relative to its span. See Fig. 19.
(2) The values of bending stiffness are not modified by the duration of load.
(3) The shear load includes a modification factor of 1.1, see text.

Table 8. *Structural Properties of Wood-based Sheet Materials General Formwork and Soffit Applications*

	Face Grain relative to span *Note (1)*	Plywood					Particle Board (chipboard)	
		Canadian 19 mm COFI Douglas Fir GIS	GIS	Finnish 18 mm (13 Ply)		American 19 mm (APA) B-C Grade: Group 1	Type III or II/III to BS 5669 18 mm	22 mm
		6 Ply	7 Ply	Birch-faced	Birch	(5 or 6 Ply)		
Bending Stiffness EI (kNm²/m)	Parallel	3.14	3.40	3.02	3.23	2.99	1.12	2.08
	Perp'r	1.54	1.54	1.58	2.23	2.99	1.12	2.08
Moment of Resistance fZ (kNm/m)	Parallel	0.393	0.426	0.655	0.834	0.423	0.217	0.286
	Perp'r	0.243	0.245	0.499	0.619	0.522	0.217	0.286
Shear Load qA (kN/m)	Parallel	7.652	6.186	10.534	15.499	10.148	4.642	5.698
	Perp'r	5.045	5.210	6.320	13.694	6.711	4.642	5.698

Notes to Table 9:
(1) The face grain relative to its span indicates the disposition of the plywood face grain relative to its span. See Fig. 19.
(2) The values of bending stiffness are not modified by the duration of load.
(3) The shear load includes a modification factor of 1.1, see text.

Table 9. *Structural Properties of Wood-based Sheet Materials Wall Formwork Applications*

When calculating the permissible span for a wood-based sheet material its support conditions may alter the theoretical values for span obtained from formulae which assume centre to centre spans with 'knife-edge' supports. On continuously spanning sheets the support conditions will be affected by the width of the bearers and walings, and at intermediate positions they will act as two supports close together. The width of the supports should always be considered when checking the shear on the sheet material. However, this is not always the case when checking the moment of resistance, reaction or deflection. It is therefore recommended that, unless a separate analysis is carried out, the following procedures are used for shear, moments, reactions and deflections.

Shear: Sheet material spans are usually relatively short and shear failure is rare. The critical section of the loaded span in shear is the clear distance between the supports with an additional reduction for the thickness of the sheet material (assuming a load dispersion of a 45° from the edge of the support). This is similar to the consideration of punching shear.

The transverse shear stress values for plywood given in BS 5268 (Ref. 4), with the appropriate modification factors, frequently give values for permissible shear load which are in conflict with a history of satisfactory practice. This is partially corrected by consideration of a reduced 'shear span' used in the formula below, and by the additional factor of 1.1 which has been included in the shear loads given in Tables 8 and 9. Further research is needed into the interaction of shear in wood-based sheet materials when subjected to the loads from high concrete pressures causing deflection in two planes on the bearers. See Section 8.1, Item 11.

BS 5268 (Ref. 4).

See Section 8.1, Item 11.

Where the face contact material has applied to it a uniformly distributed load, such as from concrete pressure, the maximum shear load in the sheet material is given by the expression:

$$S_s = 0.5 \, W_s \left(\frac{L-B-t}{L} \right) k$$

Where S_s = shear load for sheet material   kN/m

W_s = total load uniformly distributed on one span per metre length of support   kN/m

B = overall width of beam or section   m

t = thickness of sheet material   m

L = length of one span of member (measured centre to centre)   m

k = coefficient to allow for the continuity effect on multiple spans

k = 1.00 for one span

k = 1.10 for two spans

k = 1.05 for three or more spans

The calculated shear load S_s is then checked against the stated shear load capacity of the chosen material, such as those tabulated in Tables 8 and 9 for shear load (q A).

Shear caused by the application of point loads or non-uniformly distributed loads will require separate calculations.

Moments, Reactions and Deflections: Where the width of the support, **B**, is less than twice the sheet material thickness, **t**, it is reasonable to assume that the supports are 'knife-edge' single supports and thus standard loading cases, such as shown in Appendix B, Loading Cases 1 to 57, can be used.

Appendix B
Loading cases 1 to 57.

If the width of the support is greater than twice the thickness of the sheet material, and the material spans only two or three supports, then Appendix B, Loading Case 1 or 21 respectively should be used.

Loading case 1 or 21.

Face contact material usually spans over several supports, and the sheet size determines a suitable module for the support centres. For example, a 2440 mm long sheet will give 6, 7, 8, 9 or 10 spans. For wood-based sheet material, Appendix B includes a special Loading Case 58 for sheets spanning over four or more supports. This special case incorporates allowances to cater for the width of supports and for the effects of continuity on the shear and reactions. The width of the support relative to the span is an important criterion, and a practical upper limit of centre to centre span is 610 mm. Separate calculations would be required for conditions outside the limits stated for Appendix B, Loading Case 58.

Formwork sheet material
Appendix B, loading
case 58.

The increase in support reaction at some intermediate supports due to the continuity of the sheet material is normally ignored when considering the applied load on the bearer or waling, so that in Appendix B, Loading Case 58 the reaction is 1.0W at internal supports. In soffit formwork with random secondary or primary bearers an allowance of 10% is added to the calculated reactions for all bearers assumed simply supported to allow for the variations of the transferred loads. (See BS 5975 Clause 43.3.1 (Ref. 2).) This allowance includes any continuity effect from the wood-based face contact material.

See BS 5975
Clause 43.3.1 (Ref. 2).

In wall formwork using Appendix B, Loading Case 58, the walings are designed using the reactions as stated, assuming no continuity and sheet material simply supported between the walings. See also the worked example C1 in Appendix C for a typical design using the procedures above. Specific cases of sheet material not conforming with Loading Case 58 will need separate calculations.

See also the worked
example C1 in
Appendix C.

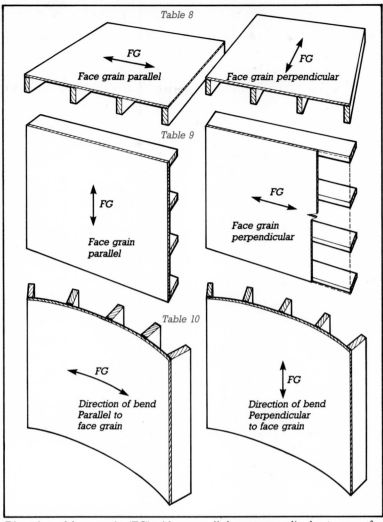

Fig. 19 *Direction of face grain (FG) either parallel or perpendicular to span for flat and curved sheet materials to Tables 8, 9 and 10.*

Formwork may be curved. Table 10 gives minimum bending radii for various thicknesses of plywood for bending parallel or perpendicular to the face grain. See Fig. 19. The references used to produce this table include Refs. 1, 30, 31 and 32.

Thickness of Plywood not exceeding	6.5 mm	9 mm	13 mm	16 mm	19 mm
Direction of bend parallel to face grain	1.5 m	2.4 m	3.6 m	4.8 m	7.0 m
Direction of bend perpendicular to face grain	0.7 m	1.5 m	2.4 m	3.6 m	4.8 m

Table 10. *Minimum Bending Radii for Plywood. See Fig. 19*

The forces required to bend and restrain plywood at the radii in Table 10 are considerable. Fastenings and supporting frameworks need to be sufficiently rigid to restrain the material in place.

A dual layer system using hardboard or thin plywood is suitable for smaller radii.

It is not normally advisable to use particle board for curved formwork.

Section 3.2.2.4 – Design Factors

Dimensions: It is important in planning formwork to arrange visible panel joints in positions appropriate to the appearance of the structure. A range of metric and imperial sizes of sheeting material is available, of which 1200 × 2400 mm (1220 × 2440 mm) is the most common.

Widths of 1200/1220 mm and 1500/1525 mm with lengths up to 3600/3660 mm are available in hardboard, plywood and particle board.

Very large panels up to 12 m and storey height, suitable for one piece wall forms, are obtainable, dimensioned and pre-drilled for ties. There is an advantage in reducing the number of visible panel joints but specifiers of non-standard sizes should be aware of the increased costs and often long delays in manufacturing non-standard sheets.

The thickness tolerance of plywood may inevitably cause a lip of up to 1 mm at joints. The permissible deviation in manufacturing thickness is usually ± 0.5 mm. Sanding of the surface to overcome this lip may cause colour variations on the concrete, particularly with faced plywood sheeting.

Lip at joints 1 mm.

Fixing: Screws, nails, staples and various mechanical fastenings can be embedded close to the edge of most wood panels without splitting. The recommended minimum edge distance is 9 mm for plywood, particle board and fibre building board used in formwork. Where possible, surfaced boards should be secured by rear fixing. Countersunk screws should be sealed and the screw heads filled for high quality concrete finishes. The allowable nail or screw lateral loads are given in BS 5268, Clauses 41 and 42 (Ref. 4).

Minimum edge distance 9 mm.

BS 5268, Clauses 41 and 42 (Ref. 4).

Edge Sealing: All edges should be sealed against moisture to prevent local swelling and to maintain flat, high quality concrete surfaces. Some boards are sealed by the manufacturer. Any edges subsequently cut should be re-sealed. Suitable sealants are: chlorinated rubber paint, neoprene, epoxy resin. Particle board may require some extra protection against mechanical damage on vulnerable edges, e.g. by hardboard or plastic lipping.

Repairs: Polyester putty can be used to fill screw holes or minor damage from poker burns etc. Larger areas of fracture can sometimes be routed and patched with a section of similar board glued in place with structural adhesive.

Any repairs to a form face will have a different porosity and surface to the 'parent' form face. This variation will be transferred as a blemish onto the concrete face. The release agent will also have differing effects due to the different absorbency of the repair material.

Section 3.3 – Metals

Section 3.3.1 – Steel

The permissible stresses for steel have hitherto been those recommended in BS 449 (Ref 33) and other appropriate current British Standards. However, the revised BS 5950: 1985 *Code of Practice for Structural Steelwork* (Ref. 34) is written in limit state terms and is unlikely to influence future design of steel formwork.

BS 449 (Ref. 33).

BS 5950: 1985 Code of Practice for Structural Steelwork (Ref. 34).

Where standard steel sections are used, they should either be clearly marked or be closely examined to ensure that they are of the quality, size and weight specified by the designer. Steel that is deformed or damaged by notches or cracks should not be used. Only in exceptional circumstances should steel be repaired on site by welding and then only by a skilled operative under the supervision of an engineer experienced in this type of work. The use of high yield steel, especially in proprietary equipment, has greatly increased in recent years and welding of such steels requires specialist knowledge. Substitution of any part, especially nut and bolt fixings, should only be allowed with knowledge of the original material specification.

The surface of the concrete produced by a steel form is smooth, of variable colour (though variations usually diminish with time) and of eggshell surface texture. Surfaces cast against formwork manufactured from strip mill quality steel will sometimes be glossy. New or relatively new highly polished steel faces may cause a characteristic black discoloration on the finished concrete, even when the correct release agents are used. To obtain high class finishes from such forms, 'pre-ageing' is recommended either by allowing them to rust (and then cleaning prior to use), or alternatively by lightly grit blasting the face. The effect of both techniques is to cause a uniform, slightly rough texture to the face prior to first use. See also Section 3.10.2.3 for pre-treatment of steel forms. Impermeability of the forms encourages occurrence of blowholes, and precautions must be taken to minimise these and to avoid crazing of the concrete and contamination from the steel face. Any marks detectable on the form face, such as those caused by diaphragm plate attachment, tack welds, plate joints welded to the back of the form, or any change of texture of the form surface will be reproduced on the concrete. If the light is oblique to the concrete surface, these marks may be apparent.

See Section 3.1.2.

See also Section 3.10.2.3.

Lightweight steel forms are liable to damage during handling unless care is exercised during striking.

See Section 3.6.
See Section 6.1.

A wide range of forms is available from various proprietary suppliers (see Section 3.6), ranging from light pressed plate constructions to large fabricated forms (see Section 6.1). Some typical examples of steel forms are shown in Figs. 1, 2, 20, 30, 34, 103 and 104.

Fig. 20   *Steel faced formwork. (Sill walls to Thames Barrier.)*

The production of the highest class of work from steel forms demands the attention of specialists in their design and use. Steel can be employed for a wide variety of classes of finish where economic factors are favourable.

See Section 2.5.

High reuse potential is in most cases the reason for the choice of a steel form. Because of its rigidity and durability of construction, it is rarely viable to adapt and modify purpose-made formwork at the termination of a contract unless provision has been made at the design stage. Provided well constructed forms are cleaned, oiled and any minor damage repaired when it occurs, form life is in the range of 100 to 600 uses for insitu work. In precast work steel has provided up to 1000 uses and is usually adopted where a large number of repetitive casts are required. Dimensional tolerances should be checked at intervals where a large number of uses are required.

Repair of forms is a highly specialised operation, best carried out by the form manufacturer. A repair to a form is likely to show on the surface of the concrete.

For economy and good results steel formwork should be kept simple.

The labour content in manufacture is not directly proportional to the steel content and depends on shape, complexity, accuracy and the repetitive nature of the work. For economy and good results steel formwork should be kept simple.

All but the lightweight proprietary systems require crane handling or mechanical lifting equipment. When used correctly the extremely long life of steel forms and their uniformity of finish can show economic advantages over other materials.

In selecting 'skin' plate thickness, lateral concrete pressures are sometimes less significant than ability to maintain tolerance after repeated rough usage from handling, impact loads, external vibration and striking. To limit distortion, welding should be kept to a minimum and, where used, careful consideration given to welding techniques.

The Control of Blemishes in Concrete (Ref. 15).

External vibration may cause aggregate transparency (the effect of coarse aggregate shape visible on the surface finish of the concrete) (See Appearance Matters No. 3. (Ref. 15)). This can be limited by attention to mix design and vibrator mounting techniques. If used, external vibrators must be rigidly mounted on the form, as close to the concrete as possible on an adequate mounting bracket designed to transmit the vibration through the form face, which should be locally stiffened to prevent 'over-flexing'. See Section 7.6.3.

See Section 7.6.3.

The high thermal conductivity and general stability of steel allows for the easy provision of supplementary heating to accelerate the curing process, by steam, hot water, electricity or warm air. See Sections 5.3.6.4 and 6.4.5. In cold weather, high thermal conductivity can be a disadvantage and some form of insulating cover may be required to limit heat loss from the concrete.

See Sections 5.3.6.4 and 6.4.5.

In hot weather and particularly in direct sunlight the temperature of the formwork may rise significantly causing difficulties in placing and compaction. This effect may be offset by spraying the outside of the form before concreting, taking care that any free water is removed.

Chemical release agents developed for use on steel forms yield good results. Application should be by spray, with light, even coating. See Section 3.10.

See Section 3.10.

Steel is also used as permanent formwork, where thin sheets are pressed into profiles to give additional strength. Section 3.7.3 details the use of such sheeting in composite deck construction.

Section 3.7.3.

Section 3.3.2 – Expanded Metal

Expanded metal made of steel is effective for stopend formwork, and is sometimes used to provide a key for bonding fresh concrete or for rendering. It is desirable to specify the mesh size. This will depend on circumstances but is normally ⅔ of the maximum aggregate size. However, it is sometimes necessary to experiment on site to find the most suitable size.

It will require suitable framing and edge treatment but there are proprietary variations which include stiffening ribs.

Fig. 21 shows a typical example of this material used as vertical stopends to slabs.

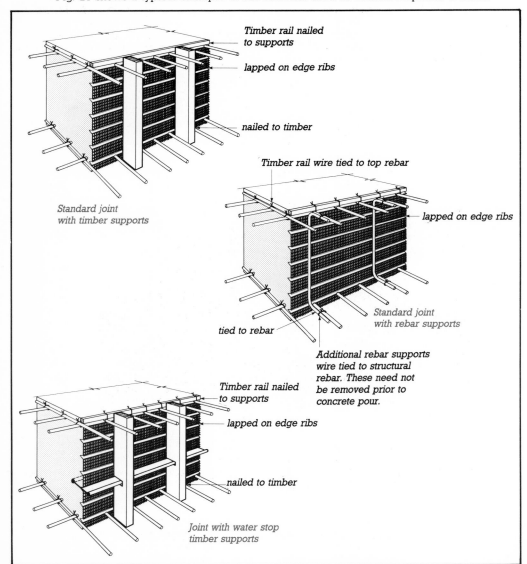

Fig. 21 based on information from the Expanded Metal Company Ltd.

Fig. 21 *Expanded metal. Typical details for use as stopends to slab formwork.*

To avoid corrosion problems on exposed surfaces, expanded metal should be given the same cover as the reinforcement. When used in watertight concrete structures, the PWD should make the necessary provisions in the form of sealants, water bars etc to ensure that a watertight structure is maintained. The need to examine expanded metal stopends carefully after concreting should be noted, to ensure that cavities do not exist behind them.

The use of expanded metal for forming no-fines concrete is a specialised technique and outside the scope of this guide.

See Section 8.1, Item 5.

It is known that the full concrete pressures are not attained when casting against open mesh products. The extent of the reduction in pressure is an item for further research. See Section 8.1, Item 5.

Section 3.3.3 – Aluminium

Aluminium has a great deal to offer the formwork designer, particularly in weight saving where there is a need to handle large assemblies of formwork; additionally savings in labour costs may be achieved by using large forms which would otherwise be impractical.

See Section 3.10.2.

When used as a face contact material there are some problems due to the reaction of alkalis in the fresh concrete with aluminium in the presence of moisture. This can be minimised by pretreatment and the use of selected release agents. See Section 3.10. Pre-etching of the face is essential before first use to ensure uniform concrete colour.

See Figs. 22, 33 and 67.

Recent years have seen a great increase in the number of proprietary sections available for structural framing in the form of walings and soldiers. Many have a timber insert for the fixing of face sheeting and there is a substantial range of accessories for joining, lifting and the spreading of tie rod loads. Typical examples of aluminium sections on wall and soffit forms are shown in the frontispiece and Figs. 22, 33 and 67.

CP 118 Code of Practice for Structural Use of Aluminium (Ref. 35).

Design work may be carried out in conformity with CP 118 *Code of Practice for Structural Use of Aluminium* (Ref. 35). However, where purpose-made sections are not specifically covered by design codes, calculations should be backed up by tests.

Fig. 22 *Aluminium walings in use on wall formwork.*

Aluminium Federation. Address in Appendix F.

Selection of the type or grade of aluminium alloy should take the likely environment into account. Certain alloys can suffer degradation and corrosion when subjected to marine environments, particularly when used in tidal zones. Advice can be obtained from the Aluminium Federation (address in Appendix F) which recommends the following alloys for particular uses:

Sheathing material	Alloy 5251 (BS 1470)
Carcassing or framing material	Alloy 6082 (BS 1474)
Cast components	Alloy LM6 (BS 1490)

Other uses of aluminium include pipe moulds, extrusions and castings for intricate feature formers where fine detail precludes the use of timber.

Special release agents are required for aluminium formwork. To keep corrosion to an acceptable minimum it is advisable to remove cement paste and fins from the form face prior to storage. Fixings to other materials are best made using galvanized or sherardized screws or bolts.

Section 3.4 – Plastic, Rubber and Fabrics

Secton 3.4.1 – General

Many plastic materials are byproducts of oil so their cost is relatively high, therefore careful consideration and planning must be given to exploit their properties.

Many plastics are extremely flexible materials with a very low 'E' value. They therefore usually require a form to back them. They are difficult to glue, and are easily separated from a concrete surface.

When used in panels, backed up by a form, it will be necessary to make allowance in the joints for the high thermal movements which will take place. These materials are generally used as form liners but recent developments have introduced techniques incorporating open meshed sheets for the containment of concrete in geotechnical applications. Some fabrics have also been used in this context. See Section 3.4.7.

See Section 3.4.7.

The application of rubber as a formwork material is covered in Section 3.4.5.

Section 3.4.5.

Section 3.4.2 – Foamed and Expanded Plastics

The most common material is expanded polystyrene (EPS). It is available in two pre-expanded forms:

(a)   As standard sized sheet (with or without a preformed profiled surface).
(b)   As block foam for hand shaping and carving. Its main use is for forming voids. See Section 3.11.1.

See Section 3.11.1.

EPS should be specified in accordance with BS 3837 (Ref. 36). It is a combustible material and some grades incorporate a fire retarding agent. Guidance on its fire characteristics and fire performance is given in BS 6203 (Ref. 37). Removal methods using heat are not recommended and non-flammable solvents and solvents which do not produce toxic fumes are preferred. See also CIRIA Special Publication 16 *A guide to the safe use of chemicals in construction* (Ref. 10).

BS 3837 (Ref. 36).

BS 6203 (Ref. 37).

A guide to the safe use of chemicals in construction (Ref. 10).

When used to form exposed surfaces care must be taken to ensure satisfactory release from the concrete. To facilitate this, it may be necessary to pretreat with either a wax, emulsion type paint or plastic coating. Furthermore, these measures can allow a limited reuse with a suitable release agent. Some proprietary linings are factory pretreated and require no additional release agent. Generally EPS is regarded as a single use material. An example of the finish obtained is shown in Fig. 9.

See Fig. 9.

Care must be taken during fixing and when placing concrete as EPS can be easily damaged by reinforcing steel, poker vibrators etc. Although it is resistant to overall compression, it is susceptible to point loads. When used as a void former, compression is generally disregarded, but when used as a form liner it may be significant and may limit the design concrete pressure.

Premoulded cylinders for void forming are available with diameters of 250 to 1000 mm and up to 2.4 m long.

Intricate sculptured shapes can be formed with most foamed plastics and profiles up to 300 mm deep can be achieved (excessive undercutting should be avoided). The overall cost of using foamed plastics will be dependent on the complexity of the finished shape, restrictions on concrete placing, methods of removal etc.

Section 3.4.3 – Glass Fibre Reinforced Plastic (GRP)

Glass fibre reinforced plastic (GRP) is a strong lightweight material generally used as formwork such as shown in Fig. 23, or as a form liner as in Fig. 24 to produce a high quality patterned surface finish. It comprises polyester resin reinforced with glass fibre. The thickness of GRP forms vary, but they are generally 5 to 16 mm thick depending on structural requirements.

Figs. 23 and 24. (Fig. 8 shows the finish obtained.)

The manufacturing process involves the production of a 'master mould', generally in timber or plaster, representing the 'as cast' concrete shape. This master mould is then pretreated with a release agent prior to the application of the first resin layer known as the 'gel coat'. After a suitable curing period subsequent layers of resin and glass fibre are added, including any stiffening members, until the required thickness is achieved.

GRP is particularly suitable for highly complex shapes but consideration should always be given to the problems of stripping. Sharp arrises should be avoided as they are both difficult to form and tend to cause brittle areas in the final form. Radii should never be less than 5 mm.

Fig. 23 *Glass fibre reinforced plastic formwork and struck 32 mm deep profiled finish concrete.*

Fig. 24 *Glass fibre reinforced plastic form liner used for the wall in Fig. 8.*

Slope 1:6.

As a general guide, positive slopes of about 1 in 6 will facilitate removal of the mould. Alternatively a split mould can be used, in which case negative slopes or undercuts can be accommodated.

The British Plastics Federation specification for polyester resins and chopped strand mat laminates (Ref. 38) is expected to form the basis of a British Standard. Guidance on structural properties of GRP is given in *Engineering Design Properties of GRP* (Ref. 39).

Engineering Design Properties of GRP (Ref. 39).

A major part of the initial cost of GRP formwork is in the master mould. Designs allowing maximum reuse of this master mould will reduce the unit cost of formwork. For example, on a simple circular column 9 m high to be cast in one lift, provided horizontal joint lines are allowed, then six semi-circular 3 m units can be obtained from a 3 m master, whereas if joint lines are prohibited only two units are achieved from a 9 m master.

With care, a GRP form can be used more than 100 times without unacceptable deterioration. However, its reuse will depend on its initial design and manufacture, the care with which it is handled on site and the use of the correct release agent. In particular, the hard wearing gel coat is subject to scour and may be affected by heat applied for accelerated curing of the concrete. Where heat is applied during curing appropriate resins should be used and specialist manufacturers' advice sought.

Minor damage to GRP forms can be repaired easily on site using polyester resin from a repair kit recommended by the manufacturer or specifically designed for this purpose.

GRP can be successfully used for the highest quality of work especially where sculptured profiles are required, and where repetition is involved. However, as the form face is impervious, a high proportion of blowholes in the concrete may be experienced; there may also be a tendency for concrete surfaces to craze. Such surface irregularities in the concrete can generally be minimised by care in placing the concrete and by the use of a suitable release agent.

Joints are generally formed with flanges whereby it is common practice to embed steel or timber sections in the laminate for additional reinforcement. In designing these joints, care must be taken to ensure that stresses are evenly distributed in the laminate, as hard spots or sudden changes of section can cause a concentration of stress.

GRP forms need adequate framing to carry the loads during concreting. This can be incorporated into the form economically provided it is taken into account during design.

GRP is a relatively flexible material and it can be used more satisfactorily for deeply profiled sections, such as troughs, where shape aids stiffness, than in flat areas.

Manufacture of GRP forms is a highly specialised process, and suitably experienced fabricators should be consulted if the use of this material is anticipated.

Fresh concrete is alkaline and can attack some fibres and resins. The use of a release agent to minimise this attack is always necessary. See Section 3.10.

See Section 3.10.

Section 3.4.4 – Polypropylene

Polypropylene formwork components are normally injection moulded, although the material can also be flow moulded and extruded. Its main use is for proprietary moulds for forming waffle and trough floors, particularly where multiple reuses are required. See Section 3.6.7 and Figs. 37 and 38.

See Section 3.6.7 and Figs. 37 and 38.

The methods of manufacture result in a uniform smooth surface to the mould which can in turn produce a smooth concrete finish. The impervious nature of polypropylene can cause blowholes but careful selection of release agent will minimise this effect.

Provided care is taken to mask joints between components it is possible to obtain a finish which is adequate for most specifications.

Polypropylene is one of the lightest of all thermoplastics. It has a high softening temperature, high flexural fatigue resistance, and good resistance to wear and abrasion. Components are very durable and can withstand the rigours of normal site use without the need for elaborate protective measures. The actual life depends on the site treatment but more than 100 uses can be expected. The use of a suitable release agent will prolong the life of a mould as well as maintaining the quality of concrete finish. Oil or hydrocarbon based release agents should not be used for extensive and repeated use as they can cause deterioration of the mould.

Although the basic material is relatively inexpensive, the initial tooling for injection moulding is very costly. Production of a few non-standard or special components is therefore prohibitively expensive but in large quantities can be very economic.

Polypropylene can be repaired by hot gas welding and this process is best carried out in factory conditions.

Section 3.4.5 – Rubber

Rubber materials – also termed 'elastomeric' materials – are generally used as form liners. A typical example is shown in Fig. 25. The finish obtained from such liners is shown in Fig.7.

Fig. 25.

(Fig. 7 shows the type of finish obtained.)

Different types and grades of material are used including polyurethane, polysulphide, silicone and polyvinyl chloride (PVC). These have varying flexibility, but all enable complex shapes (undercuts, deeply rebated profiles and textured finishes) to be cast into concrete. They are of 'solid' section, generally with a flat backing.

The materials are available both as pre-formed mats or moulds in a wide range of designs and as 'pour your own' liquid resins which enable an infinite range of designs to be produced. These are generally cold cure materials which are suitable for use in steam curing processes.

Fig. 25 *Rubber form liner in use.*

Flexible liners should be fixed to the formwork with a recommended adhesive, but where deep undercut is involved it may be necessary to devise an alternative means of fixing which allows the liner to be peeled from the concrete separately, thus avoiding any possible stripping problems. In precast work when units are cast face down the mat will often be left 'free' in the mould tray.

There are differences between the materials in flexibility, elasticity and hardness (classified using the 'Shore' hardness test). The number of uses also varies but all produce a consistent quality of concrete finish.

In most cases release agents are advised but some degree of self releasing, over a limited number of casts, is possible. All flexible mats should be handled with care, particularly if they are not supported by a rigid form. Tear strength also varies and can be improved by the use of woven cloth as reinforcement in the back, and this is often included in pre-formed mats.

Since pre-formed mats are supplied in standard sizes the joints have to be carefully made to prevent grout loss and marks on the concrete. However, it is extremely difficult to mask these joints, particularly horizontal ones, and consideration should be given to the provision of a rebate at these positions.

Overall, flexible mats offer the precaster or insitu user a wide range of design possibilities.

Section 3.4.6 – Plastic Sheet

Thermo-formed plastic sheets are used as form liners to produce low relief patterns with a smooth eggshell finish. The range of visual effects available is practically limitless.

The material can be polystyrene, acrylonitrile butadiene styrene (ABS), polyvinyl chloride (PVC) etc. Whilst flexible to varying degrees, the materials are not elastic. The pattern is produced by vacuum forming and thus there is some limitation on size, but a wide range of designs is possible. The sheet size depends on the vacuum former but is normally 2 × 1 m or 2 × 1.5 m. They should be fixed to the formwork and it is sensible to select designs which mask joints or where joint marks in the concrete are acceptable.

The actual material selected is determined by the number of uses required and the complexity of the finish but in all cases the cost of producing large numbers of linings from one master is relatively small. An advantage is that a series of easily replaceable sheets can be used to line a form; replacement of a sheet need not interrupt the construction cycle, whereas any other method of renovating a form involves at least a day out of use.

Plastics, being impermeable, tend to produce some surface blowholes and also encourage the erratic incidence of very dense mottled and glazed concrete surfaces. Surfaces cast against smooth plastics are also subject to crazing, particularly if the mix is too rich or has too high a water content. The use of the correct release agent will reduce these effects. See Section 3.10.

See Section 3.10.

Section 3.4.7 – Fabrics

Several proprietary fabric materials have been developed since the mid 1970s, principally for use in geotechnical applications such as reinforced earth. They have some applications in formwork. The two main types are open grids and woven material. The coarse open grid material is usually made from an oriented polymer. It may be used directly to contain the concrete as permanent formwork for stopends etc. An example is shown in Fig. 26. Alternatively the open grid can be used to support a finer material such as a liner (similar to hessian) to reduce loss of fines from the concrete. The material of the grids will be suitable for transmitting tensile forces only, and some limited structural framework will be required.

Fig. 26.

Left – before repair
Right – after repair.

Fig. 26 *Fabric material in use on repair of bridge pier.*

Fig. 27 *Open grid plastic material in use as containment material for concrete surround to a manhole.*

The woven material can include fibres as reinforcement and is particularly suited to repair work on existing structures and in underwater formwork. The fabric will adapt to the required containment shape needed and will generally require a structural framework for support. Typical examples are shown in Figs. 27 and 93.

Figs. 27 and 93.

The use of fabrics is a specialised application and reference should be made to suppliers for design and performance criteria. See also Section 5.6.5. The magnitude of the reduction in concrete pressure when using fabrics is not quantified and is a subject for further research. See Section 8.1, Item 5.

See also Section 5.6.5.

See Section 8.1, Item 5.

concrete
society

Section 3.5 – Cement-based Materials

Section 3.5.1 – Concrete

Moulds manufactured from concrete are occasionally used for production of precast components in the factory or on site.

Concrete moulds are durable and extremely stable, giving good dimensional accuracy. The weight of the mould may be utilised to assist in striking and demoulding.

Concrete mould modules can be built into large assemblies suitable for the casting of prestressed concrete piles on a long line basis. They also provide an economical means of casting products with intricate shapes or curves where there is a high degree of repetition, such as segments for tunnel linings and cladding panels.

Concrete moulds may be produced economically from simple master units which are manufactured to the appropriate shape and degree of accuracy from timber, plaster, clay or concrete. The concrete mould will directly reflect the quality of the master from which it is produced. Consideration must be given to the lead and draw to ensure ease of striking. The surface of the mould is usually treated to improve its smoothness and assist demoulding. Various materials including epoxies, polyurethane varnish and wax may be used for this purpose. Release agents will be required.

The concrete used in mould manufacture should be of a quality at least equivalent to that used in the final cast component.

Vulnerable features such as sharp corners may be strengthened by the introduction of steel, timber or plastic into the mould at these positions.

See also Section 6.4.2 on tilt-up moulds.

Concrete moulds may be reinforced to act as the tilting frames or strongbacks during demoulding and handling. See also Section 6.4.2 on tilt-up moulds.

Where reinforced or prestressed concrete is used as a mould or as temporary or permanent formwork, basic permissible stresses should be those recommended in the appropriate code of practice.

When concrete is used as non-structural permanent formwork, careful consideration must be given to the effects of the movement of fresh concrete setting up stresses in the permanent formwork. Joints which allow movement between the formwork units should be introduced at approximately 5 m centres. Where reinforced concrete is used as permanent formwork and also designed to act integrally with the insitu concrete, account must be taken of the stresses which will be 'locked in' during the curing of the insitu concrete.

'Double' wall and 'locked in' stresses.

Reinforced concrete permanent work may occasionally be required to act as formwork for supporting fresh concrete. An example is an expansion joint in a building with a 'double' wall. One wall is already cast with a joint material applied so that only one face of formwork is needed for construction of the second wall. The existing wall will require to resist the applied concrete pressure forces and, depending on the restraint i.e. tie rods and/or propping, may have 'locked in' stresses during the setting and strength development of the insitu concrete. The basic permissible stresses for reinforced concrete should be used from the appropriate code when designing the existing wall for the applied construction forces.

Section 3.5.2 – Glass Fibre Reinforced Cement (GRC)

Glass fibre reinforced cement (GRC) is a composite material consisting of a matrix of cement and fine aggregate which is reinforced by alkali resistant glass fibres, the length, orientation and content of which can be varied. GRC is manufactured with a wide range of matrix designs to meet particular exposure conditions, e.g. fire, abrasion, sulphates etc. Typically, the cement is grey or white ordinary or rapid hardening Portland cement. However, GRC is frequently made using sulphate resisting cement, and other special cements (such as supersulphated or high alumina cement) have occasionally been used in appropriate conditions. GRC can also include pfa or other cement replacement materials. The aggregate is typically a fine silica sand but other dense aggregates with suitable mechanical, physical and chemical properties can be used. Lightweight aggregates may be incorporated for particular purposes, e.g. fire resistance.

Admixtures can be included in GRC either to aid manufacture or to provide particular characteristics to the material, and they will generally be similar to those used in concrete.

The properties of GRC depend on the particular matrix mix design, glass fibre length, content and orientation and also on the manufacturing process used. However, at the present time, most applications of GRC for formwork are based on a standard material, Grade 1 GRC, produced by a spray process. This is a dense GRC which contains 3.6% or more by volume of alkali resistant glass fibre in the form of strands chopped to length and distributed in an essentially random two dimensional array in the plane of the material. This material is ductile, strong in shear and has a much higher impact strength than comparable asbestos-cement sheets. It has a similar bending strength to plywood but gives lower deflection, therefore designs are not normally limited by deflection. A useful guide to design of GRC permanent formwork is the GRCA Handbook No. 1 (Ref. 40).

GRCA Handbook No. 1 (Ref. 40).

Mix constituents and minimum mechanical properties of Grade 1 GRC are defined in the GRCA *Specification for Grades of Glassfibre Reinforced Cement* (Ref. 41). Methods of test for mechanical properties of GRC are defined in BS 6432 (Ref. 42).

Specification for Grades of Glassfibre Reinforced Cement (Ref. 41).

BS 6432 (Ref. 42).

Fig. 28 *Glass fibre reinforced cement permanent formwork between precast beams on roof of motorway tunnel on M25 motorway (Holmesdale tunnel).*

Fig. 29 *Glass fibre reinforced cement permanent formwork as facade formwork to sloping wall/slab of a building.*

The GRCA Specification allows for some variation in mix design and process. The effects of other variations from the Grade 1 Specification for GRC manufactured with one particular alkali resistant glass fibre are contained in a trade publication (Ref. 43), which also includes information on other physical characteristics of GRC.

Ref. 43.

Applications for glass fibre reinforced cement include permanent and reusable formwork as well as precast concrete moulds. Site tests in the UK using GRC as a reusable sheeting material have shown that conventional release agents can be used and that thirty uses without visible signs of deterioration in surface finish can be obtained.

See Section 3.7.
Figs. 28 and 29.

In the UK, GRC is used primarily for permanent formwork. See Section 3.7. Some typical examples are shown in Figs. 28 and 29. GRC permanent formwork has a wide range of applications in civil engineering and building for both new construction and renovation. Typical applications include bridge deck soffit forms and parapets, shaft and sewer linings, external wall forms, ribbed and coffered ceilings, and columns and piers.

Using batch processes, GRC is produced in a range of profiles which can include corrugations, ribs and other features for strength or stiffness. It can be shaped for appearance and include surface profile and texture as well as returns and other details. A variety of decorative treatments may be incorporated in the exposed face. Surface texture and appearance of GRC is similar to that obtained from precast concrete though the small size of the aggregate and the nature of the reinforcement may enable finer detail and texture to be reproduced. GRC can be surface coated and can also be produced with the appearance of fine exposed aggregate finish.

Section 3.5.3 – Fibre-reinforced Cement Sheet

These products are flat or corrugated sheet materials produced in standard sizes in high volume production primarily for applications other than formwork. They include boards reinforced with asbestos or other fibres. For formwork they are used as supplied, or cut to size either by the supplier or on site.

Asbestos-cement fully compressed flat sheets may be used as permanent formwork for relatively small spans up to 750 mm (for larger spans corrugated sheets can be used).

A typical use is between precast concrete bridge beams to support insitu topping.

BS 690 (Ref. 44).

Permissible stresses should be obtained from the manufacturer. The correct fully compressed grade should be selected – see BS 690 (Ref. 44). Old stock should not be used, due to brittleness increasing with age. Asbestos-cement sheets should not be used for formwork soffits if access across them is required, unless the soffit is fully decked. Walkways should be used over units and no load should be applied directly to the units. Manufacturers should also be consulted for information on deflection, where appropriate, and for any health and safety precautions. The advice of HSE Guidance Note EH36 *Work with Asbestos-Cement* (Ref. 45) must be observed when cutting the material.

Work with
Asbestos-Cement
(Ref. 45).

Fixings to anchor asbestos-cement panels in their permanent location should be considered, bearing in mind long-term durability.

Cement-based sheet products reinforced with fibres other than asbestos have recently been developed. Two which are available and which are manufactured by a similar process to asbestos-cement sheets are:

(a)   Portland cement reinforced with alkali-resistant glass fibres.
(b)   Portland cement reinforced with plastic fibres such as polyvinyl alcohol.

Use of these other fibre reinforced sheet materials is, at the time of writing, still in the development stage. The materials are ductile, strong in shear and have a higher impact strength than most comparable asbestos-cement sheets. Generally, however, they take less loading, and deflect more. Manufacturers should be consulted regarding their use as permanent formwork.

Section 3.5.4 – Wood Wool

Wood wool slabs were at one time extensively used as permanent formwork, but many problems occurred in their use. In particular, difficulties were experienced with compaction of concrete. As a result their use has declined to such an extent that it is now rarely encountered as a formwork material.

BS 3809 (Ref. 91).

The specification for wood wool permanent formwork BS 3809 (Ref. 91) is currently under review.

Section 3.6 – Proprietary Equipment

Section 3.6.1 – General

There are many varied items of proprietary formwork equipment available to limit or eliminate the need for site manufacture. This equipment is generally available on hire and, on contracts of short duration, can show appreciable economies. Although the different suppliers' items may appear similar and equally suitable for a given application, it is necessary to establish their exact characteristics. This Section deals with the general description and application of the majority of the products available.

Suppliers of equipment have design obligations, see Section 2.3, and may also have legal responsibilities, see Section 5.1.1. The extent of these responsibilities depends on the category of design. The three main categories are: *See Section 2.3.* *See Section 5.1.1.*

(a)   Design of individual items for general formwork use, e.g. formwork ties, column clamps.
(b)   Design of formwork systems which are capable of being adapted to different requirements, including design of the component parts.
(c)   Design of formwork assemblies for particular applications using proprietary equipment based on information included in the design brief. (See Section 2.9). *See Section 2.9.*

Generally, users of the equipment have little direct influence on design carried out in (a) and (b) but will have close control over design in (c) as this is carried out to their specific requirements for a particular project.

Suppliers' technical information is often intended as an introduction to the product and as a selling aid, and may not contain much technical detail. The formwork designer, however, is likely to need such detail and should ensure that up-to-date information is available. Such technical information should be obtainable from suppliers. More detailed advice or explanations should be obtained by making contact with the suppliers.

The information listed below will not be required by the formwork designer in every case, but should be available if needed:

(a)   Description of basic function of equipment with illustrations.
(b)   List of items of equipment available, giving range of sizes, overall dimensions and available spans etc with manufacturer's part numbers or other references. If items listed are only available to special order, this should be stated.
(c)   Instructions for use and maintenance, including any points which require special attention during erection or dismantling, especially where safety is concerned.
(d)   Detailed information, as follows:
    (i)   Self-weight.
    (ii)   Full dimensions of connections and any special positioning arrangements. If the item relies on an end bearing, the area of that bearing should be given.
    (iii)   Any permanent camber built into the equipment.
    (iv)   Details of any special attachments, e.g. access brackets, hand rail standards, plumbing feet.
    (v)   Locations for tie bolts or support points. If the item is a beam spanning horizontally or vertically then loading tables should be provided which give permissible spans and spacings.
(e)   Data relating to strength of equipment, as follows:
    (i)   Recommended maximum safe working loads for various conditions of use.
    (ii)   Section properties such as moment of resistance, shear capacity, bearing limitations and stiffness.
    (iii)   The basis on which the safe working loads or properties have been determined and whether the factor of safety given applies to collapse or yield.
    (iv)   Whether the characteristics are based on calculations or tests. This should be clearly stated as there can be variations between results obtained.
    (v)   Deflections under working load together with recommended precamber and limiting deflections, if relevant.

Secton 3.6.2 – Basic Panel Systems

Early systems of 'strip and re-erect' proprietary panel formwork consisted of steel panels of various imperial sizes up to 4 × 2 ft. Today these systems are available in metric sizes using the same principle but adapted to suit modern requirements. An example is shown in Fig. 30. They are particularly suitable for small, complex jobs *Fig. 30.*

such as water and sewage treatment plants. Flexible panels can be used for curved or circular walls. Special panels enable splayed or 90° corners, hoppers etc to be formed with a minimum of timber infill.

Separate channel sections are normally required between panels to accommodate the ties, and also to transmit the load from the scaffold tube walings back to the ties. These walings are an essential part of the system and are typically required at vertical spacings of between 300 and 500 mm.

On straightforward wall formwork these systems with their multiplicity of small panels are labour intensive.

To facilitate the fixing of grout checks, box-outs etc and to reduce the labour content of fixing and striking, panel systems with plywood faces were introduced. The majority of these systems use a high yield steel frame infilled with good quality 12 mm plywood available in panel sizes up to 2700 mm high and 900 mm wide. A typical example is shown in Fig. 31.

Fig. 31.

Fig. 30 *Typical proprietary steel panel formwork system.*

Fig. 31 *Typical proprietary plywood faced panel formwork system.*

The ties are either positioned within the panel frames or are 'snap ties' fitted between adjacent panels in specially machined grooves. Generally no walings are required, although a scaffold tube may be used to align the top of a form. Ancillary items include corner panels, access brackets, stabilisers etc., and components are available to facilitate the fitting of ply infills where necessary for non-modular widths.

In other systems, primarily designed for soffit work, panels can be used with beams and supporting heads to fit on props or falsework systems. Fig. 36 shows an example. There are systems of larger panels using an all steel face or plywood face with steel frames. They are heavy and more suitable for crane handling, and may have advantages for larger jobs involving long runs of straightforward walls.

See Fig. 36.

To reduce the weight of panels, aluminium frames have recently been introduced but they have not yet become popular, probably due to the high initial capital cost and cleaning and maintenance costs.

Storey height panel systems are popular in mainland Europe where standardisation of height has been adopted. Labour costs and number of ties are reduced when using such longer panels.

Panels will generally produce an F2 finish such as in Fig. 2, (see Section 2.5.4) but this may be subject to acceptance by the specifier of the regular joint markings from the panels.

See Section 2.5.4 and Fig. 2.

Section 3.6.3 – Road Forms

Road forms can be used in all types of ground slab construction to form the slab edges and stopends. They are usually inter-connecting shallow steel panels which are held both in position and upright by steel stakes driven into the sub-base. Normally they are used for slabs up to 300 mm thick and where the quality of finish is not critical except for line and level.

They are of two basic types: rigid or flexible. The rigid versions can have either radiused or square edges and both types can be supplied drilled with holes for dowel bars.

A particular type of road form is used with concrete paving trains where a rail (generally a 35 lb/yd mine rail) is attached to the top of the form for the train wheels. A quick positive end to end connection between forms is usually provided to give continuity. These are specialist items and supplier's advice should be followed.

Section 3.6.4 – Tableforms and Flying Forms

Where a soffit form and its supporting structure are struck, moved and re-erected as one unit the equipment employed is known as tableforms or flying forms. Examples are shown in Figs. 32 and 33.

Figs. 32 and 33.

'Tableform' is the original UK nomenclature, but with the advent of much larger units using aluminium frameworks or light gauge steel members the American term 'flying form' has become more used. The increased load capacity and reach of tower cranes has also made possible the considerably increased size of flying forms now in use.

Economical use is most likely on multi-storey construction with plain slabs but may also be achieved in low rise repetitive work.

Construction details most likely to hinder the use of tableforms are deep edge beams or other beams crossing the line of withdrawal of the form from the structure. Upstand beams or spandrel walls will further complicate matters and may need special adaptions, such as folding legs.

The layout and size of the forms are usually determined by the shape of the soffit and the arrangement of columns, walls and access openings, together with the limitations of crane capacity or lifting gear. The leg loading and positioning will have to be considered in relation to the capacity of the supporting slab in the permanent structure, which may require back propping. An example is given in Appendix D Example D4.

See worked example D4 in Appendix D.

The **design** of tableforms or flying forms should follow the same principles as conventional soffit support systems but the legs will normally be more widely spaced and therefore more heavily loaded. If adjustable steel props are used as part of the table framing they are usually inverted and have a purpose-made bracing system.

This may permit higher working loads than those stated in BS 5975 Clause 23.6 (Ref. 2) but the loads in any event should not exceed 35 kN for props complying with BS 4074 (Ref. 50). Designers should be aware that longer spans may make deflection a limiting criterion.

BS 5975 Clause 23.6 (Ref. 2).
BS 4074 (Ref. 50).

Fig. 32. *A tableform system being moved using a 'C' hook.*

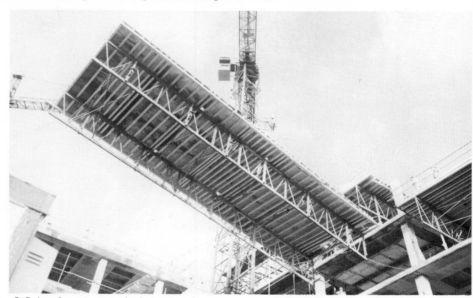

Fig. 33 *A flying form system being moved.*

All connections should be considered for the reversal of forces in lifting and striking operations.

Minimum clearance to permanent work 40 mm.

Normally the minimum clearance required between the face contact material of adjacent table tops and/or the permanent structure is 40 mm. Where props are inserted before striking the forms, greater clearance will be needed. See also Section 5.3.6.2 and Fig. 83.

Particular attention should be paid to the means of access at all stages of the movement cycle. Where practicable, guard rails and working platforms should be permanently attached to the form. Provision should be made to ensure that no component can become detached during moving operations.

Handling and moving: Table and flying forms should normally be struck by first lowering the jacks slightly, then releasing the form from the soffit, so avoiding shock loading on the slab below. Only then should lifting devices be attached and the weight taken. Attempts to take the weight of the formwork while it is still in contact with the soffit can result in lifting devices becoming over-stressed and possible damage to the crane, formwork, falsework or structure.

See Fig. 32 and Section 5.9.8.

General lifting procedures are covered by the appropriate sections of the Construction Regulations, but there is no specific reference to table formwork. Tableforms can be lifted with a purpose-designed lifting appliance such as a 'C' hook. See Fig. 32 and Section 5.9.8. The larger flying forms are usually moved with crane slings. See Section 5.9. Both methods require a safe working procedure to be established.

Section 3.6.5 – Apartment Formwork Systems

Apartment formwork systems are integral wall and soffit forms of steel face contact material which are often referred to as cell, tunnel or room forms. An example is shown in Fig. 34. The use of the expression 'tunnel forms' in this context is deprecated.   *Fig. 34.*

This system may be adopted when constructing buildings which have a large number of simple identical rectangular rooms, such as hotels or hostel bedroom blocks. The side walls are cast with the top slab in one continuous operation, often covering a width of several rooms. The outer gable wall face has a separately handled wall form. The construction method must allow easy removal by crane, from outside, of the whole formwork assembly, which generally means that the floor slab should not have upstand or downstand beams at that stage.

Fig. 34 *An apartment formwork system in use.*

It is also possible to include return or bracing walls within the single forming operation.

The joints between units are self-aligning and of precise construction, thus giving minimal visible joint marks between units. Finishing of concrete faces before decoration is minimal and plastering of the surface is not normally required. The number of uses of the formwork varies but 500 to 1000 uses per form are common.

The formwork is normally made from precision steel units arranged to form rectangular boxes. When a number of complete units are assembled and positioned, the space set between each allows for crosswalls to be placed. Ties are employed between the wall forms as determined by the supplier. Pouring continues until a floor is cast over the soffit form.

Integral formwork units are constructed from a range of panel sizes which allow for variations in length and span. The length of unit used will depend on crane capacity. Units can easily be separated into short lengths, if required, by use of quick release clamps.

To operate apartment formwork systems efficiently, consideration should be given to rationalising the structure at design stage, i.e. dimensions, location of services and openings in the structure. The objective is to establish the shortest practical cycle of operations, generally a one day cycle. Often such systems are economic due to the reductions possible in construction time. This can only be achieved by considering all aspects of construction and ensuring that a speedy method is found for all operations. For instance, provision must be made for quick attachment of electrical down drops and switch boxes immediately after the formwork units are struck, cleaned and oiled. The use of circular switch boxes instead of rectangular allows the concrete to flow around the box and reduces the need to make good the concrete.

This type of formwork is initially expensive but is designed for quick turnround with the minimum of labour. Striking time is determined by the concrete strength

Section 5.3.6.4.

See Section 5.4.3 on repropping.

developed and accelerated curing may be necessary to achieve this. Section 5.3.6.4 gives detailed guidance on the calculation for the amount of heating required. Heaters are used overnight inside the rooms which have been cast, the ends of the rooms being covered by insulating sheets, and the top face of the slab also being covered by insulating quilts. It is normally necessary to place props under the soffit immediately after the forms have been removed, and due care must be taken to ensure that props, when used, are not over-tightened and are positioned over any props in the floor below. See Section 5.4.3 on repropping.

Forms are struck by loosening the integral wall forms from the soffit forms although the wall form remains attached for handling. This allows the wall form to retract from the cast concrete. As the wall faces must strike downwards it is normal to allow a kicker to cater for this.

Separate kicker forms are often employed to cast upstands integral with the slab and for precise location during subsequent erection of formwork units.

Section 3.6.6 – Slab Support Systems

Slab support systems incorporate formwork and falsework, and cover a range of equipment from the simple, such as props with attachments for lacing and bracing, to comprehensive beam and panel systems used in conjunction with proprietary falsework. Some examples are shown in Figs. 35, 36, 39, 66 and 67. The actual face contact material may be proprietary panels or sheeting such as plywood. Some systems include facilities for the support of waffle and trough moulds.

Figs. 35, 36, 39, 66 and 67.

See Section 5.3.6.
See Section 8.1, Item 9.

Provision may be made for striking beams and panels or sheeting without disturbing the props or support system (quick strip system). This provides the opportunity of early reuse of materials and frequently a safer method of striking. For further information on concrete strength at time of striking see Section 5.3.6. Further research is needed to quantify the criteria for striking 'quick strip' systems. See Section 8.1, Item 9.

Fig. 35 *Proprietary 'quick strip' soffit system of formwork with plywood face contact material to flat slab.*

Fig. 36 *Proprietary slab support system incorporating a plywood panel system.*

For the erection and striking of slab systems a proper means of access should be provided. In most cases components are erected using a working platform fixed to the falsework or a mobile access tower.

Sometimes the panels or plywood sheets are recommended to be erected working overhead from the previously laid material. In such cases a safe system of work should be instituted so that the material is adequately supported before working on it, and that guard rails or barriers are used to protect non-working edges or to separate them from completed and secured areas.

Section 3.6.7 – Waffle and Trough Moulds

The choice of a waffle or trough floor is usually made for reasons of economy because the strength of these floors is comparable to a solid section slab but the self-weight (concrete and reinforcement) is 30 to 40% less.

The trough or ribbed floor is a 'one-way' span whereas the waffle which provides a square or rectangular grid of ribs is essentially a 'two-way' spanning structure. See Fig. 37.

See Fig. 37.

The standardisation of waffle and trough floors as recommended by The Concrete Society (Ref. 46) is largely concerned with structural and dimensional properties. Suppliers are able to offer moulds to this standard and the designer of the permanent works (PWD) should be aware of the recommendations. Special moulds of other shapes (triangular, hexagonal, etc) to non-standard grids can be made, but it is considered advisable to standardise on the 900 mm and 600 mm rib centres of waffle and trough floors respectively. The Society's recommendations satisfy the proposals of BS 4330 *Recommendation for the co-ordination of dimensions in buildings* (Ref. 47).

Ref. 46.

BS 4330 Recommendation for the co-ordination of dimensions in buildings (Ref. 47).

The fire resistance of floors using these standard waffle and trough moulds has been shown in CIRIA Report 107 (Ref. 48) to resist the applied loads for up to four hours.

CIRIA Report 107 (Ref. 48).

Fig. 37 *Example of the F1 finish obtained on the soffit of a car park using waffle forms.*

concrete society

The moulds used for forming soffits are at present generally manufactured in the following materials:

Plastics (e.g. PVC or polypropylene)
Glass fibre reinforced plastics (GRP)
Timber
Steel
Glass fibre reinforced cement (GRC)
Expanded polystyrene with suitable liner

Moulds made from polypropylene are almost invariably of standard sizes. Special, non-standard moulds can more easily be made in timber, GRP, GRC or EPS with a suitable lining. Choice of material will be influenced by the concrete finish required and the anticipated number of reuses.

See Section 5.3.6.

With suitably designed moulds it is generally accepted that slab support systems (steel beams and drop heads) offer advantages for the reuse of moulds and beams by allowing the rib soffit to be supported while the concrete cures. This allows the moulds to be struck for reuse during this period. See Section 5.3.6.

An alternative method of supporting waffle and trough moulds is to place them on a full deck of formwork, either on conventional bearers with sheeting or on a skeletal system overlaid with decking. With this method, the moulds cannot be struck until all the support work can be taken down.

Fig. 38.

The 'as struck' finish obtained is usually acceptable for such structures as car parks, warehouses and factories. It must be appreciated that moulds, whatever their means of support, will show joint marks when struck from the concrete and further work may be necessary where high quality finish and good appearance are desired. Masking or featuring of joints may be considered. An example is shown in Fig. 38.

Because both performance and economy of moulds are closely related to the method of support, manufacturers or suppliers should be consulted at the design stage for information on the possible economies and quality of finish to be attained.

Draws:
Troughs 1:8
Waffles 1:5.

A draw of 1 in 8 is recommended for troughs and 1 in 5 for waffles. It is also desirable to provide substantial radii at internal corners to assist striking.

See Section 2.6.3.

Attention is drawn to the necessity for designers and users to take due account of manufacturing tolerances and thermal movements. Long uninterrupted runs of moulds should be avoided, or allowances made at the ends for tolerance build-up (see Section 2.6.3).

Fig. 38 *Moulds in position on soffit formwork before concrete placing. Left showing trough moulds, right with waffle moulds.*

Section 3.6.8 – Adjustable Floor Centres

Floor centres are telescopic beams of lattice or solid web construction used for the support of soffit formwork. They are usually pre-cambered so that when fully loaded they give a flat soffit. A typical example is shown in Fig. 39.

Fig. 39.

In normal use the face contact material is placed directly onto the top of the floor centre and the distance apart of the centres is related to the spanning capacity of the face contact material. Where steel or steel framed proprietary panels are used directly onto the floor centres, it is necessary to ensure that they cannot slide off during initial erection. In practice it is only necessary to secure the first few panels; subsequent ones can then be laid down in safety; all the panel systems have proprietary panel/panel connecting devices.

Fig. 39 *Adjustable floor centres as soffit support to flat slab between downstand beam supports.*

Ideally there should be no construction joints above floor centres, but where these are unavoidable consideration should be given to differential deflections, especially on long spans.

See also Section 5.7.5.

Bearing tongues of floor centres produce high concentrated loads, and the wall or other support may need to be capable of carrying bearing stresses of the order of 3500 kN/m². Often the point of support is the top of side formwork and this should be adequately braced to prevent the support moving outwards, i.e. away from the centre of the floor centre e.g. see Fig. 80. If softwood beams are used for support, the load from the bearing tongues may need steel or hardwood spreaders. If the beams are in turn supported on hanger brackets the bearing stresses on the timber and wall are likely to become critical. Hanger brackets also impart eccentric loads to the wall.

See Fig. 80.

Where long span floor centres are used the lateral stability of the top compression flange will depend on the restraint provided by the frictional contact with the form sheeting. Generally the flange is sufficiently restrained by the friction connection. More detailed guidance is given in BS 5975, Clause 43.4.5 (Ref. 2).

BS 5975, Clause 43.4.5 (Ref. 2).

Where the capacity of a floor centre is to be established by test, it should be tested in accordance with BS 5507: Part 1 (Ref. 49).

BS 5507: Part 1 (Ref. 49).

Section 3.6.9 – Adjustable Steel Props

The specification for the manufacture of adjustable steel props is BS 4074 (Ref. 50). They are frequently used as inclined struts whereas the safe working loads have been derived from investigations into vertical applications.

BS 4074 (Ref. 50).

In general formwork applications the safe working loads shown in Fig. 40 are recommended. These take into account out-of-plumb or intended alignment of 1½° and 25 mm eccentricity of loading. See BS 5975, Clause 23.6 (Ref. 2).

Fig. 40.

See BS 5975, Clause 23.6 (Ref. 2).

The safe working load of props not manufactured to BS 4074 can be established by testing to BS 5507: Part 3 (Ref. 51).

BS 5507: Part 3 (Ref. 51).

concrete society

Ref. 52.

A survey of 40 construction sites (Ref. 52) found variable standards in prop erection; props erected as much as 6° out-of-plumb and timber bearers located up to 75 mm eccentrically on prop heads. Such defects seriously reduce the load-carrying capacity of props. A series of tests simulating site conditions showed that if props are erected 1½° (1 in 40) out-of-plumb and concentrically loaded their average strength is reduced to about 75% of that of props erected vertically. When the load is applied to such props by a beam placed 38 mm eccentrically, the average strength is only 50% of that of props erected vertically and concentrically loaded. As erection defects increase in magnitude, further strength reduction takes place.

Ref. 53.

Further investigations (Ref. 53) included testing additional sizes of props from several manufacturers and also secondhand and reconditioned props. The properties of such props were not significantly different from those of new props. It was also recognised that eccentricity could be eliminated by the correct use of forkheads on most proprietary systems. When using forkheads which are wider than the beam being supported, the head must either be rotated or provided with suitable packings on each side of the beam to prevent any eccentricity of loading.

See BS 5975 (Ref. 2).

If the props are erected better than 1½° out of plumb and concentric loading can be guaranteed, then higher loadings may be carried than those shown in Fig. 40. See BS 5975 (Ref. 2). Suppliers should be consulted to establish the loadings under these conditions.

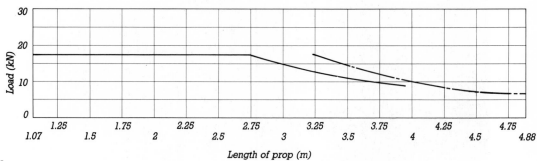

Reproduced by courtesy of The British Standards Institution and based on part of Fig. 1 of BS 5975.

—————— Nos. 0, 1, 2 and 3 size props
— · — · — No. 4 size props

Fig. 40 *Safe working load for props to BS 4074 erected to 1.5° maximum out of plumb and with up to 25 mm eccentricity of loading.*

Lacing may be required to connect the inner sliding tubes of props. This is usually done with scaffold tube and fittings fixed at a position about one-third of the distance up the inner tube. Proprietary systems are also available for this purpose.

Props exhibiting any of the following defects should **not** be used.

(a)   A tube with a bend, crease, or noticeable lack of straightness.
(b)   A tube with more than superficial corrosion.
(c)   A bent head or base plate.
(d)   An incorrect or damaged pin.
(e)   A pin not properly attached to the prop by the correct chain or wire.

Section 3.6.10 – Soldiers and Walings

Proprietary items are available which are intended to be used as backing members to plywood or similar sheeting materials and may also be suitable for use with proprietary panels. Generally the term **waling** refers to a horizontal member and **soldier** to a vertical member on a vertical wall form. However, such members may be used in other configurations.

For example, see Fig. 77.

The materials used are varied and include:

Steel in lattice configuration or cold formed sections.
Aluminium in purpose designed extrusions.
Timber in composite form with laminated sections or glued lattice arrangements.

Figs. 1, 2, 22, 24, 41 and 42.

Examples of various types are shown in Figs. 1, 2, 22, 24, 41 and 42.

The use of such members in formwork may assume certain built-in conditions of stability not necessarily present in other situations. Care should be taken to ensure that the information given by suppliers is relevant to the application. Where walings and soldiers or other backing members are used, the rigidity of the face contact material will increase as friction develops due to the concrete pressure. This may provide additional restraint to compression flanges etc which may not be present in other applications.

The moment of resistance (**M**), bending stiffness (**EI**) and bearing values should be given by the supplier.

Fig. 41 *Proprietary soldiers on a tall wall with timber walings and plywood face. An elastomeric form liner is used on the top part of the formwork.*

Fig. 42 *Proprietary soldiers and timber walings on a small wall.*

Information on shear strength will be required for walings and on allowable tie rod loads for soldiers. Note that the tie rod load is distributed generally through a waler plate into the soldier and this loading characteristic does **not** represent its shear value.

All values should be given in the context of relative conditions of loading and restraint and be verified by test results or calculations.

concrete society

It is common practice to use this type of equipment in falsework applications where not only different restraints occur but different factors of safety are necessary. An example of this is a cantilever soffit to a bridge parapet using soldiers as shown in Fig. 77. The user's attention should be drawn to factors necessary to ensure composite action where loading data rely on its occurrence.

Fig. 77.

Section 3.6.11 – Column and Beam Clamps

These are proprietary items of equipment intended for use in light construction work only. No reliable design data are available and the supplier's recommendations, based on experience, should be followed. See also the recommendations for further research in Section 8.1, Item 2.

Section 8.1, Item 2.

Column Clamps usually have four arms made from steel flat (approximately 60 × 8 mm) with wedges in slot holes at one end of each flat. They suit rectangular columns with clamping distances from about 150 to 1220 mm. The backing members spanning between clamps and face contact material are fitted within the clamping distance and should be allowed for when selecting the size of clamp. Different length arms are available for rectangular columns. An example is shown in Fig. 43.

Fig. 43. (See also Fig. 89.)

Fig. 43   *Timber formwork to column using column clamps.*

Beam Clamps generally have three parts: a horizontal bearer with an upright arm at each end to hold the side formwork to the beam. One of these arms may have a device for horizontal adjustment to facilitate setting up. The clamping distance between the insides of the arms can be from about 125 up to 875 mm. Arm heights up to about 600 mm may be obtained. Depending on the width of beam supported, provision is made for connecting one, two or three props into spigots projecting from the underside of the clamp.

The beam clamp may also be used inverted as the restraint to sideforms in ground beam construction. In this application the maximum design concrete pressure will occur at the top of the arm and some deflection can be expected. Ground beams up to 600 mm depth can be constructed using this method.

Section 3.7 – Permanent Formwork

Section 3.7.1 – General

Permanent formwork, as the name implies, becomes part of the completed structure; it is sometimes referred to as 'lost formwork' (e.g. void formers) when it is incorporated into the structure. Permanent forms, which are visible or accessible on the structure, are usually made from inert, long life materials.

The primary function of formwork is to support the concrete economically with acceptable deflections until the concrete is set and self supporting. In some cases, however, permanent formwork may have other short term or long term functions. In the long term this may include an aesthetic or a structural function either in terms of loads carried by the structure or its serviceability. In these cases the permanent form may need to act compositely with the set concrete, so adhesion or some form of mechanical connection between the two may be required.

Permanent formwork can be classified into participating and non-participating forms. The *Code of Practice for design of composite bridges* BS 5400: Part 5 (Ref. 54) further subdivides the non-participating into those for use in enclosed areas, and those for use in areas where there is a risk of falling pieces. It is outside the scope of this guide to allocate the materials of permanent formwork into the above classifications.

Code of Practice for design of composite bridges BS 5400: Part 5 (Ref. 54).

Some permanent formwork materials are available only in a limited range of sizes, thicknesses and shapes and may need cutting or temporary support on site or may only be suitable for a specialised function. Some other materials may be more versatile, or be specially designed and detailed for a particular job.

Permanent formwork may be specified to be an essential part of the construction process without which the structure could not be built. Alternatively, if the decision to use permanent formwork is an optional one, in which case it should be made at the tender stage, the contractor should study the construction process and evaluate the benefits and costs of permanent formwork. These benefits include:

(a)   Approval of the surface finish of the structure before the concrete is cast.
(b)   Site labour savings from the construction of complex forms to specified tolerances off site.
(c)   Reduction or elimination of falsework.
(d)   Economies resulting from speed in construction, due to ease of erecting tailor-made units, the relaxation of constraints on concreting rates and the elimination of striking of forms.
(e)   Protection offered to the newly cast concrete in the early stages as it cures and when it is most vulnerable.

In all cases, the presence of permanent formwork prevents inspection of the compacted concrete and greater care needs to be taken during the placing operation and this should therefore be borne in mind when considering this type of construction. Different materials have different characteristics and factors which may be of significance are water absorption of the formwork, frictional resistance to concrete flow and vibration damping characteristics. Other factors which must be considered are dimensions of the finished concrete, quantity and diameter of reinforcement, maximum aggregate size and workability of the concrete.

Section 3.7.2 – Materials

Detailed guidance on the materials used in formwork is given in other sections of this guide. The particular features of these materials in permanent formwork applications are outlined below:

(a)   **Wood-based Sheet Materials**
As permanent formwork these are primarily used for 'lost formwork' in enclosed areas, where the possibility of rotting is unimportant. In some building situations this may be undesirable due to other effects. Details of the types, specifications and structural properties are given in Section 3.2.2.

Section 3.2.2.

(b)   **Metal**
Profiled metal decking as permanent formwork is discussed in Section 3.7.3.

Section 3.7.3.

(c)   **Foamed and Expanded Plastics**
The most common material used is expanded polystyrene (EPS). It is used for void formers and is discussed in Section 3.11.1. Further details, specifications and properties are given in Section 3.4.2.

Section 3.11.1.
Section 3.4.2.

(d)   **Glass Fibre Reinforced Plastics (GRP)**
The main use of GRP for permanent formwork is for soffit forms, particularly for bridges. For formwork applications the GRP is normally stiffened with an encapsulated steel or timber strip. Properties of this material are given in Section 3.4.3.

Section 3.4.3.

(e)   **Glass Fibre Reinforced Cement (GRC)**
GRC is a very versatile material for permanent formwork and has a wide range of applications in civil engineering and building for both new construction and renovation. Typical applications include bridge deck soffit forms (see Fig. 28), parapets, shaft and sewer linings, external facade forms (see Fig. 29), ribbed soffits, and columns and piers. Details of its manufacture, specifications and properties are given in Section 3.5.2.

See Fig. 28.
See Fig. 29.
Section 3.5.2.

GRCA Handbook No. 1 (Ref. 40) is a useful guide to the design of GRC permanent formwork.

GRCA Handbook No. 1 (Ref. 40).

GRC has a number of characteristics which offer potential long term performance benefits. The cement mortar matrix in GRC has a low water/cement ratio (0.25-0.35). This produces a cement-based material with

low permeability to liquid water, vapour and air compared with most concretes. It has, therefore, the chemical resistance of a very high quality concrete. Its performance under freeze/thaw conditions is also good. In addition, because its components are inorganic it is non-combustible and is not subject to ultraviolet degradation. Produced with a rough rolled back surface, it is capable of bonding well to concrete and acting compositely with it. Finally, the fibres in GRC act to redistribute stress and to modify the early age cracking characteristics of the cement mortar matrix. With these characteristics GRC can contribute to the effective curing of concrete, cover to reinforcement and, as a surface coating, enhance the serviceability of reinforced concrete structures in terms of durability and, with the appropriate matrix, fire resistance. For example the Norwegian Concrete Association has recognised that GRC can be used to provide part or all of the cover to reinforcement.

(f) **Concrete**

Fig. 44.
See also Sections 3.5.1 and 6.4.
Refs. 122 and 124.

One of the most common materials used in permanent formwork is the reinforced concrete plank or edge form. The design of the unit is in accordance with current structural codes of practice for reinforced concrete. The units are usually precast and held in position while insitu concrete is placed around them. An example is shown in Fig. 44. Attention is necessary at the joints between units to reduce grout loss. See also Sections 3.5.1 and 6.4. Some useful references are Refs. 122 and 124.

Fig. 44 *Precast concrete units as permanent formwork on a composite slab.*

(g) **Fibre Reinforced Cement Sheet**

Section 3.5.3.

Fully compressed flat sheets can be used as permanent formwork on short spans up to about 750 mm. For longer spans corrugated sheets may be used. A typical application is between flying forms or tableforms and an adjacent insitu wall. See Section 3.6.4. The sheet material remains in place after striking of the soffit forms and is permanent formwork.

(h) **Brickwork and Blockwork**

The principal use of brickwork or blockwork formwork is as permanent formwork for retaining walls or for pile caps or ground-beams. Stresses in plain masonry should not exceed those laid down in BS 5628: Part 1 (Ref. 55) which means in most cases that falsework is needed to restrain it. Stresses in reinforced or prestressed masonry can be calculated using guidance in BS 5628: Part 2 (Ref. 56).

BS 5628: Part 1 (Ref. 55).

BS 5628: Part 2 (Ref. 56).

Consideration must be given to the effect of movement of the insitu backing concrete, especially where old brickwork is used in this manner.

Blockwork, dry stacked and surface bonded with alkali resistant glass fibre reinforced render, has been used as edge forms for ground floor slabs.

(i)   **Vitrified Clay or Concrete Pot Floors**
Hollow pots can be used in soffits to reduce the weight of the slab. The use of hollow pots in slab construction has declined in the UK, however, they are used extensively in the Mediterranean and Middle East and therefore the information has been retained in this guide. The pots are generally baked clay hollow pots of plan size 300 × 300 mm. The soffit formwork is completed and the pots laid out in rows. Hollow pots should be used to the supplier's recommendation. The pots must be firmly located in position. Slip tiles may be used for this, though the inability to inspect rib soffits after concreting should be considered. If no slip tiles are used, battens or similar means may be necessary to prevent lateral movement of the pots during concrete placing. In general a minimum rib width of 125 mm is desirable and a maximum aggregate size of 10 mm. Allowance should be made in the concrete mix design for any water absorbed into the pots. Ends of pots must be sealed before concrete is placed.

The total imposed load is the combined weight of the volume of concrete and the mass of the hollow pots. Typical masses for clay pots are given in Table 11.

Depth (mm)	Mass of Pot (Each) (kg)
100	6.8
125	7.6
150	8.6
175	9.7
200	11.2
225	12.8
250	13.9

Table 11. *Mass of Clay Hollow Pots of Nominal Size 300 × 300 mm*

For weights of materials for hollow pots other than baked clay, such as lightweight concrete, the manufacturer should be consulted.

Section 3.7.3 – Composite Floors with Steel Decking

'Composite floors' use the compressive strength and insulating properties of concrete combined with profiled steel decking as underside reinforcement to the concrete. A typical example is shown in Fig. 45. They are mainly used with a steel support framework, although they can be used with a concrete frame or brick cross-walls. The advantage of the composite deck over precast concrete flooring is that it can be lifted easily into place and fixed to the support frame.

Fig. 45.

Composite floors can also be designed to act compositely with steel beams by the use of welded shear connectors as discussed in CIRIA Report 99 (Ref. 57). The deck must perform two functions. It must be able to span between the secondary beams and support the concreting loads, and, secondly, it must be able to resist the imposed loads as a composite slab by virtue of the bond and anchorage developed with the concrete. Design is covered by BS 5950: Part 4 (Ref. 58).

CIRIA Report 99 (Ref. 57).

BS 5950: Part 4 (Ref. 58).

Various proprietary profile shapes are marketed in the UK and some are shown in Fig. 46. Most profiles are trapezoidal in form with depths of between 50 and 75 mm and sheet thicknesses of between 0.9 and 1.5 mm. Depths of the finished slab are normally controlled by fire insulation criteria and are commonly between 120 and 150 mm. Clear spans between beams of 3 to 4 m can be achieved in unpropped construction, and spans of 4 to 6 m where propping is used.

Fig. 46.

The strength of the sheeting in the construction stage can be assessed from BS 5950 (Ref. 34) but any enhancement in strength can only be assessed by testing for a given profile shape. See also CIRIA Technical Note 116, *Design of Profiled Sheeting as Permanent Formwork* (Ref. 59).

BS 5950: Part 1 (Ref. 34).

Design of Profiled Sheeting as Permanent Formwork (Ref. 59).

The degree of composite action is usually such that, except for imposed loads as high as 5 kN/m², it is the permanent formwork design which controls. In most cases, end anchorage at the edge beams is also provided by the shear connectors used to develop the composite action of the beam and slab.

Evidence on the suitability of composite slabs for fire resistance for most commercial structures is contained in CIRIA Report 107: Part 2 (Ref. 48). For example, a lightweight concrete composite slab survived 1 hour with nominal mesh reinforcement and the support steel beams were not adversely affected by the slab deflection.

CIRIA Report 107: Part 2 (Ref. 48).

Fig. 45 *Steel profile sheeting as permanent soffit formwork.*

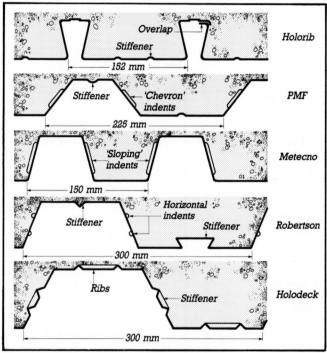

Fig. 46 *Examples of proprietary profile steel decking systems.*

Section 3.8 – Form Ties

Section 3.8.1 – General

Form ties connect opposite faces of wall formwork to restrain the applied concrete pressures. They transmit loads in tension between stiff vertical and/or horizontal members associated with the main formwork. The strength of the tie system may depend upon:

(a) Non-recoverable items lost in the concrete.
(b) Reusable components.
(c) Welding or mechanical jointing between items which form one of the components of the tie system.
(d) Transmission of the applied loads from the tie into the supporting formwork members. (Bearing stresses may be critical.)

Tie rods are also used to transmit other loads, such as in falsework applications with 'hanging' formwork. In such conditions different factors of safety may be applicable. See also Section 3.8.8 and BS 5975.

See also Section 3.8.8 and BS 5975.

Several different types of systems of tie rods are available, including:

(a) High tensile through ties which are usually reusable ties sleeved in the concrete.

(b) High tensile ties with she-bolts, where the tie is lost in the concrete.

(c) Taper ties are reusable through ties which do not require any sleeving in the concrete.

(d) Mild steel ties are generally lost ties with cones at each end acting as spacers.

(e) Coil ties are usually high tensile wires (2 or 4) welded to a wire coil at each end. They are lost ties with cones at each end acting as spacers.

(f) Snap ties are lost ties, and are wire or flat steel ties with a stress inducer allowing the end of the tie to be snapped off after concreting. They are used in building work for thin walls.

(g) Friction clamp ties are clamping devices which are attached to each end of a mild steel or high tensile bar.

Section 3.8.2 – Assessment of Loads

The assessment of loads in tie rods from the concrete pressures and their distribution through the form face and the backing members can be highly indeterminate unless simply supported systems are involved. Methods of assessing load vary and may or may not allow for continuity factors or elongation of the ties.

Section 3.8.3 – Load Capacity of Recoverable and Non-Recoverable Components

Tie components are either recoverable or non-recoverable.

In systems with non-recoverable parts, where the tie rod or part of the tie is lost in the concrete, the tie rod itself, in normal applications, is only used once and a lower factor of safety is appropriate. Where these non-recoverable ties are made of high tensile cold worked steel it is recommended that the minimum factor of safety should be 1.5 on failure load. Factors of safety as low as 1.25 on failure have been used but this is not recommended.

Factors of safety:
Non-recoverable ties –
HT cold worked steel 1.5
Mild steel 2.5
Recoverable ties –
2.0 on failure
(1.7 on yield).

The working stress of non-recoverable mild steel ties should be less than the yield point of the steel. A typical value of the factor of safety is 2.5 on failure load in such cases.

When using non-recoverable (lost) ties some components of the system will be reusable, e.g. she-bolts. These reuseable components should have a minimum factor of safety of 2.0 and should be so designed that they are not permanently strained, such as by stressing past the yield point, by a load equivalent to the failure load of the lost tie to which they connect.

Tie rods are the most critical parts in the design of wall formwork because failure of one can lead to failure of all. Despite this and the indeterminacy of load distribution from new and partly set concrete the factors of safety in Concrete Society Technical Report No. 13, 1977 (Ref. 1) and restated in this guide seem adequate. The new method of assessing concrete pressure given in Section 4.4 may mean that the previously unquantified safety margin will be reduced due to a more accurate determination of the pressure, making the tie rod more critical. Further research on this is a recommendation of this guide (see Section 8.1, Item 7).

Technical Report No. 13, 1977. (Ref. 1).

Section 4.4.

See Section 8.1, Item 7.

Where recoverable through ties are used in formwork it is recommended that the minimum factor of safety be 2.0 on failure load, or 1.7 against yield, whichever is the lower. The yield point may not be evident and in such cases the yield stress should be determined in accordance with BS 18: Part 2 (Ref. 60).

BS 18: Part 2 (Ref. 60).

Section 3.8.4 – Load Transmission

Where bearing plates or washers are used to transmit loads from the formwork to the tie unit, care should be taken to ensure that the bearing stress under the plates and washers is not excessive. The bearing stress on timber members should not exceed the values given in Section 3.2.1 and Table 4. When using timber soldiers this often limits the permissible load on the tie.

Timber bearing stress.

Section 3.2.1 and Table 4.

The allowable loads in bearing plates should be associated with the allowable gap between members, or size of hole in the member through which the load is transmitted. When one tie assembly, designed for use with a particular formwork system, is used on another arrangement of formwork, perhaps from an alternative supplier, the user may need to check the safe working load of the whole assembly.

When tie rods are jointed by mechanical methods, such as screw threads, the strength of the joint should equal or exceed that of the ties being jointed. If the joint includes welding, particular care and attention to detail is required and an adequate factor of safety on the welded joint should be included to ensure that the parent metal of the tie is the weakest component.

Section 3.8.5 – Safety Precautions

Tie rod systems are designed for tension.

No problems should be experienced with high tensile steel ties provided they are treated in a sensible way. However, the integrity of certain types of steel can be destroyed by shock loading when highly stressed by to embrittlement due to corrosion. They are unlikely to be weldable. Tie rod systems are designed **for tension** and before using them in any other way reference should be made to the supplier. Misalignment of holes in opposing formwork faces can introduce bending in tie rods and lead to premature failure. Further, incorrect assembly of non-recoverable ties, together with dirt on threads, can prevent full engagement in any assembly incorporating blind holes. It is essential that threads are kept clean when using reusable tie rod systems.

When tightening double-faced formwork against preformed kickers using tie systems without spacers there is a tendency for site operatives to overtighten the lowest row of ties and thus pretension the ties. This can lead to premature failure of the ties.

Section 3.8.6 – Elongation of Ties

For steel use $E = 2 \times 10^8 \ kN/m^2$. (Section 5.1.3.1.)

High tensile ties will be more highly stressed than mild steel ties and consequently will elongate more under load. The modulus of elasticity (**E**) for high tensile and mild steel are virtually the same. See Section 5.1.3.1. The designer should make allowance for the elastic elongation when the ties are very long on critical applications.

Section 3.8.7 – Anchor Ties

Anchor ties, hook bolts and other devices which are cast into concrete allow erection of single faces of formwork and are subjected primarily to tensile and shear loading, but there is a possibility of bending. In certain instances these devices are also used for restraint of uplift of formwork and are in pure tension. The design of the formwork can often nullify or reduce the bending stresses in the ties but it must be remembered that only allowable tensile loads are normally given by suppliers.

Factors of safety: Anchor ties – 2.0 on tie 3.0 on concrete.

BS 5080: Part 1 (Ref. 61).

It is often necessary to load the anchors at early age and before the concrete has reached full maturity. Suppliers should give details of expected pull-out values relating to concrete of various strengths. Where any doubt exists about the quality of the embedding material trials should be carried out either on site or under usage conditions as near as possible to those expected. A minimum factor of safety for the tie is 2.0 and an overall factor of safety of 3.0 for the resistance of the concrete should be used where tests simulating the conditions of use show this to be critical. The method of test for the tensile loading of structural fixings in concrete for permanent works fixings is stated in BS 5080: Part 1 (Ref. 61).

Section 3.8.8 – Hanger Ties

Factor of safety: Hanger ties – 3.0.

Where soffit formwork is suspended from beams by hanger ties the factor of safety should be at least 3.0 on failure load. A typical example is shown in Fig. 80 (c). This is to allow for accidental loads in view of the consequences of failure and the effect of bending on the tie.

Care should be taken to check stability in cases where one leg of the tie is loaded before the other.

Where hanger ties straddle a steel beam, bending stress should be considered in conjunction with the tensile stress in the vertical legs. For this reason the hanger tie should fit as tightly as possible on the top flange of the beam so that eccentricity causing bending is reduced to a minimum. Note that the size of the beam may be nominal only and the top flange width may vary with beam weight. Therefore, the physical characteristics of the beam must be known in order to arrive at the actual flange width before making or choosing hanger ties.

Section 3.9 – Reinforcement Spacer Systems

The reinforcement in a concrete structure should be fixed with appropriate accuracy in the position specified by the designer. In most structures the reinforcement cage is fixed and held in position in the formwork before the concrete is placed, by spacers placed between the reinforcement and the formwork. These spacers are normally made of either plastic, steel, concrete (site mixed or factory made) or fibre cement. A useful guide is the C&CA Construction Guide *Spacers for Reinforcement.* (Ref. 62).

Spacers for Reinforcement. (Ref. 62).

Block type spacers are more suitable for heavily reinforced and loaded slabs and beams due to their ability to withstand heavy loads without deflection with some stability against overturning. Some of the lighter plastic chairs may deform under heavy loads or indent the form face. They are also liable to overturn when used to support horizontal reinforcement. Plastic spacers compress under load and may 'grow out' later.

Block or chair type spacers may be used on vertical reinforcement, but there is a risk that they may be displaced around the bar during the erection of the formwork or the placing of the concrete, whereas the use of wheel or ring type spacers obviates this problem; in most cases the latter are quicker and easier to fix and are less likely to be seen on the surface of the concrete.

Whichever type of spacer is used, it should provide the cover specified and be firmly held in position. The correct size of clip on spacers for the particular reinforcement should be selected and used. Spacers should not be placed less than 300 mm apart, or in straight lines on parallel bars, particularly in narrow sections such as beams or columns where they could form a line of weakness. Spacers should not damage or deform the face of the formwork.

Block type spacers should have a similar strength, colour and porosity to the surrounding concrete, particularly when used on exposed surfaces.

Sufficient spacers must be used to ensure that the reinforcement does not deform under its own weight or during the concreting operation as such deformations could reduce the cover below acceptable limits. Guidance on spacing is given in Concrete Society Current Practice Sheet No. 87 (Ref. 63).

Concrete Society Current Practice Sheet No. 87 (Ref. 63).

Plastic spacers should be well perforated over at least 25% of their area, and their shape should be such that the concrete can easily surround them and fill the perforations.

Section 3.10 – Surface Treatments

Section 3.10.1 – General

Formwork surface treatments are now many and varied, from applied coatings to form linings. As a general rule it is recommended that the system chosen is tested on site, fully acquainting the operatives with the fixing and placing techniques involved and at the same time confirming the compatibility of release agent, coating, fixing system and mix design to obtain the results required. The Concrete Society Data Sheet *Notes on Formwork Release Agents and Coatings* (Ref. 64) gives guidance on UK manufacturers and also classifies the surface treatment into eight categories. This data sheet is under revision (June 1986) and may be incorporated into a future Concrete Society Digest on release agents.

Notes on Formwork Release Agents and Coatings (Ref. 64).

Polyurethanes, epoxies, chlorinated rubbers and other coatings/sealers for timber formwork are generally best applied in controlled conditions, i.e. in a factory or joiner's shop. They should always be used in accordance with manufacturer's instructions paying particular attention to the health and safety considerations set out in the CIRIA *Guide to the Safe Use of Chemicals in Construction* (Ref. 10). Careful handling and adequate ventilation are of prime importance to the operative when using a number of these products.

CIRIA Guide to the Safe Use of Chemicals in Construction (Ref. 10).

For on-site application to timber always ensure that the timber has been stored in dry conditions before treating, as the moisture content can be critical to the performance of many coatings. Form edges and tie holes should be treated to prevent moisture ingress, even to a pre-coated phenolic plywood sheet, as once this has been cut it needs to be re-sealed. This technique will extend the life of the formwork.

Temporary formwork coatings such as waxes are becoming more popular. They can reduce variations in porosity of the timber and this helps to reduce colour variations in the concrete surface, particularly with new timber or repaired sections. They can be applied on site easily and re-applied as necessary. They also have applications on steel, concrete and other formwork materials.

A release agent **must** be used with all coatings or linings.

Check with the manufacturers for compatibility of materials.

The use of coatings, sealers or precoated formwork timber is recommended in hot climates where the level of ultraviolet light can cause degradation of the timber and form hemicelluloses (wood sugars) at the surface. These can cause heavy retardation of the initial casts of concrete (this also applies to temperate zones such as the UK during a hot summer period) (Ref. 65). Where this retardation has happened already with an untreated timber form, the best remedy is a repeated lime or cement slurry wash over a period of several days and/or treatment of the form with a formwork wax, as once the form has been oiled and used proprietary products of the paint type cannot be applied successfully.

Ref. 65

Section 3.10.2 – Release Agents

Section 3.10.2.1 – Selection and Uses

Release agents are essential in the production of satisfactory concrete work, their prime function being to effect release of the form from the concrete surface and reduce the likelihood of surface damage to concrete and formwork. If painting or other treatment is to be carried out on the concrete subsequently, then information should be sought from the manufacturer of the release agent to ensure that there will be no contamination of the concrete surface.

The Control of Blemishes in Concrete (Ref. 15).

However, if applied excessively they can induce such undesirable features as staining, blowholes, poor surface durability, efflorescence and colour variation, particularly on form surfaces of variable absorbency. (See Appearance Matters No. 3 (Ref. 15)).

See Section 2.8.

As a general practice, where quality of finish is of some importance, it is desirable to conduct experiments with sample and/or trial panels before work proceeds to establish the most satisfactory release agent. See Section 2.8 on sample or trial panels.

White concrete is particularly susceptible to discoloration by mould oils, but this tendency can be reduced by the use of specially formulated high quality release agents. Chemical release agents are likely to prove the most satisfactory but specialist advice should be sought before a choice is made.

The cost of a release agent applied to a form is a small proportion of the total cost of the formwork and its omission is a false economy. The cost of application exceeds the cost of a good quality release agent itself and ease of application is therefore of great importance. Note that some release agents may be better for certain extremes of climatic conditions, with regard to application and storage.

A good release agent should:

(a)   Provide a clean and easy release or 'strike' without damage to either the concrete face or the form.
(b)   Contribute to the production of a blemish-free concrete surface.
(c)   Have no adverse effect upon either the form or the concrete surface.
(d)   Assist in obtaining maximum reuse of forms.
(e)   Be supplied ready for use from the container without site mixing.
(f)   Be easy to apply evenly at the recommended coverage.
(g)   Not inhibit adhesion of any subsequent finish applied to the formed concrete surface.
(h)   During application be inoffensive to the operative with regard to odour, skin staining, etc and be virtually free from the risk of dermatitis and allergic reactions.
(i)   Be suitable for use in the anticipated weather conditions (especially on overseas contracts).

See Section 3.10.2.4.

The types of release agent available are classified below into seven categories. The choice will depend on the face contact material and the method of application (see Section 3.10.2.4). In addition the type of concrete, the quality of finish, the area of the form, the climatic condition etc will all affect the final selection.

Ref. 95.

Ref. 96.

The address of the Water Byelaws Advisory Service is given in Appendix F.

Consideration must also be given to safety, particularly when release agents are used in enclosed spaces, e.g. in mining, tunnelling or poorly ventilated conditions. Release agents for use on potable water retaining structures may require certification (Ref. 95) for their suitability and to ensure that they have no adverse or harmful effects on the water.

The supplier of the release agent should be consulted for test certificates as appropriate and inclusion in the Water Fitting and Materials Directory (Ref. 96) of the UKWFBS. The address of the Water Byelaws Advisory Service is given in Appendix F.

Section 3.10.2.2 – Classification

Visual Concrete – Design and Production (Ref. 15).

The categories of release agents are based on those given in C&CA Appearance Matters No. 1 *Visual Concrete Design and Production* (Ref. 15) and Concrete Society Data Sheet *Notes on Formwork Release Agents and Coatings* (Ref. 64).

Notes on Formwork Release Agents and Coatings (Ref. 64).

Neat Oils   Category 1

Neat oils are usually mineral oils; they tend to produce blowholes and are not recommended for use for the production of high quality concrete surfaces. They are used in the storage of formwork and for concrete which will be hidden below ground.

Neat Oils with Surfactant   Category 2

Neat oils with the addition of a small amount of surface activating or wetting agent minimise blowholes and have good form penetration and resistance to climatic conditions.

Mould Cream Emulsions   Category 3

Emulsions of water in oil tend to be removed by rain but minimise blowholes and are good general purpose release agents, except that they are not very suitable on steel formwork.

Water-soluble Emulsions   Category 4

Emulsions of oil in water produce a dark porous skin on the concrete which is not durable. They are not recommended for good class work and are seldom used.

Chemical Release Agents   Category 5

These are small amounts of chemical suspended in a low viscosity oil distillate. The chemical reacts with cement to produce a form of soap at the interface. Recommended for all high quality work, they should be applied lightly by spray to avoid retardation. Increased cost is compensated for by better coverage compared with the oil-based materials. They generally have good weathering resistance. Certain of the proprietary chemical agents are of the 'drying type' and so are particularly suited to use in dusty, dry climates, on soffit formwork, and in prestressed concrete applications.   *(See also Section 6.4.4.)*

Paints, Lacquers, Waxes and Other Surface Coatings   Category 6

These are not strictly release agents but are sealers which prevent release agents being absorbed into the form face. Wax treatments also come into this category. They are all particularly useful where it is necessary to avoid uneven porosity with consequent colour variations in the concrete surface and to give increased usage of the formwork.

Other Specialised Release Agents   Category 7

These are various types of release agents not listed in Categories 1-6. They include chemical systems, silicones and vegetable oils for such applications as concrete forms, special heated formwork systems, spun pipe systems, etc.

Section 3.10.2.3 – Face Contact Materials

The material and the absorbency of the face contact material will affect the concrete finish and will require differing treatments for the best results. Table 12 relates the type of face contact material to the category of release agent classified in the previous section. Certain specific characteristics of the face are discussed below:

Absorbent Surfaces: With many untreated timbers or plywoods, particularly softwood species, the release agent is absorbed according to the density of the material, giving a grain patterned finish. This is most marked on the spring and summer growth rings found in softwood plywood. This problem can be overcome by giving one of the following pretreatments before use:

(a)   One or more full coats of the normal release agent.
(b)   A suitable barrier paint or varnish (on a dry surface, preferably factory applied).
(c)   A suitable proprietary formwork wax.

Before concreting for the first time, and for all subsequent pours, a normal application of the chosen release agent should be given.

Patches of barrier paint or varnish may wear off with use and generally cannot be renewed because of the absorption of release agent into the form face. This will result in a blotchy appearance to the concrete surface.

Non-absorbent Surfaces: If the surface to which it is applied is virtually impervious, the release agent may tend to migrate and dry up; this will occur where an emulsion is used. This frequently happens, for instance, on bridge decks, where the time between application and concrete placing may be prolonged. The condition is also aggravated by drying winds, strong sunlight and rain. Chemical release agents are recommended in these circumstances, or possibly neat oils with surfactant (Categories 5 and 2 respectively). One coat of release agent should be applied as near as possible to the time of the first pour and prior to each subsequent pour. Very smooth flat surfaces may require initial 'ageing' to roughen the surface to assist retention of the release agent. The use of a pretreatment wax (Category 6) will also improve the finish from the initial cast of the form.

Steel: It is recommended that a chemical release agent (Category 5) be used on steel, although for lower quality work a neat oil with surfactant (Category 2) can be used. When used in conjunction with accelerated curing and heating systems the addition of dewatering and rust inhibitors to these products will make them more suitable. New steel moulds may cause spalling for several uses until 'worn in' and the use of a formwork wax or oil (Category 6 or 2) initially will help.

Face Contact Material		Release Agent Category			
		Plain Surface Finish		Special Surface Finish	
		Pretreatment	Subsequent Applications	Pretreatment	Subsequent Applications
Timber, Sawn and Planed		2 3 5 6	2 3 5	6 2 5	2 or 5 2 5
Plywood	Unsealed	2 3 5 6	2 3 5	6 2 5	2 or 5 2 5
	Sealed	None	2 5	None	2 5
Particle Board	Unsealed	2 3 5 6	2 3 5	2 3 5 6	2 3 5
	Sealed	None	2 3 5	None	2 3 5
Fibre Building Board		5	5	5	5
Steel		None	2 5 6 (wax)	6 (5 can be used to prevent rust)	2
Plastics, GRP, Polypropylene (plain or textured), Rubber and Special Linings		None	5 7	None	5 7
Aluminium		Some specially pre-treated	5 7	Some specially pre-treated	5 7
Concrete		6 (wax) 6 (wax)	2 5 6 (wax)	·	

Notes to Table 12: *(1) Release agent categories are explained in Section 3.10.2.2.*
(2) Categories 1 and 4 are not recommended.
(3) Category 6 is considered a pretreatment only.

Table 12. *Recommended Release Agents for Different Form Face Contract Materials*

Particle Board (Wood Chipboard): Generally the material should be treated in the same way as pre-coated plywood using Categories 2, 3 or 5 of formwork release agents.

Wood-based Sheet Materials: The choice of release agent depends on the pretreatment and surface condition of the sheet.
Sheets are generally available in the following four conditions:

(a)   Sanded but otherwise untreated (the user may subsequently apply sealants to the face and edge surface).
(b)   Sanded and treated with a release agent.
(c)   Face and edge sealed (e.g. 1 or 2 coats polyurethane).
(d)   Surface overlaid with phenolic or melamine resin films, factory bonded and edge sealed.

It is recommended that pretreatments are applied in factory conditions as normal 'on-site' applications are rarely successful. The edges of cut sheets should be re-sealed with a suitable coating (Category 6).

Fibre Building Boards: Generally Category 5 is recommended by board suppliers. Some boards are available precoated with release agent.

Aluminium: Chemical release agents (Category 5) have been successfully used in conjunction with aluminium but these are generally special versions and details should be obtained from manufacturers. Pre-etching of panels is essential to give uniformity of concrete colour. There is increased adhesion between the aluminium and cement due to the the affinity of aluminium oxides and oxides formed in the cement paste. Thus careful selection and use of release agent is of particular importance.

Plastics (particularly Trough and Waffle Moulds): It is recommended that a good quality chemical release agent (Category 5) be used. It should be applied by absorbent cloth or sponge and particular attention should be paid to removal of any excess present on the base of the mould which has run down the sides.

Liners, of Plastic or Rubber: When a proprietary liner is supplied the manufacturer may recommend a suitable release agent. If this is not documented, refer to the manufacturer of release agent and conduct a trial on the material, checking for swelling, degradation, etc. In general chemical release agents will work best on these materials. A special version may be necessary for expanded polystyrene (EPS) and polypropylene, especially reusable types. Certain EPS liners are pretreated and no site application is necessary.

Concrete Moulds: The master moulds should be free of all surface blowholes and blemishes and, when fully cured, sealed either by a coating or form wax treatment. They should then have a compatible release agent applied for each cast. See Table 12.

See Table 12.

Section 3.10.2.4 – Site Work

This section discusses the method of application of release agents, the effect of the time of application and the effect during the placing of concrete.

Application by Hand: Irrespective of the quality of the release agent being applied, too much is as bad as too little. An even film applied at the recommended coverage rate, worked well into the form surface, is all that is required. In the past brushes and brooms have been the principal applicators of release agent from bucket to form. A sponge or mop, or ideally a cellulose floor mop of the type which enables the head to be squeezed out, will provide better results. The release agent should never be allowed to puddle or drain as this is both wasteful and the concrete will probably suffer retardation. Over-application, particularly on soffits, may cause the agent to be vibrated out at panel joints and so cause blemishes on the finished concrete.

Application by Spray: Chemical release agents, neat oils and some cream emulsions will spread much further if applied by spray. Best results are obtained if the spraying operation is sheltered. Misting can sometimes be a nuisance to the operative although cream emulsions are not usually a problem, despite not being really suitable for spray application. Airless spray equipment is usually more satisfactory than compressed air sprays. However, the most common type uses a hand pressurised container coupled to a lance by a flexible hose. Only spray units designed for release agents should be used. Garden sprays are not durable and may have unsuitable jets. It may be prudent to use a fresh nozzle every day to avoid 'clogging up' of the jets.

If reinforcement and/or prestressing wires and ducts are already in position before the application of the release agent, particular care should be taken to prevent coating of adjacent surfaces. If they are contaminated by release agents, refer to the manufacturer for the correct method of removal, particularly for chemical release agents. The usual method is to apply a cement/water slurry, leave it in place for 8 hours and then remove it.

'Contaminated reinforcement'.

Weather and Timing of Application: Where long waiting periods are expected between application of a release agent and concreting, it is essential to pretreat new forms to prevent their deterioration. Chemical release agents are usually best on impervious surfaces and neat oils or chemical release agents on other surfaces in these circumstances.

Proprietary rust inhibiting agents are available for steel forms where storage or long waiting times are considered. They are also particularly useful when exporting formwork in that they can be used for protection of steel equipment. They do not inhibit rust formation indefinitely and supplier's instructions should be sought. Generally to bring the forms into use it is only necessary to wipe off the excess rust inhibitor, and any contamination, prior to applying the selected release agent.

Rainfall may remove release agents. This is a very common problem to which emulsions are particularly vulnerable. Neat oils (Category 2) appear to stay on much longer, probably due to their more penetrating qualities on absorbent surfaces. Chemical release agents are very satisfactory provided the form surface is reasonably dry before application. They are therefore particularly appropriate for steel and plastic faced forms.

Strong sunlight and drying winds are detrimental to release agents, especially if they are exposed to these conditions for long periods. Neat oils and chemical release agents (Category 2 and 5) are generally most satisfactory in this respect.

Application of a release agent to a wet form face sometimes causes striking difficulties but some of the neat oils and chemical release agents have dewatering properties (Categories 2 and 5). For general use it is usually sufficient to stack forms vertically and remove as much moisture as possible from the surface prior to treatment.

Concrete Placing: Release agents may be removed from form faces by abrasion during placement of concrete in tall narrow columns, on inclined form surfaces or by mixes of low workability. Access doors or filling ports and the use of trunking can assist in reducing the risk, especially with high or inclined forms. Prior approval for their use should be obtained where the appearance of the work is important. Wax treatments can be of great assistance in reducing risk of removal by abrasion, and neat oils and chemical release agents (Categories 2 and 5) are also reasonably satisfactory in these circumstances.

Form Face Features: Any projection from the form face that prevents free movement of concrete at the interface is likely to produce defects in finish. Pronounced horizontal features in a wall need particular attention. There are many problems posed by pattern concrete finishes, the majority of which need to be dealt with on an individual basis. Specialist advice regarding their application should be sought.

Section 3.10.3 – Surface Retarders (Category 8)

Although not a release agent by definition, surface retarders are mentioned as they are applied to the form surface before concrete is placed against it, in a similar manner to release agents; their use may also assist in striking. It would not normally be necessary or advisable to use both release agent and retarder on a form surface. If a fair faced and exposed aggregate finish is required from the same mould, use of a 'drying type' chemical release agent is recommended.

Exposed Aggregate Concrete Finishes (Ref. 15).

Retarders react with the cement in the concrete against the form face and retard the setting of the surface layer. This enables the concrete surface to be removed easily, often by brushing, as soon as the form is struck. Surface retarders are used in some instances to assist in the production of an exposed aggregate finish. It is very difficult to obtain a completely consistent appearance by this method due to the many variables which can affect the degree of retardation. Although the use of surface retarders on stopend formwork is not good practice for insitu reinforced concrete work, their use in precast concrete work can be beneficial provided the reinforcement is not contaminated. Treatment of the stopend before placing in position is preferable.

Generally, the more viscous or paint type surface retarders are most satisfactory as the more fluid materials tend to run down form faces, leading to uneven application and possible excessive retardation where fluid has collected at the base of the form.

Forms once treated with retarders cannot, in general, be used for other work. However, use of latex based retarders which produce a dry film may allow the form to be cleaned and used elsewhere.

Spray-on type retarders are only used on horizontal construction joints and, if water based, are likely to affect the formwork soffit below.

Section 3.10.4 – Other Associated Treatments

Subsequent surface treatment such as water repellant coatings, bitumen sealers, paints, cementitious coatings or screeds should always be considered when choosing a release agent and the formwork finish. This is to ensure that no residual material of an incompatible nature is left on the concrete surface which could affect subsequent adhesion characteristics.

Curing membrane systems can also cause problems of this nature as well as discoloration if applied incorrectly. Resin-based materials, manufactured to correct PSA or DTp specification, will degrade within a few weeks under normal exposed weathering conditions, but check with the manufacturer before use if special finishes, white concrete or enclosed areas, etc are involved. See also Concrete Society Digest No. 3 *Curing Concrete* (Ref. 66).

Curing Concrete (Ref. 66).

Section 3.11 – Ancillary Materials and Items

Section 3.11.1 – Void Formers

The formation of openings in concrete, either to reduce the weight of the structure or to provide access for services, calls for particular attention in the selection of the former material, positioning and subsequent withdrawal if required.

The voids may or may not be sufficiently large for access and fixing of conventional formwork. With the smaller voids the choice of forming method is confined to a permanent form or one which can be removed from one or both ends of the void. Where the void is totally surrounded by concrete the use of a permanent form is unavoidable. Materials available include:

Worked example C3 in Appendix C is for a voided soffit.

    Cardboard (known as fibreboard).
    Thin sheet steel formers of various shapes.
    Thin sheet steel in helically welded tubes.
    Inflatable tubes.
    Foamed flexible and rigid plastics.

Cavities formed in the concrete should not be totally enclosed, and some provision should be made to drain the moisture which may collect within the void, leak through the concrete and cause staining. Cases have occurred where a build-up of air and vapour pressure in an enclosed bridge deck void has caused, together with shrinkage, a crack in the top deck; the subsequent release of air under pressure through the crack bubbled the waterproofing. Tests on the void former material may be necessary to ensure its stability, particularly of dyes and substances used in its manufacture. Foamed plastics have an advantage in this respect as they may be regarded as 'solid holes' which do not require draining.

Normal requirements regarding cover must be observed where steel formers which can rust are used.

Load spreaders under ties/banding

Typical void

Note
Frequency and selection of type of retraint depends on size and type of void former. Often restraint systems will alternate in use, i.e. 1 and 3, 2 and 3 etc.

Banding shown but coil ties are used

Banding

Air vents omitted for clarity

Void

Saddle

Main reinforcement

Detail

Soffit | Bearer

Bearer

1. Bolt to face contact material
2. Bolt direct to secondary bearer
3. Band to main reinforcement

Band

Plastic sleeve

Banding

Up to 400 mm

Washer
Removable bolt

4. Band singly to face

Saddle

Detail

Soffit

Fig. 47 *Typical methods of restraining void formers to soffit formwork.*

Foamed plastic formers are extremely versatile because they can be freely moulded and simply cut. But it should be remembered that this material is combustible, therefore care should be taken in its storage and use, particularly if welding or burning operations take place in close proximity.

Pneumatic duct formers are flexible cylinders with solid valved ends. These are usually employed to form cylindrical voids through the structure but they can be coupled with other components to form voids of other shapes. Inflation pressures must be sufficient to resist buckling of the tube due to pressure of the concrete. Ducts supported from the formwork must be fixed in a manner which ensures that there is no local deformation of the forms.

Factor of safety on holding down, see Section 5.3.1.

When not in use, tubes should be carefully stored and safeguarded against abrasion and contact with harmful materials. Mineral oils harm natural rubber.

The advice of the manufacturer of proprietary void formers should be obtained for methods of securing the formers to the formwork. The formers will tend to 'float' and must be anchored to the soffit formwork, the previously cast concrete or to the reinforcement. Telltales or pre-set markers will give warning of any movement during concreting. Placing and compacting the concrete may tend to displace the formers laterally, and appropriate measures must be taken to restrain them. The fixing should be made to formwork members rather than to reinforcing steel, although alternating the fixings is common practice. Examples of fixing methods are shown in Fig. 47.

Fig. 47.

Where inflatable tubes or large hollow void formers are cast into concrete, a calculation should be made of the amount of concrete required and this should be compared with the actual amount used. Any discrepancy may be evidence of failure of the formers.

Section 3.11.2 – Hole Formers

Holes or chases should preferably be formed in fresh concrete, because cutting after casting is slow and possibly more expensive. If hole formers are to be removed this should be done in a manner that avoids damage to the concrete. Great accuracy may be needed in the relative positioning and shape of the holes. This calls for efficient fixing of the former to the main formwork. Formers may sometimes be removed or released prior to striking the formwork.

Formers should be designed so that restraint to the concrete surrounding the opening is avoided. Such restraint can cause tensile forces in the concrete and even cracking at the corners of door and window openings. The insertion of a plastic gasket will allow the hole former to move with the concrete as movement takes place.

Formers constructed from concrete are stable and, when combined with an expanded plastic lagging, provide an economic means of forming holes, particularly in flat slab construction.

See also Section 3.6.7.

When forming indents or three-sided voids, such as spaces between floor ribs, the formwork should be designed with sufficient taper or 'draw' on the sides to allow its removal without damage to the concrete. See also Section 3.6.7 (Waffle and Trough Moulds).

Section 3.11.3 – Grout Checks, Sealing Grooves and Feature Strips

Grout checks, sealing grooves and feature strips are items attached to the formwork face to form rebates in the finished concrete. They usually consist of a hardwood timber or plywood strip nailed or glued to the face contact material. Care is needed to seal the joint to prevent cement fines migrating under the strip. This is particularly necessary with unsealed face contact sheet. Typical details for grout checks and sealing grooves are shown in Fig. 48.

See Fig. 48 over.

Grout checks are strips fixed to a form to define the top or end of a pour. The edge cast into the pour forms a straight clean line which may be the final top surface of a construction joint. On wall formwork the concrete may be allowed to rise up the inside edge of the grout check, allowing the top of the pour to be scabbled to remove the laitance without disturbing the clean line on the face. On opposing wall faces the placing of two grout checks allows the concrete placing operatives to 'float' the concrete to the correct level between the grout checks. A square profile will perform more satisfactorily than a rectangular shape which can cause spalling of the concrete.

Sealing grooves invariably take the same form as grout checks and will be positioned at expansion joints or at crack inducer positions in the structure. After striking, the groove is filled with an appropriate sealer. To facilitate striking, the edges of the sealing groove strip should be tapered. When both faces are cast in concrete, such as at a crack inducer, the recommended minimum draw is 1 in 5. When one side is free and only one face is in contact a draw of 1 in 8 is recommended, such as at an expansion joint. See Fig. 48.

Minimum draw.

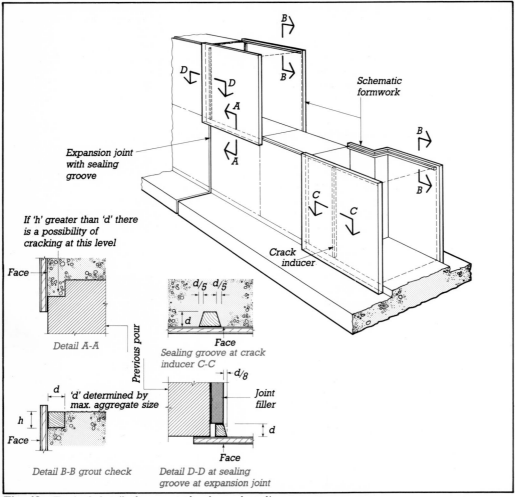

If 'h' greater than 'd' there is a possibility of cracking at this level

Face

Detail A-A

Expansion joint with sealing groove

Schematic formwork

Crack inducer

Previous pour

Face
Sealing groove at crack inducer C-C

d determined by max. aggregate size

Face

Detail B-B grout check

Joint filler

Face
Detail D-D at sealing groove at expansion joint

Fig. 48 *Typical details for grout checks and sealing grooves.*

Feature strips will usually be specified in the requirements for the finish and are discussed in Section 2.5.7. Examples of the finish obtained are shown in Figs. 10, 11 and 12. The edges of feature strips should be tapered for ease of striking. The recommended minimum draw on each side is 1 in 5. The strips will generally be struck attached to the formwork and particular care is necessary to ensure uniform permeability with all joints sealed for high quality finishes. Dissimilar materials of face and strip can cause thermal movements and 'ruckling' of the feature. In selecting the size of feature strips the temporary works designer may have to consider the implications of the form ties passing through the strip, as often these will be required to pass through the 'valley' of the concrete which is the ridge top of the strip. Selection of suitable clearances to the edge of the tie rod holes will give the minimum dimensions for the ridge top of the feature strip.

Section 2.5.7.
Figs. 10, 11 and 12.

Section 3.11.4 – Box-Outs

The term 'box-out' is used frequently to mean a hole former as discussed in Section 3.11.2. It may also mean a former planted on to a wall form to create features in the concrete. The box-out may be fixed to the form for a series of uses or, for ease of striking, may be separated from the form at each use. In the first case the box-out should be attached to only one face of the two forms.

Section 3.11.2.

Where the box-out is designed to be removed from the cast concrete in one piece, either with the form as it is struck or as a separate piece, then suitable draws or tapers should be included in its design. The minimum draw is 1 in 8.

Minimum draw 1:8.

Section 3.11.5 – Chamfers and Fillets

The forming of chamfers on external corners is frequently achieved by fixing triangular sections of timber to the form. The minimum recommended size of timber chamfer is 20 × 20 mm. On internal corners the arris can be formed by a shaped and prepared timber to give the triangular section. Accurate internal straight fillets are harder to achieve than chamfers on external corners. Where forms have a number of

Timber chamfer 20 × 20 mm.

uses it may be more satisfactory to design each one with more substantial timbers as a constant feature.

A range of proprietary sections for forming chamfers, fillets and other features is available in plastic material, usually high impact PVC. These are available in chamfer sizes of 11, 15, 20 and 25 mm.

Steel chamfers are available for use on purpose-made steel formwork. Their accurate fitting onto the form is a specialist task and designers should be aware of the cost implication, particularly in precast moulds, of specifying chamfers to corners. The difficulties of obtaining solid steel chamfer tend to limit the size; 25 × 25 mm is the most common.

Steel chamfer 25 × 25 mm.

Section 3.11.6 – Formwork Tapes and Foam Strips

Several proprietary types of tape and foam strip are available in the UK. The tapes are generally matt finish, thin PVC 45 to 50 mm wide with a special adhesive system capable of adhering to formwork surfaces which are not always completely clean or free from oil traces. Test, therefore, for good adhesive qualities before use to ensure that they will not lift before or during placement of concrete and cause blemishes. Ensure also that the chosen release agent will not affect the adhesion.

The foam strip sections, generally 12 × 6 mm, also have special adhesives and silicone paper backing. They should be of a closed cell type to ensure water tightness and reduce the incidence of sticking into the concrete matrix (usually associated with open cell structure). The denser the foam, the greater the problem with compressing so, again, test the compression over a length of the material before using. There is not usually a problem with movement once they are placed and mechanically trapped in formwork joints.

Most manufacturers will supply non-standard sizes of tape and foam strip. Lengths of roll vary considerably, so check the cost per metre length. Compared with the cost of repair after grout leakage and removal of fins they can be a worthwhile investment. When fitting to formwork they must be accurately positioned to avoid making unwanted marks on the finished concrete.

Section 3.11.7 – Cast-in Components

The selection and design of components which are to be cast into concrete requires consideration of how they will be held in position. They must be accurately positioned and rigidly held. Any removable part should be capable of being easily struck without damage to the concrete, and any final connecting components easily fitted. Protective measures should be taken to avoid damage to projections or blockage of holes and recesses.

Attachment to the formwork is normally by mechanical means such as bolting. Grout should not be allowed to get into the joint, or the embedded component may become damaged or dragged out during striking.

Where bolts are cast in to provide subsequent connections the design should allow a reasonable tolerance in positioning.

Selection and Use of Fixings in Concrete and Masonry (Ref. 67).

Further information is given in CIRIA Guide 4 *Selection and Use of Fixings in Concrete and Masonry* (Ref. 67).

Long term durability requirements may result in plated components being used. Care should be taken that the plating is not damaged during the construction operations. If plated components are threaded there will always be a risk of the plating being locally damaged when they are tightened. Refer to suppliers and specifiers for more information on the durability of cast-in components.

Section 3.12 – Form Liners

Section 3.12.1 – General

Form liners can generally be described as non-structural materials used to line the face of the structural form, with one or more of the following aims:

- to extend the life of old form faces.
- to produce a smooth and better surface finish to the concrete.
- to provide a profiled or patterned surface to the concrete.

To extend the life of old forms various liners have been used, such as thin plastic sheeting, hardboard, linoleum and sponge rubber sheeting. In most cases these types of material are not recommended because they are difficult to fix and use, and tend to give variable results. They are materials which have not been primarily designed as form liners.

There are many types of liner now available specifically designed for multiple reuse and to give good finishes. Used correctly, liners can produce excellent finishes. In view of the number of different types and finishes available to specifiers, it is a recommendation of this guide that a separate booklet be prepared relating the finishes possible to the materials used to achieve that finish. See Section 8.1, Item 10.

See Section 8.1, Item 10.

Some liners remain attached to the formwork face for several uses, while others are intended to be left on the concrete face when the form is struck.

By leaving the liner on the concrete it can be peeled off separately; this is particularly necessary in the case of sculptured forms which require the use of soft or elastic materials. Separate striking also allows the liner to be struck at a different angle to that of the main form.

The general characteristics of form liners are dependent on hardness, permeability and surface texture. See Section 3.1.2. All of these will be affected by the selection and use of release agents if necessary. See Section 3.10.

See Section 3.1.2.
See Section 3.10.

Form liners, by definition, have no structural requirements apart from transferring concrete loads into the supporting formwork. Ideally they should be supported from formwork that has a solid continuous face. Occasionally liners may be considered structural by incorporating other members, and Section 5.1.4 briefly considers this aspect.

Section 5.1.4.

Where soft flexible liners are used in wall formwork, it may be desirable to sleeve tie rod holes to prevent leakage of grout and to avoid the lateral compressive pressure of the concrete deforming the liner and jamming the recoverable items of any tie rod assembly.

Section 3.12.2 – Materials

Liners are made of such materials as fibre building board, polystyrene, rubber, neoprene and glass fibre reinforced plastic, often in the form of thick sheets, of various sizes. Some can be sculptured to produce patterns and even bas-relief pictures.

The characteristics of some form liners are given below:

Fibre Building Board (including Hardboard): There is a wide variety of fibre building board but the most usual for liners is tempered hardboard. It has oil and resin baked in during manufacture to improve water resistance and strength. See also Section 3.2.2.2.

See also Section 3.2.2.2.

Tempered hardboard used as a liner will provide a smooth surface, or alternatively the reverse side will give a fine textured pattern (see Appearance Matters No. 3 (Ref. 15)). Frequently only one use is expected but more can be achieved with care. It can be flat or curved in one plane.

The board should be mounted on a continuous support when flat, but on curved surfaces closely placed battens may be used. The edges should be nailed and the centre of the sheet should be attached by nails or glue.

Joints will show on the concrete face but the effect can be reduced by sealing the edges of the board and filling the gaps.

To avoid ruckling of the board it should be conditioned by wetting before fixing. See BS 1142: Part 2 (Ref. 28).

See BS 1142: Part 2 (Ref. 28).

Discoloration of concrete can be caused by some hardboards. Variations in colour can occur in the height of a lift due to different rates of absorption caused by pressure differences. These effects are reduced by the use of tempered hardboard or various surface treatments.

Moulded Thermoplastic Sheets: Thermoplastic sheets can be moulded by several methods to give textured or patterned finishes with features up to 60 mm deep. Sizes of sheet are usually between 3 and 7 m in length and up to 0.6 m in width although widths of 1.8 m may be available. See also Section 3.4.6.

See also Section 3.4.6.

The mouldings will have voids between the liner and the backing form; deeper sections may therefore not resist high concrete pressures and may require some filling as support. Refer to the liner supplier for more details.

Initial mould costs are high but can be offset by the production of large numbers of sheets.

See Section 3.11.6.

Joints between sheets are inevitable but either they can be masked by the pattern or a compatible form tape can be used. See Section 3.11.6.

In normal use, the liners are lightly fixed with panel pins to the form but remain on the concrete face when the forms are struck. There are conflicting claims on the extent of reuses, but the number obtainable depends on the pattern design, method of fixing, type of release agent and general handling.

Although most thermoplastic linings do not require a release agent when new, the use of a chemical release agent is recommended to ensure uniformity for all uses. With each successive use, the surface becomes scratched until eventually it may require the application of a suitable pretreatment.

Foamed and Expanded Plastics: Various materials can be used, such as expanded polystyrene (EPS), polyurethane and polyethylene. They vary in thickness up to about 25 mm and allow the production of a wide range of low relief patterns as mouldings. See also Section 3.4.2 and Fig. 9.

See also Section 3.4.2 and Fig. 9.

The materials may also be used in sheet or slab form of sufficient thickness to allow the sculpture of patterns by hand.

The materials can be hard skinned with high density material, which can increase the number of reuses depending on the concrete pressures developed in the mould. Generally with sculptured forms they are single use materials.

Rubber, Neoprene and other Plastic Liners: Rubber, neoprene and PVC can be formed by moulding into patterned mats of varying flexibility. They have characteristics suitable for many uses and can be soft enough to form undercut surfaces. See also Sections 3.4.3 and Section 3.4.5.

See also Sections 3.4.3 and Section 3.4.5.

Mats may be either carried with the form or left on the concrete after use.

An increasing range of products is currently being marketed and the producers should be approached for the latest information on methods of use and patterns available.

Figs. 7, 8, 24 and 25.

Typical liners and the finish obtained are shown in Figs. 7, 8, 24 and 25.

Absorbent Liners: Soft board, thick kraft papers and corrugated cardboards have been used with the object of providing a consistent face material by using a single use material liner.

The deliberate use of an absorbent material might assist in the reduction of blowholes, but the absorbency will vary according to weather conditions. Where materials have to be waxed or showerproofed to give a degree of wet strength the absorbent features will be lost.

The underlying form face needs to be of consistent construction. Joints in it may well show through the liner.

Section Four
Loadings

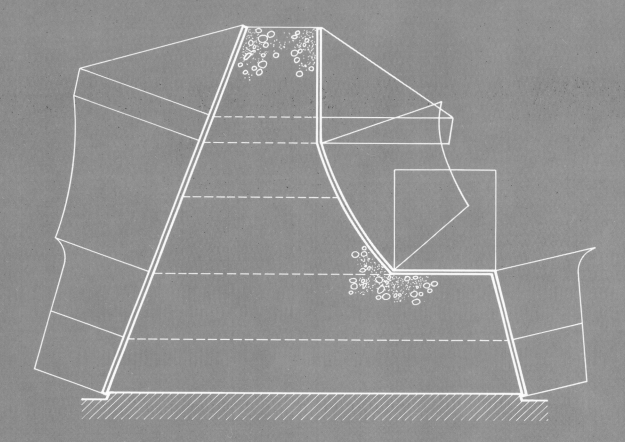

concrete
society

Section Four – Loadings

Section 4.1 – General

Five different types of load associated with formwork are considered in this guide:

Self-weight
Imposed loads
Loadings from concrete pressures
Environmental loads
Horizontal loads.

BS 5975 (Ref. 2).

Some are considered under more than one heading, for instance, wind. In accordance with BS 5975 (Ref. 2) the load of fresh concrete on soffit formwork is considered as an imposed load.

When considering the horizontal load acting on formwork, a minimum stability force should be used in design. This may exceed the calculated horizontal design load.

See Section 5.1.2.

When carrying out a design some of the loads may have to be estimated by engineering judgement. During the design check the accuracy of the estimates should be considered. See Section 5.1.2.

Section 4.2 – Self-weight of Formwork

Generally the self-weight or mass of formwork is small compared to the imposed loads.

The mass of soffit formwork should be added to the imposed and construction operation loads to give the total falsework load. The mass of wall formwork may be carried either by falsework or directly by the foundations. The mass of individual forms is of importance in assessing handling capacity.

Section 4.2.1 – Materials

The mass and density of materials commonly used in formwork are shown in Table 13.

Mass of 100 kg exerts vertical force of 1 kN (Section 1.1).

Material	Mass (kg/m³)	Mass (kg per mm thickness/m²)
Plywood (Softwood)	580	0.58
Plywood (Hardwood)	650 – 800	0.65 – 0.80
Chipboard	795	0.80
Softwood	480 – 590	
Hardwood	720 – 1050	
Steel	7850	7.85
Aluminium	2770	
Glassfibre Reinforced Cement	2000	2.0
Glassfibre Reinforced Plastic	1500	1.5
Expanded Polystyrene	16 – 32	
Reinforced Concrete (up to 2% reinforcement)	2500	

Table 13. *Mass of Materials in Common Use*

Section 4.2.2 – Wall Forms

The self-weight of wall forms tends to increase with increase in design concrete pressure; the higher the pressure the more horizontal and vertical members are required to transmit forces to a given number of ties. A further increase in mass may arise in large forms when they are stiffened to cope with twisting and racking during handling.

See Table 14.

As a general guide, the typical mass of one face of formwork for design concrete pressure between 50 and 70 kN/m² is given in Table 14. However, specific cases may need to be checked.

See Section 5.9.

For information on lifting of forms see Section 5.9.

Construction	Mass (kg/m²)
Timber and plywood (with soldiers)	60
Timber and plywood (small side forms 1 m high)	50
Plywood forms, aluminium walings, steel soldiers	50
Proprietary steel panels, tube walings for crane handling	75
Proprietary strip and re-erect panel formwork	35 – 45
Special purpose-made formwork with 5 mm steel face for multiple use	95 – 120

Table 14. *Typical Self-weight of Wall Formwork*

Section 4.2.3 – Soffit Forms

A typical arrangement of timber and plywood soffit forms for slabs up to 300 mm thick used with conventional falsework supports will have a self-weight of approximately 50 kg/m². Proprietary decking systems vary but generally weigh 50 to 85 kg/m² of soffit. However, specific cases may need to be checked.

Self-weight of approximately 50 kg/m².

Section 4.3 – Imposed Loads

The imposed loads on formwork arise from the permanent works and loads applied during construction. A full treatment of imposed loads is given in BS 5975, Clause 27 (Ref. 2). Concrete pressures are considered in Section 4.4 of this guide.

BS 5975, Clause 27 (Ref. 2).

Section 4.3.1 – Permanent Works Loads

The permanent works loads are calculated from the self-weight of the concrete structure being constructed.

In wall formwork the fresh concrete applies a pressure to the forms which is considered in detail in Section 4.4. When the wall faces are vertical no component of the mass of the concrete acts on the forms. If the wall formwork is inclined then the 'lower' face of the formwork will have to act as 'falsework' to support the mass of the fresh concrete. See Section 5.2.2 and Fig. 59.

Section 4.4

See Section 5.2.2 and Fig. 59.

In soffit formwork the permanent works load comprises the mass of the concrete. Normally a concrete density of 2500 kg/m³ should be used in the calculations for slabs having up to 2% reinforcement. When using lightweight aggregates or particularly dense aggregates separate density figures should be determined. Congested reinforcement or prestressing can significantly increase the average density of the structure to be supported.

Normally a concrete density of 2500 kg/m³ should be used.

Precast units seated on formwork should be considered as imposed loads. The effects of impact loading during placing of such units should be checked. See BS 5975, Clause 27.2 (Ref. 2).

See BS 5975, Clause 27.2 (Ref. 2).

Where the permanent works are post-tensioned whilst still being supported by formwork, the stressing force and resulting deformations of the concrete are often transferred to the supporting forms. Consideration should be given in the design to accommodating the force and the movement involved (see Sections 5.1.3.5 and 6.4.4). It should be noted that these movements can be horizontal, vertical (up or down) or rotational.

See Sections 5.1.3.5 and 6.4.4.

When multiple levels are being constructed, the sequence of operations may require future levels of permanent work to be supported by the formwork under design. See also Section 5.4.2 on backpropping and BS 5975 Appendix M (Ref. 2).

See also Section 5.4.2 on backpropping and BS 5975 Appendix M (Ref. 2).

Section 4.3.2 – Construction Operations Loads

Formwork which is part of the working area on site will require a loading allowance to cater for the operatives and their plant.

Generally, on soffit forms, 1.5 kN/m² is allowed for the operatives placing the fresh concrete, including for hand tools and small mechanical plant used in the placing operations, such as vibrator motors etc. The area considered should include all adjacent walkways around the soffit as well as the actual soffit area. This allowance of 1.5 kN/m² represents only 60 mm of extra concrete and care should be exercised on thin slabs where the relative effects of heaping of the concrete can be greater than on thick slabs (see BS 5975 Clause 27.3.1 (Ref. 2)). The method of placing will influence the heaping of concrete.

Allow 1.5 kN/m².

See BS 5975 Clause 27.3.1 (Ref. 2).

Where a soffit form is to be used only for access or inspection, the imposed load may be reduced to 0.75 kN/m².

Access only, use 0.75 kN/m².

In wall formwork, access for concreting operations should be considered; commonly only one side of the form is fitted with an access platform for use when concreting. It should be designed for an imposed load of 1.5 kN/m².

Tie rod access, use 0.75 kN/m².

Access platforms used only to place tie rods or for inspection can be designed for a reduced loading of 0.75 kN/m².

See Section 7.5.2.

All working platforms must comply with current HSE Regulations. See Section 7.5.2 on access and working platforms.

Refs. 87 and 94.

Work associated with prestressed concrete will often require platforms of higher loadings than stated to cater for jacks, pumps, fittings etc, and the advice of the specialist suppliers should be sought. Useful guides to safety in prestressing operations are published by The Concrete Society (Ref. 87 and 94).

Refer to BS 5975 Clause 27 for more details.

Pipelines from concrete pumps can produce considerable horizontal forces on forms and should be calculated separately. Other loads on soffit formwork may arise from pedestrian and vehicular traffic, and storage of materials and plant. Refer to BS 5975 Clause 27 for more details.

See Section 3.9.

It should be noted that local overloading of soffit forms can occur if reinforcement spacers are not evenly distributed. See Section 3.9.

Section 4.4 – Concrete Pressures

Section 4.4.1 – General

The maximum lateral pressure of concrete on formwork depends on six main factors:

See Fig. 49.

(a) Vertical height of the form (H) in metres. Note: This is not necessarily the pour height. See Fig. 49.

See Tables 15 and 16.

(b) Average rate of rise of the concrete vertically up the form (R) in metres per hour, taken as the average over the pour.

(c) Temperature of the concrete at time of placing (assumed to be between 5 and 30°C).

See Fig. 50.

(d) Plan dimensions of the pour. See Fig. 50.

See Table 17.

(e) Constituents of the concrete, the type of cement and/or blends, with or without admixtures, with or without retarders.

(f) Density of the concrete.

Varying any one of the above factors may alter the concrete pressure acting on the formwork. The pressure will act at right-angles to the face of the form.

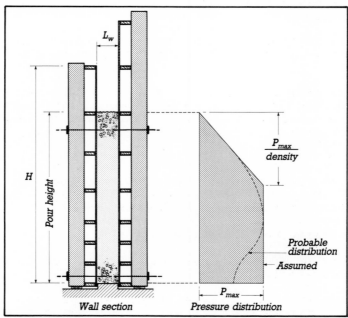

Fig. 49 *Concrete pressures on parallel forms.*

Concrete Pressure on Formwork (Ref. 3).

CIRIA Data Sheet on Design Pressures. Appendix E.

This guide is being published shortly after important new research on concrete pressures has been published in CIRIA Report 108, September 1985 (Ref. 3). The CIRIA Data Sheet on Design Pressures, which forms part of Report 108, has been reproduced in Appendix E. The results and formulae for predicting concrete pressures in Report 108 are based on extensive site evaluation and these have been adopted in this guide as the most authoritative guidance on the subject. They are hereafter referred to as the 'CIRIA method'.

Continued on page 84.

Concrete Temperature	Design Pressure (kN/m²)	Height of Form (h)							
		2 m		3 m		4 m		5 m	
5°C	40	0.3		0.2					
	45	0.8		0.2					
	50	1.5	(0.2)	0.5		0.2			
	55			0.9		0.4		0.2	
	60			1.5	(0.2)	0.7		0.3	
	65			2.4	(0.3)	1.2		0.7	
	70			3.5	(0.8)	1.9	(0.2)	1.1	
	75			4.9	(1.6)	2.7	(0.3)	1.7	
	80					3.7	(0.8)	2.5	(0.2)
	85					5.0	(1.4)	3.4	(0.4)
	90					6.4	(2.3)	4.4	(0.9)
	95					8.1	(3.5)	5.6	(1.5)
	100					10.3	(5.0)	7.0	(2.4)
10°C	30	0.3		0.2					
	35	0.6	(0.2)	0.3		0.2			
	40	1.1	(0.4)	0.6		0.3		0.2	
	45	1.8	(0.8)	1.0	(0.2)	0.6		0.4	
	50	2.8	(1.6)	1.6	(0.5)	1.0	(0.2)	0.7	
	55			2.3	(1.0)	1.6	(0.4)	1.1	(0.2)
	60			3.1	(1.6)	2.2	(0.8)	1.7	(0.4)
	65			4.1	(2.5)	3.0	(1.3)	2.4	(0.7)
	70			5.4	(3.6)	3.9	(2.0)	3.1	(1.2)
	75			7.1	(5.1)	5.0	(2.9)	4.0	(1.9)
	80					6.2	(3.9)	5.0	(2.6)
	85					7.6	(5.1)	6.2	(3.5)
	90					9.2	(6.6)	7.5	(4.6)
	95					11.0	(8.3)	8.9	(5.8)
	100					13.4	(10.5)	10.5	(7.2)
15°C	25	0.3		0.2					
	30	0.6	(0.2)	0.4		0.2		0.2	
	35	1.0	(0.5)	0.7	(0.2)	0.5	(0.2)	0.3	
	40	1.6	(1.0)	1.1	(0.5)	0.8	(0.3)	0.6	(0.2)
	45	2.3	(1.7)	1.6	(0.9)	1.3	(0.5)	1.0	(0.3)
	50	3.4	(2.7)	2.3	(1.4)	1.8	(0.9)	1.5	(0.6)
	55			3.1	(2.1)	2.5	(1.4)	2.1	(1.0)
	60			4.0	(2.9)	3.3	(2.1)	2.8	(1.5)
	65			5.1	(4.0)	4.1	(2.8)	3.6	(2.1)
	70			6.3	(5.2)	5.1	(3.7)	4.5	(2.9)
	75			8.0	(6.9)	6.3	(4.8)	5.5	(3.8)
	80					7.5	(6.0)	6.6	(4.8)
	85					9.0	(7.3)	7.8	(5.9)
	90					10.5	(8.9)	9.2	(7.1)
	95					12.4	(10.8)	10.7	(8.6)
	100					14.6	(13.1)	12.3	(10.1)

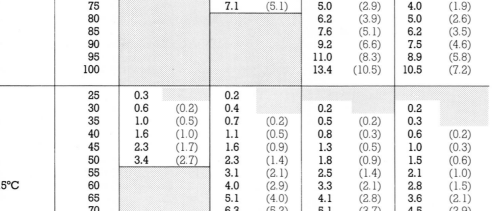

Table 15. *Rate of Rise (m/h) for Walls and Bases, height 2 – 5 m*

Notes to Tables 15 and 16:

*(1) The density of concrete is assumed to be 2500 kg/m³ (25 kN/m³) in **all** the pressure and rate calculations given in this section. When considering other concrete densities the CIRIA Report values should be used.*

(2) The tables apply to compaction by internal vibration.

(3) In the lower heights of pour the pressure cannot exceed the fluid head of the concrete and thus concreting at faster rates of rise to the highest value stated will not cause the pressure to exceed the value stated. For example, from Table 16, a column 4.0 m high with OPC concrete at 5°C, concreted with a rate of rise exceeding 4.6 m/h will still only give a maximum pressure of 100 kN/m².

*(4) A minimum rate of rise practically achievable of 0.2 m/h has been considered and rates less than this are not stated in the tables. Thus the significance of the 0.2 value in each column is that it represents the **minimum** design pressure for that height of form/pour and temperature. For example in Table 15, for a wall 8.0 m high with OPC concrete placed at 10°C, the minimum design pressure would be 50 kN/m². Note that if the concrete mix is altered to include retarders then for the same wall the minimum design pressure would increase to 70 kN/m². (See Note 5.)*

(5) The tables state the rates of rise (R) for five out of the seven main groups of cementitious materials. The user should refer to Table 17 for guidance on the figures in bold type and in brackets.

(6) The tables are not applicable to underwater concreting.

6m		7m		8m		9m		10m		Design Pressure (kN/m²)
										40
										45
										50
										55
0.2										60
0.3		0.2								65
0.7		0.4		0.2						70
1.1		0.7		0.4						75
1.7		1.1		0.7		0.5		0.3		80
2.4	(0.2)	1.7		1.2		0.8		0.5		85
3.2	(0.3)	2.4		1.8		1.3		0.9		90
4.2	(0.6)	3.2	(0.2)	2.5		1.9		1.4		95
5.3	(1.2)	4.2	(0.5)	3.3	(0.2)	2.6		2.0		100
										30
										35
										40
0.2		0.2								45
0.5		0.3		0.2		0.2				50
0.8		0.6		0.4		0.3		0.2		55
1.3	(0.2)	1.0		0.8		0.6		0.4		60
1.9	(0.4)	1.5	(0.2)	1.2		1.0		0.8		65
2.6	(0.7)	2.1	(0.4)	1.7	(0.2)	1.5	(0.2)	1.2		70
3.3	(1.2)	2.8	(0.8)	2.4	(0.5)	2.0	(0.3)	1.7	(0.2)	75
4.2	(1.8)	3.6	(1.3)	3.1	(0.8)	2.7	(0.6)	2.4	(0.3)	80
5.3	(2.5)	4.6	(1.8)	4.0	(1.3)	3.5	(0.9)	3.1	(0.6)	85
6.4	(3.4)	5.6	(2.6)	4.9	(1.9)	4.4	(1.4)	3.9	(1.1)	90
7.6	(4.4)	6.7	(3.4)	6.0	(2.6)	5.4	(2.1)	4.8	(1.6)	95
9.0	(5.5)	8.0	(4.4)	7.1	(3.5)	6.4	(2.8)	5.8	(2.2)	100
										25
										30
0.2		0.2		0.2						35
0.5		0.4		0.3		0.2		0.2		40
0.8	(0.2)	0.7		0.5		0.4		0.4		45
1.3	(0.4)	1.1	(0.2)	0.9	(0.2)	0.7		0.7		50
1.8	(0.7)	1.5	(0.5)	1.3	(0.3)	1.2	(0.2)	1.0	(0.2)	55
2.4	(1.1)	2.1	(0.8)	1.9	(0.6)	1.7	(0.5)	1.5	(0.3)	60
3.1	(1.7)	2.8	(1.3)	2.5	(1.0)	2.2	(0.8)	2.0	(0.6)	65
4.0	(2.3)	3.6	(1.9)	3.2	(1.5)	2.9	(1.2)	2.7	(1.0)	70
4.9	(3.1)	4.4	(2.5)	4.1	(2.1)	3.7	(1.8)	3.4	(1.5)	75
5.9	(3.9)	5.4	(3.3)	5.0	(2.8)	4.6	(2.4)	4.3	(2.0)	80
7.1	(4.9)	6.5	(4.2)	6.0	(3.6)	5.6	(3.1)	5.2	(2.7)	85
8.3	(6.0)	7.7	(5.2)	7.1	(4.5)	6.6	(4.0)	6.2	(3.5)	90
9.7	(7.3)	8.9	(6.3)	8.3	(5.6)	7.8	(4.9)	7.3	(4.4)	95
11.1	(8.6)	10.3	(7.6)	9.6	(6.7)	9.1	(6.0)	8.5	(5.4)	100

Table 15. *Rate of Rise (m/h) for Walls and Bases, height 6 – 10 m*

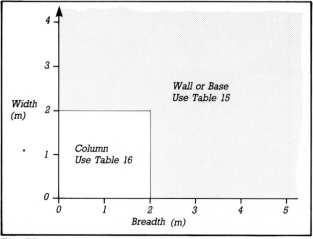

Fig. 50 *Plan dimensions for Tables 15 and 16*

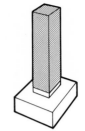

Concrete Temperature	Design Pressure (kN/m²)	Height of Form (h) 2 m	3 m	4 m	5 m	6 m
5°C	40	0.2				
	50	0.7	0.2			
	60		0.7	0.3	0.2	
	70		1.6 (0.4)	0.9	0.5	0.3
	80			1.7 (0.4)	1.1	0.8
	90			2.9 (1.1)	2.0 (0.4)	1.5 (0.2)
	100			4.6 (2.3)	3.1 (1.1)	2.4 (0.5)
	110				4.6 (2.1)	3.6 (1.2)
	120				6.6 (3.7)	5.1 (2.2)
	130					6.9 (3.6)
	140					9.1 (5.5)
	150					12.1 (8.0)
10°C	30	0.2				
	40	0.5 (0.2)	0.3	0.2		
	50	1.3 (0.7)	0.7 (0.3)	0.5	0.3	0.2
	60		1.4 (0.7)	1.0 (0.4)	0.8 (0.2)	0.6
	70		2.4 (1.6)	1.8 (0.9)	1.4 (0.6)	1.2 (0.4)
	80			2.8 (1.8)	2.3 (1.2)	1.9 (0.8)
	90			4.1 (3.0)	3.3 (2.1)	2.9 (1.5)
	100			6.0 (4.7)	4.7 (3.2)	4.0 (2.5)
	110				6.3 (4.7)	5.4 (3.7)
	120				8.3 (6.7)	7.1 (5.2)
	130					9.0 (7.0)
	140					11.3 (9.3)
	150					14.3 (12.3)
15°C	30	0.3	0.2			
	40	0.7 (0.5)	0.5 (0.2)	0.4	0.3	0.2
	50	1.5 (1.2)	1.0 (0.7)	0.8 (0.4)	0.7 (0.3)	0.6 (0.2)
	60		1.8 (1.3)	1.5 (0.9)	1.3 (0.7)	1.1 (0.5)
	70		2.8 (2.4)	2.3 (1.7)	2.0 (1.3)	1.8 (1.1)
	80			3.4 (2.7)	3.0 (2.1)	2.7 (1.8)
	90			4.7 (4.0)	4.1 (3.2)	3.7 (2.7)
	100			6.5 (5.9)	5.5 (4.5)	5.0 (3.9)
	110				7.1 (6.1)	6.4 (5.2)
	120				9.1 (8.2)	8.1 (6.9)
	130					10.0 (8.8)
	140					12.2 (11.1)
	150					15.1 (14.1)

Table 16. *Rate of Rise (m/h) for Columns, height 2 – 6 m*

Notes to Tables 15 and 16:

*(1) The density of concrete is assumed to be 2500 kg/m³ (25 kN/m³) in **all** the pressure and rate calculations given in this section. When considering other concrete densities the CIRIA Report values should be used.*

(2) The tables apply to compaction by internal vibration.

(3) In the lower heights of pour the pressure cannot exceed the fluid head of the concrete and thus concreting at faster rates of rise to the highest value stated will not cause the pressure to exceed the value stated. For example, from Table 16, a column 4.0 m high with OPC concrete at 5°C, concreted with a rate of rise exceeding 4.6 m/h will still only give a maximum pressure of 100 kN/m².

*(4) A minimum rate of rise practically achievable of 0.2 m/h has been considered and rates less than this are not stated in the tables. Thus the significance of the 0.2 value in each column is that it represents the **minimum** design pressure for that height of form/pour and temperature. For example in Table 15, for a wall 8.0 m high with OPC concrete placed at 10°C, the minimum design pressure would be 50 kN/m². Note that if the concrete mix is altered to include retarders then for the same wall the minimum design pressure would increase to 70 kN/m². (See Note 5.)*

(5) The tables state the rates of rise (R) for five out of the seven main groups of cementitious materials. The user should refer to Table 17 for guidance on the figures in bold type and in brackets.

(6) The tables are not applicable to underwater concreting.

Height of Form (h) 7 m	8 m	9 m	10 m	12.5 m	15 m	Design Pressure (kN/m²)
						40
						50
						60
0.2	0.2					70
0.5	0.4	0.2				80
1.1	0.8	0.6	0.4	0.2		90
1.9 (0.2)	1.5 (0.2)	1.2	0.9	0.5	0.2	100
2.9 (0.7)	2.4 (0.4)	2.0 (0.2)	1.6 (0.2)	1.0	0.6	110
4.1 (1.4)	3.5 (0.9)	2.9 (0.6)	2.5 (0.3)	1.7	1.1	120
5.7 (2.5)	4.8 (1.7)	4.2 (1.2)	3.6 (0.8)	2.6 (0.2)	1.9	130
7.5 (3.8)	6.4 (2.8)	5.6 (2.1)	4.9 (1.5)	3.7 (0.6)	2.8 (0.2)	140
9.6 (5.6)	8.2 (4.2)	7.3 (3.2)	6.5 (2.5)	5.0 (1.2)	3.9 (0.5)	150
						30
						40
0.2						50
0.5	0.4	0.3	0.2			60
1.0 (0.2)	0.8	0.7	0.6	0.4	0.2	70
1.6 (0.6)	1.4 (0.4)	1.2 (0.3)	1.1 (0.2)	0.8	0.5	80
2.5 (1.2)	2.2 (0.9)	2.0 (0.7)	1.8 (0.5)	1.3 (0.2)	1.0	90
3.6 (2.0)	3.2 (1.6)	2.9 (1.3)	2.6 (1.0)	2.1 (0.6)	1.7 (0.3)	100
4.8 (3.0)	4.4 (2.5)	4.0 (2.1)	3.7 (1.7)	3.0 (1.1)	2.5 (0.7)	110
6.3 (4.3)	5.8 (3.6)	5.3 (3.1)	4.9 (2.6)	4.1 (1.8)	3.5 (1.2)	120
8.0 (5.8)	7.3 (5.0)	6.8 (4.3)	6.3 (3.8)	5.4 (2.7)	4.7 (2.0)	130
10.0 (7.6)	9.1 (6.6)	8.5 (5.8)	7.9 (5.1)	6.8 (3.8)	6.0 (2.9)	140
12.2 (9.8)	11.1 (8.4)	10.4 (7.4)	9.7 (6.6)	8.5 (5.2)	7.5 (4.1)	150
						30
0.2	0.2					40
0.5	0.4	0.4	0.3	0.2		50
1.0 (0.4)	0.9 (0.3)	0.8 (0.2)	0.7 (0.2)	0.5	0.4	60
1.6 (0.9)	1.5 (0.7)	1.3 (0.6)	1.2 (0.5)	1.0 (0.3)	0.8 (0.2)	70
2.4 (1.5)	2.2 (1.3)	2.1 (1.1)	1.9 (0.9)	1.6 (0.6)	1.4 (0.4)	80
3.4 (2.3)	3.2 (2.0)	3.0 (1.8)	2.8 (1.6)	2.4 (1.2)	2.1 (0.9)	90
4.6 (3.4)	4.3 (3.0)	4.1 (2.7)	3.8 (2.4)	3.4 (1.9)	3.0 (1.5)	100
6.0 (4.6)	5.6 (4.2)	5.3 (3.8)	5.0 (3.4)	4.5 (2.8)	4.0 (2.2)	110
7.5 (6.1)	7.1 (5.5)	6.7 (5.0)	6.4 (4.6)	5.8 (3.8)	5.2 (3.2)	120
9.3 (7.8)	8.8 (7.1)	8.3 (6.5)	8.0 (6.0)	7.2 (5.1)	6.6 (4.3)	130
11.3 (9.7)	10.6 (8.8)	10.1 (8.2)	9.7 (7.6)	8.8 (6.5)	8.1 (5.6)	140
13.5 (11.9)	12.7 (10.8)	12.1 (10.0)	11.6 (9.4)	10.6 (8.1)	9.8 (7.1)	150

Table 16. *Rate of Rise (m/h) for Columns, height 7 – 15 m*

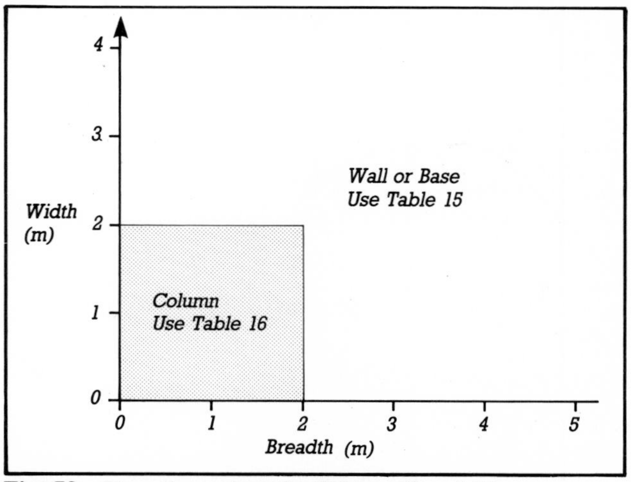

Fig. 50 *Plan dimensions for Tables 15 and 16*

Harrison (Ref. 68) introduced the concept of pore water pressure contributing to the concrete pressure and further predicted that the permeability of formwork would in theory affect the concrete pressure. This effect was not found conclusively in site readings and the permeability of the face is not now considered as a main factor. The reason is that the reuse of the formwork and its face contact materials reduces surface permeability during subsequent uses, reverting to a more impermeable face after, say, two or three uses. However, Tables 15 and 16 are not applicable to highly permeable face materials such as expanded metal or fabric.

Ref. 68.

The CIRIA method assumes nominally parallel sided forms. See Section 4.4.2. When sloping sided forms are not parallel, the rate of rise varies for a constant volume supply rate and a method of calculating the concrete pressure is given in Section 4.4.3. The pressure can be modified when concreting underwater; this is discussed in Section 4.4.4.

Section 4.4.2 – Parallel Sided Forms

The CIRIA tables give the design pressure for a given form height and rate of rise. A one-page design chart from CIRIA Report 108 is included in Appendix E of this guide. This gives different values of pressure for different cements and for changes in temperature. The formula in CIRIA Report 108 allows particular cases to be calculated.

Appendix E.

CIRIA Report 108 (Ref. 3).

The CIRIA tabular approach is well suited to the formwork designer who wishes to estimate the likely design concrete pressure. In contrast, the site staff will know the height of pour and the design pressure of the formwork (from notes on drawings etc), but will need to estimate the average rate of rise of the concrete so that the volume supply per hour can be controlled. Tables 15 and 16 allow the prediction of the rate of rise of concrete in nominally parallel sided forms at three temperatures.

Tables 15 and 16 on preceding pages.

Table 15 covers walls and bases. Table 16 covers columns. A column is defined as a section where **both** the plan dimensions are less than 2 m. See Fig. 50.

See Fig. 50.

The shape of the concrete pressure diagram is assumed to be as shown in Fig. 49. The CIRIA site tests show that when a pour is stopped below the top of the form the measured design pressure was related to the form height (**H**) and not necessarily to the height of concrete. The height of form influenced the method and rate of placing of the concrete. When double faced wall forms are of differing height the concrete will generally be placed by working from the top of the lower form, and this value should be used in determining the height (**H**) in the calculation. Where the pour is stopped significantly below the top of the form, the designer should be aware that the maximum pressure will not exceed the pour height fluid pressure.

Fig. 49.

Concrete Group	Walls and Bases	Columns
(1) OPC, RHPC or SRPC without admixtures	Use rates in **bold** in Table 15	Use rates in **bold** in Table 16
(2) OPC, RHPC or SRPC with any admixture except a retarder		
(3) OPC, RHPC or SRPC with a retarder	Use rates in brackets in Table 15	Use rates in brackets in Table 16
(4) LHPBFC, PBFC, PPFAC or blends containing less than 70% ggbfs or 40% pfa without admixtures		
(5) LHPBFC, PBFC, PPFAC or blends containing less than 70% ggbfs or 40% pfa with any admixture except a retarder		
(6) LHPBFC, PBFC, PPFAC or blends containing less than 70% ggbfs or 40% pfa with a retarder	Use formula for Pressure in CIRIA Report 108 with factor $C_2 = 0.6$	
(7) Blends containing more than 70% ggbfs or 40% pfa		

Notes to Table 17: *(1) The abbreviations are given in Section 1.4.*
(2) A blend is a concrete where a Portland cement has been combined with another cementitious material, usually ggbfs or pfa, at the batcher.

Table 17. *Guidance on Concrete Groups for Tables 15 and 16*

concrete society

Section 4.4.3 – Non-parallel Sided Forms

When considering wall forms with non-parallel sides the CIRIA method can still be used with or without a uniform rate of rise. If the volume supply of concrete can be varied during the pour, the method and rates stated at Section 4.4.2 can be used directly. The pressure at any particular level in the pour will be the same on both faces but the directions of action will be different.

Altering the volume supply rate is not always possible, in which case the following method of calculating the pressure envelope is used. Assuming the pour is split into horizontal layers, the plan area (A) at each layer can be calculated. The instantaneous rate of rise at any level is given by:

$$\text{Rate of rise } (\mathbf{R}) \text{ (m/h)} = \frac{\text{Uniform volume rate (m}^3/\text{h})}{\text{Plan area at level considered } (\mathbf{A}) \text{ (m}^2)}$$

The pressure at that level is then determined using the full height of form ($\mathbf{H}$) either from the CIRIA pressure tables or by working backwards in Tables 15 and 16.

The pressure diagram from the fluid head of concrete will be of triangular shape, and near the top of the pressure envelope will intersect with the plotted values of pressure from consideration of the layers as outlined above. Fig. 51 shows some typical pressure diagrams. The choice of thickness of layer depends on the height and cross section of the structure and generally should not exceed 1.0 m.

Fig. 51.

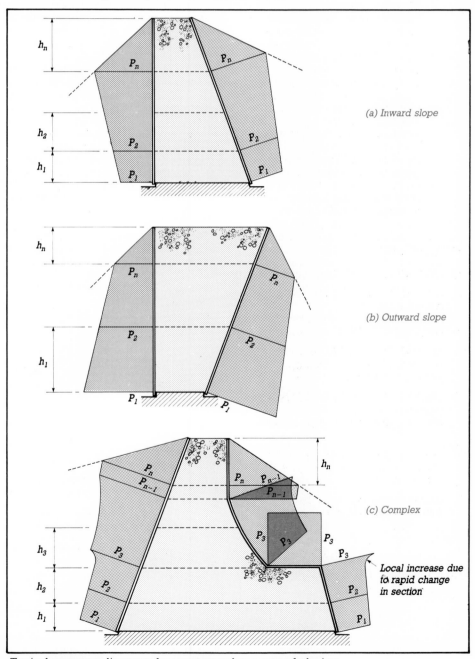

(a) Inward slope

(b) Outward slope

(c) Complex

Local increase due to rapid change in section

Fig. 51 *Typical pressure diagrams for constant volume rate of placing.*

Section 4.4.4 – Underwater Concreting

When concrete is placed underwater the pressure of concrete on formwork will be that calculated by the CIRIA method value but reduced by a factor. In water the effective weight density of concrete is reduced by the weight density of water (9.81 kN/m³). Thus for normal density concrete the underwater pressure is 0.6 × CIRIA design chart values from Appendix E. The tables of rate of rise, Tables 15 and 16, in this guide are **not** valid for underwater concrete.

Water weight 9.81 kN/m³.

*Tables 15 and 16 **not** valid.*

The calculated underwater concrete pressure values should be used with caution because they assume that the water is at the same level on both the inside and outside of the form. When there is a rapid drop in water level during concreting there will be an instantaneous change in pressure on the outside of the form, but a much slower change on the inside from the concrete due to the permeability and hydraulic gradient within. This can give a horizontal pressure **exceeding the vertical pressure**. In such cases the formwork should be designed for the calculated formwork pressure together with a surcharge equivalent to the pressure from the maximum water level difference likely to occur.

The designer should also be aware of the recommendations in Concrete Society Technical Report No. 3 *Underwater Concreting* (Ref. 69) that a more robust design for underwater use may be more practical by designing for the full concrete pressure and ignoring any reduction from submergence.

Underwater Concreting (Ref. 69).

The effective concrete pressure on fabric materials in use underwater is less than the submerged pressure values stated. The degree of reduction varies and the fabric supplier's recommendations should be sought.

Section 4.5 – Environmental Loads

The environmental loads on formwork depend on many factors such as duration of exposure, location of site, local topography, and arrangement of adjacent members, all of which will affect the loads and their magnitude.

Section 4.5.1 – Wind Loads

The basic data for wind calculations is contained in CP 3: Chapter V: Part 2. (Ref. 70). A simpler approach is contained in BS 5975 Clause 28.1 (Ref. 2).

CP 3: Chap V: Pt 2 (Ref. 70).

Soffit Formwork: When considering soffit forms, BS 5975 Clause 28.1 contains a detailed and explicit method based on CP 3 for the calculation of the maximum wind force on bearers, edge forms, parapets and reinforcement associated with soffits. This method gives the maximum wind force (W_m) and is used in the calculations for stability of the falsework system as a whole. Generally, the fixing and restraint of edge forms for concrete forces will be sufficient for transmitting any wind forces to suitable restraint in the bearers, and separate calculations are not normally required. In cases of high-sided forms and of discontinuities in the soffit formwork then further calculations may be necessary. See Fig. 52.

Use BS 5975, clause 28.1 (Ref. 2).

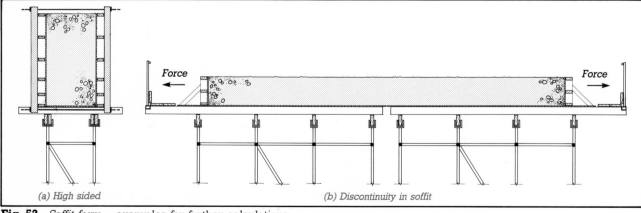

(a) High sided   (b) Discontinuity in soffit

Fig. 52   *Soffit form – examples for further calculations.*

Wall Formwork: When considering the wind forces on wall formwork, use either CP 3: Chapter V (Ref. 70) or the simplified version in Table 18 of this guide and the notes to Table 18.

Use either CP 3 (Ref. 70) or Table 18.

Table 18 gives the upper limit of likely wind forces (W_m) acting on a one metre length of a double faced set of forms. The overturning moment about the base is also stated. See Fig. 53 for details of the wall and length considered. A practical height limit of 10 m is assumed. Reference to CP 3: Chapter V and BS 5975 is required for calculating higher values.

Maximum wind W_m.

Table 18 includes the maximum wind force (W_m) for three localities (Cases A, B and C), as London and Home Counties, England and Wales only, or Great Britain and Ireland (excluding the outer islands of Scotland) respectively. The maximum wind force stated may be halved in conditions when the wall formwork is effectively shielded from the full wind, such as by already constructed walls. The wind can blow in any direction and all directions should be considered.

Working wind W_w.

A reduced value of the wind force (W_w), Case D in Table 18, is known as the working wind and is used in the stability calculations for the forms (see Section 5.1.5).

The total wind force on to the wall is made up of two components, a pressure force on the upstream face and a drag force on the downstream side.

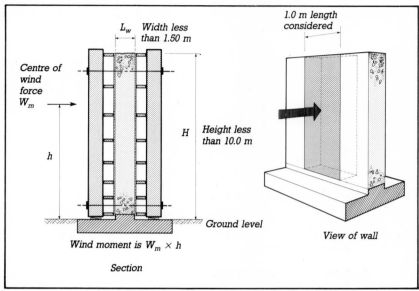

Fig. 53   *Wind force on wall forms.*

Effective Height of Forms (m)	Case A London and Home Counties (V = 42 m/s)		Case B England and Wales (V = 48 m/s)		Case C Great Britain and Ireland (Exc. Outer Islands) (V = 54 m/s)		Case D Working Wind (V = 18 m/s)	
	Force W_m (kN)	Moment (kNm)	Force W_m (kN)	Moment (kNm)	Force W_m (kN)	Moment (kNm)	Force W_w (kN)	Moment (kNm)
3	1.09	1.64	1.81	2.72	2.31	3.47	0.84	1.26
4	1.48	3.00	2.47	5.03	3.15	6.41	1.12	2.24
5	1.90	4.89	3.18	8.22	4.05	10.46	1.40	3.50
6	2.33	7.26	3.94	12.40	5.00	15.68	1.68	5.04
7	2.79	10.25	4.75	17.67	6.02	22.31	1.96	6.86
8	3.28	13.92	5.65	24.42	7.14	30.70	2.24	8.96
9	3.80	18.34	6.60	32.50	8.34	40.90	2.52	11.34
10	4.35	23.37	7.59	41.91	9.60	52.87	2.80	14.00

Notes to Table 18:   *(1) The base of wall is assumed to be at or near the ground level. See Fig. 53.*
*(2) The values of basic wind speed (**V**) are taken from BS 5975 Figure 3 (Ref. 2).*
(3) The values of topography and statistical factors S_1 and S_3 are assumed to be 1.0 and 0.77 respectively. This assumes that the site is not in a funnel shaped valley or very exposed.
(4) The surface roughness factor S_2 from BS 5975 Figure 4 (Ref. 2) assumes countryside with many wind breaks for Case A and open country with scattered wind breaks for Cases B and C.
(5) A force coefficient of 1.4 is assumed from CP3 Chapter V Part 2 Table 10 (Ref. 70) for a height/breadth ratio of 2.
(6) The length of form is considered as infinite but the values may be used for forms as short as 3.0 m.
(7) The width of the wall will affect the value of the force coefficient. It is assumed that the wall is less than 1.5 m thick.

Table 18.   *Wind Force per Metre Length of Wall with Overturning Wind Moment about Base of Wall*

The force on a single erected form, such as during erection or when one form is left in position prior to lifting its mate, will be the same as the total wind force on the wall. In such cases, ensure that the form cannot rotate inwards when temporarily propped. See Fig. 54.

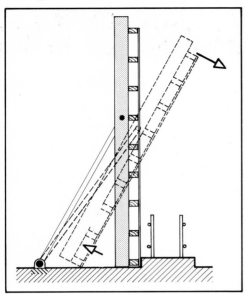

Fig. 54 *Possible overturning mode for a single erected form.*

Wind forces on to reinforcement can be significant during erection but generally are less onerous than those of the completed formwork.

Section 4.5.2 – Snow and Ice Loads

The effects of snow and ice are unlikely to cause any problems in formwork design in the UK. The platform allowable loading of 1.5 kN/m² is equivalent to approximately 1.8 m of powder snow or 160 mm of ice using densities of:

Powder snow	80 kg/m³
Ice	920 kg/m³

Section 4.6 – Horizontal Loads

Section 4.6.1 – General

Horizontal loads on to formwork should be quantified and safely transmitted to suitable restraints.

On soffit forms the horizontal loads arise from wind, imposed plant loads, stopend forces as well as possible accidental loading of the forms from, for example, skip impact. These loads are transmitted through the formwork into the falsework and are considered in detail in BS 5975 (Ref. 2).

When a wall form is erected the applied concrete pressure forces are generally restrained by tie rods or struts.

The magnitude of wind forces on walls up to 10 m in height can be obtained from Table 18.

Table 18.

Section 4.6.2 – Minimum Stability Force – Walls

The minimum horizontal stability force on a wall form shall be **10% of the total form self-weight** acting at a level midway between its centre of gravity and the top of the form. The overturning moment from any working platform should be added to this value. This is shown diagrammatically in Fig. 56 (c). The use of this minimum stability force in design of formwork is covered in Section 5.1.5.

Minimum wall stability force, 10% of total form self-weight.

Fig. 56 (c).
Section 5.1.5.

Section Five
Design

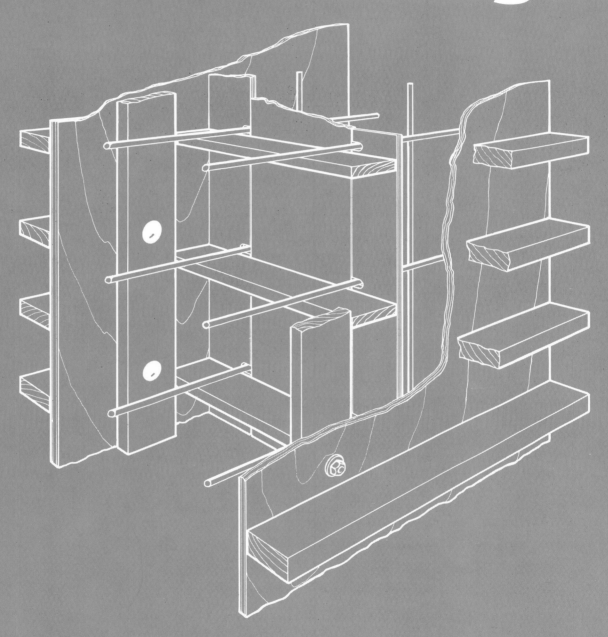

Section Five – Design

Section 5.1 – General Design Considerations

The design of formwork involves the same structural principles as the design of the permanent works, but there are fundamental differences in approach between them:

(a)   The formwork usually supports loads for short durations only until the permanent work is able to support itself.
(b)   Higher working stresses are often used.
(c)   The formwork often relies upon its own self-weight for stability and is rarely tied down to firm foundations, except in exposed conditions.
(d)   The components used in formwork are normally reuseable in whole or in part.
(e)   The formwork system when erected will include manufacturing and assembly tolerances.

The design and detailing of formwork should be supervised by persons with the relevant design and practical experience. Particularly on a major structure, the designer needs a knowledge not only of engineering design methods but also of the many formwork/falsework systems available and experience in their selection and use on site. On major projects the construction organisation may appoint a 'formwork coordinator' to supervise all the formwork procedures. This is similar in concept to the appointment of a 'falsework coordinator' stated in BS 5975, Clause 10.2 (Ref. 2).

BS 5975, Clause 10.2 (Ref. 2).

See Section 2.9.

Before commencing to design, the formwork designer (TWD) should collect the necessary information and data as set out in the formwork designer's brief (see Section 2.9).

Incomplete information will necessitate the designer making assumptions which could prove incorrect and lead to an unsatisfactory design. It is essential that close co-operation between the formwork designer and the user (and where necessary, engineer and client) be encouraged and maintained. Contractors should recognise that detailed design of formwork by experienced designers will lead to economies. (Additional economic factors are discussed in Section 1.6.)

Additional economic factors are discussed in Section 1.6.

Appropriate design checks should be carried out. With the increasing use of computers and other design aids the importance of simple rule-of-thumb checks should not be overlooked.

Structural design of formwork is usually aided by reference to charts and tables. These may be published either by design offices, suppliers of equipment, or by trade associations such as the National Association of Formwork Contractors.

See also Section 2.2.

Section 5.1.1 – Responsibility of Formwork Design Organisations

Formwork design may be undertaken in a number of ways depending on the contractual arrangements. Examples are:

(a)   Design by main contractor

> In own design office
> In own site office
> By subletting to a sub-contractor
> By subletting to a supplier of equipment
> By subletting to an independent design office
> By accepting a nominated sub-contractor.

(b)   Design by employer.

(c)   Design by manufacturer (e.g. precast beams).

Each of these arrangements will impose a set of legal responsibilities on the various parties concerned. Temporary works designers (TWD) should carefully check their legal responsibilities and ensure they have the necessary competence and are adequately protected. It is therefore recommended that in all cases proper communications are set up between the parties involved.

The formwork designer should make himself aware of the terms of the contract under which the formwork design is being prepared. In the case of design under a sub-contract this will often mean being aware of the terms of the main contract as well as those in the sub-contract.

The formwork designer and the formwork coordinator (if appointed) should be clearly identified and the formwork designer's brief should be established. The same system can be used where items are manufactured off site.

Communication of the design is most conveniently done using drawings or sketches although it may be necessary to supplement these with written specifications and method statements. The formwork coordinator or site supervisor will be responsible for ensuring that the erection of the formwork is carried out in accordance with the design.

If revisions are made to the design, the date should be recorded and the relevant documents re-issued as appropriate.

Section 5.1.2 – Checking of Formwork Design

Before starting any construction work the proposed formwork design should be subject to a check for concept, adequacy and correctness. The ability of the checker and his remoteness or independence from the formwork designer should be greater where new ideas are incorporated or the structure is complex. The check may be carried out in the same office by someone not involved in the design. In cases where failure of formwork can have major consequences, such as collapse of sliding or climbing forms intended for use at a height or over public areas, it may be desirable to obtain a more independent and comprehensive check.

In certain instances a specification will require an independent check. See for example the DTp Specification Clause 8A (Ref. 11). This check usually refers to the falsework but will occasionally be a requirement for the formwork.

DTp Specification Clause 8A (Ref. 11).

Section 5.1.3 – Deformations

All the elements of formwork, i.e. face contact materials, bearers/walings, soldiers/supports, tie rods etc, will move as load is applied or released. This movement will be elastic **(within the limits of working stresses)** which means that deflections will be increased or reduced in direct proportion to the load changes.

Calculations of deflections or movements are made in respect of the modulus of elasticity (**E**) of the material (also known as Young's modulus) where

$$E = \frac{\text{Stress}}{\text{Strain}} = \frac{\text{Load/Cross-sectional area}}{\text{Change in length/Original length}}$$

or

$$\frac{\text{Change in length}}{\text{(deflection or movement)}} = \frac{\text{Stress} \times \text{Original length}}{E}$$

It is **most important** to check that the terms are expressed in compatible units; steelwork sections, in particular, often have properties listed in centimetre (cm) units.

When the units of stress are in kN/m² and lengths and change in length are in m, then the modulus of elasticity (**E**) is in kN/m². Note that a stress in kN/m² is equivalent to N/mm² × 1000.

1 kN/m² = 1 N/mm² × 1000.

Values of modulus of elasticity (**E**) for timber are given in Table 3 and for concrete in BS 5975, Table 25 (Ref. 2). For steel use $E = 2 \times 10^8$ kN/m².

E:
Timber – use Table 3
Concrete – use BS 5975, Table 25
Steel – use 2×10^8 kN/m².

For members in direct tension or compression the above will enable appropriate calculations to be done. For members in bending, it is crucial to establish the support conditions and the loading conditions, and then the appropriate formulae from Appendix B can be used to calculate the deflections. Where continuous beams/bearers are loaded the notes to Appendix B, Part 2 should be studied.

Appendix B.

In both wall and soffit formwork the designer will need to be aware of the theoretical magnitude of the elastic deformation of each element.

Experience shows that a deflection of individual formwork members not exceeding 1/270 of the span between centrelines of supports produces an acceptably flat concrete surface. This is shown diagrammatically in Fig. 55. However, sometimes other magnitudes are specified; see also Section 2.7. It should be noted that the total deflection of the face and that of any one component are not the same; if a specification requires a dimensional limit,

δ = 1/270 of span.
See Fig. 55.
See also Section 2.7.

*Deflections of Formwork
(Ref. 20).*

this should be compared with the total deflection of the various components. NAFC Data Sheet No. 4, *Deflections of Formwork* (Ref. 20), gives more information on this point.

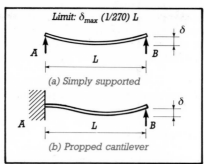

Fig. 55 *Limits of elastic deformation. (Unless specified otherwise)*

Provided the elements of the formwork are not overloaded (allowable safe working stresses not exceeded) they will return to their original shape when the imposed load is removed, i.e. on striking.

It should be noted that a timber subjected to heavy loads for long periods (several weeks) may become permanently deflected, which may preclude its further use.

Section 5.1.3.2 – Creep

Since formwork loads are usually short term, creep deformations are rarely considered in design.

Section 5.1.3.3 – Moisture Movement

Drying shrinkage of concrete occurs over a time scale of months and years and is therefore not usually a problem for formwork. In the case of permanent formwork or moulds made of concrete it could affect units in store and should be considered in their design. If timber forms are subject to severe drying, some shrinkage across the grain may occur. For this reason, timber boards are seldom selected as face contact material. Particle board can be particularly affected by moisture movement. (See Section 3.2.2.2).

See Section 3.2.2.2.

Section 5.1.3.4 – Thermal Movement

See Section 6.4.5.

Thermal movement either as expansion or contraction may be significant, particularly if heating is applied. See Section 6.4.5. The most serious problems are likely to arise from differential expansion between form and concrete.

When timber is subject to change in temperature, the resulting change in dimension is more likely to be caused by change in its moisture content than by thermal movement.

Although plastics generally have much higher coefficients of thermal expansion, their modulus of elasticity is lower, and thus residual stresses from thermal changes are rarely a problem. When timber or plywood is bonded to one side of a plastic material, thermal or moisture movement may cause the unit to bow. This is particularly apparent on thin sections.

Section 5.1.3.5 – Stressing Movement

See Section 6.4.4.

See Section 6.4.4 for guidance on moulds for prestressed concrete.

Formwork associated with post-tensioning needs careful consideration as stressing loads are often transferred through the concrete into the supporting formwork and falsework. Allowance should be made in the formwork design to accommodate the forces or movements involved. Engineering judgement is required to assess at what time the permanent structure may be considered self-supporting, as accommodating the full stressing movement on the formwork and falsework may be uneconomic.

Prior to stressing, the falsework will support the entire load of the permanent work. But at full stress the permanent work will be capable of carrying its own weight plus the design imposed load.

In certain cases of continuous structures with differing spans the **vertical movement can be downwards** with consequential rotation at supports, and possible increase in vertical loads, on the falsework/formwork support structure.

Section 5.1.4 – Form Liners

Materials used in linings to forms are covered in Section 3.12 but several of the other materials mentioned can be used as form liners to impart a particular visual feature. It is good practice to consider the material as non-structural and to use a structural framework as the load-carrying members. An example is shown in Fig. 24. Care should be exercised in considering the additional weight of the forms for crane handling, and also in adequately securing the form liner to the backing material to avoid detachment.

Section 3.12.

Fig. 24.

Where form liners are used as formwork directly onto framework the liner material is structural and must be designed to carry the load. Use the advice and stresses given in Section 3.

Section 3.

Section 5.1.5 – Stability

During assembly, erection, use and dismantling, formwork should be stabilised from overturning and from lateral or vertical movement. Often the friction between members is sufficient to prevent movement and detailed calculations may only be required in special cases.

The stability of **soffit formwork** erected at the top of falsework is covered in BS 5975 (Ref. 2) where the formwork is considered an integral part of the whole falsework structure. Special checks on the formwork may be required if the soffit is inclined.

BS 5975, Clause 43.4 (Ref. 2).

Wall formwork, when erected, provides large surface areas for the wind and may need to be stabilised. The magnitude of the wind force is covered in Section 4.5.1. The minimum value of stability force is stated in Section 4.6.2. In addition to the wind force/minimum stability force, an overturning moment on the formwork is applied by any working platform with the loading from operatives and plant etc.

Section 4.5.1.
Section 4.6.2.

It is unrealistic to expect sites to operate under extreme weather conditions, therefore an upper limit on wind force is established. This is known as the **working wind.** Working operations are normally limited to gale force 6 on the Beaufort scale. This corresponds to a dynamic wind pressure of 0.2 kN/m² and is shown in Table 18, Case D for walls up to 10 m high.

Working wind:
Gale force 6,
Wind pressure
0.2 kN/m²
(Table 18, Case D).

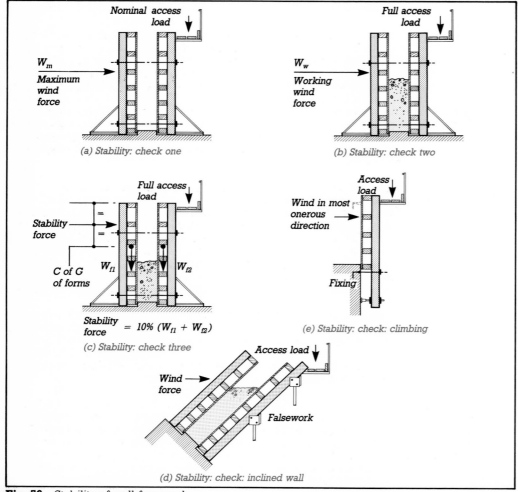

Fig. 56 *Stability of wall formwork.*

Minimum factor of safety on overturning 1.2.

In the design of freestanding wall formwork, the minimum factor of safety on overturning is 1.2. Three design checks on stability should be considered:

See Fig. 56 opposite.

1.   With the maximum wind and nominal access loading on any working platform. See Fig. 56 (a).
2.   With the working wind and full construction operations loading on the working platform. See Fig. 56 (b).

Section 4.6.2.

3.   With minimum stability force (from Section 4.6.2) and full construction operations loading. See Fig. 56 (c).

Section 4.5.1.

It should be remembered that the wind can blow in any direction, so the most onerous condition should be considered. If the forms are sheltered from the wind and a reduction in the maximum wind force can be applied (Section 4.5.1), it only relates to the first check 1 above, as shown in Fig. 56 (a).

See Fig. 56 (d).

To ensure stability on **inclined formwork** requires consideration of the falsework loads on the lower face in addition to the stability and overturning forces. See Fig. 56 (d). The same design checks are applied.

Fig. 56 (e).
Section 5.2.3.3.

In **climbing formwork** the stability under wind loads depends upon the fixings to the lower level. The most onerous condition is with the wind from the direction as shown in Fig. 56 (e). Separate consideration of the factor of safety on the supporting fixings is given in Section 5.2.3.3.

Section 5.2.3.
Fig. 54.

The method of stabilising wall forms to resist the overturning forces can be by propping, extended feet on the forms, or by bolting to foundations. Generally, it will be by propping, and care must be taken in the connection of the props to the form. Note also that as the prop takes load it can create an uplift on the form which consequently may require anchoring down. In most cases the self-weight of the form is adequate to satisfy this requirement. See also single face formwork, Section 5.2.3 and Fig. 54.

Section 5.1.6 – Factors of Safety

Factors of safety will allow for variations in materials and loadings, including the likelihood of accidental loadings. A factor of safety used in the element design of formwork members will often be different from the value used when considering the stability of the whole system.

The working stresses recommended in Section 3 incorporate the factors of safety for the short term loads associated with formwork. Reusable components will generally require a larger factor of safety. For example, an expendable item such as a tie rod which may be used once and left embedded in the concrete will have a lower factor of safety than when used as a reusable item such as a suspender for falsework/formwork.

e.g. tie rod safety, see Section 3.8.3.

The location and environmental conditions of a form may dictate that economically the most adverse conditions need not be considered, e.g. the effect of a severe storm on a wall form on a remote site could be considered differently to its effect on the same form used on an urban site. The TWD should exercise great caution in deciding the relevant design criteria.

Wherever possible, formwork should be designed so that damage due to large accidental loads is confined to local areas and does not bring about progressive collapse. The nature of formwork with reusable components often has sufficient built-in stiffness and rigidity to distribute any accidental loading to adjacent supports, such as ties in a wall or vertical supports in a soffit, thus reducing the incidence of a catastrophic failure. The forms may deflect excessively, but often collapse is averted. Generally it is uneconomic to design on the philosophy that all members will be of sufficient strength to withstand the failure of any one member in the system. The recommendation of a universal factor of safety is not considered prudent for formwork.

A universal factor of safety is not recommended.

Failure is the result of either of two conditions:

(a)   One or more components collapse completely.
or
(b)   One or more components exhibit excessive movement or deflection under applied loads or forces.

In case (b) the deflection renders the item unserviceable although its factor of safety on final collapse could be high. The designer should consider most carefully the properties of components and materials when making a selection. Published test results on components may illustrate a mode of failure which will not occur in the particular application, so that further reference to a proprietary supplier or manufacturer may be necessary.

When carrying out a particular test to determine properties of a reusable component for a particular application a minimum factor of safety on collapse of 2.0 should be used. Care should be exercised, as already stated, in the interpretation of the test results. For example, if the item is in mild steel, such as a tie rod, the use of a factor of safety of 2.0 on final collapse would give a working stress value above the yield point which is unlikely to be acceptable. Random site testing of elements is not recommended, particularly proof testing of timber.

Section 5.1.7 – Design Concept

The concept of the design will be formulated by the TWD, having due regard to the many factors outlined in the preceding sections of this guide. The amount of design involvement in a scheme will depend on its complexity and its scale; for example, formwork for a small cantilever beam projecting at the top of a tall building would generally require more consideration than the same beam on the inside of a small building at low level. The area of formwork may be the same but the engineering solution would be different.

Perhaps the factor having the most influence on the formwork concept is the consideration of the final surface of the concrete that will be acceptable to the client. In Section 2.5 the various surface finishes are described, with particular reference to the DTp method of classification.

*Section 2.5.
(See also Table 2.)*

Having considered the location and dimensions of the form from the drawings, together with the client's requirement for finish, usually from the specification, the designer (TWD) will then select the materials that will achieve the most economic engineering solution. Section 3 gives guidance on this choice. Having selected the materials, the applied loads onto the formwork can be evaluated and the engineering concept and design developed.

The following sections outline the main points to be considered in the design.

Section 5.2 – Wall Formwork

Section 5.2.1 – General

Having established the design brief, the designer will formulate the most economic design: some particular parameters may already have been dictated, such as tie rod centres to suit a specified finish. Particular attention to details, reuse of forms, safety, stability and operation of the formwork system should also be considered.

The designer (TWD) will make assumptions about the rate of rise, volume of pours, temperature, mix design etc and will calculate the maximum design concrete pressure (see Section 4.4). The design pressure will influence all the element sizes, face contact materials, walings, soldiers, tie rods etc. For this reason the maximum design pressure together with the design criteria of the formwork should be made known to the site, generally by notes on the drawing.

See Section 4.4.

State design pressures on drawings.

The site operatives should be aware that changes in concrete temperature, use of admixtures, change of mix, use of cement replacement materials etc., will all affect the pressure. For these reasons the site should check the actual conditions relating to the pour to ensure that the design pressure of the form is not exceeded. For example, a fall in concrete temperature of 10°C, such as the difference between summer and winter working, can in certain cases increase the actual pressure by 50%.

Wall form designs can be for single sided or double sided formwork, and the following sections give some of the main factors to be considered in each case. However, there is no difference in the calculation of the concrete pressure envelope.

Structural formulae for some typical loading cases for beams and members of constant section are given in Appendix B.

Typical loading cases. Appendix B.

Section 5.2.2 – Double Face Formwork

Section 5.2.2.1 – General

The most common wall formwork is double sided. Some typical examples are shown in Figs. 41 and 42. The concrete pressure on each face can be balanced using a tie rod system, generally leaving no out-of-balance forces. An imbalance of forces occurs at outside corners where the surface area is greater than on the inside corner. See Fig. 57. However, for walls of width less than 300 mm the effect can be ignored. If diagonal ties are placed across the corner then the forces on the two outside faces may be balanced, which provides an adequate corner connection. Dimensional accuracy is needed in placing and locating such ties to ensure that they are not loaded eccentrically. Skew wall intersections need careful attention.

Figs. 41 and 42.

See Fig. 57.

See Section 3.8.
Fig. 57 (b) and 57 (c).

Wherever possible tie rods should be placed so that the load is in tension only in the tie. See Section 3.8. When the ties are not perpendicular to the form face, such as in Fig. 57 (b) and 57 (c) at the corners, suitable packs are necessary to prevent bending being induced into the ties. Tie rod holes not exactly opposite each other on opposing form faces will also result in bending in the ties.

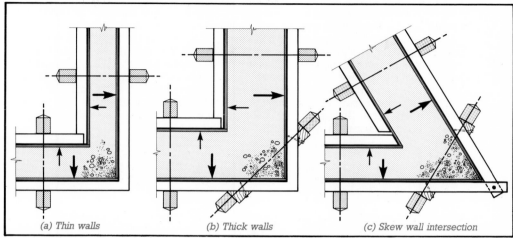

(a) Thin walls   (b) Thick walls   (c) Skew wall intersection

Fig. 57   *Typical wall corner plans.*

For details at joints see
Section 5.7.2.

See Fig. 94(a).

See Fig. 58.

The design of the stopend will need separate consideration, particularly on wide wall sections, as the concrete pressure is the same on the stopend as on the wall itself. For details at joints see Section 5.7.2. On a long wall form the horizontal force from the stopend can generally be safely restrained by adequate fixing to the main wall form, particularly on narrow walls less than 450 mm wide, such as illustrated in Fig. 94 (a), provided that there is no discontinuity of the wall formwork in the length. The stopend forces are distributed through the face into the kicker, and there is in addition some frictional restraint between the face and the stiffening concrete. If casting subsequently onto an existing wall pour (see Fig. 58), then provided that the wall is longer than the overall height of the stopend, this arrangement for the stopend is satisfactory, but if, for example, the last pour in a long line of pours is very short, then there may not be sufficient restraint from the formwork and external strutting of the stopend may be required.

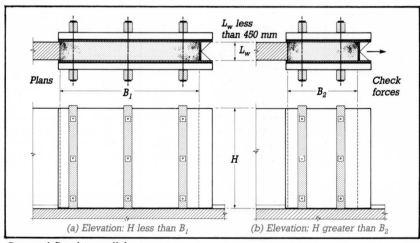

(a) Elevation: H less than B_1 (b) Elevation: H greater than B_2

Fig. 58   *Stopend fixed to wall form.*

On very tall wall pours access for concreting and vibration of the concrete should be considered. If the wall is less than 500 mm wide and reinforced on both faces, internal access from the top may be impossible and access doors may need to be provided. This practice should be avoided wherever possible as refitting an access door will always leave a mark on the finished wall face.

Example C1 in
Appendix C.

Example C1 in Appendix C works through the design of a typical double faced wall form.

The differences between the design of parallel and non-parallel formwork are discussed in the following sections.

Section 5.2.2.2 – Parallel Sided Formwork

When forms are parallel sided the rate of rise of the concrete up the form face during placing will generally be constant. The concrete pressure will be determined as described in Section 4.4.2. The tie rods will be perpendicular to the face and standard waler plates etc can be used.

Section 4.4.2.

If the whole wall section (see Fig. 59) is inclined, the maximum achievable concrete pressure will be the actual vertical fluid head of concrete from the free surface of the pour, and the rate of rise (**R**) will be the vertical rate of rise and not the rate up the slope distance of the face. The CIRIA method of predicting concrete pressure may be used. (See Section 4.4.2). The lower formwork face will also require to be designed to transmit the weight of the concrete (W_c) into the supporting falsework, in addition to the applied concrete pressure. Note that the pressure, of course, still acts at right angles to the face. The upper face will be similar to a top form. See also inclined soffits with top form in Section 5.3.3.3 and Fig. 73.

See also worked example C4 in Appendix C.

See Section 4.4.2.

Section 5.3.3.3.
Fig. 73.

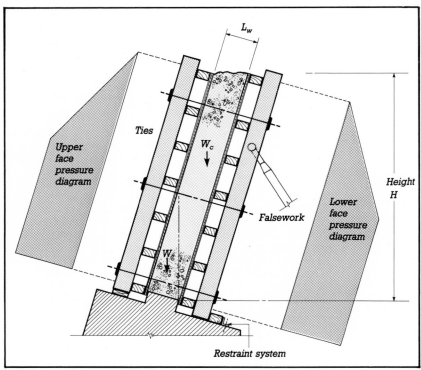

Fig. 59 *Typical parallel face sloping wall – concrete pressure diagrams.*

Section 5.2.2.3 – Non-parallel Sided Formwork

Typical examples of wall forms with faces that are not parallel are wave walls such as on a dam crest (see Fig. 101) and gravity dam walls. The pressure of the concrete (see Section 4.4.3) will act at right angles to the formwork face and create a force equal to the pressure multiplied by the area of the face considered. Some typical examples are shown in Fig. 60.

Fig. 101.
See Section 4.4.3.

The design may be considered either as a double face form with connecting ties or as two independent single face forms. (See Section 5.2.3 and Fig. 61(e)). The distance between the forms will determine the solution.

See Section 5.2.3 and Fig. 61(e).

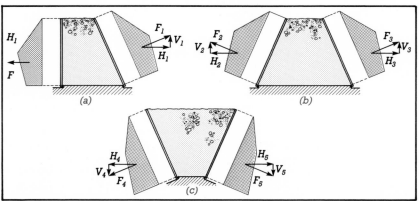

Fig. 60 *Typical force diagrams for walls; non-parallel faces.*

Refers to Fig. 60.

Inward sloping faces will be adjusted to an uplift force arising from the vertical component of the force on the face, $\mathbf{V_1}$, $\mathbf{V_2}$, $\mathbf{V_3}$. Note that the horizontal forces will always balance and $\mathbf{H} = \mathbf{H_1}$ and $\mathbf{H_2} = \mathbf{H_3}$ and $\mathbf{H_4} = \mathbf{H_5}$, so long as the top and bottom surfaces are level. For a small deviation from level any difference is absorbed in internal friction in the concrete.

Delivery rate.

It is **most important** to establish with the site whether concrete will be delivered at a steady uniform rate in m^3 per hour **or** at a rate which varies with the section to be filled. The delivery rate should be established and then maintained. These agreed conditions should be made known to the site, generally by notes on drawings.

Whilst maximum pressures from fluid concrete act only for a short time during stiffening, loads from the weight of concrete acting vertically on the forms must be considered for a longer time until the structure is self-supporting and stable (such as in Fig. 60 (c)).

Fig. 60 (c).

In addition to considering the forces on the sloping sides, the design should allow for the practical implications of placing and compacting the concrete. Special provisions for the surface finish may be required such as allowance for release of trapped air and selection of a suitable release agent to minimise blowholes.

Section 3.10.2.

The method of handling the sloping form will require separate consideration. See Section 5.9. During erection some spacer assemblies will be needed to hold the form in its correct alignment.

See Section 5.9.

The restraint of the vertical, or uplift component can be in one of three ways: kentledge, tie rods or external strutting. These solutions can apply to both single or double faced forms. Typical methods are shown in Fig. 61.

Fig. 61.

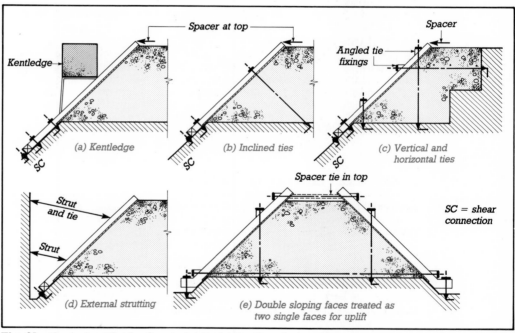

Fig. 61   *Typical methods of restraint to sloping face formwork.*

Kentledge. The self-weight of the form face that is acted on by the uplift force may be sufficient restraint. The effect of any friction restraint force at the kicker should be ignored in this case. A suitable factor of safety applied to the uplift force is 1.5, thus:

Factor of safety on uplift forces 1.5.

$$\text{Self-weight} + \text{Kentledge} = \text{Uplift} \times 1.5$$

When using kentledge there is no hidden safety factor in case of accidental overloading of the form. See Fig. 61 (a). The form has also to be designed to transmit the vertical weight of the kentledge before any fluid concrete has been placed. This method is not economic for large sloping forms.

Tie Rods: Uplift forces can be restrained using tie rods connecting into previously cast concrete. Examples are shown in Fig. 61 (b) and (c). Although it is possible to use inclined ties into fixings such as in (b), it is more practical to restrain the uplift by casting fixings into the first pour and to use vertical ties with suitable angled connections to the formwork, as shown in Fig. 61 (c).

The former case requires the precise locating of angled fixings. When the design incorporates two sets of tie rods, i.e. one horizontal and one vertical such as in Fig. 61 (c), it assists erection if they are at right angles to each other so that adjustment of one set does not significantly alter the length of the other set.

See Fig. 61(c).

The use of bolts or tie rods through backing members directly into cast-in fixings, such as in kickers, to restrain uplift forces is not recommended as it can induce bending into the connections unless specifically designed.

When connecting into previous pours it is necessary to check that the applied forces can be restrained, and in particular that the previously poured concrete has sufficient strength and is large enough to obtain a satisfactory fixing. In addition to cast-in fixings, the use of self-drill type anchors, resin anchors etc can be considered. When using tie rods for restraining uplift, design the fixings and ties for the actual calculated value of the uplift forces. The factor of safety of the fixings and ties will provide adequate safety against uplift.

External Strutting: In certain cases it is possible to restrain the uplift by external strutting. See Fig. 61 (d). This is covered in the considerations of a top form in Section 5.3.3.3. The magnitude of restraint depends on the arrangement of any through ties. Particular care is necessary in assessing the direction of the external struts as they may induce additional forces into the formwork.

Fig. 61 (d).
Section 5.3.3.3.

Section 5.2.3 – Single Face Formwork

Section 5.2.3.1 – General

Whenever site conditions or the specification preclude the use of through ties on walls, the additional cost implications of single face formwork should be carefully considered by the specifier, and the contractor should take particular care in the design.

On pours up to about 2 m high, such as on foundation bases, one solution is external strutting using standard props. When the wall is between 2 and 5 m high then external strutting by heavy proprietary equipment or its equivalent is possible provided low design concrete pressures can be guaranteed.

Alternatively, walls up to 2 m high can be cantilevered from previous pours. Cantilevering can be used on very tall walls when successive pouring in lifts up to 2 m high is acceptable.

Section 5.2.3.2 – Externally Strutted Formwork

Horizontal Struts: The force from the concrete pressure acting normal to the face must be resisted by external props. If these props are fitted normal to the face then the formwork is designed conventionally. Ideally the prop lengths should be limited so that self-weight bending does not reduce their capacity.

If the props are strutted onto an opposite face of similar single face construction, such as in a pit wall, then the effect of the props in equalising the applied concrete forces relies on **both walls being concreted simultaneously** to balance the force in the props. This may be difficult to achieve and other methods should be considered.

Inclined Struts: The most common external strutting involves the arrangement with inclined struts. The top strut(s) will be at an angle to the face to resist the force of the concrete and will result in an uplift force on the formwork. See Fig. 62 (Strut 'B').

See Fig. 62 (Strut 'B').

The magnitude of the uplift force depends on the position and angle of the prop. The uplift force to be restrained is the calculated vertical component from the strut(s) less the form self-weight (W_f). The effects of any friction connection with the kicker should be ignored. The method of fixing the lower ends of the struts must be considered.

The uplift can be restrained by suitable fixing into the previously cast base, preferably at each soldier or prop position, by using a vertical fixing connected directly to the soldier. The use of horizontal fixings into the kicker to restrain uplift is not recommended.

Fixings into kicker not recommended.

The magnitude of the uplift force can be significant. For example, on a wall 2.0 m high with Strut 'B' at 45° and assuming full fluid concrete pressure, the total uplift is 16.7 kN per metre length of wall. This is slightly reduced by the self-weight of the formwork.

When designing for single face walls up to 5 m in height the concrete pressure may need to be very considerably reduced, possibly to 35 kN/m², to keep the uplift force down to a reasonable value. In such cases the effects of elastic movement of the fixing at the base is magnified at the top of the pour to give larger values of deflections than initially calculated for the formwork alone. Further, the longer the restraining struts, the larger their own elastic shortening and the larger the top deflection. As a rule-of-thumb a steel strut stressed to working capacity will shorten by 0.5 mm per metre of its length plus 0.5 mm for each joint in its length.

Steel struts shorten by 0.5 mm per metre plus 0.5 mm per joint.

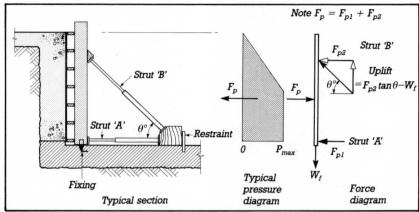

Fig. 62 *Single face: inclined struts.*

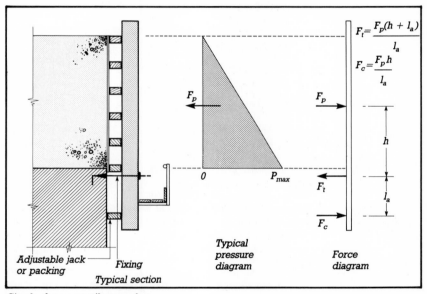

Fig. 63 *Single face: cantilevered.*

Section 5.2.3.3 – Cantilevered Formwork

When successive single faced vertical pours are to be cast, the formwork may be cantilevered from the previous pour, provided that the anchorages in the previous pour can safely withstand the forces. The restraint force F_t in Fig. 63 will always be greater than the concrete pressure force F_p. Furthermore the position of the packing at F_c will affect the restraint force. On site, supervision should ensure that the position of packing F_c is as designed.

When considering wind forces on the form, allowance should be made for wind from all directions. See Section 5.1.5 and Fig. 56 (e). The principal design consideration for single face forms in cantilever is the deflection of the top of the formwork. This is a function not only of the elastic property of the soldier on the formwork but also the overall rotation of the system due to elongation of the tie at F_t and compression of any packings etc fitted at F_c. For these reasons the length of cantilever is often restricted to between 1.5 and 2 m and the top of the form may need to be preset inwards to compensate for the deflection.

See Section 5.1.5 and Fig. 56 (e).

Restrict length to 1.5/2.0 m.

When the cantilevered form is sloping outwards, in addition to the wind loads and stability considerations, the design must also allow for the weight of the wet concrete supported as the forms are now acting as falsework. Special connections to the previous pour to transmit shear loads may have to be included in the design.

During erection of cantilevered forms a small bracket (seating cleat) already fitted to the previous pour in predetermined positions will assist location during erection. These are not required at all soldier positions but there should be at least two per crane-handled unit.

Seating cleats.

Special attention should be paid in the formwork design to the provision of safe and adequate access arrangements. See Section 7.5.2. Access to lifting connections, fixing points and for concreting operations is necessary, in particular, at the start and at final release of formwork. Where access may be limited, provision of safety nets, safety belts or an independent bracket scaffold fixed to the wall previously constructed should be considered.

See Section 7.5.2.

Section 5.2.3.4 – Dam Formwork

A particular case of single face forms in cantilever occurs in dam construction. The infrequency of such work undertaken and its very special nature leaves only a small number of contractors with the experience to carry out the work. Formwork design for dams should only be undertaken with the appropriate specialised knowledge.

The design pressure is usually low due to the large mass of concrete being placed, but can increase near the top of the structure if it becomes narrower and the rate of rise increases. Impact loading on forms is more severe due to the use of larger concrete skips and tracked machines which may be used to suspend 150 mm diameter concrete poker vibrators which operate on the working horizontal surface when close to the formwork. An allowance of up to 30 kN/m^2 may be appropriate.

The design may be influenced by the magnitude of the tie load $\mathbf{F_t}$. (Fig. 63). The rapid turnround of the formwork and the use of relatively weak hearting concrete (often used in the dam centre because of its low heat characteristic) may result in a low pull-out value for any cast-in fixings.

See Fig. 63.

Many of the problems associated with the use of dam formwork occur when the shape changes rapidly or is non-standard. This usually occurs at the start of lifts close to the rock faces which slope at varying angles and also when the introduction of other features occur abruptly as with scour pipes, stop-log slots, gates, grillages, adjoining structures etc.

Section 5.2.4 – Curved Wall Formwork

Formwork curved in plan in one plane, such as a circular tank wall, is designed as previously described, either as double face or single face. Typical examples are shown in Fig. 65 and Fig. 104. Usually the inside face is erected first, so that reinforcement can be more easily fixed.

Fig. 65.
Fig. 104.

The face contact material for the forms will either be made up in straight sections as chords, or bent to the required radius. Bending radii for plywood are given in Table 10. Suitable fixings will be required to maintain the radii of the forms.

Table 10.

Fig. 64 shows the chord offsets when making up a curve in short straights. In certain cases the effective radii and thicknesses of the wall may need to be adjusted to ensure that the cover to reinforcement is maintained; the wall kicker will also have to be adjusted in width to suit.

Fig. 64.

Face contact material may have differing properties in two directions. Care is necessary to ensure that on site it is used as designed.

(See also Fig. 19.)

Formwork that is curved in section, such as tunnel walls, needs particular care in design. See Section 5.6.2.

See Section 5.6.2 and Fig. 101.

Where a wall is curved in plan but has an inclined face in section, then the sloping (batter) face is part of a large cone section. The radii in plan alter as the level changes, thus square items fitted to the batter face require to be warped to fit. The use of climbing formwork on such a wall requires extremely careful design and different make-up pieces at each lift, unless overlaps are permitted. A typical example is cooling tower construction. The positions of tie rods need careful consideration.

The cost of the formwork for an inclined wall to a circular tank will always be more than that for an equivalent vertical wall. The specifier should be aware of the cost implications.

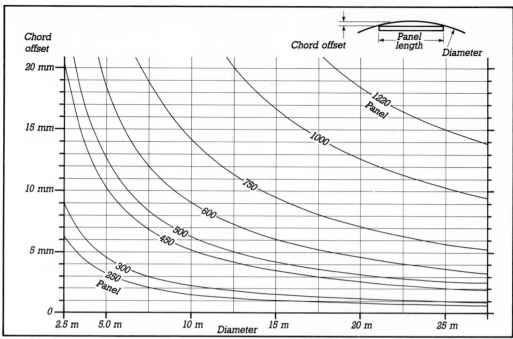

Fig. 64 *Chord offset for straight panels on circular formwork.*

Fig. 65 *Circular formwork to insitu silo.*

Striking piece.

On all curved formwork the inside form may become fully trapped when a complete ring is erected, and a removable striking piece up to 300 mm wide should be incorporated. If curved walings are used, their length should be less than the semi-circular length, particularly if crane-handled units are used.

There is an inherent increased strength in curved members as they start to act in hoop tension on the outside and as compression arches on the inside. The amount of increase is difficult to quantify and the experience of designers with suitable knowledge and judgement should be sought.

Section 5.2.5 – Striking

Tables of Minimum Striking Times for Soffit and Vertical Formwork (Ref. 71).

Curing Concrete (Ref. 66).

The time at which striking of vertical formwork can be carried out should be carefully controlled. CIRIA Report 67 (Ref. 71) gives guidance for the more common materials used in formwork in a range of conditions. However these tables are not applicable to concretes containing ggbfs or pfa. The main concern for vertical forms is to eliminate frost and mechanical damage to the concrete and reduce thermal shock. The time at which the forms can safely be removed is related to the material of the form and the gain of strength of the concrete. This strength gain is governed by the mean air temperature, the mix design, the release agent and the subsequent method of curing. A useful guide on curing of concrete is Concrete Society Digest No. 3 (Ref. 66).

Where finish and uniform colour are important, a consistent timing regime of striking and curing will be critical. Often forms 'left on the pour over the weekend' will produce different colour and surface to those struck during the week due to inconsistency in the timing of striking.

A concrete strength of 2 N/mm² is a generally recommended minimum requirement to reduce risk of mechanical damage to F3 and F4 finishes while striking wall forms.

F_3 and F_4 finish, minimum strength 2 N/mm².

Generally, for F1 and F2 finishes, provided the mean air temperature and concrete temperature are above 10°C overnight, the form can be struck next morning. In the case of sloping sections of concrete, for example shown in Fig. 73, then in addition to the possibility of mechanical damage, the concrete has to support itself on striking and a minimum structural strength will need to be achieved before striking can commence. See soffit form striking in Section 5.3.6.

F_1 and F_2 finish, strike next morning if above 10°C overnight.

Soffit, see Section 5.3.6.

The method of quantifying the concrete strength at the time of striking is outside the scope of this guide but some guidance is given in Section 5.3.6.3 and in Refs. 72 and 73. On a large site the use of temperature matched curing baths may justify the initial investment in giving faster striking times, whereas on a smaller site, cubes cured alongside might be more appropriate.

Section 5.3.6.3.
Refs. 72 and 73.

See also BS 8110, Clause 6.9.3 (Ref. 14).

The required surface finish and shape will also affect the striking time; suitable draws on features and correct choice of suitable release agents will facilitate easy stripping. Leaving forms in place for longer than necessary may have the advantage of greater strength in the concrete but can adversely affect the final colour by leaving patches and/or discoloration on the surface and, in certain cases, restrain concrete shrinkage to the extent of inducing cracking. An example is a post-tensioned concrete beam with frequent web stiffeners.

The use of a crane to strike formwork is not recommended, although handling the form by crane immediately after release is normal practice. Ideally the form should be designed and connected to the crane so that the form's own weight assists removal. The crane connection point should be located between the centre of gravity of the form and the wall face. Screw jacks built into the formwork face with 100 × 100 mm square face area will aid initial release.

See Section 5.9.

Careful attention to detail in the form design will considerably reduce the likelihood of damage during striking.

Section 5.3 – Soffit and Beam Formwork

Section 5.3.1 – General

This section of the guide considers the temporary works necessary to support the fluid concrete for slabs. Generally such support will comprise two elements: firstly the face contact material and its immediate backing, and secondly the supporting framework transmitting those forces to suitable foundations. The latter is generally known as falsework and its design is covered by BS 5975 (Ref. 2). The face contact material forming the concrete mould is considered as soffit formwork and considerations for its design are given in this guide. Some examples of soffit formwork are shown in Figs. 66 and 67. There is obviously overlap between formwork and falsework but the design parameters are the same for the backing members whether they are considered as part of the formwork or as part of the falsework. For example, the structural properties of individually loaded timbers in Table 4 are identical to those for falsework stated in BS 5975.

BS 5975 (Ref. 2).

Compare Table 4 and BS 5975, Clause 18.3 (Ref. 2). (Note: at the time of writing (Aug. 1986) BS 5268 Part 2 (Ref. 4) grade stresses are being incorporated in a third amendment to BS 5975.)

Fig. 66 *Soffit formwork with timber bearers and plywood.*

Fig. 67 *Soffit formwork with aluminium bearers and plywood.*

In falsework, allowance is not normally made for the stiffness of the face contact material to transmit horizontal restraint forces to the supports. When it is necessary to utilise the face for this purpose consideration must be given to its direction of lay, as the properties of some face contact materials vary according to their orientation. For examples, see Tables 8 and 9. The face will generally be butt jointed, in which case it is suitable for transmitting compression forces only.

See Tables 8 and 9.

Typical loading cases, Appendix B.

Support reactions: 10% increase for random bearers.

When considering the design of the bearers supporting the face, if the layout is known then the actual values of the reactions at supports, bending moments, deflections etc can be calculated. Some typical loading arrangements are shown in Appendix B. The working stresses of the materials can be obtained from Section 3 of this guide. If the support positions are known but the precise length of bearers is not known, it is recommended that the support reactions are analysed for all bearers as simply supported and the resulting reaction at the supports increased by 10% to allow for the variations in the transferred loads. If there is more than one level of random length bearers, such as secondary and primary, all random bearers are considered simply supported and the support reaction is calculated from the unit area, and the 10% is only added once to allow for all the random transferences of forces. Where a specific case can be identified, such as over three supports, then a more detailed analysis may be justified.

The site practice of lapping primary support timbers may introduce eccentric loading at the support, particularly if continuous over more than three supports. It is therefore preferable to use twin bearers with staggered joints, to minimise eccentricity.

See Section 3.11.1.

Factor of safety on holding down 2.5.

See Fig. 47.

Certain slab designs will incorporate void formers such as duct tubes (see Section 3.11.1). The flotation of such items should be considered in the design of the soffit forms. If fluid concrete is placed around such voids, the flotation force upwards is equivalent to the weight of the displaced concrete less the self-weight of the void. When internally vibrating the concrete, this force can be locally increased; a factor of safety of at least 2.5 is therefore recommended on any holding-down details.
The weight of reinforcement is rarely sufficient to withstand the uplift forces.
The recommended solution is to strap the voids through the soffit forms and connect to suitable restraints below. See Fig. 47.

Worked example C3 in Appendix C.

If the slab is concreted full depth, including voids, the force in the soffit face contact material will locally be equivalent to the full mass of the concrete section **excluding** the voids. The uplift force will also be present until the concrete ceases to be fluid. If the alternative approach of casting the slab below the void in an initial stage is adopted, the uplift forces on the formers in the second stage will still be present. Worked example C3 in Appendix C includes the soffit formwork for a voided bridge deck cast in one stage.

Concrete Society Data Sheets (Ref. 46).

See Section 3.6.7.

Floors may incorporate waffles or troughs in the permanent design. Guidance on dimensions may be obtained from the Concrete Society Data Sheets (Ref. 46) and some further details are given at Section 3.6.7. In areas of solid slab a separate design may be needed for the face contact material to support the full depth of concrete.

Proprietary moulds are available and, depending on the system selected, the method and degree of support to the rib soffit will vary. Where a partly flanged mould is used, which forms only part of the rib, the make-up could either be a proprietary skeletal decking system or a single strip of face contact material. The latter may require more support than its adjacent mould to minimise differential deflections. The advice of the specialist supplier should be sought.

In multi-storey construction the structural design loads should be stated, preferably on the drawings, so that the contractor can provide the most economic system of support. For example the *Standard Method of Measurement of Building Works* includes this requirement in SMM6: Clause F.1.2.c (Ref. 74). The effect of backpropping and repropping is discussed in more detail in Section 5.4.

State structural design loads.

Ref. 74.

Section 5.4.

Section 5.3.2 – Nominally Level Soffits

For the purposes of this guide a nominally level soffit is one whose gradient does not exceed a slope of 1 in 20.

Maximum slope 1 in 20.

Formwork for flat slabs is invariably more economic than for beam and slab type construction. Consideration should therefore be given to the design by the permanent works designer (PWD) of integral beam strips within the depth of the slab and the omission of drop slabs at columns. However, it should be appreciated that many factors, other than formwork considerations, affect the choice of structural form.

Where layouts are not governed by other considerations, the designer of the permanent structure can promote economy by using multiples of the currently available soffit systems, face contact materials and bearers etc. Due consideration should be given for manufacturing, erection and construction tolerances.

Discontinuity of the face contact materials and soffit supports such as shown in Figs. 52 and 68 can result in out-of-balance horizontal forces which require to be stabilised. Note that these forces occur whether the soffits are level or inclined, as in Fig. 68.

See Fig. 52

Fig. 68.

Out-of-balance forces can also occur during placing of concrete due to impact or surge effects against stationary concrete such as at joints. See Fig. 69. Generally the minimum lateral stability force requirements from BS 5975 Clause 43.4.1 (Ref. 2) will cater for these locally induced forces, but the conditions should always be checked.

See Fig. 69.

BS 5975 Clause 43.4.1

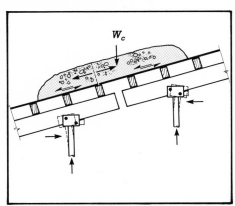
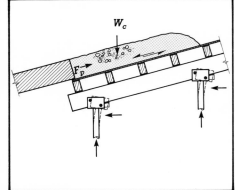

Fig. 68 *Discontinuity in face and soffit: concrete at rest.*

Fig. 69 *Soffit against fixed face.*

Section 5.3.3 – Inclined Soffits

Section 5.3.3.1 – General

The selection of a support system to an inclined soffit will affect the formwork details. If the choice is to design the supports to be perpendicular to the inclined soffit then the falsework will be 'out of vertical by design' and additional components of force are introduced into the bracing system. See BS 5975, Clause 42.1.3.3. In this situation all the formwork connections are normal to each other (e.g. face contact to bearers) and the use of wedges in the formwork is eliminated. Checks should be made to ensure that any bearers acting at right angles to the slope, i.e. across it, are stable. They may require noggins or cross struts for stability. See Fig. 70. This arrangement is often simple to detail and design but can be difficult to erect due to the inherent problem of deliberately setting up items out of vertical and to an exact slope.

See BS 5975, Clause 42.1.3.3.

See Fig. 70.

The more usual arrangement for an inclined soffit, when using conventional forkheads, is to install the falsework in the vertical position and accommodate the inclination by wedging the primary bearers. Proprietary rocking forkheads are available which can eliminate the need for wedges. See Fig. 71.

See Fig. 71.

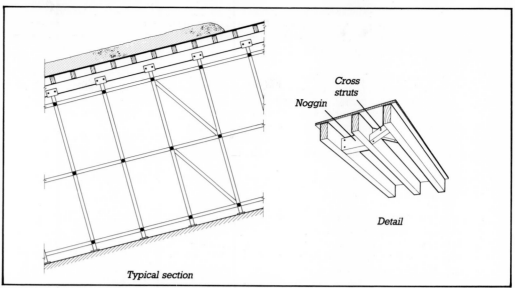

Fig. 70 *Inclined soffit: falsework out of vertical by design.*

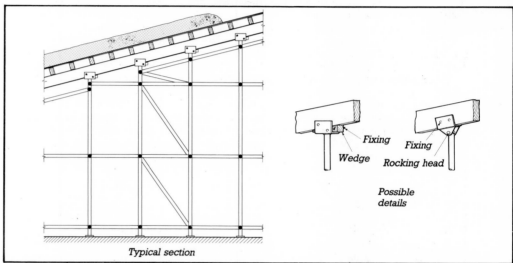

Fig. 71 *Inclined soffit: falsework vertical.*

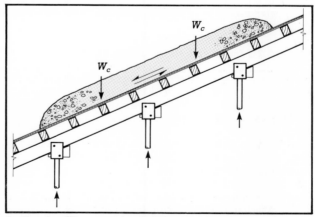

Fig. 72 *Inclined soffit: concrete at rest.*

When using wedges, particular care should be taken to use the correct angle so as to ensure concentric loading of the supports.

Fig. 72.

Concrete at rest on an inclined soffit, as shown in Fig. 72, imparts **only vertical forces** onto the supports. Horizontal components of force will arise only from impact, flowing materials or wind forces. Concrete remains at rest because internal friction within the material prevents it flowing and friction between the wet concrete and the face contact material prevents it sliding. However, it is recommended that the face contact material for inclined soffits is fixed to bearers or supports with suitable wedges, nails or fasteners to withstand such horizontal forces. (Lateral bracing may be required for the supports.)

Experience shows that for formwork using softwood bearers on nominally level soffits, i.e slope less than 1 in 20, the shear at the interfaces does not exceed the safe frictional limits stated in BS 5975 Clause 43.4.6, using a factor of safety of 2.0.

BS 5975 Clause 43.4.6.

Softwood timber bearers in soffit formwork can be sloped up to 11° to the horizontal (1 in 5 slope) before special considerations are necessary for designed fixings to prevent sliding. This figure is based on a coefficient of static friction for softwood on softwood of $\mu = 0.4$ and a factor of safety of 2.0.

Softwood/softwood slope 11° (1 in 5).

μ = coefficient of static friction = $\tan \theta$ (where θ is the angle of inclination to the horizontal). Thus for $\mu = 0.4$, $\theta = 21.8°$.

Applying a factor of safety of 2.0 gives

$$\mu = \frac{0.4}{2.0} = 0.2 \quad \text{thus} \quad \theta = 11.3°$$

Lateral stability of members may require separate checks to be carried out.

The design depends on whether or not a top form is required.

Section 5.3.3.2 – Inclined Soffit without Top Form

Generally for slopes up to 20° a top form is unnecessary. For slopes between 20° and 30° the use of a top form depends on several factors which are discussed at Section 5.3.3.3.

In the exceptional cases of very thin shells or domes it may be possible to concrete at angles in excess of 30° without a top form, up to angles of 80°.

The design of the soffit forms without a top form will be covered by the points already mentioned above; in addition the method of finishing the top face of the concrete will need to be considered. The choice of screeding method may dictate the pour size in order to obtain the required finish. The use of low workability concrete for an inclined soffit will also affect the finishing trades output.

The choice of release agent on the face contact material is also important. Certain agents can produce very slippery surfaces.

Safe access for operatives during reinforcement placing should be provided, and the angle of slope is critical. Where the soffit form projects outside the stopends of the form, such as at the sides of a ramp, the use and fixing of stepping lathes is suggested. *The Code of Practice for access and working scaffold structures in steel* BS 5973 (Ref. 75), gives recommendations for stepping lathes on slopes.

BS 5973 (Ref. 75).

Section 5.3.3.3 Inclined Soffit with Top Form

A top form will increase the cost of the work and should be avoided wherever possible, but for slopes steeper than 30° a top form is recommended. As a rule-of-thumb, for slopes between 20° and 30° the following factors favour the use of top forms

(a)   Fluid concrete (with or without a superplasticiser).
(b)   High rate of pour along the inclined plane, giving a relatively high design pressure.
(c)   Unacceptability of a trowelled finish.
(d)   Ambient temperature below 10°C.
(e)   Possibility of heavy vibration.
(f)   Little or no top face reinforcement.
(g)   Complex geometry and high dimensional accuracy.

If none of the above conditions apply, top forms may be omitted for slopes up to 30°.

When using inclined top forms, the designer should consider:

(a)   Trapping of air. Top forms tend to encourage the formation of blowholes. The choice of suitable release agent can reduce but not eliminate this effect.
(b)   Mix design. In particular the proportion of fines may affect the finish when using a top form.
(c)   Access for placing and compacting the concrete.

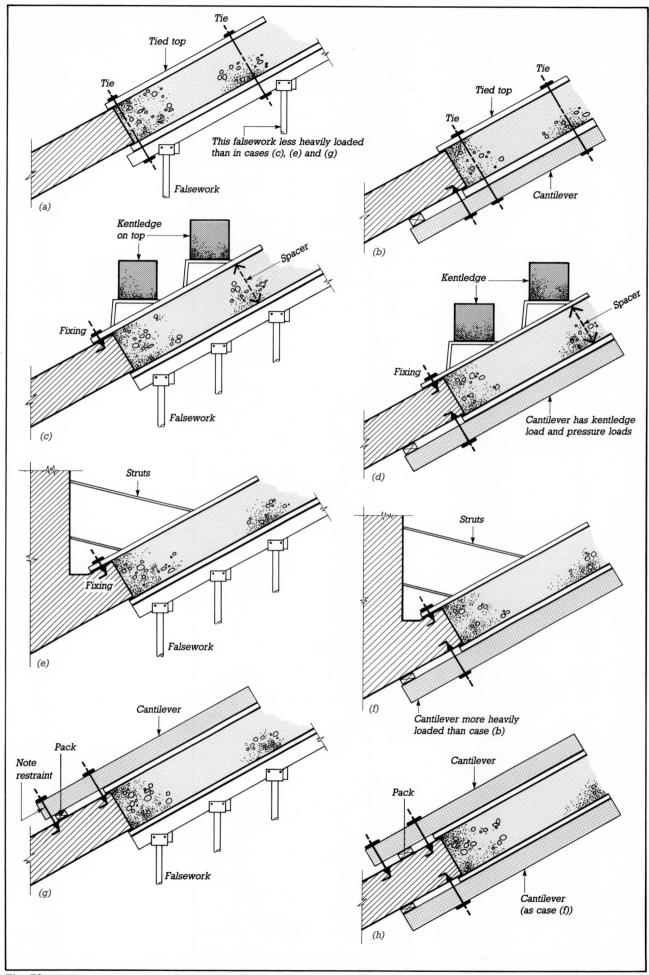

Fig. 73 *Inclined double faced formwork: possible solutions for restraint.*

(d)   Care in design of lifting points for ease of striking and handling. The position of the centre of gravity will often need to be established by site trials before use (see Section 5.9).

See Section 5.9.

(e)   Flotation of the form due to uplift.

(f)   Method of spacing the form from the inclined soffit to the top form. If a tie rod system is used for spacing it will be in compression, becoming tensioned as the concrete is placed.

The method of restraint of the top form from concrete pressure forces will affect the design of the inclined soffit form. When calculating the concrete pressure for constant thickness soffits using the CIRIA method in Section 4.4.2 the following should be noted:

Section 4.4.2.

(a)   The fluid concrete pressure (maximum) at any point uses the value of head as the **vertical** dimension to the level of the free surface of concrete.

(b)   The rate of rise (**R**) is the **vertical** rise in m/h and **not** the slope rise per hour.

(c)   If using Table 15, the value of **H** for the form height will be the projected vertical total form height and **not** the length of the form.

There are many design solutions for formwork for inclined soffits. Some are shown in Fig. 73. The solutions to the design of the top form will be in one of three ways:

See Fig. 73 on preceding page.

        Through ties, similar to an inclined wall.
        External strutting or kentledge.
        Cantilever construction.

Top Form with Through Ties: Design of an inclined soffit with top form and ties, as shown in Fig. 73 (a) and (b), is the same as that for an inclined double face wall with the addition of the imposed construction operations load.

(Compare Fig. 59.)

The pressure diagrams for the more typical cases are shown in Fig. 74. The diagram for the top face is as shown and the resulting force is restrained by tie rods connected to the soffit formwork. Generally a spacer type tie rod is used to ensure the correct thickness of inclined soffit, and to assist during erection of the top form. The forces are distributed to the tie rods which are kept normal to the face.

Fig. 74.

The imposed construction operations loading acting on the top form is unlikely to affect the top form design as it acts in the opposite direction to the concrete pressure. However, it is additive to the soffit form loading.

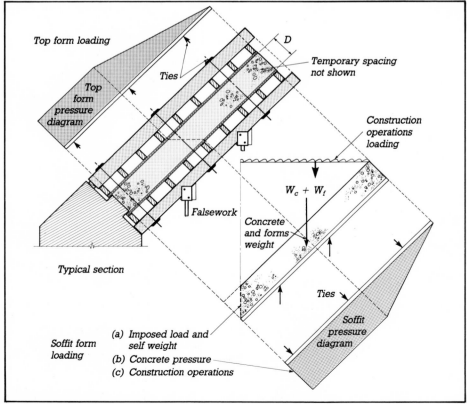

Fig. 74   *Inclined soffit with top form and ties.*

concrete society

The total load on the inclined soffit form is the sum of several applied loading cases. First there is the applied concrete pressure, acting at right angles to the face as shown in Fig. 74 and distributed through the forms to the tie rods in a similar manner to the top form.

In addition the soffit formwork has to support the self-weight (W_t) of the combined top and bottom forms, together with the total actual weight of the wet concrete (W_c). This load system is vertical and is distributed to the falsework supports. An additional load is the imposed construction operations loading on the form area. It is only applied to one of the two faces and is ‒ considered for convenience along the horizontal length but is applied vertically as shown in the figure. Because the lower soffit form is longer the different magnitudes of the pressure diagrams produce a slight loading imbalance and a small horizontal force. This is generally ignored.

The separate load cases described above all occur together. However it is important not to duplicate the forces from the concrete by taking both the mass and the pressure. When the design parameters have been established from the various loading and support patterns, suitable materials should be chosen so that the design stresses are not exceeded. The pressure system is contained within the framework and the ties. The mass (the permanent works load) must be carried to 'earth'. A quick conservative approximation can be made by adding the loads, but, particularly on slabs thicker than 1.0 m, a more rigorous treatment will provide a more economic solution.

Top Form with External Strutting or Kentledge: The use of external strutting or kentledge to restrain the top form against the applied concrete pressure significantly alters the loading condition for design of the soffit form. Typical examples are shown in Fig. 73 (c), (d), (e) and (f). When there is no connection between the top form and the inclined soffit form, the full concrete pressure force will be exerted on the soffit form and will be required to be supported by the falsework. A typical example is shown in more detail in Fig. 75.

See Fig. 73.

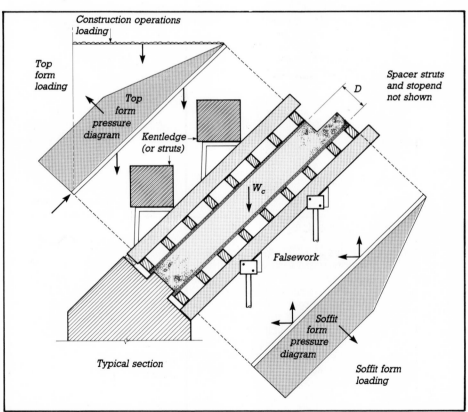

Fig. 75 *Inclined soffit with top form and kentledge (no ties)*

The top form will be designed to resist the outward forces which will be distributed to the struts or kentledge. When using kentledge the support of the kentledge itself should be taken into account. Depending on the distribution of the struts and restraints, the elements of the top form will be designed to suit. In this case the construction operations loadings will be acting onto the top form. The soffit form will be subjected to the pressure, as shown in the diagram, which will give a force normal to the face. The resulting force can be resolved into vertical and horizontal components.

The vertical component of this force is usually greater than the mass of the permanent work being supported. The formwork will need to be designed to transmit these larger forces to the supporting falsework members.

When kentledge is used a spacer system may be incorporated to transfer the self-weight of the kentledge into the falsework prior to concreting. Care should be taken to ensure that the soffit forms are not locally overstressed. A factor of safety of at least 1.5 should be used when calculating the required kentledge. It should be noted that the kentledge will be supported by the falsework even after the concrete has set.

Factor of safety on kentledge 1.5.

Top Form in Cantilever: The concrete pressures can be restrained on a top form by cantilevering the top form from the previous section of work. See Fig. 73 (g) and (h). As with all cantilever constructions the strength of the anchorage and the tip deflection of the top form are both design considerations to be checked. Generally the length of cantilever should not exceed a slope length of 1.5 m to minimise the tip deflections. Details of one typical arrangement with the concrete pressure diagrams are shown in Fig. 76.

See Fig. 73.

Maximum cantilever slope length 1.5 m.

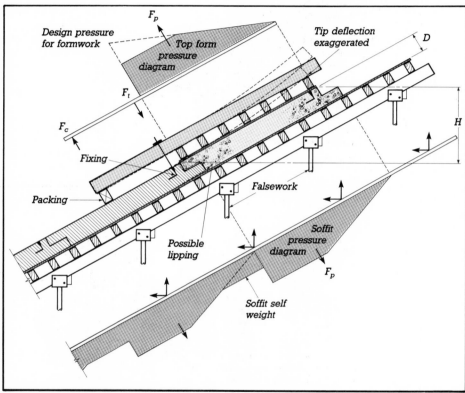

Fig. 76 *Cantilever top form to inclined soffit.*

The design of the soffit formwork requires particular care to ensure that all the forces are restrained correctly. The soffit form will have a concrete pressure diagram similar in shape and magnitude to the top form. The face contact material and bearers on the soffit will need to resist a force that is generally **larger** than that of the permanent works load. Ideally, a cast-in fixing or through tie at position F_t on Fig. 76, to **connect** to the soffit form, will ensure that the soffit also acts partially in cantilever to balance the top form cantilever. If such a through connection is not fitted, i.e. as in Fig. 76, there is an out-of-balance force and the previously cast permanent works section will be stressed by an upwards force reacting against the soffit form; this may cause unacceptable lipping at the underside joint between the two pours. The permanent works designer should be aware of the applied forces on the structure if this method of construction is adopted.

Generally the forces transferred from the formwork into the falsework supports will be the vertical forces from the mass of the permanent works, form self-weight and construction operations loadings plus any environmental and stability loads. The design of the formwork for the inclined soffit will have to allow for the separate load cases described all occurring together. See *Top Form with Through Ties* on previous pages.

Section 5.3.4 – Cantilever Soffits

Fig. 73

Fig. 77.

An alternative solution to conventional falsework support on short projections of soffit is to cantilever support from the existing structure, to form the soffit formwork for insitu concrete. Some examples are shown in Fig. 73 (b), (d), (f) and (h). In certain cases there is no actual soffit formwork but only side formwork such as the insitu parapet side to precast beams. An example of cantilever soffit forms is shown in Fig. 77.

Notify PWD.

All types of formwork and falsework constructions which are cantilevered from the permanent structures will create forces and moments in the structures. It is therefore important that these conditions are notified to the designer of the permanent works so that the structure can be checked and modified if necessary.

Fig. 77 *Cantilever soffit formwork for a bridge parapet cantilevered from precast beams.*

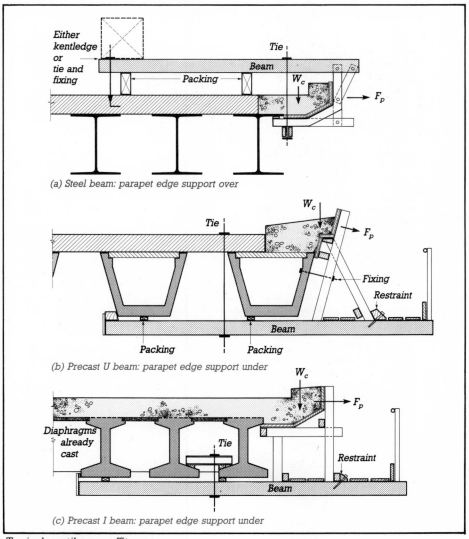

(a) Steel beam: parapet edge support over

(b) Precast U beam: parapet edge support under

(c) Precast I beam: parapet edge support under

Fig. 78 *Typical cantilever soffit cases.*

The two solutions generally used for the support are to suspend beams from the underside of the existing structure or cantilever beams over the top. Fig. 78 shows some typical cases. The side forms exert horizontal forces which are resisted by strutting from the cantilevered beams. In both solutions this side form force adds an additional applied moment and horizontal force into the cantilevers. Even when there is no soffit, there will be applied forces to be resisted.

Fig. 78.

When the cantilever is over the top of the structure (see Fig. 78(a)) it is held down either by ties or by kentledge into the existing structure. With kentledge (shown dotted) the support packing under the cantilever should be designed for the full kentledge load when the applied concrete force is not present. A factor of safety of at least 3.0 should be used in determining the kentledge. If the system is tied down the factor of safety in the ties and any cast-in fixings generally will be adequate. Consideration should be given to the stability of the system prior to fixing of ties, particularly if the beam is part of a traveller.

See Fig. 78(a).

Factor of safety on kentledge for cantilever soffits 3.0.

When the cantilever projects from the underside of the structure (see Fig. 78(b) and (c)) the beams forming the cantilever will be connected by fixing directly to the structure, either by bolts into previously cast-in sockets or by tie rods. When using a formwork tie rod system a minimum factor of safety of 3.0 for tensile forces is recommended. Particular care is necessary in the detailing of the system to provide restraint for the shear forces generated by horizontal concrete pressures. The designer may need to check the effects of combined tension and shear in the ties and bolts. Where high yield steels are used bending stresses in the ties/bolts should be avoided.

See Fig. 78(b) and (c).

Factor of safety on tie rods 3.0. (See also Section 3.8.8.)

The most significant design consideration with this type of support is the effect of deflections of the cantilever. In addition to the calculable deflected shape of the cantilever beams, additional movement will take place due to elastic lengthening of ties, crushing of any compressive packs etc, resulting in further rotation of the cantilever about its original position. This is shown diagrammatically in Fig. 79. All these movements are functions of the properties of the cantilever support system and can be minimised but not avoided entirely. The specifier of such a system should be aware of the implications of these movements and make suitable allowances such as presetting the system to allow for the anticipated deflections and allowing realistic tolerances.

Fig. 79.

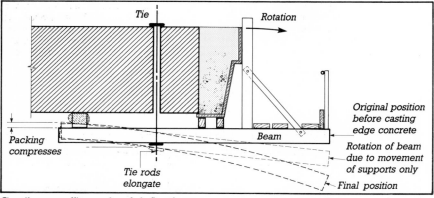

Fig. 79 *Cantilever soffit: mode of deflection.*

Deflections shown exaggerated for clarity.

The differential movement of the formwork against the permanent structure should be considered by the formwork designer and, wherever possible, details considered to reduce the effects. The use of planned fixings into the edges of the precast beams as shown in Fig. 78 (b) will reduce the effects of local differential movements of the formwork.

Differential movement.

Fig. 78 (b).

Section 5.3.5 – Beam Formwork

Uniformity of beam and column sizes and good beam to column junction details can lead to economy in formwork in both manufacture and fix/strike operations. Beams and columns should preferably be of the same width.

Consideration should be given to whether the beams are to be concreted separately or monolithically with the slab. In the former case the beam sides are subjected to horizontal pressure only. In the latter case both horizontal pressure and vertical loads are encountered. In addition to any camber specified by the permanent works designer, allowance should be made for deflection and settlement of formwork and falsework, as well as beam sides. Where they are designed to support adjustable floor centres, they should be detailed with struts under the floor centre positions. Typical examples are shown in Figs. 39 and 80.

Figs. 39 and 80.

In deep, heavily reinforced beams it may be necessary to specify the centres of the soffit reinforcement spacer blocks in order to avoid excessive local bearing pressures on the soffit forms.

See Section 3.6.11.

Proprietary beam clamps are available and can provide an economic solution for beams up to approximately 600 mm deep. See Section 3.6.11.

See Fig. 81.

Beam sides are generally strutted off the soffit bearers; alternatively they may be tied through, or above and below, to provide more positive connections. See Fig. 81.

Beam formwork should be detailed to allow the sides to be struck without disturbing the soffit as this will normally be required to stay in position for a much longer period. However, in certain circumstances it may be desirable to hang the beam soffit from the beam sides, in which case the complete form can be struck as a single unit, provided that a suitable striking angle is incorporated in the side forms.

When beams are poured integrally with the slab, as in tableform construction, it is advisable to splay the beam sides to allow a vertical strike without dismantling.

See Fig. 80(c) and Section 3.8.8 on hanger ties.

In steel frame buildings where beams are to be cased, support can be taken from the beam itself by the use of proprietary hangers; however, access and working platforms must always be considered. See Fig. 80 (c). See also Section 3.8.8 on hanger ties.

In general, beam formwork is subjected to very similar pressures to wall and slab formwork and their design approach should be similar.

Fig. 82.

Typical examples of beam and edge formwork are shown in Fig. 82.

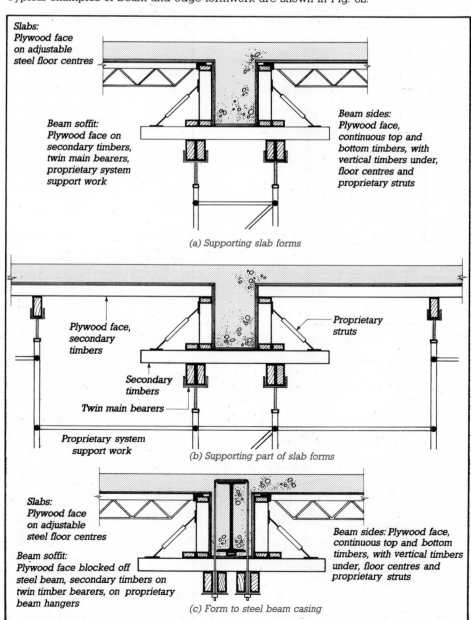

(a) Supporting slab forms

(b) Supporting part of slab forms

(c) Form to steel beam casing

Fig. 80 *Examples of beam formwork supporting soffit falsework and forms.*

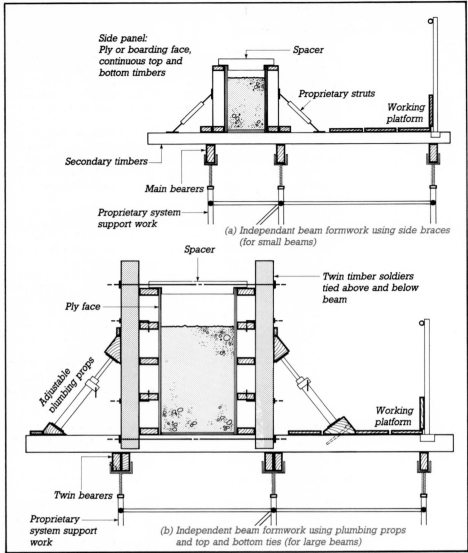

(a) Independant beam formwork using side braces
(for small beams)

(b) Independent beam formwork using plumbing props
and top and bottom ties (for large beams)

Fig. 81 *Examples of independent beam formwork.*

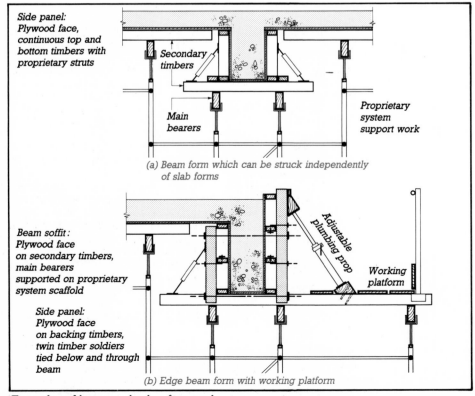

(a) Beam form which can be struck independently
of slab forms

(b) Edge beam form with working platform

Fig. 82 *Examples of beam and edge formwork.*

concrete
society

Section 5.3.6 – Striking

Section 5.3.6.1 – General

Tables of Minimum Striking Times for Soffit and Vertical Formwork (Ref. 71).

The time and procedure by which beam and soffit formwork can be struck should be carefully controlled and should be carried out in accordance with the requirements of the contract specification and drawings. The main consideration is the gain of strength of the concrete to ensure that the member, when released, can support its own weight together with any imposed construction operations loads. Additional considerations are the elimination of frost and mechanical damage, reduction in thermal shock, and limiting excessive deflections. CIRIA Report 67 (Ref. 71) gives guidance on the striking of soffit forms related to design concrete strength and temperature for the more common materials used in formwork, but is limited to plain Portland cement concretes and might not be applicable to concrete containing ggbfs or pfa.

Minimum strength 10 N/mm² or twice stress subjected.

BS 8110, Clause 6.9.3 (Ref. 14).

It is recommended that the minimum concrete strength at time of striking be specified. Where this is not the case it is recommended that whichever is the greater value of either 10 N/mm² or twice the stress to which the member will be subjected at striking is used as the criterion. Calculation to justify a lower value at striking should be approved by the permanent works designer. BS 8110 (Ref. 14) provides some guidance on concrete strengths when striking forms. This guidance gives the structural capacity of the member so that it is self-supporting; in certain situations, such as in 'quick strip' support systems, items of soffit formwork may be removed without disturbing the supports in contact with the slab. In such cases the striking criterion for the removal of soffit form items will be frost or mechanical damage when a minimum concrete strength of 5 N/mm² is recommended. It is necessary to check that the member can span between the remaining supports when the forms are removed. The criteria for striking the final supports will be the gain of strength of the concrete.

Quick strip: minimum strength for mechanical damage 5 N/mm².

Particular care is necessary when striking soffit forms to cantilevers, where the overall stability as well as the gain of concrete strength must be considered.

Section 5.3.6.2 – Striking Procedure

Safety when striking.

Formwork and falsework should be designed so that striking may be carried out safely without causing damage to either concrete or formwork. Areas of soffit formwork about to be struck should be guarded to prevent persons walking into the area. This is particularly relevant at edges of slabs and at large openings. Having established that striking may commence, the site will adopt a procedure based on the method statement stipulated by the designer for the removal of the soffit formwork. For example:

(a)   Where slabs are spanning between beams, the slabs on both sides of a beam should be released before the supports under the beam are disturbed.

(b)   In striking soffit formwork to any single slab or beam the risk of overloading the supports must be avoided. Striking should be undertaken in two stages. First, ease all the supports by about the same amount (e.g. if using adjustable props by one or two turns) and, second, start at mid-span, remove supports working towards the columns or walls.

(c)   Where the soffit form is part of a cantilever, start the removal of supports from the tip of the cantilever and work towards the column, beam or wall.

(d)   Where a clear span system of falsework is used the amount of striking clearance will need to allow for both the instantaneous deflection of the permanent work and the subsequent relaxation of the clear span falsework member as it returns to its unstressed state.

(e)   Where a 'quick strip' proprietary system is used care should be taken to ensure that the structural supports, left undisturbed while the formwork is removed, are clearly distinguishable to the site operatives. The manufacturer's recommendations should be followed.

Soffit formwork should never be allowed to fall to the level below (a practice known as 'crash striking').

See Fig. 83.

To assist in the striking process the inclusion of a purpose designed initial striking piece can be particularly helpful. Such striking pieces can take the shape of a flat sided striking bar, usually solid in section, up to 25 mm wide, or they can be tapered and incorporated into a repropping procedure, thus allowing the section of permanent works to remain supported (see Fig. 83). Striking pieces are generally required in long clear spans of formwork, particularly if they are precambered, and in arch forms of tight radius.

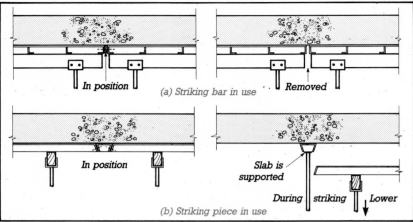

Fig. 83 *Striking bar and striking piece in use.*

The practice of striking certain waffle or trough moulds with compressed air should be carefully controlled. The moulds will have been fitted with air valves during manufacture and if this method of release is used it is necessary to check before placing the concrete that there is an air passage through the face into the gap between mould and concrete. This method is more suited to the larger areas of one-piece mould because large forces can be set up.

Section 5.3.6.3 – Quantifying Concrete Strength

There are several methods by which the gain of strength of the concrete can be quantified. The subject of strength evaluation is covered by Harrison (Ref. 72). Methods of testing concrete are covered by BS 1881 (Ref. 76), and in particular a summary of non-destructive methods of test is given in BS 1881: Part 201. The following list of methods is intended for background information:

Ref. 72.

BS 1881 (Ref. 76).

(a) **Cubes Cured Alongside Structure**

The strength of cubes cured alongside the member will only give indicative results as the temperature history will not be reproduced exactly. An exposed cube will follow the ambient temperature and will tend to be more representative of the temperature history for a thin section than for a thicker section. Temperature rise in thick sections can be substantial (up to 50°C) and can accelerate the gain of strength of the concrete. This method is appropriate for thin suspended slabs without insulation and on small sites where the cost of the more sophisticated methods cannot be justified.

(b) **Temperature Matched Curing**

A temperature sensor probe is placed at a suitable position in the pour. This is linked to a control system and a curing tank accurately follows this sensor. Into this tank are placed cubes in their moulds and lightly covered with steel or glass plates. Curing the cubes by this system results in them having the same maturity as the concrete at the sensor and this method overcomes the limitations of curing alongside the structure. See DD92:1984 (Ref. 73).

See DD92:1984 (Ref. 73).

The method suits larger sites where significant economies can be made by shortening the formwork cycle time. Some reinstatement of the concrete finish after removing the probe may be necessary depending upon its location. It is also used to investigate the insitu properties of concrete which has been through a thermal cycle, as in a mass pour.

(c) **Rebound Hammers**

These measure the surface hardness by mechanically applying a known force and measuring the rebound. At low concrete strengths up to 10 N/mm^2 they tend to dent the concrete surface and are also sensitive to the aggregate being used. Test results should be used with care when assessing striking times. Because the method is simple it is useful for corroborative testing on a site, provided the mix design and a procedure for striking have been previously evaluated by other means.

(d) **Penetration Tests**

A probe is fired into the surface and the depth of penetration is a measure of the hardness. The most common of these tests is the Windsor probe which fires a hardened steel bolt into the concrete. The test needs calibrating for each mix and is more suited to a larger site. Damage to the finish will occur.

(e) **Pull-out and Break-off tests**

Rings, bolts etc are cast into the pour and are then physically removed or deformed, the energy to remove them being a function of the concrete strength. From 5 to 10 tests are needed to obtain a satisfactory result. A calibration is needed to convert the instrument reading into concrete strength. These methods were developed for evaluation of striking times, and particularly for the larger site with fast construction cycle times. The damage to the finish will require reinstatement.

(f) **Maturity Meter**

Ref. 77.

A recently introduced method of measuring concrete strength is to cast into the concrete, patented disposable devices containing a chemical in a sealed phial. Breaking the phial and observing the evaporation of the compound is a measure of the maturity of the concrete (see Ref. 77). The system requires initial calibration for the particular mix in use, and several devices are needed to obtain a satisfactory result. Some making good of the face of the concrete will be involved. Meters are available which perform a similar task using a temperature sensing probe in the concrete. All of these devices might not be suitable for concretes containing ggbfs or pfa due to their different activation energies.

(g) **Striking Time Tables**

BS 8110, Table 6.6 (Ref. 14).

Tables quantifying the time at which striking can commence can be established, either from sources of reference, e.g. BS 8110, Table 6.6 (Ref. 14), or by the site management from testing etc. These tables will all consider the characteristic strength of the concrete at the time considered and will be the lower bound of strength for the grade of concrete. Actual test results by other means will often give significantly shorter striking times.

Tables should state both the grade of concrete and the temperature conditions assumed.

Section 5.3.6.4 – Accelerated Curing

To reduce the cycle times in reuse of formwork, it may be necessary to accelerate the curing of the insitu concrete slab to increase early strength. A typical striking time for a 24 hour cycle would be only 14 hours. To obtain this early strength the mix design may need modifying and the soffit form and slab may need heating.

(An example is apartment formwork systems, Section 3.6.5.)

If the solution is to heat the concrete insitu then heat is directed at the unstruck soffit and concrete slab, while insulating the top of the slab with quilts to reduce the thermal loss. In addition curtains are often provided to reduce heat loss out of the end of the structure being heated. In preparing proposals for accelerated curing, the TWD should check the flexural strength of the slab at striking, and the local bond stress with the reinforcement as detailed. At early age the bond strength develops at a slower rate than the ultimate moment, and bond failure can be the controlling criterion, particularly where the reinforcement is not fully embedded in concrete. A C&CA Advisory Note (Ref. 78) describes a method for checking local bond stress at early age.

The Application of Accelerated Curing to Apartment Formwork Systems (Ref. 78).

(Ref. 78).

Energy 0.75 kW/m³/°C up to 54°C.

Table 19.

The quantity of heat to be applied may be estimated by considering the energy necessary to raise the temperature of the concrete mass. A recommended rule-of-thumb is to consider raising the temperature of the concrete from time of placing to 54°C using an energy of 0.75 kW per cubic metre of concrete per degree rise. Some energy will be absorbed by the formwork; Table 19 gives the heat needed assuming 10% absorption by the forms.

Concrete Starting Temperature (°C)	Degree Rise to 54°C	Energy Needed °C × 0.75		Total Heat Needed (kW per Cubic Metre of Concrete)
		Concrete	Forms	
5	49	36.8	3.6	40.4
10	44	33.0	3.3	36.3
15	39	29.3	2.9	32.2
20	34	25.5	2.5	28.0
25	29	21.8	2.2	24.0

Notes to Table 19:   *(1) The volume of concrete includes both the slab and supporting columns or walls.*
(2) Assumed insitu reinforced concrete of density 2500 kg/m³.
(3) Steel formwork assumed with 10% absorption. (The approximate absorption of heat for steel forms is 12 kW/tonne of formwork.)

Table 19. *Heat Needed for Accelerated Curing based on Volume of Concrete*

The number and layout of the heaters will depend on factors such as the dimensions of the formwork, the duration of heating, the type of heater and the likely loss of heat to the outside air. The duration of heating will be approximately related to the air temperature; Table 20 gives values on a European site for a slab placed at a concrete temperature of 10° to 15°C.

Air Temperature (°C)	Heating Time (h)
+ 15	5.0
+ 10	5.5
+ 5	6.0
0	6.5
− 5	7.0
− 10	7.5

Table 20. *Approximate Heating Time for Accelerated Curing*

The heater selected will be rated for capacity in kilowatt hours (kWh) and the number of heaters calculated from the formula:-

$$\text{Number of heaters} = \frac{\text{Heat need (kW/m}^3) \quad \times \quad \text{Volume (m}^3)}{\text{Heating time (h)} \quad \times \quad \text{Heater capacity (kWh)}}$$

Using the above rules-of-thumb the heating can be applied shortly after finishing concreting. See Ref. 79. Limits have been proposed for temperature, rate of temperature rise, delay on start of heating and so on. Economic methods for site accelerated curing of concrete are unlikely to cause any short or long term problems with the heated members. Further, the high cost of applying enough heat to harm the structure make this unlikely to happen. In precast work (see Section 6.4.5 on heated moulds) the mass is smaller and the heating environment more efficient so that the criteria for heat application are different.

Ref. 79.

See Section 6.4.5 on heated moulds.

The time at which striking can commence will rely on quantifying the concrete strength. See Section 5.3.6.3.

See Section 5.3.6.3.

There are four main heating systems used for accelerated curing:

Steam – either in pipes or in a tent enveloping the structure. The latter is generally not suited to site application and is more widely used in precast factories. When using piped steam, dry steam is preferable.

Gas heating – either infra-red heaters, which are directed up at the soffit, or convector heaters. Generally, with both types, a system of end curtains is employed to reduce wind and convection losses. The gas can be controlled and gives a heating system which is easily transportable.

Electric heating – generally either by overblankets or internal convector heating, although low voltage resistance wires cast into the concrete have been used with well insulated forms. Particular attention to wiring and safety is required. The methods are easily controlled by timers.

Turbo heaters – space heaters fuelled either by gas or oil to heat the soffit by convection. They heat the whole form area and supporting structure. To reduce thermal losses a system of end curtains is employed.

Section 5.4 – Backpropping and Repropping

Section 5.4.1 – General

Section 5.3.6.

It is economically desirable to strike and remove soffit formwork and its supporting falsework as soon as practicable after the permanent work has become self-supporting. Guidance on striking of soffit formwork is given in Section 5.3.6. Reinstatement of falsework to carry loads after the formwork has been removed may be required, either to reduce longer term creep deflections or to transfer loads from subsequent levels of construction. In certain fast construction cycles the supporting falsework may have to be left in an undisturbed and loaded condition for loading from future construction. Wherever such through propping is considered necessary a detailed sequence should be laid down which should be subject to the approval of the designer of the permanent works. Site staff should be aware that changing a sequence of propping without due consideration of the detailed effects of such a change can result in overloading of falsework or additional unforeseen stresses in the permanent works.

Detail the sequence.

Vertical falsework members giving extra support to a soffit which has already been cast may generally be assumed to have a fixed end condition, both top and bottom. Both ends will be effectively held in position, but if a slab being cast does not immediately have continuity to its ultimate supports then it will need separate consideration. It may be necessary to check the sliding friction between slab and supporting falsework at the soffit level; vertical members would be assumed to have an effective length of their clear height – pin jointed – for calculating their load capacity. Provided the applied load does not exceed the capacity of the single strut, bracing is not required, but where the load exceeds the safe single full height strut capacity, a structurally efficient bracing system will be needed to reduce the effective strut lengths by introducing node points within the strut length. See BS 5975, Clause 43.4.3 (Ref. 2) for calculation of the falsework.

See BS 5975, Clause 43.4.3 (Ref. 2).

In multi-storey construction, where a prop is at a position not directly over the line of supports below, then the effect on the slab or beam should be considered. This is particularly important with trough or waffle type slabs where the supports must be positioned over rib-lines and not on the relatively thin topping concrete to the moulds, unless calculated otherwise. The permanent works designer using such flooring layouts should be aware of the implications of changing the mould grid in plan from one level to another and the consequent implications for the falsework support. Where it is not possible to ensure that supports are positioned over ribs or other supports, suitable spreaders should be incorporated.

Early release of individual supports to allow striking, followed by immediate propping, is normally only advised when careful control can be exercised and when explicitly permitted by the contract specification. Excessive stress and deflection may be accidentally induced in the completed work.

Section 5.4.2 – Backpropping

In multi-storey construction the speed of construction vertically will often dictate that the slab level immediately below the level to be supported has not gained full maturity and construction loads will require to be distributed through several levels. This is known as **backpropping.** With fast construction cycles the level immediately below the falsework may not be allowed to take up its instantaneous deflected shape, and unstruck falsework will require supporting through several levels.

BS 5975 Appendix M (Ref. 2).

The load in the falsework will vary significantly depending on the exact sequence of loading and unloading of the supports at each level. A detailed appraisal is given in BS 5975 Appendix M (Ref. 2), which shows the cumulative build-up of loads that can occur. A more rigorous analysis to compute the actual falsework loads would need to consider both the relative stiffness of the supporting slabs as they elastically deflect under applied loads, together with the elastic shortening of the falsework supports. The latter effect is generally ignored in backpropping calculations.

Section 5.3.1 and Section 2.2.1 (d).

See worked examples D1 to D5 on propping in Appendix D.

To enable the falsework coordinator and the formwork designer to make engineering judgements and calculations necessary to assess the need and magnitude of propping for a given structure, they should have access to the design loads for the slabs, including allowances for imposed loads, finishes, partitions etc. The design concrete strength will be known so that the loading characteristics of any slab at a given time can be accurately assessed. The surplus capacity of the slab at a given age may then be used to carry any additional construction loads. See Worked Examples D1 to D5 on propping in Appendix D.

Section 5.4.3 – Repropping

The permanent work once struck will take up its instantaneous deflection. If left unsupported the structure may continue to deflect (creep) and it is often considered necessary to replace some supports, particularly on long spans or if the concrete has not gained sufficient maturity. This practice is known as **repropping** and the initial load in the falsework supports will be nominal.

The repropping of a beam or slab may also be carried out to avoid accidental overloading.

The falsework supports will be placed after the beam or slab has been allowed to deflect under self-weight and care should be taken to ensure that such supports are not overtightened. The most onerous condition is on relatively thin members which could be damaged by reverse bending arising out of overzealous repropping.

Use of repropping for future additional loads is covered in Section 5.4.2 on backpropping.

Section 5.4.2.

Concrete that has not achieved full maturity will be subject to further deflections after the instantaneous deflection has taken place and may require repropping. As a guide, if a beam or slab is loaded after the concrete has achieved 40% or more of its characteristic strength, the ultimate deflection will not be significantly increased, (Refs. 72 and 90).

40% characteristic strength.

Refs. 72 and 90.

The prevention of accidental overloading of a slab, e.g. by inadvertently placing a heavy bundle of reinforcement onto the newly cast slab at midspan, depends on site supervision. To reprop the slab for such an eventuality, it is suggested that, as a rule of thumb, supports having a capacity of 25% of the slab self-weight be provided.

Minimum reprop for 25% of self-weight.

Whenever repropping is used, it should not be allowed to remain in place for too long because creep loading may cause overstressing of the propping members.

Section 5.5 – Column Formwork

Section 5.5.1 – General

Because of their comparatively small cross section and relatively high rates of rise, column forms are subject to higher concrete pressures than walls. See Section 4.4 and Table 16. Due to the confined space into which the concrete is placed, tall and inclined columns may require pockets or windows at intervals to facilitate placing and compacting of the concrete. A cleanout opening may be required at the column base for removal of debris before concreting takes place.

See Section 4.4 and Table 16.

Columns may have circular, square, rectangular or other irregular cross sections. These irregular cross sections can often be formed by placing inserts or box-outs within standard square or rectangular column moulds. See Fig. 84. A range of proprietary column forms is available and some are designed to cater for different rectangular or circular shapes by adjustment on site.

For a column design see worked example C2 in Appendix C.

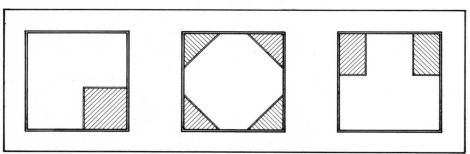

Fig. 84 *Forming different shaped columns by boxing-out.*

Variations in column shapes and sizes, particularly on the same project, should be kept to the minimum, thereby reducing the number of forms required and increasing the number of uses. Ideally column sizes should be selected in modular increments of 75 mm e.g. 300, 375, 450 etc, thus enabling both the designer and the builder to standardise and hence economise.

75 mm module e.g. 300, 375, 450 etc.

An example of a purpose-made octagonal column form is shown in Fig. 85.

Fig. 85.

Circular column moulds are usually manufactured in steel or GRP with a reuse potential in excess of 100, but occasionally timber moulds are used where the number of uses is smaller. Some details are shown in Fig. 86.

Fig. 86.

Fig. 85 *Special octagonal column form.*

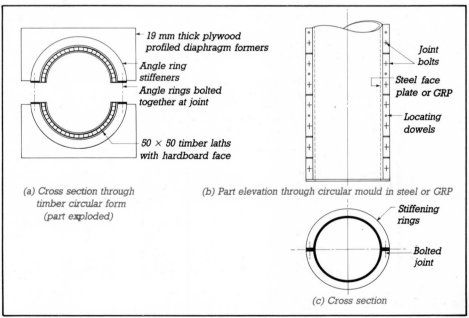

19 mm thick plywood
profiled diaphragm formers

Angle ring
stiffeners

Angle rings bolted
together at joint

50 × 50 timber laths
with hardboard face

*(a) Cross section through
timber circular form
(part exploded)*

Joint
bolts

Steel face
plate or GRP

Locating
dowels

(b) Part elevation through circular mould in steel or GRP

Stiffening
rings

Bolted
joint

(c) Cross section

Fig. 86 *Circular columns: typical details.*

Fig. 87.

Square and rectangular columns are usually manufactured in steel, GRP or timber, depending on the number of uses and the finish required. An example is shown in Fig. 87. Proprietary column clamps and system panels will often provide an economic solution. Column clamps are proprietary items of equipment intended for light construction work and care should be taken to ensure that the allowable bearing stress in the timber is not exceeded. This will prevent the legs of the clamps from twisting under load due to instability and make certain that the clamp is subjected to mainly shear and tensile forces. Spacing of clamps will depend on the concrete pressure and the timber stud sizes, but with low design pressures the spacing will be about 200 mm with the bottom clamp not more than 150 mm up from the bottom of the mould to ensure a grout-tight seal. See also Fig. 43 and Section 3.6.11.

*See also Fig. 43 and
Section 3.6.11.*

Fig. 87 *A square column form with square column head.*

A suitable system for small columns is the use of proprietary steel banding. The bands of steel resist the applied concrete pressure in hoop tension. Various rules-of-thumb are used to calculate the spacing, and supplier's recommendations should be followed.

Some of the more common arrangements are shown in Figs. 88 and 89.   *Figs. 88 and 89.*

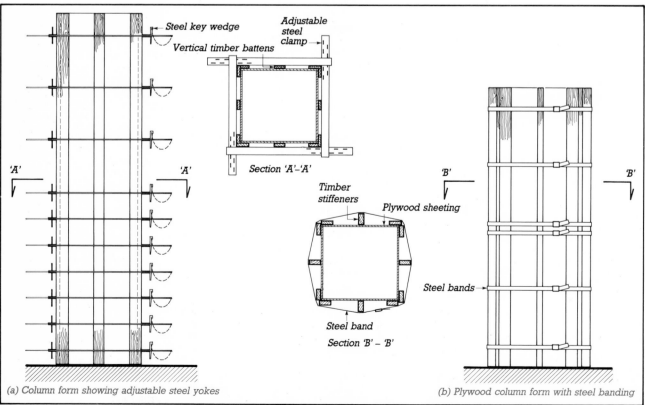

(a) Column form showing adjustable steel yokes   (b) Plywood column form with steel banding

Fig. 88 *Typical square column details.*

concrete society

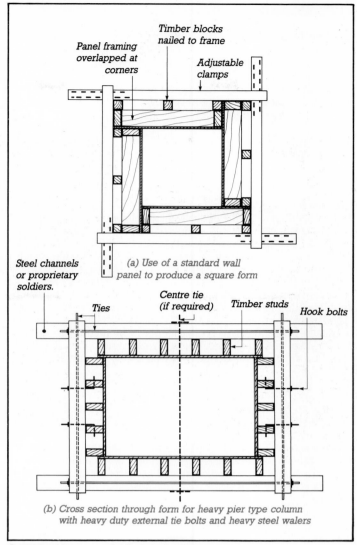

Panel framing overlapped at corners

Timber blocks nailed to frame

Adjustable clamps

Steel channels or proprietary soldiers.

(a) Use of a standard wall panel to produce a square form

Ties

Centre tie (if required)

Timber studs

Hook bolts

(b) Cross section through form for heavy pier type column with heavy duty external tie bolts and heavy steel walers

Fig. 89 *Square column: typical plan details.*

Section 5.5.2 – Erection

See Fig. 96.

Square or rectangular column moulds in timber are generally made in four separate panels and erected panel by panel around a previously cast kicker or spacer system. Some typical details for the arrangements of column kickers are shown in Fig. 96. Clamps or yokes are then placed at the appropriate positions which, ideally, will have been marked on the panels by projecting nails. The complete form is then aligned, plumbed and stabilised with suitable props, preferably on all faces, to eliminate the possibility of twist when concreting. Props should be placed against suitably stiffened portions of the form and not against clamps or yokes.

Square, rectangular and circular column moulds in steel or GRP are generally manufactured in halves with flanged and bolted joints and are usually erected in two pieces around a pre-positioned reinforcement cage. Alternatively, where reinforcement detail permits, they can be preassembled and lowered over the cage on to the kicker and finally tightened, aligned, plumbed and stabilised. Suitable propping brackets or stiffened portions should be incorporated in the design.

Columns 20 mm high.

See also Section 2.6.4.

Columns cast slightly above the soffit of the slab they are to support (say 20 mm) will allow tolerance on levels when the soffit formwork is erected and facilitate a clean grout-tight joint. See also Section 2.6.4.

Section 3.11.5.

Sharp corners on columns are prone to damage during and after stripping. It is therefore desirable that all sharp corners shall be avoided by the introduction of a chamfer fillet into the corners of the form. Section 3.11.5 states recommended fillet sizes depending on the material of the form.

On certain types of construction it is necessary to build inserts and fixing points into columns for the attachment of various permanent works items; e.g. in car parks, the bottom 1.5 to 2.0 m of columns often have a steel insert at the corners to protect against vehicle impact. These inserts need to be fixed to the column form and will inevitably reduce the life of timber forms.

Section 5.6 – Special Applications

Section 5.6.1 – Arch Formwork

The forming of arches may be considered as a special type of sloping soffit. Reference should also be made to Section 5.3.3. The design of the arch soffit depends upon whether or not a top form is required. This significantly affects the load in the supporting falsework. A typical arrangement is shown in Fig. 90. The concrete pressure will act at right angles to the form face.

Section 5.3.3.

The design of falsework for arches is given in BS 5975, Clause 45.3 (Ref. 2) and an analysis of the forces acting is given in Appendix J of the same Code.

BS 5975, Clause 45.3 and Appendix J (Ref. 2).

Two major design points should be considered:

(a) **Waler Spacing**
The face contact material has to be bent into the required curve between walers if short straights are not accepted. (See Fig. 64 for chord offset dimensions.) Although the arch shape is only a curved wall form rotated, the effect of fluid concrete pressures is different. With a wall, the concrete pressure is uniform at the same level and the inherent stiffness of the bent face contact material can be used. In an arch the effect of placing and vibrating fluid concrete will locally cause increased pressures which will tend to ripple the face material between horizontal walings; alternate spans will hog. Thus when considering the bending radii of the face contact material on arch forms they are designed for the full force spanning the actual distance between walers with no allowance for any effect from the curving of the material. (An allowance is accepted in wall formwork curved in plan see Section 5.2.4.)

See Fig. 64 for chord offset dimensions.

Minimum bending radii for plywood, Table 10.

See Section 5.2.4.

(b) **Striking**
Small radius arches may be struck in one piece. A full semi-circle cannot be struck and a striking piece must be incorporated. Provision to ease the arch form vertically downwards, say 25 mm, would be suitable on most arch forms. Even on a large arch form the provision for striking the form downwards is suggested. Where the arch falsework is in one piece and the sides of the formwork are steep, consideration should be given to hingeing the formwork at its lowest points to give side clearance before overall lowering. See Fig. 90.

(See also Section 5.3.6 on striking of soffits.)

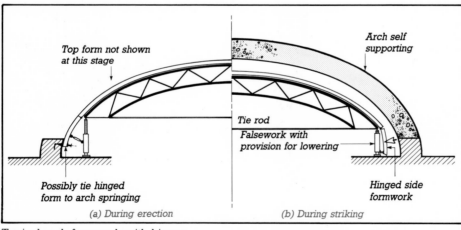

Fig. 90 *Typical arch formwork with hinges.*

An arch form will always have its centre of gravity above its support position. Particular care is necessary during erecting and striking to ensure that the form is always stable.

Formwork for skew arches can be geometrically very complex with the use of conventional square section walings, bearers etc., and the economic implications should be considered by the permanent works designer. Wherever possible, a skew arch should be designed as a more conventional arch about its axis of skew, but concreted only over a part of its plan area.

The method of placing concrete should, wherever possible, balance the loading on the arch. An out-of-balance limitation is given in BS 5975, Clause 45.3 for the falsework. Access doors for inspection and placing of concrete should, if required, be incorporated into the top form only.

BS 5975, Clause 45.3.

Section 5.6.2 – Tunnel Formwork

The essential difference between arch formwork and tunnel formwork is in the methods of placing concrete and the way the form is moved. The design of the members and calculations of the concrete pressures will be similar.

Tunnel formwork will form the lining concrete to a tunnel. Different uses of the completed tunnel will dictate varying qualities of surface finish and positions of construction joints. A high pressure water tunnel will require minimum lipping between pours, whereas a lower standard of finish would be acceptable on a service tunnel. Ideally, the invert will be poured first with a framework for screeding to the correct profile of the tunnel and to give stability for the main tunnel form. The remaining cross section of the arch will normally then be cast in one pour (see Fig. 91). The concrete will be poured equally both sides to avoid out-of-balance forces. The type of ground through which the tunnel is being dug will also affect the basic concept. Resin-type anchors, sometimes used in hard ground, are difficult to fix to, unless the lining concrete is sufficiently thick to give access behind the form for connection of the ties. An alternative is to design the formwork in a compression ring and react the forces by strutting off the rock face using 'spud' bars. As the concrete rises up the arch these spud bars can be withdrawn and the concrete made good.

See Fig. 91.

Although most tunnel forms will be balanced pours, the case can occur when only one side of a tunnel form is concreted, such as at a pedestrian opening in a station tunnel. One side should be treated as a single face pour and separate calculations carried out.

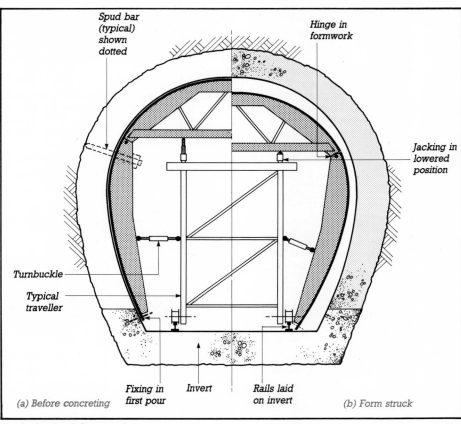

Fig. 91 *Typical tunnel formwork.*

In long lengths of tunnel one end of the pour will usually be connected to previous work. The method of concreting will generally be by pneumatic placer or concrete pump with flexible pipes. Access doors in the face of the forms will be used for most of the placing, with the final concreting of the crown completed through the stopend. In large tunnels the crown sections may be removable, allowing concrete to the sides to be fed in over the crown. Compaction of the concrete will usually be with internal vibrators, due mainly to the limited penetration depth of surface vibrators (see Section 7.6).

See Section 7.6.

The use of superplasticisers and retarders in tunnel formwork may have a more significant effect on the design than in, say, wall formwork. The designer should be aware of the mix design and its implications for tunnel forms. See Section 4.4.

See Section 4.4.

The method of moving a tunnel form depends upon the circumstances and tunnel size. A small diameter tunnel form may have its own integral traveller with wheels ahead of the form on the ground and with its rear wheels on the last pour. It is retracted to a smaller size and is moved forward and then opened out for reuse, rather like an expanding mandrel (see Section 5.6.3). A larger tunnel may use a central traveller running on the previously cast invert pour such as shown in Fig. 91; depending on the type of tunnel, mucking out trains from the face may need to pass through the formwork system. Often jacks are installed on such a traveller for lowering the crown. This type may also incorporate side-hinged sections for striking prior to the lowering of the entire form and moving forward. In certain cases the traveller may require to be removed when concreting to gain better access for the concrete pump.

See Section 5.6.3.
Fig. 91.

The design of tunnel forms is a specialist task and only people with suitable experience should undertake this operation.

Section 5.6.3 – Telescopic Tunnel Formwork

When a long tunnel of constant diameter is to be concreted, as in many hydro-electric schemes, it is often advantageous to the contractor to concrete continuously day and night without a break. Often no stopends are needed with this method of work unless a break in the concreting is planned. The principle can of course be used with stopends and the work split into separate pours as necessary. The speed of operation is achieved by 'telescoping' the formwork. In principle, this involves the formwork section at the leading end of the pour being held in position by spuds and the traveller being withdrawn to the last section of formwork at the tail end of the pour (see Fig. 92). The traveller is attached to the rear section of formwork which is designed so that it articulates and collapses to a reduced size and thus passes through all the sections of formwork already erected. The section is taken to the front of the pour, which may be interrupted for a short period while the new section is expanded to the required size and attached to the last section of formwork so that concreting can continue. The traveller then returns to the rearmost section of formwork again to continue the cycle at appropriate intervals. Due to the arch effect of the concrete and the ideal curing conditions underground, the formwork can often be stripped earlier than would be possible above ground.

See Fig. 92.

A 24 hour cycle is not uncommon under these circumstances and a total length of form of 96 m comprising sixteen 6 m lengths each moved forward every 1½ hours, would not be unreasonable.

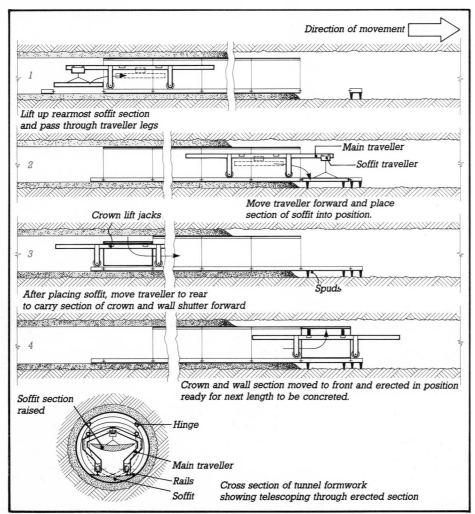

Fig. 92 *Typical telescopic tunnel form operation.*

concrete society

Section 5.6.4 – Domes, Shells and Folded Plate Formwork

For complex insitu concrete structures the formwork design, erection and striking should be carried out by personnel having the necessary qualifications and experience. Close liaison with the designer of the permanent works is always necessary so that any limitations on procedure or deflection is specified by the PWD.

In the design of the forms, consideration should be given to the lateral forces from wind loads, including suction on the leeward side, unsymmetrical or eccentric loadings during form erection, method of placing concrete, striking, movement of plant, and special tolerances based on functions of the shapes (deflections of the permanent work may cause binding of formwork).

The self-weight of the formwork may be larger than the imposed design live load of the permanent work. In such a case the forms should not be suspended from the structure, e.g. in a climbing form.

The degree of complexity outlined above suggests that the details of the formwork and concreting procedure should be discussed and approved with the designer of the permanent works to ensure that the structure, as designed, is not overloaded during construction.

Section 5.6.5 – Underwater Formwork

Underwater Concreting (Ref. 69).

The placing of concrete underwater for protection, repair or structural purposes is a specialist task and should be carried out by persons experienced in such work. Concrete Society Technical Report No. 3 *Underwater Concreting* (Ref. 69), is currently being revised. Whenever specifying underwater formwork the cost implications should be considered. The work will be carried out under very difficult conditions, often by divers working by touch only (because lighting is ineffective in cloudy water). Tolerances should be set with due regard to these conditions. Guidance on wave forces is given in BS 6349 *Code of Practice for Maritime Structures* (Ref. 80). Before concreting it is often necessary to check that excessive silt has not collected within the forms. Air lifts provide the most satisfactory means of removing excess silt if present in objectionable quantities.

Code of Practice for Maritime Structures (Ref. 80).

Two solutions to the problem of ensuring that the concrete remains in its designed location underwater are to use either flexible or rigid forms. The choice will depend on factors such as whether the water is tidal, whether there is scouring due to currents, the timescale and the complexity of the structure.

Flexible Formwork: A common way of containing cementitious mixes underwater is to use flexible formwork made from fabric materials. A typical example is shown in Fig. 93. Fabrics are available with different degrees of permeability. The products are available from specialist suppliers who will tailor the form to suit the application. The principle when using permeable fabrics is to reduce the concrete pressure by controlled filtration of the excess water in the concrete while preventing loss of the solids in the mix. The effect is to control very accurately the position of the concrete. Because of the permeability of the fabric, the rate of strength gain is often increased. With developments and improvements in materials and applications, the advice of specialist suppliers should be sought. When using impermeable fabrics the concrete pressure will be similar to the calculated value for rigid forms used underwater. The fabrics can take the shape of double sided mats, with intermediate connections for the shaping of 'slab' type forms. Reinforcement can be included to construct underwater structural members. Alternatively, for single faced repair work, the fabrics can be connected to existing structures, e.g. jetty walls, using simple tie assemblies, and carefully placed concrete between the fabric and the damaged structure.

Fig. 26.

An example is shown in Fig. 26.

Left – in position on pipe

Right – inflated with cementitious material.

Fig. 93 *Fabric material as flexible form to pipe saddle for underwater placing of concrete. Photographed in trial erection.*

Rigid Formwork: For rigid formwork a steel form will be preferable to timber or aluminium, as the latter needs to be weighed down to keep in place. Underwater the weight of items is reduced to the submerged density values. The forms will have to be placed and positioned by divers and the forms must therefore be very simple, with as few additional components as possible. If the forms require connecting underwater, then quick connection details will reduce costly diving time. The permanent works designer should assist by keeping the details simple and, where possible, avoiding corbels and other complex details. Items such as through ties will be hard to assemble in position underwater and can also interfere with concreting .

Recommendations for the concrete pressures for rigid forms are given in Section 4.4.4. The designer should be aware when designing forms in tidal areas that not only should the forms be designed for the concrete pressures acting outwards (during placing), but that prior to concreting, an inwards force may occur. This is due to the differential water levels as waves and tide rise up the form on the outside.

Section 4.4.4.

Section 5.7 – Construction Joints

Section 5.7.1 – General

A construction joint is the temporary face of a concrete pour, against which subsequent concrete will be placed. Its function is to divide the concrete into practicable pour sizes.

The construction joint should form a clean line in the exposed concrete face, particularly if surface finish is visually important. The construction joint will always be evident, and where appearance is important it should be featured in the design or disguised by other prominent features. Consideration should be given by the PWD to featuring both vertical and horizontal joints so as to mask colour variations. See Section 3.11.3. It is essential that construction joint formwork is designed for ease of erection and striking, as these operations are time consuming.

See Section 3.11.3.

Attention should be paid to the design, construction and erection of stopend forms, bearing in mind that the pressure of concrete on the construction joint form is the same as that on the main formwork with which it is associated. The main types of construction joint are considered in the following subsections.

Section 5.7.2 – Vertical Stopends to Walls and Beams

Stopends should be fixed to main forms and not to external struts or supports. (See also Section 5.2.2.1.) Congested reinforcement leads to difficult formwork fixing and striking, so stopends should be located where steel is least congested. If a joint can be located adjacent to a lap, the minimum length of reinforcement will project from the joint thus facilitating removal of joint formwork. In congested reinforcement it might be more suitable to adopt expanded metal formwork and leave it cast-in place. See Section 3.3.2. Adequate cover should be given to non-protected materials.

See also Section 5.2.2.1.

See Section 3.3.2.

Typical details for vertical stopends to walls are shown in Fig. 94.

Fig. 94.

Key joggles are rarely necessary other than in radiation shields and so should not be specified for normal situations. If they are required then particular care should be taken to ensure that the stopends can be easily removed.

Key joggles rarely necessary.

Section 5.7.3 – Vertical Stopends to Slabs

Careful detailing of reinforcement, especially at laps, is important in relation to construction joints in thick slabs and large beams. Where possible, laps should be detailed to suit construction bays so that only a lap length of reinforcement projects beyond the joint.

Allowances should be made for access to stopends for striking. Lap positions can assist this facility.

Typical details using expanded metal formwork are shown in Fig. 21.

See Fig. 21.

The concrete pressures on stopends are not usually critical in thin slabs. The design of stopends for thick slabs should be treated as single faced walls (see Section 5.2.3).

See Section 5.2.3.

Section 5.7.4 – Horizontal Joints in Walls, Beams and Thick Slabs

These are outside the scope of this guide. For the treatment of concrete at construction joints reference should be made to BS 8110 (Ref. 14) and the Cement & Concrete Association's *Construction Joints in Concrete* (Ref. 98).

BS 8110 (Ref. 14).

Construction Joints in Concrete (Ref. 98).

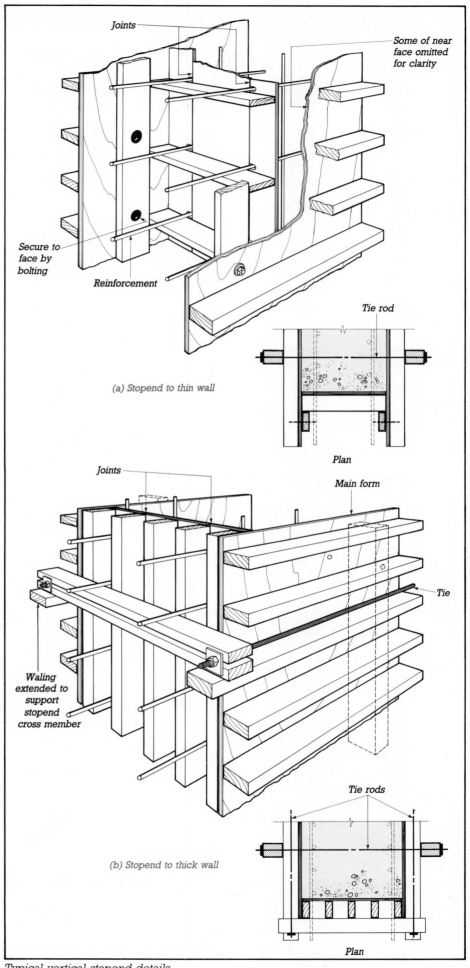

Joints

Some of near
face omitted
for clarity

Secure to
face by
bolting

Reinforcement

Tie rod

(a) Stopend to thin wall

Plan

Joints

Main form

Tie

Waling
extended to
support
stopend
cross member

Tie rods

(b) Stopend to thick wall

Plan

Fig. 94 *Typical vertical stopend details.*

Section 5.7.5 – Construction Joint Positions

When construction joint positions are not indicated on the drawings or in the specification the following rules provide a general guide.

(a)   Horizontal joints should be formed at the top of foundations with or without a kicker. Typical arrangements are shown in Figs. 95 and 96. Several proprietary systems are available for aligning forms without a cast-in-situ kicker. But leakage below the formwork may make it preferable to use a kicker.   *See Figs. 95 and 96.*

(b)   Horizontal joints in columns should be formed at or slightly above the lowest soffit of beams meeting at the head of a column.

(c)   Horizontal joints formed in the ribs of large 'T' or 'L' beams can be at or slightly above the slab soffit.

(d)   Concrete in an upstand, starter or kicker at the bottom of a wall or column should preferably be placed at the same time as the work from which the upstand projects.

(e)   If a construction joint in a beam is unavoidable, its position should be approved by the PWD having given due consideration to point loads or high shear stress.

(f)   Construction joints should be placed at positions of low stress.

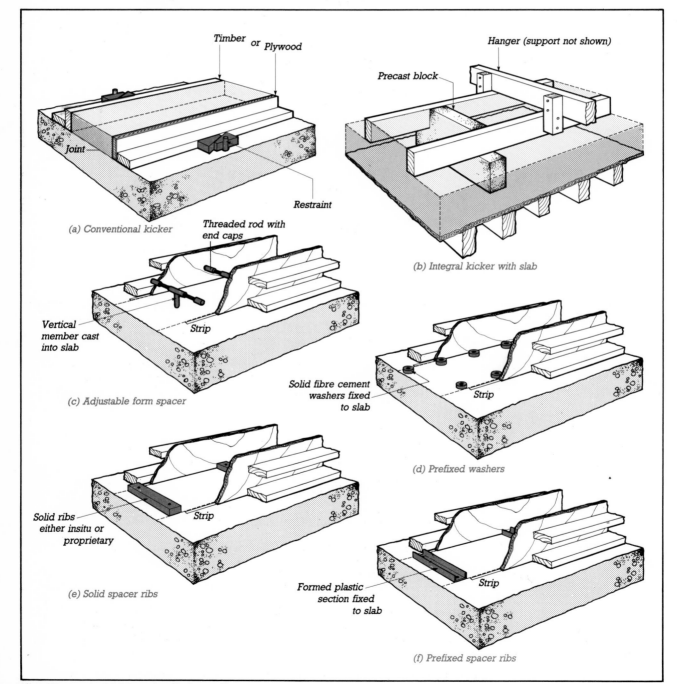

(a) Conventional kicker

(b) Integral kicker with slab

(c) Adjustable form spacer

(d) Prefixed washers

(e) Solid spacer ribs

(f) Prefixed spacer ribs

Fig. 95 *Typical kicker details for walls.*

concrete society

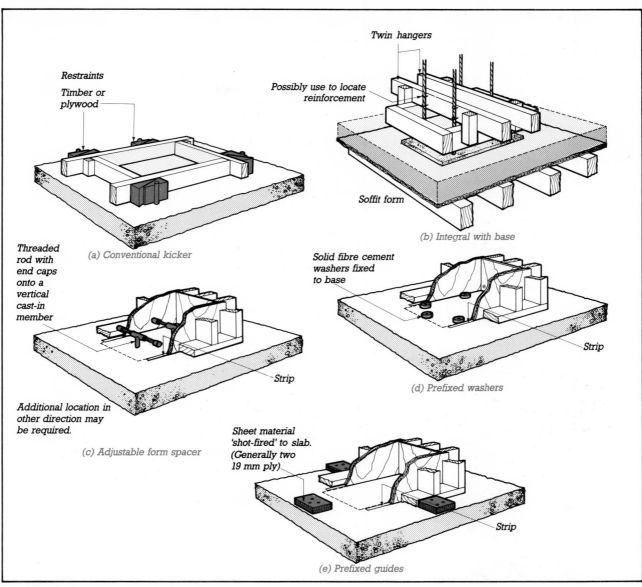

Fig. 96   *Typical kicker details for columns.*

Section 5.7.6 – Movement Joints

See Section 3.11.3 and Fig. 48.

Formwork for expansion and contraction joints requires the same general treatment as a construction joint. Design of joint formwork should make allowance, where necessary, for dowels, rebates for sealants (see Section 3.11.3 and Fig. 48) or any special joint assemblies.

Section 5.8 – Watertight Construction

Section 5.8.1 – General

Concrete may fail to be watertight for several reasons:

(a)   It may be porous.
(b)   It may leak along construction joints.
(c)   Cracks may be formed by thermal cracking, for example due to restraint of the movement caused by heat of hydration (often inaccurately referred to as drying shrinkage).
(d)   Cracks may form by shrinkage.
(e)   Ties and other inserts may provide leakage paths.

BS 5337: 1976 (Ref. 82).

Early Age Thermal Crack Control in Concrete (Ref. 83).

Guidance on suitable concrete technology and reinforcement detailing can be found in BS 5337: 1976 *Code of Practice for the Structural Use of Concrete for Retaining Aqueous Liquids* (Ref. 82) and in CIRIA Report 91, *Early Age Thermal Crack Control in Concrete* (Ref. 83).

Along construction joints the leakage path is frequently extended and made more tortuous by the use of water bars, which are discussed in the next section. Plates of steel or other materials can be put into the centre of non-recoverable ties for the same reason. A reduction in the safe working load of such 'lost' ties may be necessary if the plates are welded to the ties to seal the hole in the plate.

Reduce tie SWL if welded water bar.

Tie rods of the recoverable type will leave holes in the structure. Proprietary compounds are available for sealing effectively any holes in the concrete, such as those made by tie rods, and supplier's advice should be sought.

When selecting the positions of tie rods in the form, suitable clearance should be allowed from the edge of any water bar. This occurs particularly at the kicker joint and at vertical stopends.

Section 5.8.2 – Water Bars

The desirability and effectiveness of water bars is outside the scope of this guide. Where they are specified, careful design of the stopend formwork is necessary. In some cases they may be disadvantageous, due to the difficulty of holding them in position while ensuring full compaction of concrete around them. Careful cleaning is always required around water bars before the adjacent concrete pour is cast. This is particularly important with surface type water bars in slabs.

Water bars should not be nailed or punctured to hold them in position except where provision is made for this. Consideration should be given to the use of the type with pierced flanges to assist with location in relation to the reinforcement.

Split forms with water bars projecting through are preferred to water bars folded against the inside face of the joint form during the initial pour.

Section 5.9 – Mechanical Handling of Formwork on Site

Section 5.9.1 – General

Methods of moving formwork on sites have changed with the improvements in available lifting equipment and have resulted in more economic use of materials and reductions in labour and plant content per unit area of formwork. Both the use of travellers (see Section 6.2) and cranes in the handling of formwork requires an understanding by the formwork designer of mechanical lifting. This section is intended for guidance only as all lifting gear i.e. hooks, eyebolts, slings, shackles, 'C' hooks etc, is covered by the Construction Regulations (Ref. 9). Some or all of the lifting gear may require certification and regular inspection. This is outside the scope of this guide but recommendations for rating of lifting gear for general purposes are given in BS 6166 (Ref. 84). A useful reference for all lifting operations is given in the Construction Safety Manual, Section 9 (Ref. 85).

See Section 6.2.

Construction Regulations (Ref. 9).

BS 6166 (Ref. 84).

Construction Safety Manual, Section 9 (Ref. 85).

Certain components are commonly used with formwork and a brief description is included below, together with particular points for consideration and the relevant British Standard number and title for information.

All lifting points on formwork should be designed with suitable factors of safety to take into account shock loading as well as any additional loading that may be imposed during striking of the formwork from the concrete face. A useful design guide on lifting points is published by the Engineering Equipment and Material Users Association (Ref. 86). The Chain Testers Association's *Code of Practice for the Safe Use of Lifting Equipment* gives useful advice on a wide range of lifting equipment (Ref. 92).

Design guide on lifting points. (Ref. 86).

Code of Practice for the Safe Use of Lifting Equipment. (Ref. 92).

Where formwork is repeatedly handled by mechanical plant the attachments and lifting gear should be regularly inspected visually with particular reference to the actual connection to the formwork. In addition, attention must be given, when designing the formwork panel, to ensure that the forces from the lifting/handling operation will not pull it apart. Where inclined slings are used, the resolution of the horizontally induced force will need to be considered.

On particularly large or heavy forms several lifting points may need to be used at one time. In such cases the relative stiffness of the formwork may alter the assumed load distribution into the lifting points. In addition, the use of multiple connections from one continuous lifting beam can also give rise to local overloading if the effects of stiffness and continuity are not considered.

When selecting the pick-up height of the mechanical lifting equipment, consideration should be given to the overall height of the lifting appliance together with the lifting gear and the form height to ensure clearance for placing the forms in position and again for striking. A particularly onerous condition may arise during striking of wall formwork when the form may have to be lifted over the partially completed works with possible projecting reinforcement for subsequent levels of work; this reinforcement may not have been in place when the forms were initially positioned.

Form height is not lifting height.

Section 5.9.2 – Lifting Beams/Spreader Beams

The design of lifting beams is a specialist task and should only be carried out by a person with the relevant experience. Some typical examples of lifting beams used in formwork are shown in Fig. 97 (a), (b), (c) and (d).

See Table 21 and Fig. 98.

Fig. 97 (e).

Fig. 97 (f).

When two-legged slings are used the angle of the sling legs induces a horizontal force. See Table 21 and Fig. 98. This can be resisted by a spreader beam such as in Fig. 97 (e), in which case the spreader will be in direct compression and the vertical load lifted will not be subjected to a horizontal component of force. An alternative, if the form is not stiff horizontally, is to connect a beam or something similar direct to the formwork as shown in Fig. 97 (f). The magnitude of the horizontal component is given in Table 21.

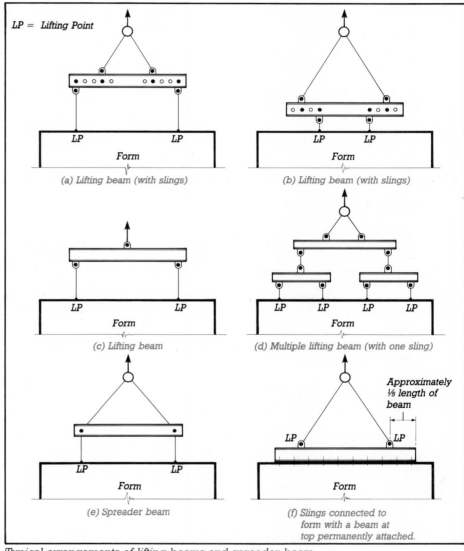

Fig. 97 *Typical arrangements of lifting beams and spreader beam.*

Section 5.9.3 – Slings

The three types of sling in common use are the chain sling, the steel wire rope sling and the flat woven sling. Some relevant references are:-

BS 2902:1957 (1985)	Higher tensile steel chain slings and rings
BS 3458:1962 (1985)	Alloy steel chain slings
BS 1290:1983	Specification for wire rope slings and sling legs for general lifting purposes
BS 6210:1983	Code of practice for the safe use of wire rope slings for general lifting purposes
BS 3530:1968	Small wire ropes
BS 302:1968	Wire ropes for cranes, excavators and general engineering purposes
BS 3481: Pt. 2:1983	Specification for flat woven webbing slings made of man-made fibre for general service
BS 6304:1982	Specification for chain slings of welded construction. Grades M(4), S(6) and T(8).

It is strongly recommended that two-legged slings are marked with a safe working load applicable to an angle of no more than 90° between the legs and that, in practice, the safe working load and angle **must not** be exceeded. As the angle is increased, so the load which the sling can lift is proportionally decreased. Furthermore there will always be a horizontal compression force acting between the lifting points which is restrained either by a spreader beam as in Fig. 97 (e) or by the lifting beam or the formwork itself. Table 21 gives values of the compression force and tension load in each leg related to the load to be lifted. See also BS 6166 (Ref. 84).

Fig. 97 (e).

See also BS 6166 (Ref. 84).

The Construction Regulations (Ref. 9) give guidance on the use of slings; for example prohibiting contact at sharp corners. They should be consulted.

Ref. 9.

Angle Between Legs, $\theta°$	Tension Per Leg, F_t (kN)	Compression in Spreader, F_c (kN)
30	0.52 W	0.13 W
40	0.53 W	0.18 W
50	0.55 W	0.23 W
60	0.58 W	0.29 W
70	0.61 W	0.35 W
80	0.65 W	0.42 W
90	0.71 W	0.50 W

Table 21. *Leg and Compression Loads in Two-legged Slings or Chains*

Fig. 98 *Force diagram for slings.*

When formwork is lifted off its resting place it will adjust its angle, once clear, to hang from the crane with its centre of gravity vertically beneath the main hook. Generally the symmetrical position of lifting points and lifting gear as shown in Fig. 97 will be suitable, but if the form is asymmetric its centre of gravity will not be central. See Fig. 99 (a). If this form is lifted using equal-legged slings then it will tilt as shown in Fig. 99 (b). This may not be acceptable and two ways of hanging the form horizontally are shown in Fig. 99 (c) and (d). In the first case the equal-legged slings are attached at points on the form to give the correct position above the centre of gravity. This may not be practical and the second case uses unequal length slings attached to the form. In both cases of Fig. 99 (b) and (d) the angles of the sling to the vertical will not be equal producing increased tension in the leg adjacent to the smallest angle. In an extreme case, one leg could be vertical and therefore take the full load.

Fig. 97.

Fig. 99

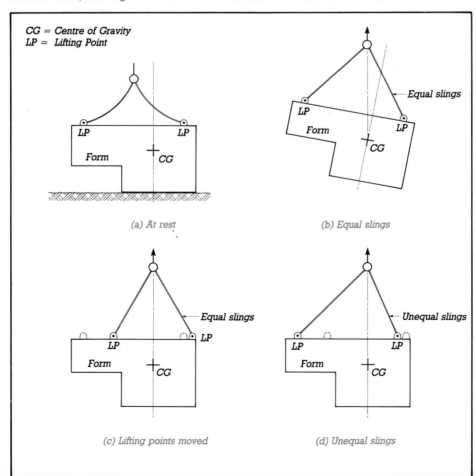

CG = Centre of Gravity
LP = Lifting Point

(a) At rest

(b) Equal slings

(c) Lifting points moved

(d) Unequal slings

Fig. 99 *Slinging of assymetric formwork.*

Legs of chain slings must be shortened only by the use of shortening claws attached to the head fittings. Claws can be supplied by manufacturers as part of the chain sling.

An even distribution of the load between all the legs of a multi-leg sling is essential and allowances should always be made for the possible effects of variation in angles. It will be necessary to include some form of spreader if there are more than three legs.

Section 5.9.4 – Hooks

Loads should only be applied to the hooks at the position specifically designed to take it, i.e. the bed of the hook. Loading at any other position, e.g. the point, can only result in overstressing the hook, causing it to open or even break. To avoid overloading the point of any hook, all lifting rings or holes should be large enough to take the whole hook.

L.O. Regulations (Ref. 9).

Particular attention is also drawn to the requirements of Lifting Operations Regulation 37 (Ref. 9) which requires that all rope or chain slings be properly attached to the crane hook by ring, link or shackle of adequate strength (so that unstable conditions resulting from the sling slipping over the hook surface cannot arise).

Refer to BS 2903 for higher tensile steel hooks for chains, slings, blocks and general engineering purposes.

Section 5.9.5 – Shackles

Shackles are widely used for making connections in slinging. They should be matched to the grade of rope or chain in use. They must be tested, certified and marked with their safe working load.

Refer to BS 3032:1958 for higher tensile steel shackles and BS 3551:1962 for alloy steel shackles.

Section 5.9.6 – Chain

Section 5.9.3.

When chain is used in lifting, its application will be similar to that for slings as covered in Section 5.9.3. Some additional references for chain are:

BS 4942: Pts 1 to 6:1981	Short link chain for lifting purposes
BS 1663:1950 (1985)	Higher tensile steel chain Grade 40
BS 3113:1959	Alloy steel chain, grade 60 for lifting purposes
BS 3458:1962 (1985)	Alloy steel chain slings

Section 5.9.7 – Eyebolts

Cause of accidents.

Eyebolts are probably the cause of more accidents than any other single item of lifting gear because the effect on the safe working load of loading at an angle to the shank is not properly appreciated. It cannot be too strongly stressed that home-made eyebolts are highly dangerous.

The three main types of British Standard eyebolt are the dynamo, the collared eyebolt, and the eyebolt with link. Dynamo eyebolts are only suitable for axial loads and are therefore not recommended. Two references are:

BS 4278:1984	Specification for eyebolts for lifting purposes
PM 16	HSE Guidance Note: Eyebolts

Section 5.9.8 – 'C' Hooks

See Fig. 32.

Certain large soffit formwork systems can be handled by the use of large 'C' hooks. Fig. 32 shows the application to a tableform system. The method of connecting the 'C' hook to the formwork soffit must be adequate and the combined weight of hook and formwork must be within the capacity of the crane.

When used on a structure where table sizes vary in length and width, the 'C' hook should be designed to suit all cases, or clearly designated with its limitations.

Proof load = 1.5 × SWL.

All 'C' hooks should be tested with a proof load of 50% above safe working load. The test should be applied to simulate the table giving the most arduous loading condition, when the centre of gravity is likely to be near the tip of the 'C'.

Sections Six~Ten

Section 6
Special Formwork

Section Six – Special Formwork

Section 6.1 – General

Figs. 100 and 101.

(See also Section 1.6.)

The term 'special formwork' is applied to formwork which is not 'off the shelf' proprietary equipment, but which is purpose-made for a particular application. Some examples are shown in Figs. 100 and 101.

Economies may be achieved from the use of special formwork when one or more of the following conditions occur:

(a)   A substantial number of reuses is envisaged.
(b)   Where the formwork shape required becomes uneconomical or impracticable for site fabrication.
(c)   If the specification requires the number of ties to be kept to a minimum, or prohibited, e.g. large unsupported spans.
(d)   Where, due to difficulty of crane access, formwork is required to be self-contained, e.g. incorporating its own traveller or gantry unit.
(e)   Where high concrete pressures are developed which cause high stresses in the formwork.
(f)   Where very tight/small dimensional tolerance is specified.

See Fig. 102.

Special formwork will be commissioned only if it will reduce the total cost. As with all formwork the cost per use – the best measure for comparison – falls as the number of reuses increases; repair and maintenance costs will also have to be included. This is illustrated in Fig. 102, which also shows how the proportion of the labour element of the cost per use varies.

Fig. 100 *Falsework and special formwork in use on construction of trapezoidal bridge piers. (M25 Motorway – Gade viaduct.)*

137

Frequently a reduction in programme time will result in financial savings, and a well built special form which can reduce maintenance time to a minimum will reduce the time loss due to site hold-ups. Further economies can be made with a mobile self-sufficient structure to reduce crane time and costs for the moving of the forms. The next section discusses the use of such travellers in formwork.

Section 6.2.

Fig. 101 *Special formwork in use on a dam crest.*

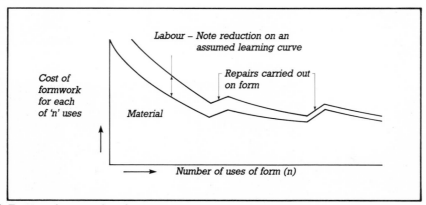

Fig. 102 *Formwork cost related to use.*

Section 6.2 – Travellers

A travelling form is formwork set up on, or suspended from, a mobile structure, with or without built-in motive power. Examples are shown in Figs. 103, 104 and 105.

In general, the traveller is not a structural component of the formwork. After fixing the forms in position for concrete placing, the traveller may be required to strike and move other formwork on the same line of construction. Within the traveller, provision must be made for the supported formwork to be jacked into position vertically and horizontally. The moving parts (jacks and turnbuckles) must have sufficient range of movement to allow for misalignment of the traveller in relation to the intended position of the formwork in use.

Normal design and use criteria apply to travelling forms provided the traveller connection points are suitably strengthened. The fewer connection points the better, making it easier to position the formwork for concrete placing. All lifting and suspension equipment must be suitable for the loads concerned and the connections must be easy to make and dismantle (see Section 5.9).

See Section 5.9.

In cantilever-type travellers, kentledge (counterweight) may be necessary. An example is shown in Fig. 104. The factor of safety for the kentledge design should be at least 1.5, though the nature of the work may dictate a higher figure.

Minimum factor of safety on kentledge 1.5.

In certain cases the traveller is an integral structural part of the formwork system, such as in the cantilever construction of the insitu bridge shown in Fig. 105.

Fig. 105.

On exposed sites, users of travelling formwork should be aware of the risks of instability from quite moderate winds onto large 'sail' areas of formwork. This is particularly relevant on cantilever travellers where holding-down devices or extra kentledge may be required.

(Windloads in Section 4.5.1.)

Fig. 103 *A straddle traveller for tall wall during trial erection.*

Fig. 104 *A cantilever traveller for steel faced formwork to tank walls.*

Fig. 105 *A cantilever traveller and formwork for cantilever construction of insitu concrete bridge (Kylesku Bridge).*

When a traveller is being moved towards an open edge from which it could fall a significant distance, e.g. as shown in Fig. 105, then the arrester system on the traveller should be backed up in a positive way by trailing chains or stop blocks.

Operatives must not ride on the formwork while it is moving.

A fail safe system should be built into the hauling lines by means such as an idle loop, so that if the traveller jams the hauling line will not be overloaded and fail.

Section 6.3 – Slipforms

Slipforming is the process of continuous concrete construction, and is normally carried out vertically with a constant cross section. The forms are raised and the concrete placed at such a rate that the concrete achieves specified physical properties before the forms expose it. Rates of rise of 150 to 450 mm per hour can be achieved, and construction usually continues around the clock.

Further information on slipforming is contained in Concrete Society Current Practice Sheets Nos 108 and 109 (Ref. 97).

Concrete Society Current Practice Sheets Nos. 108 and 109 (Ref. 97).

The process has been used for constructing chimneys, silos, shaft linings, towers and building cores, as well as bridge piers. The layout is normally simple. It is possible to vary the wall thickness and layout over the height, though each complication will increase the overall cost. An example of slipforming the 183 m core of a major building is shown in Fig. 106. The ideal structure should have significant dimensions in both major axes to ensure stability. Variants of the process operate horizontally, and on sloping structures.

Fig. 106 *Slipform in use on National Westminster Tower in London.*

concrete society

Slipforming may be economic for structures as low as 12 m, or lower still if several identical structures can be constructed in sequence. While there are some limitations on the structural design which are unavoidable, the following factors will be amongst those leading to the adoption or rejection of a slipforming concept on a structure:

(a)   Concreting will take place in a very short time.

(b)   The initial setting up of the process insitu will be longer than for conventional forms, but can be reduced on critical programmes by prefabricating the slipforms in large sections, either adjacent to the slip or off site.

(c)   The cost per square metre of the equipment – forms, framework, climbing equipment – will be more than for conventional formwork.

(d)   Labour costs per hour will be higher due to shift working, but productivity will be good.

(e)   There are no construction joints. This is particularly important for leak-free structures such as water tanks, chimneys and reactor shields.

(f)   The process is less weather sensitive than conventional working. The working platforms can be protected so that disruptions caused by inclement weather, heavy rain, low temperatures or high winds are kept to a minimum. This enables work to continue when conventional work would have ceased. When working in noxious atmospheres, say adjacent to working chimneys, slipform assemblies have been cocooned and pressurised by fans to prevent ingress of fumes.

(g)   Standby plant and operatives are needed.

(h)   The surface finish will be peculiar to the process, whether 'off the form' or treated. It is easy to obtain a good key for subsequent finishes.

(i)   The final tolerance of the slipform structure will be similar to that for the conventionally cast work. Recent improvements in control techniques and supervision have almost eliminated problems associated with 'spiralling' and non-verticality.

(j)   Cutting corners in formwork design or selection of lifting/climbing equipment capacity may result in major and expensive problems in the slipform process.

The typical arrangement of slipforms comprises two panels, held in position by a yoke with two legs and a cross member over the top. To the cross member is fixed a jack, which climbs a rod whose base is in the structure. As the slip proceeds the rods are subsequently withdrawn from the concrete as a part of the process, thus leaving no climbing equipment cast in the structure. The various walls are braced together, and working areas and access scaffolds are added. The reinforcement must be detailed to suit the method.

The forms are generally only 1.2 m high and are set up with a slight taper to prevent the form gripping the concrete and lifting it at the trailing edge. It is set up with the correct wall thickness at approximately mid-height. The face contact material will most likely be proprietary steel panels, although where vertical striations are needed film-faced plywoods with hardwood features have been used.

Openings can be formed using timber or expanded polystyrene formers arranged to allow a film of concrete on each face, thus avoiding displacement of the former vertically as sliding proceeds. An allowance of 18 mm less than the nominal wall thickness will clear any build-up of hardened concrete on the upper edge of the form. Door frames and opening formers tend to become displaced during concreting and care must be taken to avoid their becoming lifted with the form face by friction.

Slipforming is a specialised process and advice should be sought from people with the relevant experience.

Section 6.4 – Moulds for Precast Concrete

Section 6.4.1 – General

The design of moulds for precast concrete is governed by somewhat different criteria from those relating to insitu form design. Those criteria regarding pressures and structural design of the mould apply, but due to the higher number of uses generally required, mould construction is more substantial. Many moulds for precast work incorporate some degree of mechanisation to aid either casting or release.

Special finishes, or the degree of accuracy specified in the precast component, call for special attention to design of mould surface and sub-structure.

'Face up' or 'face down'.

An important consideration in obtaining a special finish is the decision to cast the unit either 'face up' or 'face down'. This will depend on the final location of the unit in the structure, the method of handling and securing embedded items, and any secondary fixtures and fittings to be applied later.

Whilst precasting can be carried out either in a works or on site, the quality of product is governed by the degree of mechanisation, the mould quality, dedication and the working conditions in which it is produced. High quality items such as cladding and decorative structural panels are generally manufactured in a works.

The materials used in precast mould construction are similar to those employed in formwork generally. In addition, as the casting is often carried out in such a way that featured faces and recesses are formed horizontally, a number of materials can be utilised which might not be considered for insitu concrete. For example, exposed aggregate finishes, decorative finishes, composite panels incorporating GRC or artificial stone are all ideally suited to precast work. For further reading see Section 10 and, in particular, Refs. 122 and 124.

Further reading, Section 10.

Refs. 122 and 124.

The reader's attention is drawn to the difference between tilt-up moulds and tilt-up construction. The former refers to the precast mould for making multiple units and is discussed in the next section, whereas tilt-up construction is a method of work used on site and is discussed in Section 6.6.

Section 6.6.

Section 6.4.2 – Tilt-up Moulds

A tilt-up mould is one in which a unit is cast horizontally and may subsequently be tilted through an angle for the following purposes:

(a)   The mould may be tilted to approximately the vertical to facilitate early handling and vertical stacking.
(b)   It may be tilted through a minor angle to facilitate brushing, washing and acid treatment to achieve special surface finishes on the trowelled face.
(c)   It may be tilted through an angle greater than 90°, against an adequate support, for surface treatment to the face cast from the mould.
(d)   It may be tilted during the casting process to allow placing and compaction of the concrete where the casting has to be carried out in various stages.

Fig. 107 *A crane handled tilt-up mould.*   **Fig. 108** *An hydraulic tilt-up mould.*

The adoption of tilted moulds in manufacture may offer the following advantages:

(a)   The vertical position of the cast unit on completion of demoulding facilitates easy and early striking, with subsequent benefits as the unit is in an advantageous position for early handling and vertical stacking, leading to a faster production cycle.
(b)   Vertical handling of the unit may offer design economies.
(c)   Horizontal manufacture may allow the adoption of thin veneers of expensive facings such as tiles, mosaic and similar materials.
(d)   Horizontal manufacture may facilitate the casting of sandwich and hollow units.

Examples of tilt-up moulds are shown in Figs. 107 and 108.

Figs. 107 and 108.

Provision should be made to lock the mould automatically when it is moved to the tilt-up position. The lock mechanism should be designed to resist displacement, should it be pulled as the concrete unit is removed by the crane.

Section 6.4.3 – Gang and Battery Moulds

Gang and battery casting is the mass production technique whereby numbers of units are cast within a main mould having sub-dividing partitions which may be of steel, concrete or timber-based materials. A free-standing battery should be of self-supporting, stable construction, adequately anchored to resist accidental horizontal impact.

Outer mould panels must be designed to withstand full fluid concrete pressure, and division panels must be capable of withstanding the pressure resulting from differential rates of filling of adjacent sections of the battery.

The mould designer must take into account the high rates of filling and the intensive vibration normally employed in battery casting.

Inserts and fittings to be cast into the concrete unit should be designed in conjunction with the mould manufacturer, particularly those which may affect the flow of concrete within the mould and so impair the surface finish of the unit. Stopends and soffits should be assembled onto division panels so that the grout loss from the concrete unit is reduced to a minimum.

See Section 7.5.2.

Access should be provided so that mould cleaning, oiling, steel fixing, assembly, concreting and striking can be carried out. See Section 7.5.2.

At all times the mould components and concrete units must be secured to ensure that operatives may work in safety.

Fig. 109.

A battery mould with integral heating system and external vibration (photographed during trial erection) is shown in Fig. 109.

Fig. 109 *A battery mould.*

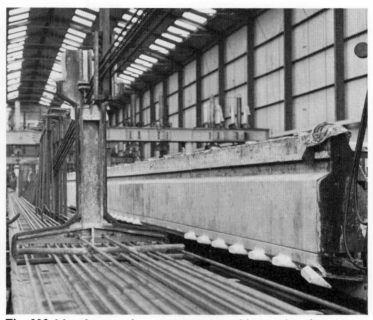

Fig. 110 *Manufacture of precast prestressed beams in a factory.*

Section 6.4.4 – Moulds for Prestressed Concrete

Special considerations apply to the design of moulds used to produce both post-tensioned and pre-tensioned concrete units. Side forms which cannot be removed before prestressing operations commence should be designed to allow for vertical and horizontal movement of the cast member during prestressing operations. A typical prestressed beam factory is shown in Fig. 110.

Fig. 110.

Safety in prestressing operations (pre-tensioning) (Ref. 94).

Whenever stressing operations have to be carried out, safety considerations should be of paramount importance to all the personnel concerned. A useful guide is published by The Concrete Society, *Safety precautions in prestressing operations (pre-tensioning)* (Ref. 94).

For example, while tensioning is proceeding all persons not directly concerned with the operation, should be kept clear by tape barriers or similar. When pre-tensioning, guards should be placed over the stressing beds to catch any flying broken strand.

See Section 3.10.2.

Selection of a suitable release agent is essential, and during application care must be taken to avoid contamination of tendons and wires. A 'drying' type of chemical release agent is most suitable. See Section 3.10.2.

Special considerations for post-tensioned and pre-tensioned units are as follows.

Section 6.4.4.1 – Post-tensioned Concrete

Moulds for post-tensioned concrete units should permit strains or deflections due to prestressing without detriment to the concrete.

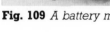

Great care must be taken to ensure that anchorage assemblies are correctly aligned with the ducts through the concrete, and that the bearing plates are accurately fastened to the end former.

The method of positioning the ducts within the unit to the design tolerance should be suitable to resist flotation or any displacement. Where pins or through-bolts are used, care must be taken to avoid local loss of grout.

The bed of the mould, or pallet as it is called, should be designed to accommodate the load pattern which will vary from a uniformly distributed load before stressing to point loads at the bearings, as the beam hogs during stressing.

Section 6.4.4.2 – Pre-tensioned Concrete

Moulds for 'long-line' pre-tensioned concrete should accommodate and permit strains or deflections due to transfer of prestress without detriment to the concrete.

When groups of units are to be cast in parallel or in series the soffit or pallet should be arranged so that movement of units due to elastic shortening can take place.

Where bearing plates or similar components project from the prestressed unit, it will be necessary to allow for movement of such projections relative to the pallet.

Pallet members will need to be designed to resist local downward forces transmitted by stopends used as deflector plates.

Tendons should be as straight as possible but any bends should be smooth.

Stopend and divider plates should be designed to allow free movement of the tendons during stressing operations, but should not allow grout loss at the ends of the unit.

Whenever units are cast around deflected tendons, the tendon deflection devices must be directly coupled to the main prestressing floor, or balanced against other tendons. Should the mould be used to transmit any reaction it must be designed and anchored accordingly.

Irregularities at intermediate mould joints should be arranged in such a way that units are free to move along the bed at the time of transfer of prestress.

Section 6.4.5 – Heated Moulds

Increased rates of precast concrete production can be achieved by heating the concrete or the mould or both. Hot concrete may be produced by using steam or hot water in the mixing process, and using heated aggregates. Heat may also be introduced into the concrete in the form or mould, using steam or electrical heating applied externally or through the mould. Various electrical systems are available where the current is passed through the reinforcing steel or stressing tendons or the steel sheathing. See Section 5.3.6.4 for the accelerated curing of insitu concrete.

See Section 5.3.6.4.

When hot air heating systems are employed, care should be taken over possible fire risks, particularly where plastics or spirit-based adhesives or solvents are being used.

The formwork should be designed to accommodate strains due to differential expansion resulting from differences in temperature, moisture content or thermal movement, without detriment to the concrete. Strains which have not been anticipated may cause movements of formwork joints, either closing them, causing buckling of the form, or opening them with resulting loss of material.

Due to the relatively smaller mass of concrete material to be heated compared to heating insitu construction, the applied heating to precast moulds should be controlled to ensure that:

(a) The rate of rise in temperature of the concrete does not exceed approximately 15°C per hour for the first three hours.
(b) Thereafter the rate of rise and fall of temperature of the concrete should be limited to 35°C per hour.
(c) The temperature of the concrete should not exceed 80°C.

The forms should allow the concrete to be cured at elevated temperatures with a minimum loss by evaporation of water from the surface. This loss could lead to cracking due to differential shrinkage caused by differences in moisture content, differential thermal movement caused by lowering of the surface temperature by evaporation, and reduction in durability of the concrete at the surface due to insufficient hydration of the cement.

Polythene sheeting, insulation boards or insulating quilts should therefore be applied to exposed surfaces of the concrete. It is important that the temperature of the concrete is maintained and an assessment made of the maturity of the concrete. A correlation can be established (for a specific concrete mix) between maturity and strength and this relationship can be used to determine economic striking times. Some guidance on quantifying concrete strength is given in Section 5.3.6.3.

Section 5.3.6.3

Release agents for heated moulds should be selected such that they do not cause obnoxious fumes at high temperatures. Chemical release agents, Category 5, are recommended (see Section 3.10.2).

See Section 3.10.2.

Section 6.5 – Stairs and Staircases

Stair flights in buildings can be large in number, fairly small in size and with a number of common dimensions. Precasting can often provide an economic solution. They may be cast in a number of orientations.

Section 6.6 – Tilt-up Construction

Tilt-up construction employs the insitu ground or foundation slab as the soffit on which wall elements are precast. The system is weather sensitive as it relies on an 'out of doors' flooring operation which in an unpredictable climate may cause problems. The units, which may be cast manually or by paving machine, are formed using simple edge moulds. The machine cast elements are subsequently sawn to size. Where necessary, feature formers and precast beam units can be incorporated to meet architectural and structural requirements. An example is shown in Fig. 111.

Fig. 111 *Tilt-up construction – wall unit being raised into position.*

Anchors embedded in the precast element in conjunction with specially designed spreader beams and lifting connections facilitate the rotation of the panels into their final vertical location at the perimeter of the slab. Push-pull props support the elements whilst insitu stitching concrete is placed. Provision should be made to lock the unit in position when erected to avoid accidental dislodgement by the crane. A possible overturning mode for the erected unit is similar to that shown in Fig. 54 for a formwork panel. The props to the unit will be required to withstand the full wind force/moment (for units up to 10 m high Table 18, Cases A, B or C could be used) together with an allowance for the unit not being erected exactly vertical.

See Fig. 54.
Wind in Table 18.

The technique takes advantage of readymix supply and provides an economy in form and access requirements.

Great care is necessary in the selection and application of the bond breaker to the insitu concrete prior to the precasting operation.

Section Seven – Work on Site

Section 7.1 – General

As stated in Section 2.6.1, the prime consideration of all members of the design team is to construct a concrete structure which complies with the drawings and the specification.
To achieve this requires coordination of design, workmanship, supervision and inspection. Furthermore, the vibration of the concrete will contribute significantly to the quality of the end product. Section 5 gives guidance on design and this section gives general guidance on work on site. More detailed information on site work is available in construction guides such as the Cement and Concrete Association 'Man on the Job' leaflets (Ref. 88) and the Concrete Society Digests.

'Man on the Job' leaflets (Ref. 88).

Concrete Society Digests.

When soffit formwork is under consideration the design team will also need to refer to 'Section seven. Work on site' in BS 5975 (Ref. 2). The whole assembly will be a combination of formwork with its supporting falsework.

'Section seven. Work on site' in BS 5975 (Ref. 2).

Formwork assembly may be approached either:

(a)   From detailed fabrication drawings normally prepared in a formwork design office, the forms being constructed on or off the site. When fabricated off site, serious consideration should be given to transportation requirements.

or

(b)   Contructed on site in accordance with information available from design charts and standard details. Often a general arrangement drawing of the various components is produced to assist assembly. Proprietary systems are in this category.

Usually the nature of the job, the facilities available, the required quality and the standard of finish will decide which approach is adopted. In some cases, requirements of the specifying authority may influence the decision, for example the submission of formwork drawings to the PWD prior to construction taking place may be a contractual requirement, and this may require a formwork design office to be involved.

Section 7.2 – Workmanship

To produce concrete of a high standard of appearance and precision, a high standard of site workmanship is required, and this will apply even if formwork is specially constructed for the job in question. The very highest standards of site workmanship will be required where high quality concrete work is required. Where the amount of work does not justify specially designed and fabricated formwork, the degree of success in achieving the required result will depend solely on the skill and expertise of the site operatives. In a few cases the economic solution may be to fabricate a quality form for only one or two uses.

There are cases, however, when good quality work can be achieved with unskilled labour. These will normally be cases where work is simple, of a highly repetitive nature, and where the size of the job justifies the use of sophisticated special purpose formwork which is designed for simplicity. A considerable amount of work does not demand good appearance or close tolerances. Such work does not place such heavy demands on workmanship, although appreciable skill and experience are still necessary to ensure that the formwork is stable, safe and to the required standard.

The future standards of workmanship in the industry will depend on the quality of training provided. Courses provided by organisations such as the Construction Industry Training Board and the National Association of Formwork Contractors are to be encouraged.

Addresses in Appendix F.

Section 7.3 – Supervision

Work is usually supervised by both the contractor's staff and representatives of the client. The contractor's staff supervises the execution of the work, the client's supervision being more concerned with the acceptability of the results. The supervision of formwork is mainly performed by the contractor's staff.

Operatives will fabricate the equipment and erect and strike it at the point of use. Supervision will be needed:

(a)   To interpret and/or amplify the design drawings.
(b)   To ensure that the quality of the formwork being produced will enable the concrete finish to be as specified.
(c)   To ensure smooth continuity in planning and progressing the work.

Where details are being evolved at operative level, it is particularly important that they are checked.

Check details.

The supervisor is responsible for ensuring that the formwork is satisfactory before concreting commences; on a major contract a 'permit to load' procedure may be desirable.

'Permit to load'.

Different emphases of skill are needed by the supervisor for shop fabrication in metal or timber, and on site for erection and dismantling.

On major works, personnel experienced in formwork may be required to attend during concrete placing to ensure early recognition of local over-stress and carry out remedial action if necessary. A supply of suitable material such as adjustable props should be available.

Section 7.4 – Inspection and Checking

A close watch should be maintained during the various stages of formwork construction and a thorough inspection should be carried out by the supervisor as soon as the work is finished and before the concrete is placed. On crucial areas of formwork a 'permit to load' procedure may be desirable.

'Permit to load'.

The nature of the inspection will depend upon the type of work. The following are some of the more important items:

(a)   Access and working platforms comply with the Regulations.
(b)   Materials are in accordance with the TWD's design specification.
(c)   The formwork complies with design drawings (when appropriate).
(d)   All ties, props, scaffold fittings and other connections are checked for tightness and security against vibration both before and during concreting operations.
(e)   Stopends are properly restrained.
(f)   Forms are correctly aligned and levelled and adequate allowance is made for take-up and deflection.
(g)   Release agent has been applied.
(h)   The form can be struck without damaging the concrete.
(i)   The formwork is grout-tight.
(j)   All bearing points and lifting points are adequate.
(k)   Inserts, void formers and cast-in fixings are properly positioned and secured.

Appendix A lists common failures of formwork.

Appendix A, Common Failures of Formwork.

It should be noted that, although formwork may be examined by a member of the client's supervisory staff, under the usual contract conditions this does not absolve the contractor in any way from his responsibility for ensuring that the formwork is capable of meeting the specification, particularly that of producing the required standard of finish, safely.

Section 7.5 – Safety

Section 7.5.1 – General

As stated in Section 2.3, the Health and Safety at Work etc, Act (Ref. 7) places a responsibility for safety on all parties in the construction industry. This guide highlights some of the relevant safety matters in connection with formwork. A useful guide to all aspects of safety is the Construction Safety Manual published by the Building Employers Confederation (Ref. 85).

Ref. 7.

Construction Safety Manual (Ref. 85).

The following are some aspects which must be considered from the point of view of safety:

(a)   Working platforms, guard rails, toe boards etc must be incorporated into the formwork design where no other means of access is provided. This is covered in more detail in Section 7.5.2.

See Section 7.5.2.

(b)   Safety considerations should be included in any inspections of formwork, and these inspections should be formalised and recorded.
(c)   The formwork should be stable at all stages in its assembly, erection, use and dismantling. (See Section 5.1.5 and Fig. 56 for wall formwork.)

See Section 5.1.5 and Fig. 56.

(d)   Provision should be made to ensure the safety of men working beneath the forms from the danger of falling tools and components; nets alone may be inadequate. Deeper toeboards or substantial screens or 'fans' may be required, depending on the size and weight of items that may fall; it should be borne in mind that only a very substantial shield will stop a reinforcing bar or scaffold tube falling end-on from a height. See BS 5973 (Ref. 75).

See BS 5973 (Ref. 75).

(e)   Extra care should be taken when the construction method requires working up to 'open edges'. Often the open edge is a temporary condition and is a function of the overall construction system. In such cases an operating procedure should be established to minimise the time of exposure of the open edge. For examples see Figs. 32, 33, 34 and 67.

Figs. 32, 33, 34 and 67.

(f)   Safety helmets should be provided and worn on site.

(g)   Nails should be removed from timber after use or bent over so that they cannot cause injury.

(h)   Where the forms are crane handled, the users of the form should be aware of its weight and the correct method of handling the formwork. See Section 5.9.

(i)   Openings left in soffit forms or slabs should be provided with guard rails or with adequately secured and supported sheeting.

See Section 5.9.

Section 7.5.2 – Access and Working Platforms

The Regulations require safe access to be provided when erecting, filling or striking forms. Working platforms placed more than 2 m above the ground must be at least 600 mm wide when nothing is to be stored on them. Where some storage is required, say for a vibrator motor, then the platform should be at least 800 mm wide, leaving a 430 mm clear unobstructed passageway.

All platforms are to be fitted with guardrails between 915 and 1150 mm above the level of the decking and toeboards with a minimum height of 152 mm; they are to be inspected before being used, and where they remain in use they should be inspected at 7 day intervals. The gap between toeboard and rail should not exceed 762 mm.

BS 5973, Clauses 15.5 and 15.6 (Ref. 75).

When platforms are mounted on tall forms or slipforms, then their decking units must be securely fixed down to prevent accidental displacement or being lifted by wind forces. Access through these platforms should be by a hinged trapdoor, to ensure that it can always be properly relocated.

Careful attention should be paid to the construction of the working platforms, that they do not become unserviceable and that they have been designed for any incidental loadings. Access ladders, walkways etc should be securely held in place and should be the length or width required by the Construction Regulations. If there is danger that loose debris could accumulate on gangways these should also be fitted with toeboards.

Loose sheet materials, plywood, battens etc must be fully secured if there is any risk of these being blown by the wind.

Where access may be limited, provision of safety nets, safety belts or an independent bracket scaffold fixed to the wall previously constructed should be considered.

Section 7.6 – Vibration of Concrete

Section 7.6.1 – General

Vibration is the most common method of compaction in both insitu, and precast work. A useful guide is the C&CA 'Man on the Job' booklet *Placing and Compacting Concrete* (Ref. 88).

Placing and Compacting Concrete (Ref. 88).

The amplitude and frequency of vibration employed varies according to the type of vibration and method of application but normally lies within the range 3000 to 18000 cycles/min. The effect of such rapid vibration is to produce a mobile condition within the concrete. The static friction acting between the particles of the mix when they are at rest (the internal friction) is eliminated when the particles are set in motion by the vibration. The result is that the mix temporarily assumes characteristics very similar to those of a liquid. The force of gravity then causes resettlement and compaction of the concrete.

The individual particles tend to seek the position in which they leave the least possible air void volume. The flowing mass of concrete closely surrounds the reinforcement and penetrates narrow and confined parts of the form.

Voids reduce the strength and durability of concrete. For every 1% of entrapped air the concrete strength will be reduced by about 5% (see Fig. 112).

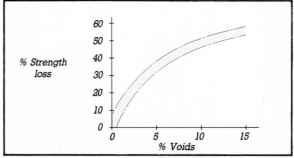

Fig. 112 *Relationship between loss of strength and air voids in concrete.*

Section 7.6.2 – Internal Vibration

Most insitu concrete is compacted by means of internal poker vibration for which a methodical and systematic approach is essential to achieve the desired result.

Mainly vertical insertions of the vibrator(s) at equal intervals will best ensure that all the concrete is uniformly and effectively compacted. Insertions should be made at intervals not greater than 8 to 10 times the poker diameter, and in the case of walls, columns and beams where the finish is of special importance even closer insertions may be necessary, say 200 to 300 mm.

The poker should be withdrawn slowly, particularly near the surface. Internal vibration which is carried out carefully and systematically with closely spaced insertions will produce concrete of high density, high strength and with very good surface finish.

When impermeable form faces such as steel and plastic-faced plywoods are used, more vibration may be needed than with ordinary plywood forms if a good quality finish is to be achieved.

The concrete should be placed in horizontal layers 300 to 600 mm deep and vibrated as above with the poker penetrating at least 100 mm into the previously vibrated layer, which must still be plastic. This will ensure a satisfactory bond between the layers.

When vibrating thin slabs the poker will have to be held at an angle or even horizontally, in order to achieve adequate contact between tube and concrete.

With internal vibration, care must be taken not to damage the form face ('burning') or disturb 'cast-in' items or reinforcement.

The choice of poker diameter depends on a number of factors such as wall thickness, density of steel, concrete mix design and rate of placing. The practice of applying the poker to the reinforcement to increase the sphere of influence is undesirable as it may displace the steel from its position and may even break the wire ties. It will also reduce the bond of the concrete to the steel.

Table 22 gives guidance based on vibration poker capacity.

Internal Vibrator Diameter (mm)	Capacity (m³/h)	Application
25	1 – 5	Exceptionally narrow and densely reinforced structures
35 – 50	10 – 15	Narrow and heavily reinforced structures
50 – 70	20 – 25	Normal walls and floors in housing, industrial buildings and bridges
over 70	over 25	Heavy construction including deep bases, plinths and slabs

Table 22.   *Internal Vibration – Poker Capacities*

Section 7.6.3 – External Vibration

External vibration is used mainly for precast work and occasionally for insitu work where internal vibration would be difficult or impossible to operate, such as culverts and tunnel linings. Where the apprearance of the concrete is important the use of internal vibrators is preferred.

External surface vibrators have the effect of assisting the compaction of the concrete adjacent to the face, but thick sections would also require internal vibration.

Formwork must be designed to withstand the effect of external vibration and the advice of the vibrator and formwork manufacturer should be sought.

Externally vibrated forms are best made in steel but in any case extreme care must be taken to ensure that all fixings, joints and ties are of a 'vibration proof' type as forms have been known to shake apart under the effects of external vibration. It is equally important to adopt a strict systematic method of vibration, particularly where multiple levels of vibrators are employed.

External vibrators are energised by direct electric drive, or by hydraulic or air power.

Electricity. Direct current is rarely used. Alternating current is normally used and gives a constant speed related to the frequencies and input. 50 cycles/sec provides frequencies of 1500 and 3000 rev/min. For higher frequency vibrators, frequency converters are needed and give frequencies up to 12000 rev/min. These are all of the rotary type.

Hydraulic vibrators are normally a derivation of hydraulic impact rock and concrete breakers, using a reciprocating piston. The hoses to the power source are heavy and less flexible than air hoses.

Air vibrators often use a steel ball blown round a track by an air jet. They are usually of high and variable frequency depending upon air pressure. They are noisy but quite effective.

Section 7.7 – Striking Procedures

The procedure for striking formwork together with any associated falsework should be carefully considered to avoid excessive stress or damage to the completed structure or the formwork.

Soffit striking, see Section 5.3.6.2.

See Section 5.3.6.2 on detailed procedures for striking of soffit formwork.

Wall striking, see Section 5.2.5.

On striking, hardwood wedges should be used to separate form and concrete surfaces if special means such as jacks have not been provided. Using nailbars to lever forms from the concrete will cause damage to both concrete and form. Cranes should be employed to take the weight of forms only, not to release formwork from concrete.

Section Eight – Recommendations

Section 8.1 – Further Research

The following items are carried forward from the previous edition (Ref. 1) of this Report:

1. Investigate further the prevention of water penetration at tie rod positions in water retaining structures. The work should compare the effectiveness of tie rods 'lost' in the concrete (with or without devices for increasing the water path) with methods of sealing the tie rod holes used on both recoverable and non-recoverable tie systems. The slight settlement of concrete during placing of tall walls and its effect on cast-in ties at lower levels of the wall should be studied. Inspection of the performance of existing structures would be included. Section 5.8 of this guide discusses watertight construction.

Section 3.8.

Section 5.8.

2. Establish the design basis for both proprietary beam and column clamps used in light construction work. The items are described in Section 3.6.11.

Section 3.6.11.

3. Review the practicability of a procedure of 'signing for' formwork for crucial areas of work similar to that recommended in BS 5975, Clause 10.2 (Ref. 2) for falsework. This is also a recommendation from Section 7.4 of this report.

BS 5975, Clause 10.2
Section 7.4.

4. Investigate the current specifications which include formwork and make recommendations for their revision to suit the practical details in this report. (At the time of writing this guide, the 6th Edition of the Department of Transport's specification (Ref. 11) was being finalised for publication.

Ref. 11.

In addition the following items are now considered significant:

5. Investigate the mechanism and magnitude of the reduction in concrete pressure when casting against open meshed products, such as expanded metal (Section 3.3.2) and fabric materials (Section 3.4.7). The materials are often used in stopends in wall formwork, and an understanding of their effect on concrete pressures could lead to economies in design.

Section 3.3.2.
Section 3.4.7.

6. Investigate on site the pressure of concrete on inclined formwork faces and measure the resultant uplift forces associated with this pressure. The work would be an extension of CIRIA Report 108 *Concrete Pressures on Formwork* (Ref. 3) and is to confirm or modify the method stated in Section 4.4.3.

CIRIA Report 108 (Ref. 3).
Section 4.4.3.

7. Investigate on site any failures which occur in wall formwork that has been designed to the 1985 CIRIA method of calculating concrete pressure. This investigation should enable the recommended tie rod factors of safety in Section 3.8 to be verified.

Section 3.8.

8. Investigate the application of the minimum stability force on wall formwork stated in Section 4.6.2. The concept is similar to that for falsework and the investigation should verify the magnitude and position of the force.

Section 4.6.2.

9. Further investigate the required structural criteria for striking beam or soffit formwork when 'quick strip' systems are used. The work should quantify the striking times when operating such systems. Section 5.3.6 gives limited guidance on 'quick strip' support systems.

Section 5.3.6.

10. Commission a booklet on form liners with photographs of the actual finishes obtained and the method of achieving the standard shown. The booklet to be complementary to this guide and is intended for architects and specifiers as a guide to the finishes available. In the preparation of this guide one of the major changes identified during the past decade has been the introduction of form liners of different materials, finishes, methods of application etc. Section 3.12 outlined the main features relevant to the materials but there is a requirement for further visual information for specifiers that could be regularly updated to keep pace with developments in form liners.

Section 3.12.

11. Investigate on site the effect of shear limitations on wood-based sheet materials for wall formwork. This investigation should verify the increased factor for shear capacity for wood-based sheet materials in Section 3.2.2.3.

Section 3.2.2.3.

Section 8.2 – Training

The availability of training facilities for both operatives and engineers has improved over the last decade. In particular, the Construction Industry Training Board, in conjunction with the National Association of Formwork Contractors, have set up a three-year apprenticeship scheme with time divided between the site and full time college training. This course should be patronised more fully in view of the long term benefits to both employers and employees.

See Appendix F for addresses.

The training of engineers and supervisors in the profession should continue, both by in-house courses and by design/appraisal courses at the Cement and Concrete Association. This guide should supplement this training.

The general training of prospective Chartered Engineers should include Formwork as a specific subject and not as part of the generality of temporary works.

concrete
society

Section Nine – References

1. THE CONCRETE SOCIETY, *Formwork*, Report of the Joint Committee, The Concrete Society and Institution of Structural Engineers, London, March 1977, 77pp, Technical Report No. 13, Publication No. 51.075.

2. BRITISH STANDARDS INSTITUTION, *Code of practice for falsework*, BS 5975: 1982, London, 80 pp, inc AMD 4057, August 1982, and AMD 5415 to be published late 1986. (A third amendment is in course of preparation.)

3. HARRISON, T. A. and CLEAR, C., *Concrete pressure on formwork*, Construction Industry Research and Information Association, Report 108, London, September 1985, 32pp.

4. BRITISH STANDARDS INSTITUTION, *Structural use of timber*. Code of practice for permissible stress design, materials and workmanship, BS 5268: Part 2: 1984, 108pp, (inc. AMD 4723, September 1984).

5. *THE CONCRETE YEAR BOOK*, Published annually, Palladian Publications, London, Publication No. 06.086.

6. BRITISH STANDARDS INSTITUTION, *Glossary of formwork terms*, BS 4340: 1968, London, 28pp, (Currently under revision, to be published as BS 6100 *Glossary of building and civil engineering terms*, Section 6.5 *Formwork*).

7. GREAT BRITAIN LAW STATUTES, *Health and Safety at Work etc, Act 1974*, HMSO, London, 1975, 109pp.

8. STATUTORY INSTRUMENTS 1966. No. 94. *Construction (Working Places) Regulations 1966*, HMSO, London.

9. STATUTORY INSTRUMENTS 1961. No. 1581. *The Construction (Lifting Operations) Regulations 1961*, HMSO, London.

10. CONSTRUCTION INDUSTRY RESEARCH AND INFORMATION ASSOCIATION, *A guide to the safe use of chemicals in construction*, CIRIA Special Publication 16, London, 1981, 25pp.

11. DEPARTMENT OF TRANSPORT, SCOTTISH DEVELOPMENT DEPARTMENT and WELSH OFFICE, *Specification for Road and Bridge Works*, Sixth Edition 1986, HMSO, London, 195pp.

12. DEPARTMENT OF THE ENVIRONMENT, Property Services Agency, *General Specification*. Volume 1 Section 3.05 concrete work. Formwork 3, Finishes and tolerances 8, Croydon, 1984 (available for PSA contracts only).

13. CENTRAL ELECTRICITY GENERATING BOARD, *Specification for Constructional Work*, Specification Civil /4A, 1975, London, CEGB Technical Documentation Branch.

14. BRITISH STANDARDS INSTITUTION, *Structural use of concrete*, Code of Practice for design and construction, BS 8110: Part 1: 1985, London, 184pp. (Supersedes CP110: Part 1: 1972).

15. MONKS, W., Appearance Matters Series, Cement and Concrete Association, Slough:
    1. *Visual concrete: Design and production*, 1980, 29pp, Publication No. 47.101.
    3. *The control of blemishes in concrete*, 1981, 21pp, Publication No. 47.103.
    7. *Textured and profiled concrete finishes*, 1986, 12pp, Publication No. 47.107.
    8. *Exposed aggregate concrete finishes*, 1985, 16pp, Publication No. 47.108.
    9. *Tooled concrete finishes*, 1985, 8pp, Publication No. 47.109.

16. HAWES, F. L., *The weathering of concrete buildings*, Cement and Concrete Association, Slough, Appearance Matters No. 6, 1986, 48pp, Publication No. 47.106.

17. MONKS, W. and WARD, F. W., *External rendering*, Cement and Concrete Association, Slough, Appearance Matters No. 2, Seventh Edition 1982, 32pp, Publication No. 47.102.

18. WARD, F. W., *Striated finish for insitu concrete using timber formwork*, Cement and Concrete Association, Slough, May 1972, 5pp, Publication No. 47.018.

19. BRITISH STANDARDS INSTITUTION, *Code of practice for accuracy in building*, BS 5606: 1978, London, 60pp, (inc. AMD 4166, February 1983).

20. NATIONAL ASSOCIATION OF FORMWORK CONTRACTORS, Data Sheet No. 4, *The deflection of formwork*, London, 1983, 2pp.

21. BRITISH STANDARDS INSTITUTION, *Timber grades for structural use*, BS 4978: 1973, 20pp, London (inc. AMDs up to AMD 4567, September 1984).

22. TIMBER RESEARCH AND DEVELOPMENT ASSOCIATION, *Simplified rules for the inspection of secondhand timber for load bearing use*, booklet, Timber in Temporary Works High Wycombe, February 1981, 1p, TBL 54.

23. BRITISH STANDARDS INSTITUTION, *Specifications for tropical hardwoods graded for structural use*, BS 5756: 1980, London, 8pp.

24. NATIONAL LUMBER GRADES AUTHORITY, *The National Grading Rules for Dimension Lumber*, Joist and Plank Rules, Ganges, Canada, 1979.

25. TIMBER RESEARCH AND DEVELOPMENT ASSOCIATION, *Comparative testing of wood-based formwork linings*, Timber in Temporary Works, Research Report 1/81, High Wycombe, April 1981, 16pp.

26. TIMBER RESEARCH AND DEVELOPMENT ASSOCIATION, *Plywood. Its manufacture and uses*, High Wycombe, June 1981 with 1984 Addendum, 58pp, TBL 7.

27. BRITISH STANDARDS INSTITUTION, *Specification for wood chipboard and methods of test for particle board*, BS 5669: 1979, London, 28pp, (inc. AMD 3764, 1981, AMD 3858, 1981 and AMD 4770, 1985).

28. BRITISH STANDARDS INSTITUTION, *Medium board and hardboard*, BS 1142: Part 2: 1971, London, 16pp, (inc. AMD 4769, 1985).

29. BRITISH STANDARDS INSTITUTION, *Specification for bond performance of veneer plywood*, BS 6566: Part 8: 1985, London, 12pp.

30. FINNISH PLYWOOD INTERNATIONAL, FPI technical Publication No. 25, Issue 2, *Handbook of Finnish plywood, blockboard and laminboard*, Helsinki, April 1984.

31. AMERICAN PLYWOOD ASSOCIATION, Form No. B 360A, Product Guide, *HDO/MDO plywood*, Tacoma, October 1984, 11pp.

32. AMERICAN PLYWOOD ASSOCIATION, Form No. F 200A, Industrial use guide, *Applications Summary*, Tacoma, May 1983.

33. BRITISH STANDARDS INSTITUTION, *The use of structural steel in building*, BS 449: Part 2: 1969, Metric units, London, 120pp, (inc. AMDs up to AMD 4576, August 1984).

34. BRITISH STANDARDS INSTITUTION, *The structural use of steelwork in building*, Part 1. Code of practice for design in simple and continuous construction: hot rolled sections, BS 5950: Part 1: 1985, London, 111pp.

35. BRITISH STANDARDS INSTITUTION, *The structural use of aluminium*, CP118: 1969, London, 188pp, (inc. AMD 1129, March 1973).

36. BRITISH STANDARDS INSTITUTION, *Specification for expanded polystyrene boards*, BS 3837: 1977, London, 4pp.

37. BRITISH STANDARDS INSTITUTION, *Guide to fire characteristics and fire performance of expanded polystyrene (EPS) used in building applications*, BS 6203: 1982, London, 20pp.

38. BRITISH PLASTICS FEDERATION, BPF Publication No. 285/1, Part 1 – *Specifications for unsaturated polyester resins*, Part 2 – *Polyester chopped strand mat laminates*, London, 26pp.

39. BRITISH PLASTICS FEDERATION, BPF Publication No. 215/1. *Engineering design properties of glass-fibre reinforced plastic (GRP)*, London, 1979, 181pp.

40. GLASSFIBRE REINFORCED CEMENT ASSOCIATION, *GRCA Handbook No. 1 – Permanent Formwork*, London, July 1985, 36pp.

41. GLASSFIBRE REINFORCED CEMENT ASSOCIATION, *Specification for grades of glassfibre reinforced cement (Grade One)*, London, March 1980, 20pp, (under revision).

42. BRITISH STANDARDS INSTITUTION, *Methods for determining properties of glass fibre reinforced cement material*, BS 6432: 1984, London, 8pp.

43. PILKINGTON REINFORCEMENTS LIMITED, *CEM-FIL GRC Technical Data*, St. Helens, 1985, 60pp.

44. BRITISH STANDARDS INSTITUTION, *Specifications for asbestos-cement and cellulose-asbestos-cement flat sheets*, BS 690: Part 2: 1981, London, 4pp.

45. HER MAJESTY'S STATIONERY OFFICE, *Work with asbestos cement*, Guidance Note EH36, Health and Safety Executive, London.

46. THE CONCRETE SOCIETY, Trough and waffle floors, *Concrete*, Part 1, Vol. 12, No. 11, November 1978, pp 29-31. Part 2, Vol. 12, No. 12, December 1978, pp 25-27.

47. BRITISH STANDARDS INSTITUTION, *Recommendations for the co-ordination of dimensions in building. Controlling dimensions*, BS 4330: 1968, London, 20pp.

48. LAWSON, R. M., *Fire resistance of ribbed concrete floors*, Construction Industry Research and Information Association, Report 107, London, 1985, 44pp.

49. BRITISH STANDARDS INSTITUTION, *Methods of test for falsework equipment*, Part 1, Floor centres, BS 5507: Part 1: 1977, London, 8pp, (inc. AMD 5360 to be published August 1986).

50. BRITISH STANDARDS INSTITUTION, *Specification for metal props and struts*, London, BS 4074: 1982, 8pp

51. BRITISH STANDARDS INSTITUTION, *Methods of test for falsework equipment*, Part 3, Props, BS 5507: Part 3: 1982, London, 4pp.

52. BIRCH, N., BOOTH, J. G. and WALKER, M. B. A., *Effect of site factors on the load capacities of adjustable steel props*, Construction Industry Research and Information Association, Report 27, London, 1971, 48pp.

53. BIRCH, N., WALKER, M. B. A. and LEE, C. T., *Safe working loads for adjustable steel props; the influence of prop conditions and site workmanship*, Construction Industry Research and Information Association, Technical Note 79, London, 1977, 32pp.

54. BRITISH STANDARDS INSTITUTION, *Steel, concrete and composite bridges*, BS 5400, *Code of practice for design of composite bridges*, BS 5400: Part 5: 1979, London, 36pp, (inc. AMD 3998, May 1982).

55. BRITISH STANDARDS INSTITUTION, *Code of practice for structural use of unreinforced masonry*, BS 5628: Part 1: 1978, London, 40pp, (inc. AMD 2747 October 1978, AMD 3445 September 1980 and AMD 4800 March 1985).

56. BRITISH STANDARDS INSTITUTION, *Code of practice for structural use of reinforced and prestressed masonry*, BS 5628: Part 2: 1985, London, 44pp.

57. LAWSON, R. M., *Composite beams and slabs with profiled steel sheeting*, Construction Industry Research and Information Association, Report 99, London, 1983, 48pp.

58. BRITISH STANDARDS INSTITUTION, *Structural use of steelwork in buildings*, BS 5950, *Code of Practice for design of floors with profiled steel sheeting*, BS 5950: Part 4: 1982, London, 20pp.

59. BRYAN, E. R. and LEACH, P., *Design of profiled sheeting as permanant formwork*, Construction Industry Research and Information Association, Technical Note 116, London, 1984, 32pp.

60. BRITISH STANDARDS INSTITUTION, *Methods for tensile testing of materials: Steel: General*, BS 18: Part 2: 1971, London, 28pp.

61. BRITISH STANDARDS INSTITUTION, *Methods of test for structural fixings in concrete and masonry*, BS 5080, *Tensile loading*, BS 5080: Part 1: 1974 (1982), London, 12pp, (inc. AMD 3821, April 1982).

62. ROBERTS, R. F., *Construction Guide – Spacers for reinforcement*, Cement and Concrete Association, Slough, 1981, 8pp, Publication No. 47.007.

63. LANCASTER, R. I., Steel reinforcement accessories, *Concrete*, Vol. 17, No. 9, September 1983, pp 32-36, Current Practice Sheet No. 87.

64. THE CONCRETE SOCIETY, Data Sheet, *Notes on formwork release agents and coatings*, April 1981, 6pp, Publication No. 53.035 (under revision).

65.   BUILDING RESEARCH ESTABLISHMENT, *Shuttering plywood, factors affecting choice of species*, December 1973, Information Sheet IS 21/73.

66.   BIRT, J. C., *Curing concrete*, Concrete Society Digest No. 3, The Concrete Society, London, 6pp, March 1985, Publication No. 53.047.

67.   PATERSON, W. S., *Selection and use of fixings in concrete and masonry*, Construction Industry Research and Information Association, Guide 4, London 1977, 30pp.

68.   HARRISON, T. A., *Pressure on vertical formwork when concrete is placed in wide sections*, Cement and Concrete Association, Research Report No. 22, Slough, March 1983, 30pp, Publication No. 41.022.

69.   THE CONCRETE SOCIETY, *Underwater concreting*, Technical Report No. 3, London, 1971, 13pp, Publication No. 52.018, (under revision).

70.   BRITISH STANDARDS INSTITUTION, *Loading – Wind Loads*, CP3: Chapter V: Part 2: 1972, London, 52pp, (inc. AMD 4952, January 1986 and AMD 5152, March 1986).

71.   HARRISON, T. A., *Tables of minimum striking times for soffit and vertical formwork*, Construction Industry Research and Information Association, Report 67, London, 1977, reprinted 1979, 23pp.

72.   HARRISON, T. A., *Formwork striking times – Methods of assessment*, Construction Industry Research and Information Association, Report 73, London, 1977, 38pp. (Under revision, August 1986.)

73.   BRITISH STANDARDS INSTITUTION, *Method for temperature matched curing of concrete specimens*, London, DD92: 1984, 4pp.

74.   ROYAL INSTITUTION OF CHARTERED SURVEYORS, *Standard Method of Measurement of Building Works*, SMM6, Sixth edition, Eyre and Spottiswoode, London, 128pp, 1979, (inc. Amendment, April 1984).

75.   BRITISH STANDARDS INSTITUTION, *Code of Practice for access and working scaffolds and special scaffold structures in steel*, BS 5973: 1981, London, 72pp, (inc. AMD 3962, April 1982).

76.   BRITISH STANDARDS INSTITUTION, *Testing concrete*, BS 1881. The 100 series (i.e. Parts 101, 102, 103 etc) deal with sampling and testing for workability, strength etc. The 200 series deals with non-destructive testing, see in particular, BS 1881: Part 201: 1986, *Guide to the use of non-destructive methods of test for hardened concrete*, 22pp.

77.   HANSEN, A. J., Strength indication with a simple maturity meter, *Proceedings of International Conference on Forming Economical Concrete in Buildings*, Lincolnshire (Chicago), Illinois, USA, 8-10 November 1982, Portland Cement Association (USA).

78.   HARRISON, T. A., *The application of accelerated curing to apartment formwork systems*, Cement and Concrete Association, Advisory Note, Slough, 1977, 9pp, Publication No. 45.032.

79.   FEDERATION INTERNATIONALE DE LA PRECONTRAINTE, *Guide to Good Practice – Acceleration of concrete hardening by thermal curing*, Slough, March 1982, 16pp, Publication FIP/9/7.

80.   BRITISH STANDARDS INSTITUTION, *Code of practice for maritime structures – General criteria*, BS 6349: Part 1: 1984, London, 164pp.

81.   BAMFORTH, P., *Mass concrete*, Concrete Society Digest No. 2, The Concrete Society, London, March 1985, 8pp, Publication No. 53.046.

82.   BRITISH STANDARDS INSTITUTION, *Code of practice for the structural use of concrete for retaining aqueous liquids*, BS 5337: 1976, London, 16pp, (inc. AMD 2344, September 1977 and AMD 3870, June 1982).

83.   HARRISON, T. A., *Early-age thermal crack control in concrete*, Construction Industry Research and Information Association, Report 91, London, 1981, 48pp.

84.   BRITISH STANDARDS INSTITUTION, *Recommendations for rating of lifting gear for general purposes*, BS 6166: 1981, London, 4pp.

85.   BUILDING EMPLOYERS CONFEDERATION, *Construction Safety*, The Building Advisory Service Publication, London, amended annually (31 Sections).

86.   ENGINEERING EQUIPMENT AND MATERIAL USERS ASSOCIATION, *A design guide – lifting points*, London, 1984, 13pp, Publication No. 101.

87.   THE CONCRETE SOCIETY, *Safety precautions for prestressing operations, (Post-tensioning). Notes for guidance*, London, 1980, 2pp, Publication No. 53.031.

88.   CEMENT AND CONCRETE ASSOCIATION, *Man on the Job*, Set of 18 booklets, Slough, Publication No. 45.100 (may be purchased individually) (*Formwork*, 20pp, Publication No. 45.115).

89.   MAJUMDAR, A. J. and NURSE, R. W., Glass fibre reinforced cement and fire resistance, *Materials Science and Engineering*, Vol. 15, 1974, pp 107 to 127.

90.   SADGROVE, B. M., *The strength and deflection of reinforced concrete beams loaded at early age*, Construction Industry Research and Information Association, Technical Note 31, London, 1971, 29pp.

91.   BRITISH STANDARDS INSTITUTION, *Specification for wood wool cement permanent formwork and infill units*, BS 3809: 1971, London, 8pp, (under revision).

92.   CHAIN TESTERS' ASSOCIATION, *Code of practice for the safe use of lifting equipment*, 12 sections, London, 1981, 98pp.

93.   NATIONAL BUILDING SPECIFICATION, *Formed finishes*, Section E13.4, Newcastle upon Tyne, NBS Services, published annually.

94.   THE CONCRETE SOCIETY, *Safety precautions for prestressing operations (Pre-tensioning). Notes for guidance*, London, 1982, 4pp, Publication No. 55.036.

95.   UNITED KINGDOM WATER FITTINGS BYELAWS SCHEME, *Requirements for the testing of non-metallic materials for use in contact with potable water.* Information and Guidance Note No. 5-01-02, London, September 1984, Issue 2, 4pp.

96.   WATER RESEARCH CENTRE, *Water Fittings and Materials Directory*, two issues published annually by Unwin Brothers Limited, Old Woking.

97.   ROSS, P. S., Slipforming, *Concrete*, Vol. 20, Part 1: No. 1, January 1986, pp 25 and 26, Part 2: No. 2, February 1986, pp 21 and 22, Concrete Society Current Practice Sheets Nos. 108 and 109.

98.   BROOK, K. M., *Construction joints in concrete*, Cement and Concrete Association, Technical Report, Slough, May 1969, 8pp, Publication No. 42.414.

99.   BRITISH STANDARDS INSTITUTION, *Safety rules for the construction and installation of electric lifts*, BS 5655: Part 1: 1979, London, 68pp, (inc. AMD 3303, February 1980 and AMD 4564, May 1984).

concrete
society

Section 10
Bibliography

Section Ten – Bibliography. (The numbers follow in sequence from Section Nine).

100. AMERICAN CONCRETE INSTITUTE COMMITTEE 347, *Recommended practice for concrete formwork*, Detroit, 1978, reaffirmed 1984, 37pp, 347-78.

101. BROOK, K. M., *Placing concrete in deep lifts*, Cement and Concrete Association, Slough, Technical Report No. 413, May 1969, 12pp, Publication No. 42.413.

102. GAGE, M., *A guide to exposed concrete finishes*, Architectural Press/Cement and Concrete Association, London, 1970, 164pp, Publication No. 15.334.

103. GILCHRIST WILSON, J., *Specification clauses covering the production of high quality finishes to in situ concrete*, Cement and Concrete Association, Slough, 1970, Publication No. 47.010.

104. GILCHRIST WILSON, J., *White concrete – with some notes on black concrete*, Cement and Concrete Association, Slough, 28pp, Publication No. 48.010.

105. GILCHRIST WILSON, J., *Abrasive blasting of concrete surfaces*, Cement and Concrete Association, Slough, 1971, 16pp, Publication No. 47.008.

106. HARRISON, T. A., *Permanent GRC soffit formwork for bridges*, Cement and Concrete Association, Interim Technical Note 9, Slough, February 1986, 12pp.

107. HIGGINS, D. D., *Efflorescence on concrete*, Cement and Concrete Association, Appearance Matters No. 4, Slough, 1982, 10pp, Publication No. 47.104.

108. HIGGINS, D. D., *Removal of stains and growths from concrete*, Cement and Concrete Association, Appearance Matters No. 5, Slough, 1982, 11pp, Publication No. 47.105.

109. HURD, M. K., *Formwork for concrete*, American Concrete Institute, Detroit, 4th Edition, 1979, Cat. No. 78-72045, 464pp.

110. HURST, M. P., *Formwork*, Construction Press, Harlow, 1983, 271pp.

111. INSTITUTE OF BUILDING, *Pricing formwork*, London, 1974, 12pp, IOB Booklet No. 14, Publication No. 15.241.

112. INSTITUTION OF STRUCTURAL ENGINEERS, The structural use of chipboard for flooring, State of the art report jointly by the Institution of Structural Engineers and the Timber Research and Development Association, *The Structural Engineer*, Volume 62A, No. 1, January 1984, 4pp.

113. INTERNATIONAL COUNCIL FOR BUILDING RESEARCH STUDIES AND DOCUMENTATION, CIB Report No. 24, *Tolerances on blemishes in concrete*, Rotterdam, 1980, 18pp.

114. IRWIN, A. and SIBBALD, W., *Falsework – Handbook for civil engineers*, Granada, London, 1984, 192pp.

115. KIRK, G. and VENABLES, R. K., *Development of improved stopends: Report on preliminary testing and scheme for further work*, Construction Industry Research and Information Association, Technical Note 67, London, 1976, 51pp.

116. LEE, I. D. G. and HALL, A. B., Wood chipboard as a structural lining for formwork, *Concrete*, Vol 14, Part 1: No. 1, January 1982, pp39 and 40; Part 2: No. 2, February 1982, p31. Current Practice Sheets 72a and 72b.

117. LUCKETT, P. R., Special steel formwork and precast moulds, *Concrete*, Vol. 13, No. 6, June 1981, pp41 and 42, Current Practice Sheet No. 65.

118. MAYNARD, D. P., Chipboard for concrete forms, *Conference on Chipboard Structures*, 1980, Chipboard Promotion Association, London.

119. NORTH, B. H., Appearance Matters, *Concrete*, Vol. 7, No. 5, May 1973, pp 18-23.

120. PORTLAND CEMENT ASSOCIATION, Proceedings of an International Conference, *Forming Economical Buildings*, Lincolnshire, Illinois, 8-10 November 1982.

121.   READING, T. J., Effects of release agents used on plywood forms, *Concrete International*, Vol. 7, No. 7, July 1985, pp 15-22.

122.   RICHARDSON, J. G., *Formwork construction and practice*, Viewpoint Publications, London, 1977, Publication No. 13.019, 274pp.

123.   RICHARDSON, J. G., *Concrete notebook*, Viewpoint Publications, London, 1974, 92pp, Publication No. 12.063.

124.   RICHARDSON, J. G., *Precast concrete production*, Viewpoint Publications, London, 1973, 232pp, Publication No. 13.014.

125.   RICHARDSON, J. G., *Formwork notebook*, Viewpoint Publications, London, 1982, Second Edition, 120pp, Publication No. 12.082.

126.   RICOUARD, M. J., *Formwork for concrete construction*, Macmillan Press, London, English edition, 1982, 185pp.

127.   SOMMERS, P. H., *Simplified design of formwork*, Paper at ACI Convention, Kansas City, 27 September 1983, Illinois, Concrete Construction Publications.

128.   SOMMERS, P. H., Charts aid in design of horizontal formwork, *Concrete Construction*, Vol. 30, No. 7, July 1984, pp 648-650.

129.   TIMBER RESEARCH AND DEVELOPMENT ASSOCIATION, *Timber in temporary works – A guide to available literature*, High Wycombe, 1981, TBL 53.

130.   TIMBER RESEARCH AND DEVELOPMENT ASSOCIATION, *Moisture content of timber, its importance, measurement and specification,*, Wood Information Sheet 14, Section 4, High Wycombe, 1985, 8pp.

131.   TRUE, G. F., *The production of glassfibre reinforced cement*, Viewpoint Publications, London, 1985, 150pp, Publication No. 13.023.

132.   TRUE, G. F., Glassfibre reinforced cement permanent formwork, *Concrete*, Vol. 19, No. 2, February 1985, pp 31-33, Concrete Society Current Practice Sheet No. 98.

133.   CONSTRUCTIONAL STEEL RESEARCH AND DEVELOPMENT ORGANISATION, *Steel Designers' Manual*, Fourth Edition (Revised) 1983, Collins Professional Technical, 1089pp.

Appendices

concrete
society

Appendix A – Common Failures of Formwork

Fault	Possible Design Deficiency	Possible Construction Deficiency
Dimensional Inaccuracy *Joints Opening and Deflection of Forms*	Excessive deflection. Supports too far apart or section of support members too small. Excessive elongation of ties, incorrect or insufficient ties. Bearing area of plate washers or prop heads/base plates too small. Insufficient column or beam clamps. Failure to provide adequately for lateral pressures on formwork. Insufficient allowance for incidental loadings due to placing sequences. On cantilever soffits; rotational movement and elastic deformation of system.	Metal locking devices not tight enough in column or beam clamps. Forms filled too rapidly. Vibration from adjacent loads. Insufficient allowance for live loads and shock loads. Void formers and top forms floating due to insufficient fixing. Plywood not spanning in the direction of its greater strength. Use of lower strength class members than designed. Change of concrete pressure group by use of retarders etc., or reduction in placing temperature.
Lifting of Single Faced Forms	Forms not adequately tied down to foundations to resist uplift force generated by raking props.	Ties not tight enough. Ties omitted. Forms filled too rapidly. Wedging and strutting not adequately fixed.
General	Props inadequate. Failure to provide adequately for lateral pressures on formwork. Lack of proper field inspection by qualified persons to see that form design has been properly intepreted by form builders. Lack of allowance in design for such special loadings as wind, dumper trucks, placing equipment. Inadequate provision of support to prevent rotation of beam forms where slabs frame into them on one side only.	Failure to regulate the rate or sequence of placing concrete to avoid unbalanced loadings on the formwork. Failure to inspect formwork during and after placing concrete, to detect abnormal deflections or other signs of imminent failure which could be corrected. Insufficient nailing, screwing, bolting. Inadequately tightened form ties or wedges. Premature removal of supports, especially under cantilevered sections. Failure to comply with recommendations of manufacturers of standard components and to keep within the limits required by the designer. Use of defective materials. Failure to protect paper and cardboard forms (particularly tubes) from weather or water, (or damage) before concrete is placed into or around them. Studs, walings, etc. not properly spliced.

Continued overleaf

Fault	Possible Design Deficiency	Possible Construction Deficiency
Loss of Material *At Kicker*	Ties or props incorrectly spaced, not close enough to existing concrete. Insufficient ties or props. Incorrect tie, possibly causing elongation of tie. Single faced forms lifting due to inadequate anchorage. Failure to provide adequately for lateral pressures on formwork.	Ties, props or wedges not tight enough. Dirty forms with concrete from previous pour left on (ill-fitting joint). Out of alignment kicker with stiff form. Grout check omitted or placed incorrectly.
At Tie	Incorrect tie.	Hole in panel too large. Cones, if used, not square to panel face or not tight enough. Failure to inspect and improve tightness during pouring.
Surface Blemishes *Scabbing*	Incorrect release agent.	Dirty forms, lack of release agent.
Staining	Incorrect release agent.	Incorrect release agent, over or under application, incorrect mixing of release agent.
Colour Difference	Wrong sheeting used, wrong treatment specification. Wrong specification of sealer for grain of timber or plywood based forms with paint, wax or similar treatment (Category 6 – see Section 3.10)	As above. Form surfaces of different absorbencies. Sealants applied to damp timber or plywood surfaces. Lack of curing of concrete. Forms struck at different times.
Crazing	Very smooth, impermeable formwork surfaces may produce this effect.	
Dark Staining	Can be caused by use of impermeable formwork surfaces.	
Between Panels	Insufficient panel connectors.	Badly fitting joints or panel bolts, loose wedges, metal locking devices not tightened. Incorrectly erected crane handled panel of formwork.

concrete society

Appendix B – Typical Loading Cases

General

The following notation applies to the loading cases in this appendix:

Notation	Unit	Notes
E	kN/m^2	Modulus of elasticity for material. When using steel use $2 \times 10^8 kN/m^2$ (Values are often quoted in other forms: e.g. N/mm^2, kN/cm^2, lb/in^2)
EI	kNm^2	Bending stiffness. (Note that the values of **EI** for timber for five basic sizes are given in Section 3.2.1.3 and for plywood in Section 3.2.2.3)
I	m^4	Moment of Inertia of member. **All** cases assume that a constant section member is used
L	m	Length of one span of member
L_c	m	Length of cantilever member from its support
M_n	kNm	Bending moment at support position 'n'
M_{mm}	kNm	Maximum bending moment occurring in the span 'nm'. (Note this will not always be at mid-span position)
P	kN	An individual load as a concentrated point load
R_n	kN	Support reaction at position 'n'
range	m	Total of the largest positive and negative deflection in a multi-span member
S_{mm}	kN	Value of vertical shear force in member at position 'n' on the side of span 'nm'
T	kN	**Total** load with triangular distribution on one span or one cantilever, with one end reducing to zero
W	kN	**Total** load uniformly distributed on one span or one cantilever
w	kN/m	Distributed load per unit length on one cantilever
δ or δ_{mm}	m	Deflection in one span, or tip deflection in case of cantilever, measured from the line of supports
⫢	–	Built in fully fixed end condition, i.e. no rotation possible
▲	–	Simply supported condition

When using the loading cases stated it is important that the units of the items are compatible. It is suggested that where possible kilonewtons (kN) and metres (m) be used for consistency.

The loading cases in Appendix B, Part One all relate to single spans whereas those in Appendix B, Part Two relate to multiple spans. The reader's attention is drawn to the introductory notes to Part Two.

Appendix B – Part 1 – Single Spans

Case Condition	Moment (kNm)	Reaction (kN)	Shear Force (kN)	Deflections Distance from A	Value (m)
1	$M_{AB} = 0.125\,WL$	$R_A = R_B = 0.50\,W$	$S_{AB} = S_{BA} = 0.50\,W$	0.50 L	$\delta_{AB} = 0.0130\,\dfrac{WL^3}{EI}$
2	$M_A = M_B = -0.0833\,WL$ $M_{AB} = 0.0417\,WL$	$R_A = R_B = 0.50\,W$	$S_{AB} = S_{BA} = 0.50\,W$	0.50 L	$\delta_{AB} = 0.00260\,\dfrac{WL^3}{EI}$
3	$M_A = -0.50\,WL_c$ $M_B = 0$	$R_A = W$	$S_{AB} = W$	L_c	$\delta_B = 0.125\,\dfrac{WL_c^{\,3}}{EI}$
4	$M_A = -0.125\,WL$ $M_B = 0$ $M_{AB} = 0.0703\,WL$	$R_A = 0.625\,W$ $R_B = 0.375\,W$	$S_{AB} = 0.625\,W$ $S_{BA} = 0.375\,W$	0.579 L	$\delta_{AB} = 0.00541\,\dfrac{WL^3}{EI}$
5 w = unit load	$M_A = M_B = -0.50\,wL_c^{\,2}$ $M_{AB} = -0.50\,wL_c^{\,2}$	$R_A = wL_c$ $R_B = wL_c$	$S_A = S_B = wL_c$ $S_{AB} = S_{BA} = 0$	$-L_c$ 0.5 L	$\delta_C = \dfrac{wL_c^{\,3}}{8EI}(2L + L_c)$ $\delta_{AB} = -\dfrac{wL^2\,L_c^{\,2}}{16EI}$
6 Total load = 1.667 W	$M_A = M_B = -0.0556\,WL$ $M_{AB} = 0.0694\,WL$	$R_A = 0.833\,W$ $R_B = 0.833\,W$	$S_A = S_B = 0.333\,W$ $S_{AB} = S_{BA} = 0.50\,W$	0.50 L −0.333 L —	$\delta_{AB} = 0.00608\,\dfrac{WL^3}{EI}$ $\delta_{up} = -0.00309\,\dfrac{WL^3}{EI}$ range $= 0.00917\,\dfrac{WL^3}{EI}$

Case Condition	Moment (kNm)	Reaction (kN)	Shear Force (kN)	Deflections — Distance from A	Deflections — Value (m)
7	$M_A = +0.25\, wL_c^2$ $M_B = -0.50\, wL_c^2$	$R_A = -0.75\,\dfrac{wL_c^2}{L}$ $R_B = wL_c + 0.75\,\dfrac{wL_c^2}{L}$	$S_{AB} = S_{BA} = R_A$ $S_{BC} = wL_c$	$0.667\, L$ $L + L_c$	$\delta_{AB} = -\dfrac{wL^2 L_c^2}{54EI}$ $\delta_C = \dfrac{wL_c^3}{8EI}(L_c + L)$
8	$M_{AB} = 0.128\, TL$	$R_A = 0.667\, T$ $R_B = 0.333\, T$	$S_{AB} = 0.667\, T$ $S_{BA} = 0.333\, T$	$0.519\, L$	$\delta_{AB} = 0.0130\,\dfrac{TL^3}{EI}$
9	$M_A = -0.10\, TL$ $M_B = -0.0667\, TL$ $M_{AB} = 0.0429\, TL$	$R_A = 0.70\, T$ $R_B = 0.30\, T$	$S_{AB} = 0.70\, T$ $S_{BA} = 0.30\, T$	$0.475\, L$	$\delta_{AB} = 0.00262\,\dfrac{TL^3}{EI}$
10	$M_A = -0.333\, TL_c$	$R_A = T$	$S_{AB} = T$	L_c	$\delta_B = 0.0667\,\dfrac{TL_c^3}{EI}$
11	$M_A = -0.667\, TL_c$	$R_A = T$	$S_{AB} = T$	L_c	$\delta_B = 0.183\,\dfrac{TL_c^3}{EI}$
12	$M_A = -0.133\, TL$ $M_{AB} = 0.0596\, TL$	$R_A = 0.80\, T$ $R_B = 0.20\, T$	$S_{AB} = 0.80\, T$ $S_{BA} = 0.20\, T$	$0.553\, L$	$\delta_{AB} = 0.0047\,\dfrac{TL^3}{EI}$
13	$M_A = -0.117\, TL$ $M_{AB} = 0.0846\, TL$	$R_A = 0.45\, T$ $R_B = 0.55\, T$	$S_{AB} = 0.45\, T$ $S_{BA} = 0.55\, T$	$0.598\, L$	$\delta_{AB} = 0.0061\,\dfrac{TL^3}{EI}$

concrete society

Case Condition	Moment (kNm)	Reaction (kN)	Shear Force (kN)	Deflections	
				Distance from A	Value (m)
14	$M_A = -PL_c$	$R_A = P$	$S_{AB} = P$	L_c	$\delta_B = 0.333\,\dfrac{PL_c^3}{EI}$
15	$M_{AB} = 0.25\,PL$	$R_A = 1.50\,P$ $R_B = 1.50\,P$	$S_{AB} = 0.50\,P$ $S_{BA} = 0.50\,P$	0.50 L	$\delta_{AB} = 0.0208\,\dfrac{PL^3}{EI}$
16	$M_A = M_B = -0.125\,PL$ $M_{AB} = 0.125\,PL$	$R_A = 0.50\,P$ $R_B = 0.50\,P$	$S_{AB} = 0.50\,P$ $S_{BA} = 0.50\,P$	0.50 L	$\delta_{AB} = 0.00521\,\dfrac{PL^3}{EI}$
17	$M_A = -0.188\,PL$ $M_{AB} = 0.156\,PL$	$R_A = 0.688\,P$ $R_B = 0.312\,P$	$S_{AB} = 0.688\,P$ $S_{BA} = 0.312\,P$	0.553 L	$\delta_{AB} = 0.00932\,\dfrac{PL^3}{EI}$
18	$M_{AB} = 0.333\,PL$	$R_A = 2\,P$ $R_B = 2\,P$	$S_{AB} = P$ $S_{BA} = P$	0.50 L	$\delta_{AB} = 0.0355\,\dfrac{PL^3}{EI}$
19	$M_A = M_B = -0.222\,PL$ $M_{AB} = 0.111\,PL$	$R_A = P$ $R_B = P$	$S_{AB} = P$ $S_{BA} = P$	0.50 L	$\delta_{AB} = 0.00772\,\dfrac{PL^3}{EI}$
20	$M_A = -0.333\,PL$ $M_{AB} = 0.222\,PL$	$R_A = 1.33\,P$ $R_B = 0.67\,P$	$S_{AB} = 1.33\,P$ $S_{BA} = 0.67\,P$	0.577 L	$\delta_{AB} = 0.0152\,\dfrac{PL^3}{EI}$

Appendix B – Typical Loading Cases
Part Two – Continuous Members on Multiple Spans

The typical loading cases 21 to 58 are given as a guide only for use on multiple span conditions of loading. To assist the reader case 30 is shown in Fig. 113 with the position of the deflections. It is **most important** that the following constraints are considered to apply to the member and loading case for the values stated to be valid.

1. All the spans are of equal length.

2. The members shown are fully continuous over **all** spans and supports with a constant moment of inertia.

3. The loads are identical on each of the spans indicated **and** are assumed to be applied simultaneously.

4. The supports remain rigid without any settlement (no sinking supports).

5. The total reactions at supports are stated, together with the shear force value at points adjacent to the supports. In cases 40 to 57 a point load is considered to be applied at the support position. (This represents loading conditions of groups of point loads at half or third span spacing.) The designer should be aware that moving the relative position of the spaced loads to one side of the supports will increase the shear force values and also alter the bending moment and deflection stated.

6. In certain situations the loads may only be applied to some of the spans of a system of continuous members. This situation of incidental imposed loads may produce bending moments, deflections and shear forces of greater magnitude or in different directions than those resulting from all spans loaded simultaneously. These situations require either a rigorous analysis for a solution or the application of simplistic approximations based on experience and engineering judgement. Some of the more common cases have been identified and are shown in this appendix.

7. The effects of incidental loading conditions outlined in Note 6 can produce different analyses depending on the support conditions. For example, in cases 41 and 42 the analysis depends on whether or not the member at support C is tied down and able to transfer tension into the support system. In practice, with soffit forms, the self-weight and some load from the reinforcement, which will have been considered as dead load in case 21, can produce a reaction which exceeds the uplift value at support C. (The most likely occurrence of incidental loading causing uplift will be in soffit systems where the self-weight is light compared to the applied loads. The increasing use of long lengths of aluminium beams, resulting in low self-weight of the formwork, suggests that checks should be made to ensure that the loading conditions assumed do apply.)

8. When summarising several load conditions on the same member, for example dead load and then incidental live loads, it should be remembered that it is correct to algebraically sum the bending moment, reaction and shear force **at supports** only. The maximum bending moments in the spans may occur at different positions and engineering judgement is required when combining the values. In considering the deflections these can **not** be considered as algebraically cumulative.

9. The values for maximum deflections and the position considered (measured from the support A) are for guidance for the specific loading case considered. The deflection is measured from the line of the supports. In certain cases the member will hog upwards (shown as a negative deflection.) As an example the deflection positions for loading case 30 are illustrated in Fig. 113.

The total of the largest positive and negative deflections is referred to as the range, and is shown in the last column of the tables. It should be noted that when checking the finished concrete face with a straight edge it is the range which is the most likely to be measured.

In practice it should be remembered that the nature of formwork, with its variability of material, reuse capability, assembly accuracy etc, makes it inevitable that the reality will diverge somewhat from the theoretical performance. In wall formwork, elasticity of tie rods will alter the theoretical straight soldier to a different shape. The soffit form will be on falsework which will shorten due to elasticity, together with additional ground consolidation as the load is applied, making the formwork beams deform. Thus, detailed and rigorous analysis of the members may not always be justified and sound engineering judgement based on simpler rule-of-thumb assumptions, such as 'all spans are simply supported' etc. may give more realistic and economic solutions. See also BS 5975: Clause 43.3.1 (Ref. 2).

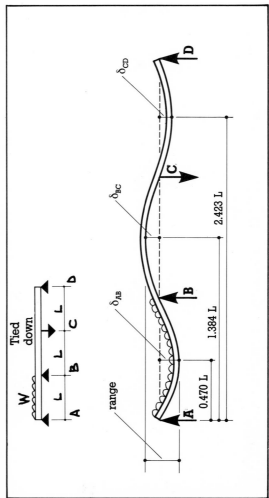

Fig. 113 *Diagram of deflections of loading case 30.*

Appendix B – Part 2 – Multiple Spans

Case	Condition	Moment (kNm)	Reaction (kN)	Shear Force (kN)	Deflections — Distance from A	Value (m)
21		$M_B = -0.125\ WL$ $M_{AB} = M_{BC} = 0.070\ WL$	$R_A = R_C = 0.375\ W$ $R_B = 1.250\ W$	$S_{AB} = S_{CB} = 0.375\ W$ $S_{BA} = S_{BC} = 0.625\ W$	0.421 L	$\delta_{AB} = 0.00541\ \dfrac{WL^3}{EI}$
22	Tied down	$M_B = -0.063\ WL$ $M_{AB} = 0.096\ WL$	$R_A = 0.438\ W$ $R_B = 0.625\ W$ $R_C = -0.063\ W$	$S_{AB} = 0.438\ W$ $S_{BA} = 0.562\ W$ $S_{BC} = 0.063\ W$ $S_{CB} = -0.063\ W$	0.472 L 1.423 L —	$\delta_{AB} = 0.00915\ \dfrac{WL^3}{EI}$ $\delta_{BC} = -0.00401\ \dfrac{WL^3}{EI}$ range = 0.0132 $\dfrac{WL^3}{EI}$
23	Self-weight not included	$M_B = 0$ $M_{AB} = 0.125\ WL$	$R_A = 0.50\ W$ $R_B = 0.50\ W$ $R_C = 0$	$S_{AB} = S_{BA} = 0.50\ W$ $S_{BC} = 0$	0.50 L 2.0 L —	$\delta_{AB} = 0.0130\ \dfrac{WL^3}{EI}$ $\delta_C = -0.0417\ \dfrac{WL^3}{EI}$ range = 0.0547 $\dfrac{WL^3}{EI}$
24	Tied down, Unit load. If B is not tied down see case 5 i.e. span considered is AC	$M_A = M_C = -0.50\ wL_c^2$ $M_B = 0.25\ wL_c^2$ (Note + ve)	$R_A = R_C = wL_c + 0.75\ \dfrac{wL_c^2}{L}$ $R_B = -1.5\ \dfrac{wL_c^2}{L}$	$S_A = S_C = wL_c$ $S_{AB} = S_{BC} = 0.75\ \dfrac{wL_c^2}{L}$	$-L_c$ —	$\delta_{tip} = 0.125\ \dfrac{wL_c^3}{EI}(L_c + L)$
25	Total load = 2.667W	$M_A = M_C = -0.0556\ WL$ $M_B = -0.0972\ WL$ $M_{AB} = M_{BC} = 0.04\ WL$	$R_A = 0.791\ W$ $R_B = 1.08\ W$ $R_C = 0.791\ W$	$S_A = 0.333\ W$ $S_{AB} = S_{CB} = 0.458\ W$ $S_{BA} = S_{BC} = 0.627\ W$	0.465 L -0.333 L —	$\delta_{AB} = 0.0035\ \dfrac{WL^3}{EI}$ $\delta_{tip} = -0.00077\ \dfrac{WL^3}{EI}$ range = 0.00427 $\dfrac{WL^3}{EI}$

Case Condition	Moment (kNm)	Reaction (kN)	Shear Force (kN)	Deflections Distance from A	Value (m)
26	$M_B = M_C = -0.10$ WL $M_{AB} = M_{CD} = 0.080$ WL $M_{BC} = 0.025$ WL	$R_A = R_D = 0.40$ W $R_B = R_C = 1.10$ W	$S_{AB} = S_{DC} = 0.40$ W $S_{BA} = S_{CD} = 0.60$ W $S_{BC} = S_{CB} = 0.50$ W	0.446 L 1.113 L 1.50 L —	$\delta_{AB} = 0.00688 \dfrac{WL^3}{EI}$ $\delta_{BC} = -0.000417 \dfrac{WL^3}{EI}$ $\delta_{BC} = 0.000521 \dfrac{WL^3}{EI}$ range = 0.00730 $\dfrac{WL^3}{EI}$
27	$M_B = M_C = -0.050$ WL $M_{BC} = 0.075$ WL	$R_A = R_D = 0.050$ W $R_B = R_C = 0.550$ W	$S_{AB} = S_{DC} = 0.05$ W $S_{BA} = S_{CD} = 0.05$ W $S_{BC} = S_{CB} = 0.50$ W	0.577 L 1.50 L —	$\delta_{AB} = -0.00321 \dfrac{WL^3}{EI}$ $\delta_{BC} = 0.00677 \dfrac{WL^3}{EI}$ range = 0.00998 $\dfrac{WL^3}{EI}$
28	$M_B = M_C = 0$ $M_{BC} = 0.125$ WL	$R_A = R_D = 0$ $R_B = R_C = 0.50$ W	$S_{BC} = S_{CB} = 0.50$ W	1.50 L	$\delta_{BC} = 0.0130 \dfrac{WL^3}{EI}$
29 Self-weight not included	$M_B = M_C = -0.050$ WL $M_{AB} = M_{CD} = 0.101$ WL $M_{BC} = -0.050$ WL	$R_A = R_D = 0.45$ W $R_B = R_C = 0.55$ W	$S_{AB} = S_{DC} = 0.45$ W $S_{BA} = S_{CD} = 0.55$ W $S_{BC} = S_{CB} = 0$	0.479 L 1.50 L —	$\delta_{AB} = 0.00992 \dfrac{WL^3}{EI}$ $\delta_{BC} = -0.00625 \dfrac{WL^3}{EI}$ range = 0.0162 $\dfrac{WL^3}{EI}$
30	$M_B = -0.067$ WL $M_C = +0.017$ WL $M_{AB} = 0.094$ WL	$R_A = 0.433$ W $R_B = 0.65$ W $R_C = -0.10$ W $R_D = 0.017$ W	$S_{AB} = 0.433$ W $S_{BA} = 0.567$ W $S_{BC} = S_{CB} = 0.083$ W $S_{CD} = S_{DC} = 0.017$ W	0.470 L 1.384 L 2.423 L —	$\delta_{AB} = 0.00890 \dfrac{WL^3}{EI}$ $\delta_{BC} = -0.00334 \dfrac{WL^3}{EI}$ $\delta_{CD} = 0.00107 \dfrac{WL^3}{EI}$ range = 0.0122 $\dfrac{WL^3}{EI}$

concrete society

Case	Condition	Moment (kNm)	Reaction (kN)	Shear Force (kN)	Deflections Distance from A	Value (m)
31	Tied down	$M_B = -0.117\,WL$ $M_C = -0.033\,WL$ $M_{AB} = 0.073\,WL$ $M_{BC} = 0.054\,WL$	$R_A = 0.383\,W$ $R_B = 1.200\,W$ $R_C = 0.450\,W$ $R_D = -0.033\,W$	$S_{AB} = 0.383\,W$ $S_{BA} = 0.617\,W$ $S_{BC} = 0.583\,W$ $S_{CB} = 0.417\,W$ $S_{CD} = S_{DC} = -0.033\,W$	0.431 L 1.025 L 1.567 L 2.423 L —	$\delta_{AB} = 0.00590\,\frac{WL^3}{EI}$ $\delta_{BC} = -0.000034\,\frac{WL^3}{EI}$ $\delta_{BC} = 0.00376\,\frac{WL^3}{EI}$ $\delta_{CD} = -0.00214\,\frac{WL^3}{EI}$ range $= 0.00804\,\frac{WL^3}{EI}$
32		$M_B = -0.125\,WL$ $M_C = 0$ $M_{AB} = M_{BC} = 0.070\,WL$	$R_A = 0.375\,W$ $R_B = 1.250\,W$ $R_C = 0.375\,W$ $R_D = 0$	$S_{AB} = S_{CB} = 0.375\,W$ $S_{BA} = S_{BC} = 0.625\,W$ $S_{CD} = 0$	0.422 L 1.578 L 3.00 L —	$\delta_{AB} = 0.00542\,\frac{WL^3}{EI}$ $\delta_{BC} = 0.00542\,\frac{WL^3}{EI}$ $\delta_D = -0.0208\,\frac{WL^3}{EI}$ range $= 0.0263\,\frac{WL^3}{EI}$
33	w = load per unit length Tied down	$M_A = M_D = -0.50\,wL_c^2$ $M_B = M_C = +0.10\,wL_c^2$ $M_{BC} = 0.10\,wL_c^2$	$R_A = R_D = wL_c + \dfrac{0.60\,wL_c^2}{L}$ $R_B = R_C = -\dfrac{0.60\,wL_c^2}{L}$	$S_A = S_D = wL_c$ $S_{AB} = S_{DC} = \dfrac{0.60\,wL_c^2}{L}$ $S_{BA} = S_{CD} = -\dfrac{0.60\,wL_c^2}{L}$ $S_{BC} = S_{CB} = 0$	$-L_c$	$\delta_{up} = \dfrac{wL_c^3}{40EI}(6L + 5L_c)$
34	Total load = 3.667 W	$M_A = M_D = -0.056\,WL$ $M_B = M_C = -0.089\,WL$ $M_{AB} = M_{CD} = 0.053\,WL$ $M_{BC} = 0.036\,WL$	$R_A = 0.800\,W$ $R_B = 1.033\,W$ $R_C = 1.033\,W$ $R_D = 0.800\,W$	$S_A = S_D = 0.333\,W$ $S_{AB} = S_{DC} = 0.467\,W$ $S_{BA} = S_{CD} = 0.533\,W$ $S_{BC} = S_{CB} = 0.50\,W$	0.474 L 1.034 L 1.50 L -0.333 L —	$\delta_{AB} = 0.0040\,\frac{WL^3}{EI}$ $\delta_{BC} = -0.000046\,\frac{WL^3}{EI}$ $\delta_{BC} = 0.00191\,\frac{WL^3}{EI}$ $\delta_{up} = -0.00123\,\frac{WL^3}{EI}$ range $= 0.00523\,\frac{WL^3}{EI}$

Case	Condition	Moment (kNm)	Reaction (kN)	Shear Force (kN)	Deflections Distance from A	Value (m)
35		$M_B = M_D = -0.107\ WL$ $M_C = -0.071\ WL$ $M_{AB} = M_{DE} = 0.077\ WL$ $M_{BC} = M_{CD} = 0.036\ WL$	$R_A = R_E = 0.393\ W$ $R_B = R_D = 1.143\ W$ $R_C = 0.929\ W$	$S_{AB} = S_{ED} = 0.393\ W$ $S_{BA} = S_{DE} = 0.607\ W$ $S_{BC} = S_{DC} = 0.536\ W$ $S_{CB} = S_{CD} = 0.464\ W$	0.440 L 1.066 L 1.541 L —	$\delta_{AB} = 0.00646\ \dfrac{WL^3}{EI}$ $\delta_{BC} = -0.000184\ \dfrac{WL^3}{EI}$ $\delta_{BC} = 0.00189\ \dfrac{WL^3}{EI}$ range $= 0.00664\ \dfrac{WL^3}{EI}$
36	 W = Load/Unit length	$M_A = M_E = -0.50\ wL_c^2$ $M_B = M_D = 0.143\ wL_c^2$ $M_C = -0.071\ wL_c^2$	$R_A = R_E = wL_c + \dfrac{0.642\ wL_c^2}{L}$ $R_B = R_D = -\dfrac{0.858\ wL_c^2}{L}$ $R_C = \dfrac{0.43\ wL_c^2}{L}$	$S_A = S_E = wL_c$ $S_{AB} = S_{ED} = \dfrac{0.643\ wL_c^2}{L}$ $S_{BA} = S_{DE} = \dfrac{0.643\ wL_c^2}{L}$ $S_{BC} = S_{DC} = \dfrac{0.215\ wL_c^2}{L}$ $S_{CB} = S_{CD} = \dfrac{0.215\ wL_c^2}{L}$	$-L_c$	$\delta_{tip} = \dfrac{wL_c^3}{56EI}\ (8L + 7L_c)$
37	Total load = 4.667 W 	$M_A = M_E = -0.0556\ WL$ $M_B = M_D = -0.0911\ WL$ $M_C = -0.079\ WL$ $M_{AB} = M_{DE} = 0.052\ WL$ $M_{BC} = M_{CD} = 0.040\ WL$	$R_A = 0.798\ W$ $R_B = 1.048\ W$ $R_C = 0.976\ W$ $R_D = 1.048\ W$ $R_E = 0.798\ W$	$S_A = S_E = 0.333\ W$ $S_{AB} = S_{ED} = 0.465\ W$ $S_{BA} = S_{DE} = 0.535\ W$ $S_{BC} = S_{DC} = 0.513\ W$ $S_{CB} = S_{CD} = 0.487\ W$	0.471 L 1.023 L 1.512 L -0.333 L —	$\delta_{AB} = 0.00387\ \dfrac{WL^3}{EI}$ $\delta_{BC} = -0.000023\ \dfrac{WL^3}{EI}$ $\delta_{BC} = 0.00236\ \dfrac{WL^3}{EI}$ $\delta_{tip} = -0.0011\ \dfrac{WL^3}{EI}$ range $= 0.00497\ \dfrac{WL^3}{EI}$

concrete society

Case	Condition	Moment (kNm)	Reaction (kN)	Shear Force (kN)	Deflections	
					Distance from A	Value (m)
38		$M_B = M_E = -0.105$ WL $M_C = M_D = -0.079$ WL $M_{AB} = M_{EF} = 0.078$ WL $M_{BC} = M_{DE} = 0.033$ WL $M_{CD} = 0.046$ WL	$R_A = R_F = 0.395$ W $R_B = R_E = 1.132$ W $R_C = R_D = 0.974$ W	$S_{AB} = S_{FE} = 0.395$ W $S_{BA} = S_{EF} = 0.605$ W $S_{BC} = S_{ED} = 0.527$ W $S_{CB} = S_{DE} = 0.473$ W $S_{CD} = S_{DC} = 0.50$ W	0.441 L 1.076 L 1.533 L 1.969 L 2.500 L —	$\delta_{AB} = 0.00657 \frac{WL^3}{EI}$ $\delta_{BC} = -0.000233 \frac{WL^3}{EI}$ $\delta_{BC} = 0.00153 \frac{WL^3}{EI}$ $\delta_{BC} = -0.00003 \frac{WL^3}{EI}$ $\delta_{CD} = 0.00315 \frac{WL^3}{EI}$ range $= 0.00680 \frac{WL^3}{EI}$
39	Total load = 5.667 W 	$M_A = M_F = -0.0556$ WL $M_B = M_E = -0.091$ WL $M_C = M_D = -0.082$ WL $M_{AB} = M_{EF} = 0.052$ WL $M_{BC} = M_{DE} = 0.039$ WL $M_{CD} = 0.043$ WL	$R_A = R_F = 0.798$ W $R_B = R_E = 1.044$ W $R_C = R_D = 0.991$ W	$S_A = S_F = 0.333$ W $S_{AB} = S_{FE} = 0.465$ W $S_{BA} = S_{EF} = 0.535$ W $S_{BC} = S_{ED} = 0.509$ W $S_{CB} = S_{DE} = 0.491$ W $S_{CD} = S_{DC} = 0.50$ W	0.472 L 1.026 L 1.509 L 2.500 L -0.333 L —	$\delta_{AB} = 0.0039 \frac{WL^3}{EI}$ $\delta_{BC} = -0.000028 \frac{WL^3}{EI}$ $\delta_{BC} = 0.00224 \frac{WL^3}{EI}$ $\delta_{CD} = 0.00279 \frac{WL^3}{EI}$ $\delta_{tip} = -0.00114 \frac{WL^3}{EI}$ range $= 0.00504 \frac{WL^3}{EI}$
40		$M_B = -0.188$ PL $M_{AB} = M_{BC} = 0.156$ PL	$R_A = R_C = 1.313$ P $R_B = 2.375$ P	$S_{AB} = S_{CB} = 0.313$ P $S_{BA} = S_{BC} = 0.687$ P	0.447 L —	$\delta_{AB} = 0.00932 \frac{PL^3}{EI}$ range $= 0.00932 \frac{PL^3}{EI}$

Case Condition	Moment (kNm)	Reaction (kN)	Shear Force (kN)	Deflections Distance from A	Value (m)
41	$M_B = -0.094\ PL$ $M_{AB} = 0.203\ PL$	$R_A = 1.406\ P$ $R_B = 1.688\ P$ $R_C = -0.094\ P$	$S_{AB} = 0.406\ P$ $S_{BA} = 0.594\ P$ $S_{BC} = S_{CB} = 0.094\ P$	0.480 L 1.423 L —	$\delta_{AB} = 0.0150\ \dfrac{PL^3}{EI}$ $\delta_{BC} = -0.00601\ \dfrac{PL^3}{EI}$ range $= 0.0210\ \dfrac{PL^3}{EI}$
42	$M_{AB} = 0.250\ PL$ $M_B = 0$	$R_A = R_B = 1.50\ P$ $R_C = 0$	$S_{AB} = S_{BA} = 0.50\ P$ $S_{BC} = 0$	0.50 L 2.00 L —	$\delta_{AB} = 0.208\ \dfrac{PL^3}{EI}$ $\delta_C = -0.0625\ \dfrac{PL^3}{EI}$ range $= 0.271\ \dfrac{PL^3}{EI}$
43	$M_B = M_C = -0.150\ PL$ $M_{AB} = M_{CD} = 0.175\ PL$ $M_{BC} = 0.100\ PL$	$R_A = R_D = 1.35\ P$ $R_B = R_C = 2.15\ P$	$S_{AB} = S_{DC} = 0.35\ P$ $S_{BA} = S_{CD} = 0.65\ P$ $S_{BC} = S_{CB} = 0.50\ P$	0.463 L 1.100 L 1.500 L —	$\delta_{AB} = 0.0116\ \dfrac{PL^3}{EI}$ $\delta_{BC} = -0.000583\ \dfrac{PL^3}{EI}$ $\delta_{BC} = 0.00208\ \dfrac{PL^3}{EI}$ range $= 0.0122\ \dfrac{PL^3}{EI}$
44	$M_B = M_C = -0.075\ PL$ $M_{BC} = 0.175\ PL$	$R_A = R_D = -0.075\ P$ $R_B = R_C = 1.575\ P$	$S_{AB} = S_{DC} = 0.075\ P$ $S_{BA} = S_{CD} = 0.075\ P$ $S_{BC} = S_{CB} = 0.50\ P$	0.577 L 1.50 L —	$\delta_{AB} = -0.00481\ \dfrac{PL^3}{EI}$ $\delta_{BC} = 0.0115\ \dfrac{PL^3}{EI}$ range $= 0.0163\ \dfrac{PL^3}{EI}$

Case Condition	Moment (kNm)	Reaction (kN)	Shear Force (kN)	Deflections	
				Distance from A	Value (m)
45 Self-weight not included	$M_B = M_C = 0$ $M_{AB} = 0.250\,PL$	$R_A = R_D = 0$ $R_B = R_C = 1.50\,P$	$S_{BA} = S_{CD} = 0$ $S_{BC} = S_{CB} = 0.50\,P$	0 1.50 L —	$\delta_A = -0.0625\,\dfrac{PL^3}{EI}$ $\delta_{BC} = 0.0208\,\dfrac{PL^3}{EI}$ range $= 0.0833\,\dfrac{PL^3}{EI}$
46	$M_B = M_C = -0.075\,PL$ $M_{AB} = M_{CD} = 0.213\,PL$ $M_{BC} = -0.075\,PL$	$R_A = R_D = 1.425\,P$ $R_B = R_C = 1.575\,P$	$S_{AB} = S_{DC} = 0.425\,P$ $S_{BA} = S_{CD} = 0.575\,P$ $S_{BC} = S_{CB} = 0$	0.485 L 1.50 L —	$\delta_{AB} = 0.0162\,\dfrac{PL^3}{EI}$ $\delta_{BC} = -0.00938\,\dfrac{PL^3}{EI}$ range $= 0.0256\,\dfrac{PL^3}{EI}$
47	$M_B = -0.100\,PL$ $M_C = 0.025\,PL$ $M_{AB} = 0.200\,PL$	$R_A = 1.40\,P$ $R_B = 1.725\,P$ $R_C = -0.15\,P$ $R_D = 0.025\,P$	$S_{AB} = 0.40\,P$ $S_{BA} = 0.60\,P$ $S_{BC} = S_{CB} = 0.125\,P$ $S_{CD} = S_{DC} = 0.025\,P$	0.479 L 1.384 L 2.423 L —	$\delta_{AB} = 0.0146\,\dfrac{PL^3}{EI}$ $\delta_{BC} = -0.00501\,\dfrac{PL^3}{EI}$ $\delta_{CD} = 0.00160\,\dfrac{PL^3}{EI}$ range $= 0.0196\,\dfrac{PL^3}{EI}$
48	$M_B = -0.175\,PL$ $M_C = -0.050\,PL$ $M_{AB} = 0.163\,PL$ $M_{BC} = 0.138\,PL$	$R_A = 1.325\,P$ $R_B = 2.30\,P$ $R_C = 1.425\,P$ $R_D = -0.050\,P$	$S_{AB} = 0.325\,P$ $S_{BA} = S_{BC} = 0.625\,P$ $S_{CB} = 0.375\,P$ $S_{CD} = S_{DC} = 0.05\,P$	0.453 L 1.025 L 1.540 L 2.423 L —	$\delta_{AB} = 0.0101\,\dfrac{PL^3}{EI}$ $\delta_{BC} = -0.00005\,\dfrac{PL^3}{EI}$ $\delta_{BC} = 0.00687\,\dfrac{PL^3}{EI}$ $\delta_{CD} = -0.00321\,\dfrac{PL^3}{EI}$ range $= 0.0133\,\dfrac{PL^3}{EI}$

Case Condition	Moment (kNm)	Reaction (kN)	Shear Force (kN)	Deflections — Distance from A	Value (m)
49	$M_B = M_D = -0.161\,PL$ $M_C = -0.107\,PL$ $M_{AB} = M_{DE} = 0.170\,PL$ $M_{BC} = M_{CD} = 0.116\,PL$	$R_A = R_E = 1.339\,P$ $R_B = R_D = 2.214\,P$ $R_C = 1.893\,P$	$S_{AB} = S_{ED} = 0.339\,P$ $S_{BA} = S_{DE} = 0.661\,P$ $S_{BC} = S_{DC} = 0.553\,P$ $S_{CB} = S_{CD} = 0.447\,P$	0.459 L 1.062 L 1.520 L —	$\delta_{AB} = 0.0109\,\dfrac{PL^3}{EI}$ $\delta_{BC} = -0.000267\,\dfrac{PL^3}{EI}$ $\delta_{BC} = 0.00411\,\dfrac{PL^3}{EI}$ range $= 0.0112\,\dfrac{PL^3}{EI}$
50	$M_B = M_E = -0.158\,PL$ $M_C = M_D = -0.119\,PL$ $M_{AB} = M_{EF} = 0.171\,PL$ $M_{BC} = M_{DE} = 0.110\,PL$ $M_{CD} = 0.130\,PL$	$R_A = R_F = 1.340\,P$ $R_B = R_E = 2.20\,P$ $R_C = R_D = 1.96\,P$	$S_{AB} = S_{FE} = 0.34\,P$ $S_{BA} = S_{EF} = 0.66\,P$ $S_{BC} = S_{ED} = 0.54\,P$ $S_{CB} = S_{DE} = 0.46\,P$ $S_{CD} = S_{DC} = 0.50\,P$	0.460 L 1.071 L 1.515 L 1.971 L 2.50 L —	$\delta_{AB} = 0.0111\,\dfrac{PL^3}{EI}$ $\delta_{BC} = -0.00033\,\dfrac{PL^3}{EI}$ $\delta_{BC} = 0.00358\,\dfrac{PL^3}{EI}$ $\delta_{CD} = -0.000047\,\dfrac{PL^3}{EI}$ $\delta_{CD} = 0.00603\,\dfrac{PL^3}{EI}$ range $= 0.0114\,\dfrac{PL^3}{EI}$
51	$M_B = -0.334\,PL$ $M_{AB} = M_{BC} = 0.222\,PL$	$R_A = R_C = 1.667\,P$ $R_B = 3.667\,P$	$S_{AB} = S_{CB} = 0.667\,P$ $S_{BA} = S_{BC} = 1.333\,P$	0.423 L —	$\delta_{AB} = 0.0152\,\dfrac{PL^3}{EI}$ range $= 0.0152\,\dfrac{PL^3}{EI}$
52 (Tied down)	$M_B = -0.167\,PL$ $M_{AB} = 0.278\,PL$	$R_A = 1.834\,P$ $R_B = 2.340\,P$ $R_C = -0.174\,P$	$S_{AB} = 0.834\,P$ $S_{BA} = 1.166\,P$ $S_{BC} = S_{CB} = 0.174\,P$	0.473 L 1.423 L —	$\delta_{AB} = 0.0252\,\dfrac{PL^3}{EI}$ $\delta_{BC} = -0.0107\,\dfrac{PL^3}{EI}$ range $= 0.0359\,\dfrac{PL^3}{EI}$

Case Condition	Moment (kNm)	Reaction (kN)	Shear Force (kN)	Deflections	
				Distance from A	Value (m)
53	$M_B = M_C = -0.266\,PL$ $M_{AB} = M_{CD} = 0.244\,PL$ $M_{BC} = 0.066\,PL$	$R_A = R_D = 1.734\,P$ $R_B = R_C = 3.266\,P$	$S_{AB} = S_{DC} = 0.734\,P$ $S_{BA} = S_{CD} = 1.266\,P$ $S_{BC} = S_{CB} = 1.00\,P$	0.446 L 1.103 L 1.50 L —	$\delta_{AB} = 0.0191\,\dfrac{PL^3}{EI}$ $\delta_{BC} = -0.00106\,\dfrac{PL^3}{EI}$ $\delta_{BC} = 0.00216\,\dfrac{PL^3}{EI}$ range $= 0.0202\,\dfrac{PL^3}{EI}$
54	$M_B = -0.178\,PL$ $M_C = -0.090\,PL$ $M_{AB} = 0.274\,PL$	$R_A = 1.822\,P$ $R_B = 2.400\,P$ $R_C = -0.266\,P$ $R_D = 0.044\,P$	$S_{AB} = 0.822\,P$ $S_{BA} = 1.178\,P$ $S_{BC} = S_{CB} = 0.222\,P$ $S_{CD} = S_{DC} = 0.044\,P$	0.470 L 1.384 L 2.423 L —	$\delta_{AB} = 0.0245\,\dfrac{PL^3}{EI}$ $\delta_{BC} = -0.0089\,\dfrac{PL^3}{EI}$ $\delta_{CD} = 0.00285\,\dfrac{PL^3}{EI}$ range $= 0.0334\,\dfrac{PL^3}{EI}$
55	$M_B = -0.312\,PL$ $M_C = -0.090\,PL$ $M_{AB} = 0.230\,PL$ $M_{BC} = 0.170\,PL$	$R_A = 1.690\,P$ $R_B = 3.534\,P$ $R_C = 0.866\,P$ $R_D = -0.089\,P$	$S_{AB} = 0.690\,P$ $S_{BA} = 1.310\,P$ $S_{BC} = 1.224\,P$ $S_{CB} = 0.776\,P$ $S_{CD} = S_{DC} = 0.09\,P$	0.431 L 1.566 L 2.423 L —	$\delta_{AB} = 0.0165\,\dfrac{PL^3}{EI}$ $\delta_{BC} = 0.0108\,\dfrac{PL^3}{EI}$ $\delta_{CD} = -0.0057\,\dfrac{PL^3}{EI}$ range $= 0.0222\,\dfrac{PL^3}{EI}$
56	$M_B = M_D = -0.286\,PL$ $M_C = -0.192\,PL$ $M_{AB} = M_{DE} = 0.238\,PL$ $M_{BC} = M_{CD} = 0.112\,PL$	$R_A = R_E = 1.714\,P$ $R_B = R_D = 3.380\,P$ $R_C = 2.810\,P$	$S_{AB} = S_{ED} = 0.714\,P$ $S_{BA} = S_{DE} = 1.286\,P$ $S_{BC} = S_{DC} = 1.094\,P$ $S_{CB} = S_{CD} = 0.906\,P$	0.440 L 1.063 L 1.541 L —	$\delta_{AB} = 0.0180\,\dfrac{PL^3}{EI}$ $\delta_{BC} = -0.000479\,\dfrac{PL^3}{EI}$ $\delta_{BC} = 0.00581\,\dfrac{PL^3}{EI}$ range $= 0.0185\,\dfrac{PL^3}{EI}$

Case	Condition	Moment (kNm)	Reaction (kN)	Shear Force (kN)	Deflections	
					Distance from A	Value (m)
57		$M_B = M_E = -0.281\,PL$	$R_A = R_F = 1.719\,P$	$S_{AB} = S_{FE} = 0.72\,P$	$0.442\,L$	$\delta_{AB} = 0.0183\,\dfrac{PL^3}{EI}$
		$M_C = M_D = -0.211\,PL$	$R_B = R_E = 3.351\,P$	$S_{BA} = S_{EF} = 1.28\,P$	$1.073\,L$	$\delta_{BC} = -0.000602\,\dfrac{PL^3}{EI}$
		$M_{AB} = M_{EF} = 0.240\,PL$	$R_C = R_D = 2.930\,P$	$S_{BC} = S_{ED} = 1.07\,P$	$1.533\,L$	$\delta_{BC} = 0.00484\,\dfrac{PL^3}{EI}$
		$M_{BC} = M_{DE} = 0.10\,PL$		$S_{CB} = S_{DE} = 0.93\,P$	$2.50\,L$	$\delta_{CD} = 0.00918\,\dfrac{PL^3}{EI}$
		$M_{CD} = 0.122\,PL$		$S_{CD} = S_{DC} = 1.00\,P$	—	range $= 0.0189\,\dfrac{PL^3}{EI}$
58	**Formwork use only:** face contact material continuous over four or more supports with L < 610 mm and width of support B wider than 2t	$M_B = -0.095\,WL$	$R_A = 0.5\,W$	$S_{max} = S_{BA} = S_{BC}$	—	Approximate
		$M_{AB} = 0.085\,PL$	$R_B = 1.0\,W$	$= 0.525\left(\dfrac{L-B-t}{L}\right)W$	—	$\delta_{AB} = 0.0066\,\dfrac{WL^3}{EI}$
						range $= 0.0068\,\dfrac{WL^3}{EI}$

Appendix C
Worked Examples of
Formwork Design

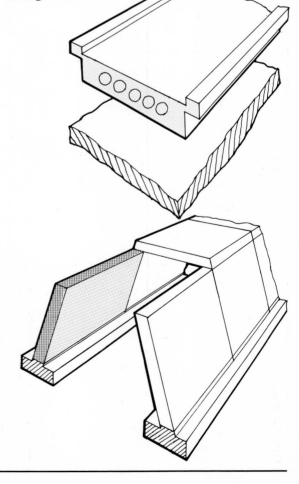

	Project	Sheet
APPENDIX C1 **WORKED EXAMPLE OF** **FORMWORK DESIGN**	**LICHFIELD**	**1 of 11**
	Part of Structure	Drg Ref
	DOUBLE-FACED WALL FORMWORK	**APP.C1**
	Job Ref **A/C1**	Calc by **T·C·L.**	Date **3.2.86**	Check by **P.F.P**	Date **24.5.86**

Ref	Calculations	Output

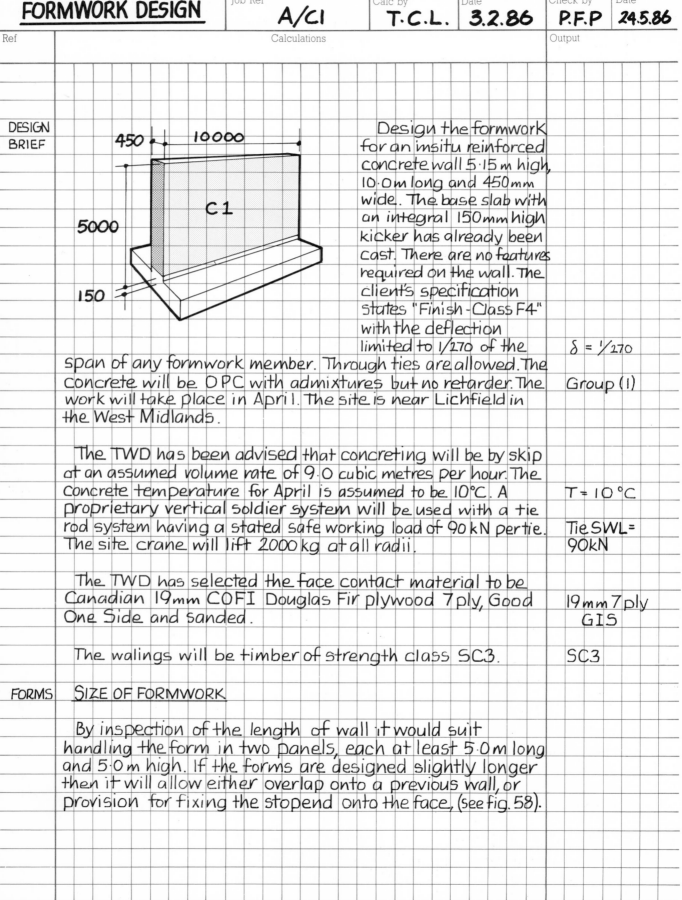

DESIGN BRIEF

Design the formwork for an insitu reinforced concrete wall 5·15 m high, 10·0 m long and 450 mm wide. The base slab with an integral 150 mm high kicker has already been cast. There are no features required on the wall. The client's specification states "Finish - Class F4" with the deflection limited to 1/270 of the span of any formwork member. Through ties are allowed. The concrete will be OPC with admixtures but no retarder. The work will take place in April. The site is near Lichfield in the West Midlands.

$\delta = 1/270$

Group (1)

The TWD has been advised that concreting will be by skip at an assumed volume rate of 9·0 cubic metres per hour. The concrete temperature for April is assumed to be 10°C. A proprietary vertical soldier system will be used with a tie rod system having a stated safe working load of 90 kN per tie. The site crane will lift 2000 kg at all radii.

$T = 10\,°C$

Tie SWL = 90 kN

The TWD has selected the face contact material to be Canadian 19 mm COFI Douglas Fir plywood 7 ply, Good One Side and sanded.

19 mm 7 ply GIS

The walings will be timber of strength class SC3.

SC3

FORMS

SIZE OF FORMWORK

By inspection of the length of wall it would suit handling the form in two panels, each at least 5·0 m long and 5·0 m high. If the forms are designed slightly longer then it will allow either overlap onto a previous wall, or provision for fixing the stopend onto the face, (see fig. 58).

concrete society

Ref	Calculations	Output.
CONCRETE PRESSURE	**CONCRETE AND CONCRETE PRESSURE CALCULATION**	

Using the concrete information in the design brief and the CIRIA method 1985 for ascertaining the concrete pressure (reproduced in Appendix E) gives :-

Concrete density of 25 kN/m³
Concrete classified as Group 1
Volume rate of delivery is 9.0 m³/h
Plan area of pour = 10 × 0.45 = 4.5 m² (A)
Hence rate of rise (R)

$$= \frac{\text{Volume rate}}{\text{Plan Area}} = \frac{9.0}{4.5} = 2.0 \, m/h \quad (R)$$

Thus from Appendix E, for temperature 10°C and extrapolating for H = 5.0 m, gives :-

$$P_{max} = \text{Maximum concrete pressure} = 62.5 \, kN/m^2$$

Output: $P_{max} = 62.5 \, kN/m^2$

The equivalent fluid head is

$$\frac{\text{Pressure}}{\text{Density}} = \frac{62.5}{25.0} = \underline{2.5 \, m}$$

The concrete pressure diagram is as opposite.

5000

2500

62.5 kN/m²

| PLY | **PLYWOOD** | |

From brief use 19mm COFI 7 ply GIS plywood. Thus from section 3.2.2.3 Table 9 the structural properties for wall formwork assuming the plywood spanning in its strong direction with the sheets vertical on horizontal walings gives :-

Bending stiffness (EI) = 3.40 kNm²/m
Moment of resistance (fZ) = 0.426 kNm/m
Shear load (qA) = 6.186 kN/m

Ref	Calculations	Output
	The plywood will span over several walings and each waling will be say 75mm wide. Thus B > (2×t) i.e. 75 > (2×19mm) use Appendix B loading case 58. Thus if centre/centre ply span is L the load on one span per metre is $$W = 62.5 \, L$$	
	Maximum moment in plywood is $$M_{max} = -0.095 \, WL = -0.095 \times 62.5 \times L^2$$ thus $0.426 = 5.938 \times L^2$ $\therefore L = 0.268 \, m$ (Note the −ve sign indicates the hogging moment at the support. The plywood is symmetrical so the limit is ± 0.426 kNm)	
	Using sheets actually 2440mm long × 1220mm wide, standard modules of the bearers gives 9 spans of 271mm or 10 spans of 244mm. Thus select the 9 spans with 1% overstress. This is normal practice with engineering judgement considering the accuracy of the selected value of 62.5 kN/m² concrete pressure. (See note (2) below.) Thus W = 62.5 × 0.271 = 16.94 kN	L = 271 mm
	The maximum shear force is thus :− $$S_{max} = 0.525 \left(\frac{L-B-t}{L} \right) W = 0.525 \left(\frac{271-75-19}{271} \right) W$$ $$= 0.525 \times 0.653 \times 16.94 = 5.807 \, kN$$ cf allowable is 6.186 kN $\therefore$ OK	
	Check deflection in a span to limit 1/270th thus $\delta = 0.0066 \dfrac{WL^3}{EI} = 0.0066 \times \dfrac{16.94 \times 0.271^3}{3.40}$ $$= 0.00065 \, m = 0.65 \, mm$$ cf allowable is $\dfrac{271}{270} = 1 \, mm$ $\therefore$ OK	$\delta = 0.65 \, mm$
	Notes : (1) Actually checking the face finish with a straight edge would measure the range. (See Appendix B.) This would increase the value from 0.65mm to 0.67mm. In practice it is the single span member deflection that is used as a design criterion. (2) The waling spacing was calculated for the maximum concrete pressure that occurs in the lower 2.5m of the form. In setting out the	

concrete society

Ref	Calculations	Output

waling positions it is normal practice to increase the spacing towards the top, thus reducing the number of walings. It is important at the design stage to consider the detail of the plywood on the walings. If the bottom of the form overlaps the kicker by say 50mm the form length is 5050mm. If the bottom sheet of plywood has a waling flush to the edge and there is a butt joint at its top then the <u>actual</u> plywood span is now

$$\frac{2440 - (75/2)}{9} = 267mm$$

and the overstress is cancelled. Assume for this example that the ply lap position is <u>not</u> known and the bottom centres are 271mm. Thus assuming the height at 5050 gives a possible waling spacing of :-

$$(10 \times 271) + (3 \times 305) + (4 \times 356)$$

(3) When using values from Appendix B, for Moment, Reactions, Shear etc the factors are <u>ALL</u> in decimals and the <u>maximum</u> value for a particular case will be the <u>largest</u> factor. For example at case 38 the maximum moment is 0.105 WL as the factor 0.105 is larger than 0.079, 0.078, 0.033 and 0.046.

WALINGS

WALINGS

Assume 75 x 150 timbers of strength class SC3 will be used.

The permissible structural values are taken from Section 3.2.1.3 Table 6 which assumes wall formwork with load sharing as four or more walings will be in contact with the plywood.

Allowable moment of resistance	= 2.017 kNm
Allowable bending stiffness	= 139.14 kNm²
Allowable shear load	= 10.80 kN
Allowable bearing stress	= 3100 kN/m²

Applied loading on one waling

Maximum distributed load on waling = 62.5 x 0.271

$$W = 16.94 \text{ kN/m}$$

Each waling will be at least 5.0m long. Select by inspection soldier centres of say 1.1m with walings spanning between. The form length, split into two for handling, will need to suit ideal plywood modules. Assume one central join and the necessity to cut one plywood sheet gives a panel length of 5.49m

Ref	Calculations	Output.

(i.e. four + one cut in half = 4.5 × 1220 = 5490 mm)
From section 5.2.2.1 and fig 58 for wall thickness up to 450mm and panel lengths greater than form heights the stopends may be secured to the panel ends. In waling design, limit any cantilever to about one third of the span.
(i.e. $\frac{1100}{3}$ = 367mm approximately in this case.)

Consider one panel with five soldiers (A to E) with walings for the loading case 37 from Appendix B2. Cantilevers assumed to be equal at a value of about one third span.

This assumption gives results which, although approximate, are sufficiently accurate for the general design of members in formwork.

$L = 1.10\,m$, $w = 16.94\,kN/m$, $W = wL = 16.94 \times 1.1 = 18.63\,kN$

$M_A = M_E \quad = -0.0556\ WL = -0.0556 \times 18.63 \times 1.1 = -1.14\,kNm$

$M_B = M_D \quad = -0.0911\ WL = -0.0911 \times 18.63 \times 1.1 = -1.87\,kNm$

$M_C \qquad = -0.079\ WL = -0.079 \times 18.63 \times 1.1 = -1.62\,kNm$

$M_{AB} = M_{DE} = 0.052\ WL = 0.052 \times 18.63 \times 1.1 = 1.07\,kNm$

$M_{BC} = M_{CD} = 0.040\ WL = 0.040 \times 18.63 \times 1.1 = 0.82\,kNm$

Thus the maximum waling B.M. (see note (3) on sheet 4) occurs at support 'B' and will be approximately −1.87 kNm (< allowable moment of resistance 2.017 kNm.)

(In practice it is not necessary to write down all the values of B.M.)

Max B.M. = −1.87 kNm

concrete
society

Ref	Calculations	Output.

CHECK SHEAR VALUES

$S_A = S_E \qquad = 0.333w = 0.333 \times 18.63 = 6.20\,kN$

$S_{AB} = S_{ED} = 0.465w = 0.465 \times 18.63 = 8.66\,kN$

$S_{BA} = S_{DE} = 0.535w = 0.535 \times 18.63 = 9.97\,kN$

$S_{BC} = S_{DC} = 0.513w = 0.513 \times 18.63 = 9.56\,kN$

$S_{CB} = S_{CD} = 0.487w = 0.487 \times 18.63 = 9.07\,kN$

The maximum shear value is 9.97 kN and the permissible shear load is 10.80 kN   ∴ O.K.
(In practice it is not necessary to write down all the values of shear force.)

Output: Max.shear = 9.97 kN

CHECK THE REACTIONS AT SUPPORTS (i.e. SOLDIER POSITION)

$R_A = R_E \qquad = 0.798w = 0.798 \times 18.63 = 14.87\,kN$

$R_B = R_D \qquad = 1.048w = 1.048 \times 18.63 = 19.52\,kN$

$R_C \qquad = 0.975w = 0.975 \times 18.63 = 18.16\,kN$

Total = 86.94 kN

Output:
14.87 kN
19.52 kN

As a check the total actual applied load is
$5.00 \times 16.94 = 84.70\,kN$. Thus the actual is 2.6% less than the assumed design load. Note that the shear values do not sum exactly to the reactions due to certain rounding up/down in the formulae for the shear forces.

CHECK DEFLECTIONS

By inspection of loading case 37 the maximum deflection occurs in span AB.
Thus deflection in 1100mm is $0.00387\dfrac{WL^3}{EI}$

$= 0.00387 \times \dfrac{18.63 \times 1.1^3}{139.14} = \delta = 0.69\,mm$

$\dfrac{\delta}{1100} = \dfrac{1}{1594} < \dfrac{1}{270}$ (Section 2.7)   ∴ O.K.

Output: $\delta = 0.69\,mm$

Ref	Calculations	Output.
SOLDIERS AND TIES		

SOLDIERS AND TIES

Assume a proprietary soldier is used and that it comprises two parts each 2.7m long, placed on the panels at five positions A to E. The selection of the vertical spacing of the tie rods will be influenced by many factors and will often be determined by experience. The principal factors are:-
1. Proprietary supplier's soldier data giving predetermined positions for the ties.
2. Concrete pressure diagram with reduction of pressure near to top of wall.
3. Size and load capacity of ties.
4. Predetermined positions as specified by client to coincide with horizontal features.
5. Economics of material and labour costs for fixing and subsequently making good tie rod positions.

Max. point load from walings at 271mm ℅ is their reactions R_B and R_D of 19.52 kN on rows B and D. By interpolation the max. equivalent U.D.L. on soldier is w = $\frac{19.52}{0.271}$ = 72.03 kN/m

SOLDIER LOADING DIAGRAM

Σw = 270.12 kN

Ref	Calculations	Output.

Consider as a beam loaded with pressure diagram and supported at tie positions. The spans are not equal and there is a variation of load shape so that a moment distribution is necessary to find the tie loads and the soldier characteristics.

Consider end spans PQ and NM as propped cantilevers.

$k_{QP} = 0.75 \;\; \frac{1}{1.5} = 0.5, \quad k_{PO} = k_{ON} = \frac{1}{1.2} = 0.83$

$k_{NM} = 0.75 \;\; \frac{1}{1} = 0.75$

$\therefore DF_{PQ} = 0.5/(0.5 + 0.83) = 0.38 \qquad DF_{OP} = 0.5$

$\quad DF_{NM} = 0.75/(0.75 + 0.83) = 0.47$

FEM PQ Approximately = −0.133 TL = −6.04 kNm (case 12)
FEM PO Approx. = −0.0833 WL − 0.0667 TL = −6.65 kNm (case 2+9)
FEM OP —— " —— = −0.0833 WL − 0.10 TL = −7.46 kNm (case 2+9)
FEM ON,NO — " —— = −0.0833 WL = −8.64 kNm (case 2)
FEM NM — " — = −0.125 WL = −9.00 kNm (case 4)
FEM MN — " — = −0.50 WL = −0.81 kNm (case 3)

(cases refer to Appendix B)

	Q	P (0.38)	P (0.62)	O (0.50)	O (0.50)	N (0.53)	N (0.47)	M	M
								+0.81	−0.81
FEM / DIST	+6.04	−6.65	+7.46	−8.64	+8.64	+8.64 / +0.40	−9.00		
	+0.23	+0.38	+0.59	+0.59	−0.02	−0.02			
CO / DIST		+0.30	+0.19	−0.01	+0.30				
	+0.11	−0.19	−0.09	−0.09	−0.16	−0.14			
CO / DIST		−0.04	−0.10	−0.08	−0.04				
	+0.02	+0.02	+0.09	+0.09	+0.02	+0.02			
	+6.18	−6.18	+8.14	−8.14	+8.74	−8.74	+0.81	−0.81	

Max. B.M. = 8.74 kNm

ELASTIC SHEAR:
```
              4.12↑5.15    6.78↑6.78    7.28↑8.74    0.81↑
↓4.12           ↓6.78    5.15↓7.28    6.78↓0.81    8.74↓
```

STATIC SHEAR:
```
↑9.76    20.54    25.07↑25.07    43.27↑43.27    36.01↑10.8
                    6.62   9.27
                    0.30   4.25
```

TOTAL SHEAR:
```
↑5.64    24.66↑30.36    40.22↑42.72    43.77↑43.94    28.08↑10.8
```

TOTAL REACTIONS:
```
 5.64        55.02          82.94          87.71          38.88
  Q            P              O              N              M
```

Max. Reaction 87.71 kN

Ref	Calculations	Output.

∴ Max. Tie load = 87.71 kN at support N

Check Σ reactions = 270.12 cf sheet 7 = Σw

∴ O.K.

From brief, tie SWL = 90 kN

∴ O.K.

Free span bending moments :−

M_{QP} approx. = 0.128 TL = $0.128 \times \frac{41.78}{2} \times 1.45 \times 1.5$ = 5.82 kN (case 8)

M_{PO} —"— = 0.125 WL + 0.128 TL = 7.52 + 3.14 = 10.66 kNm (case 1 + 8)

M_{ON} —"— = 0.125 WL = $0.125 \times 72.03 \times 1.2 \times 1.2$ = 12.97 kNm (case 1)

M_{NM} —"— = 0.125 WL = $0.125 \times 72.03 \times 1.0 \times 1.0$ = 9.00 kNm (case 1)

B.M. DIAGRAM SHOWING NET B.Ms.

The max. B.M. is 8.74 kNm occurring at support N. The net B.M. at the joint in the soldier is established by inspection from the diagram and is approx. 2.0 kNm

Hence select a tie rod system with a tie safe working load of 88 kN (See section 3.8 on form ties.)

The selection of the soldier may be made at this stage, see also section 3.6.10, or it may have been predetermined in the design brief. If the latter case, then it would be necessary to check the characteristics of the soldier as designed against the soldier suppliers information. Factors to be considered would be :−

A. Maximum positive moment in span (4.53 kNm approx)

B. Maximum negative (support) moment (8.74 kNm approx.) which occurs in combination with tie load of 87.64 kN

C. Moment at joint (2.0 kNm approx.)

WEIGHT

WEIGHT OF WALL FORM

The weight of one form panel 5.0m high and 5.49m long will be 5.0 x 5.49 x 60 = 1650 kg

$= \frac{1650}{100}$ = 16.50 kN (one face)   (Section 4.2.2. table 14)

Output: Max. tie load 87.71 kN (N)

Output: 16.5 kN/face

Ref	Calculations	Output.
STABILITY	**WALL FORM STABILITY**	

(Site is in Lichfield in the West Midlands) consider the overturning moment and/or stability moment for one panel of double face forms 5.5 m long (say) (see section 5.1.5). This assumes in the worst case one form panel erected and left on its own during a maximum wind.

Wind Moment: from section 4.5.1.2 table 18 the max. overturning moment with the full wind force will be $8.22 \times 5.50 = 45.21 \,kNm$ (case B for H = 5.0m).

(The reduced working wind overturning moment will be $3.5 \times 5.50 = 19.25 \,kNm$.)

Minimum stability moment on a wall form will be $(16.5 \times 2 \times 10\%) \times 5 \times \frac{3}{4} = 12.38 \,kN\,m$.

Consider one working platform 800mm at top of form on the outside of the soldier. It will have a lever arm about the face of the form of approximately:–
$20 + 150 + 225 + \frac{800}{2} = 795 \,mm$ (Assuming the soldier is 225mm deep).

Thus moment from platform with nominal access load from operatives (see section 4.3.2) will be:–
$5.5 \times 0.8 \times 0.795 \times (0.75 \,kN/m^2) = 2.62 \,kNm$.

When the full construction operation load is applied during concreting this increases to:–
$5.5 \times 0.8 \times 0.795 \times (1.5 \,kN/m^2) = 5.25 \,kNm$.

Consider the three stability checks (section 5.1.5) gives:–

(1) Full wind + nominal access load

    45.21   +   2.62   = 47.83 kNm.

(2) Working wind + full platform

    19.25   +   5.25   = 24.50 kNm.

(3) Min. stability + full platform

    12.38   +   5.25   = 17.63 kNm.

Thus on each panel 5.5m long supply propping for an overturning moment of $47.83 \times 1.2 = 57.40 \,kNm$ where 1.2 is the minimum factor of safety on overturning stated in section 5.1.5.

Output: 57.40 kNm

Use 2 N° proprietary push-pull props connected to a point 3.0 m up the form on <u>one</u> side only, at an angle of 60° to the horizontal.

Ref	Calculations	Output.
	Horizontal force / prop $= \dfrac{57 \cdot 40}{3m \times 2 N^{o}} = 9.57\,kN$	
	$\therefore$ Load in prop $= \pm\ 9.57 \times \dfrac{2}{1} = 19.14\,kN$	19.14 kN/prop
	The anchorage for each prop will be required to resist the design forces as follows :–	
	Vertical $= \dfrac{19.14}{2} \times \sqrt{3} = 16.58\,kN$	
	Horizontal $= 9.57\,kN$	
	Note: The factor of safety has already been included and these values are the required restraint forces at the anchorage.	

APPENDIX C2 WORKED EXAMPLE OF FORMWORK DESIGN	Project **WOLVERHAMPTON**	Sheet **1 of 9**
	Part of Structure **SQUARE COLUMN FORMWORK**	Drg Ref **APP.C2**
	Job Ref **A/C2** · Calc by **T.C.L** · Date **4.2.86**	Check by **P.F.P.** · Date **26.6.86**

Ref	Calculations	Output

DESIGN BRIEF

975 · 975

4600

C2

COLUMN (SQUARE)

Design the formwork for an insitu reinforced concrete column of square plan 975mm x 975mm and 4.60m high. There are six columns to be constructed. The client's specification requires an F3 high class finish without ties and no features on the faces. The corners are to be cast with 20x20 mm chamfers. The base to each column will have a small kicker for alignment of the formwork.

Output: 20×20 chamfers

The concrete will contain a blend of OPC with less than 40% pulverised fuel ash and will have a pumping admixture, but no retarder. The work will be carried out during a short construction period in summer and the expected concrete temperature will be 15°C. The form will be filled in just over one hour.

Output: Group (5)

Output: T = 15°C

The contract has already purchased stocks of 18mm Finnish Birch plywood in 1200 x 2400 sheet sizes. It is 13 ply.

Output: 18mm Birch 13 ply

The TWD has decided to use Strength Class SC4 backing timbers placed vertically and with structural steel yokes at varying centres horizontally to suit the concrete pressure. Stability and alignment will be from an erected scaffold around the column form, previously used for fixing the reinforcement.

Output: SC4 timber

(This example only designs the forms.)

CONCRETE PRESSURE

CONCRETE PRESSURE CALCULATIONS

The volume of concrete is small (4.37m³) and it is placed quickly in just over one hour. Thus the vertical rate of rise is about 4 metres per hour. The concrete is Group 5 at a temperature of 15°C.

Ref	Calculations	Output

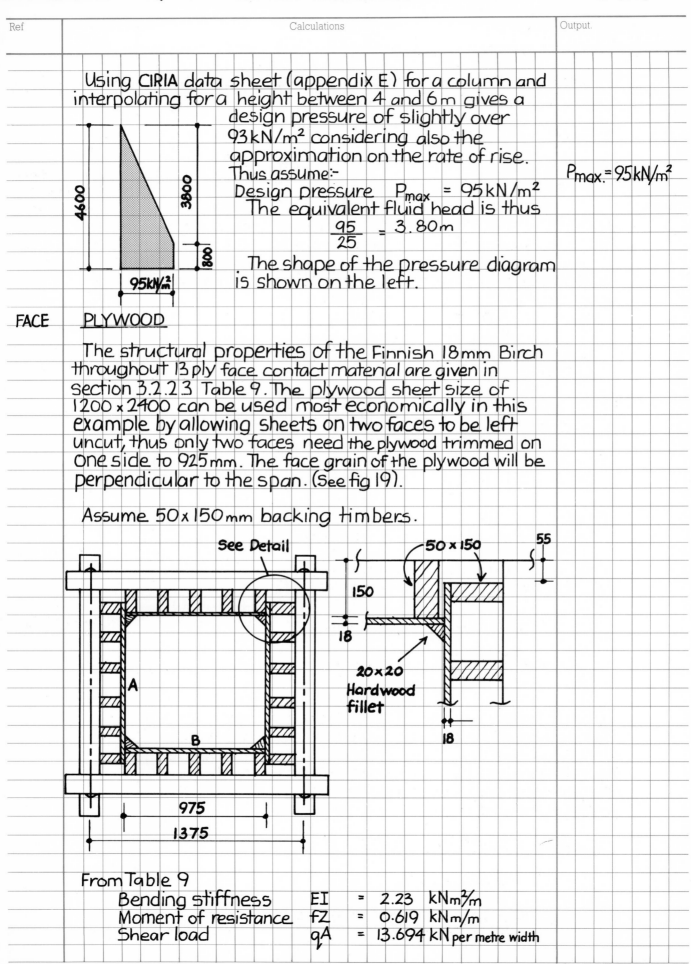

Using CIRIA data sheet (appendix E) for a column and interpolating for a height between 4 and 6 m gives a design pressure of slightly over 93 kN/m² considering also the approximation on the rate of rise. Thus assume:-

Design pressure P_{max} = 95 kN/m²

The equivalent fluid head is thus

$$\frac{95}{25} = 3.80 \, m$$

The shape of the pressure diagram is shown on the left.

$P_{max} = 95 \, kN/m^2$

FACE PLYWOOD

The structural properties of the Finnish 18mm Birch throughout 13 ply face contact material are given in section 3.2.2.3 Table 9. The plywood sheet size of 1200 x 2400 can be used most economically in this example by allowing sheets on two faces to be left uncut, thus only two faces need the plywood trimmed on one side to 925mm. The face grain of the plywood will be perpendicular to the span. (See fig 19).

Assume 50 x 150 mm backing timbers.

From Table 9

Bending stiffness	EI	=	2.23	kNm²/m
Moment of resistance	fZ	=	0.619	kNm/m
Shear load	qA	=	13.694	kN per metre width

Ref	Calculations	Output.

Inspection of the proposed layout of the vertical timbers gives plywood spans of :-

Side (A) of $\dfrac{1200-50}{5}$ = 230 mm

Side (B) of $\dfrac{975-50-5}{4}$ = 230 mm

Plywood span
230mm

(Often the spacing will be different from side to side and the timbers designed for the worst case.)

Using loading case 58 (Appendix B) for the plywood across either 5 or 6 supports gives :-

Maximum moment = 0.095 WL

where W = 95 × L

Thus limiting span of the plywood is

$0.095 \times 95 \times L^2$ = 0.619

∴ L_{max} = 0.262 m = 262 mm

Checking the shear in the plywood gives

$S = 0.525 \left(\dfrac{L-B-t}{L}\right) W$

$= 0.525 \left(\dfrac{230-50-18}{230}\right) \times 95 \times 0.23$

Shear = 8.08 kN

cf allowable 13.69 ∴ O.K.

Checking deflection of the plywood gives

$\delta = 0.0066 \times \dfrac{WL^3}{EI} = 0.0066 \times \dfrac{95 \times 0.23 \times 0.23^3}{2.23}$

= 0.00079 m = 0.79 mm

Ply δ = 0.79mm

Allowable is $\dfrac{230}{270}$ = 0.85 mm

∴ O.K.

Check to see whether two timbers can be omitted near the top. The plywood would span three supports at 460 mm centres. Thus from loading case 21 (Appendix B) the relationship between the moment of resistance of the plywood and the concrete pressure at the limiting point (P_L) is given by :-

Moment = 0.125 WL = $0.125 \times P_L \times 0.46^2$

= 0.619 kNm/m

Thus $P_L = \dfrac{0.619}{0.125 \times 0.46^2}$ = 23.4 kN/m²

Ref	Calculations	Output.

Thus the timbers could be reduced at a level $\dfrac{23.4}{25}$

= 936 mm from the top, by considering the moment of resistance only. In practice on such a column of 4.6m height the timbers would be taken full height and not stopped short.

The reaction onto the backing timbers is thus a maximum at the bottom of the form.

UDL on timbers = 95 x 0.23 x 1.0 = 21.85 kN/m

(The factor 1.0 is from loading case 58.)

VERTICAL TIMBERS

VERTICAL BACKING TIMBERS

The design brief assumes 50 x 150 timbers of strength Class SC4. There are more than 4 timbers and load sharing can be assumed. The structural properties of the timber are given in Section 3.2.1.3 Table 6, ie:

Bending stiffness   EI   =   101.79 kNm²
Moment of resistance fZ   =   1.868 kNm
Shear load   qA   =   7.47 kN
Bearing stress   =   3370 kN/m²(no wane)

The selection of the yoke centres vertically is by experience, and will vary to suit the height of the column and the design concrete pressure. They will be closer together near to the bottom of the column. The design procedure involves selecting an arrangement and carrying out a moment distribution to establish the design criteria for the vertical timber members.

LOADING DIAGRAM

concrete society

Ref	Calculations	Output.

Assume 5 No yokes at A, B, C, D and E.

The fixed end moments are calculated using Appendix B and loading Cases 2, 3, 4, 9 and 10.

FEM

FEM
$M_{AB} = 0.33$ $M_{BA} = 0.92 + 0.94 = 1.86$
$M_{BC} = 0.98 + 0.19 = 1.17$ $M_{CB} = 0.98 + 0.29 = 1.27$
$M_{CD} = 0.82 + 0.08 = 0.90$ $M_{DC} = 0.82 + 0.12 = 0.94$
$M_{DE} = 0.98$ $M_{ED} = 0.44$

Stiffness $k_{AB} = \frac{3}{4} \, {}^{I}\!/_{1.35} = 0.556$ $k_{BC} = {}^{I}\!/_{1.0} = 1.00$
$k_{DE} = \frac{3}{4} \, {}^{I}\!/_{0.60} = 1.250$ $k_{CD} = {}^{I}\!/_{0.75} = 1.333$

DF

Distribution factors
BA/BC 0.36/0.64
CB/CD 0.43/0.57
DC/DE 0.52/0.48

Ref	A		B		C		D		E		Output
DF	1		0.36	0.64	0.43	0.57	0.52	0.48			
Co	+0.33	−0.33							+0.44	−0.44	
			−0.17				+0.22				
FEM			+1.86	−1.17	+1.27	−0.90	+0.94	−0.98			
			−0.19	−0.33	−0.16	−0.21	−0.09	−0.09			
Co				−0.08	−0.17	−0.05	−0.11				
			+0.03	+0.05	+0.09	+0.13	+0.06	+0.05			
Co				+0.05	+0.02	+0.03	+0.06				
			−0.02	−0.03	−0.02	−0.03	−0.03	−0.03			
BM	+0.33	−0.33	+1.51	−1.51	+1.03	−1.03	+0.83	−0.83	+0.44	−0.44	MOMENTS
SHEAR (Static)	1.41↑	2.72↑	2.72↑	5.90↑	5.90↑	6.58↑	6.58↑	6.55↑	6.55↑	4.37↑	
		1.75↑	3.49↑	0.96↑	1.92↑	0.54↑	1.08↑				
(Elastic)		0.87↓	0.87↑	0.48↑	0.48↓	0.26↑	0.26↓	0.65↑	0.65↓		
	1.41	3.60	7.08	7.34	7.34	7.38	7.40	7.20	5.90	4.37	SHEARS
	A		B		C		D		E		
	5.01 kN		14.42 kN		14.72 kN		14.60 kN		10.27 kN		REACTIONS

The maximum Negative Bending moment is 1.51 kNm
(Allowable is 1.868 ∴ O.K.)

Max. B.M.
1.51 kNm

Ref	Calculations	Output.
	The maximum Shear Force is 7.40 kN at S_{DC} (Allowable is 7.47 kN ∴ O.K.)	Shear 7.40 kN
	The maximum load onto the yoke will be at yoke C of 14.72 kN per timber (230 %)	
	Check design of yoke and include a check on the bearing stress of the timber onto the yoke flanges.	
YOKE	<u>DESIGN OF STEEL YOKES — HORIZONTAL</u>	
	Consider the use of twin 127 x 64 mm rolled steel channel sections in Grade 43 mild steel for the horizontal yokes. End tie rods of 20mmØ mild steel all thread rod will connect opposite pairs of channels	

Properties of 127 x 64 mm RSC from Property Tables are

Weight		=	14.90 kg /m
Depth of Section	(D)	=	127.0 mm
Width of Section	(B)	=	63.5 mm
Web thickness	(t_w)	=	6.4 mm
Flange thickness	(T)	=	9.2 mm
Radius of Gyration	r_y	=	18.8 mm
Moment of Inertia	I_{xx}	=	482.5 cm^4
Elastic Modulus	Z	=	75.99 cm^3

Thus $D/T = \frac{127}{9.2} = 13.80$

Consider Side A and Side B. The loading patterns with approximate reactions will be :–

See Sheet (2)

7.36kN	14.72kN	7.36kN

14.72kN   14.72kN

227.5 ↓   230 ↓ 230 ↓ 230 ↓230 ↓227.5   (B)

F   1375   G

14.72 kN   14.72 kN

14.72kN   14.72kN

342.5 ↓   230 ↓ 230 ↓ 230 ↓ 342.5   (A)

H   1375   J

$$R_F = R_G = R_H = R_J = \frac{4 \times 14.72}{2} = 29.44 \text{ kN}$$

Thus the tie load is 29.44 kN. From section 3.8.3 the minimum factor of safety on mild steel ties is 2.5 thus the required minimum failure load is
29.44 kN x 2.5 = 74 kN.

Tie Load 29.44 kN

Ref	Calculations	Output.

(Note: Typical proprietary M20 ties state failure loads of 120 kN.)

Check the actual bending moment for both case A and case B. Use typical loading formula from 'Steel Designers Handbook' (Ref. 133.) gives :-

$$M_{FG} = \left(\frac{14.72}{2} \times 0.688\right) + (14.72 \times 0.458)$$
$$+ (7.36 \times 0.228)$$
$$= 5.06 + 6.742 + 1.678$$
$$= 13.48 \, kNm$$

$$M_{HJ} = (14.72 \times 0.573) + (14.72 \times 0.343)$$
$$= 8.435 + 5.049 = 13.48 \, kNm$$

Thus maximum BM is 13.48 kNm

Output: BM = 13.48 kNm

From BS 5975, Table 34 (Ref. 2) the effective length of the twin channels is

$$L = 1.2 \, (L + 2D) = 1.2 \, (1375 + (2 \times 127))$$
$$= 1955 \, mm$$

Thus $\frac{L}{r_y} = \frac{1955}{18.8} = 104$

Hence from BS 5975 Table 21 (Ref. 2) the permissible bending stress is

$$P_{bc} = 165 \, N/mm^2$$

Actual bending stress is

$$f = \frac{M}{Z} = \frac{13.48}{75.99} \times \frac{10^6}{2 \times 10^3} = 88.7 \, N/mm^2$$
$$\therefore \underline{O.K.}$$

Output: Bending Stress 88.7 N/mm²

(Note the x2 in bottom line for the twin channels.)

Check bearing stress on backing timbers

$$f_b = \frac{14.72}{50 \times 63.5 \times 2} \times 10^6 = 2318 \, kN/m^2$$

Output: Bearing Stress 2318 kN/m²

(Allowable is 2670 with wane and 3370 without wane.)
$$\therefore \underline{O.K.}$$

Ref	Calculations	Output.

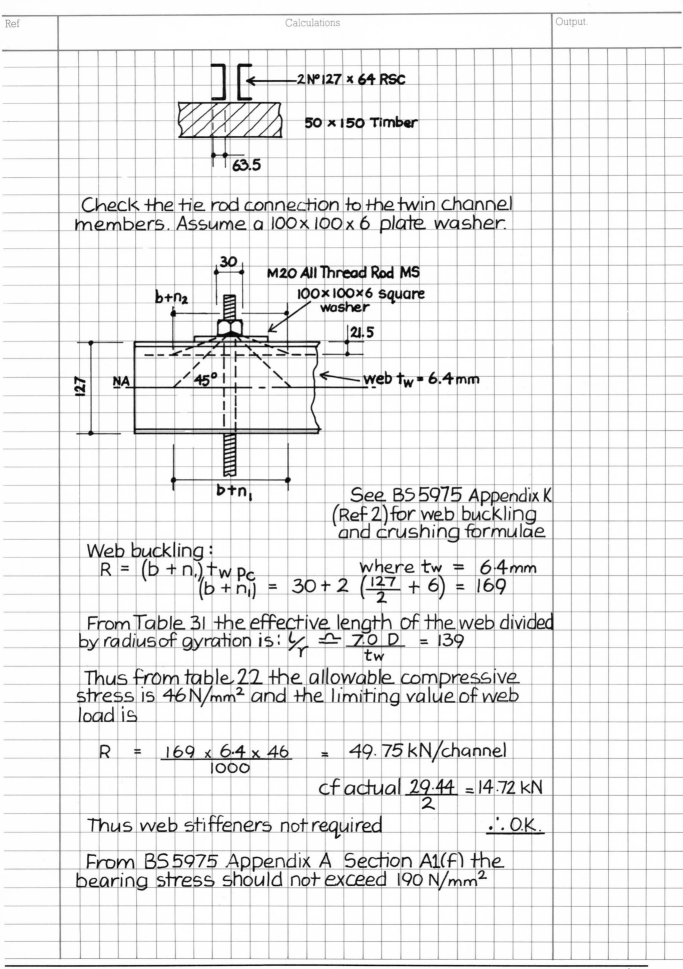

2 N° 127 × 64 RSC

50 × 150 Timber

63.5

Check the tie rod connection to the twin channel members. Assume a 100 × 100 × 6 plate washer.

30

M20 All Thread Rod MS

100 × 100 × 6 square washer

$b + n_2$

21.5

127

NA   45°

web t_w = 6.4 mm

$b + n_1$

See BS 5975 Appendix K (Ref 2) for web buckling and crushing formulae

Web buckling:
$$R = \frac{(b + n_1) \, t_w \, p_c}{}$$

where t_w = 6.4 mm

$$(b + n_1) = 30 + 2\left(\frac{127}{2} + 6\right) = 169$$

From Table 31 the effective length of the web divided by radius of gyration is: $\dfrac{l}{r} \simeq \dfrac{7.0 \, D}{t_w} = 139$

Thus from table 22 the allowable compressive stress is 46 N/mm² and the limiting value of web load is

$$R = \frac{169 \times 6.4 \times 46}{1000} = 49.75 \text{ kN/channel}$$

cf actual $\dfrac{29.44}{2} = 14.72$ kN

Thus web stiffeners not required ∴ O.K.

From BS 5975 Appendix A Section A1(f) the bearing stress should not exceed 190 N/mm²

concrete society

Ref	Calculations	Output.
	The dispersion angle for web crushing is 30° and gives a length $(b + n_2)$.	

(See BS 5975 Appendix K2 (b) (Ref 2) and Figure 27 in the same standard.)

$$(b + n_2) = (30 + 2) \times 21.5 / \tan 30°$$

$$= 104mm$$

Thus web crushing is critical at a load of

$$R = \frac{104 \times 6.4 \times 190}{1000} = 126kN$$

Actual is $\frac{29.44}{2} = 14.72\ kN$

∴ O.K.

Hence twin 127 x 64 RSC Mild Steel twin channel sections acceptable.

Output: Use] [twin 127 x 64 RSC

APPENDIX C3 **WORKED EXAMPLE OF** **FORMWORK DESIGN**	Project **BRIDGE, POLSTRONG**		Sheet **1 of 6**
	Part of Structure **SOFFIT FORMWORK TO DECK (WITH VOIDS)**		Drg Ref **APP.C3**
	Job Ref **A/C3**	Calc by **T.C.L** Date **5.2.86**	Check by **P.F.P.** Date **1.4.86**

Ref	Calculations	Output
	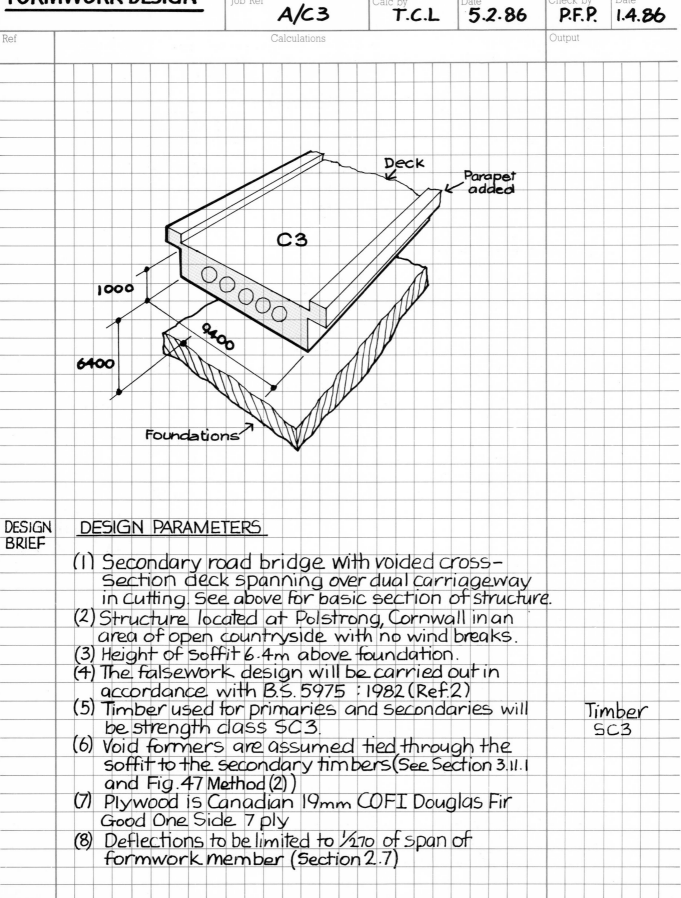	
DESIGN BRIEF	<u>DESIGN PARAMETERS</u>	

(1) Secondary road bridge with voided cross-section deck spanning over dual carriageway in cutting. See above for basic section of structure.

(2) Structure located at Polstrong, Cornwall in an area of open countryside with no wind breaks.

(3) Height of soffit 6.4m above foundation.

(4) The falsework design will be carried out in accordance with B.S. 5975 : 1982 (Ref.2)

(5) Timber used for primaries and secondaries will be strength class SC3.

(6) Void formers are assumed tied through the soffit to the secondary timbers (See Section 3.11.1 and Fig.47 Method (2))

(7) Plywood is Canadian 19mm COFI Douglas Fir Good One Side 7 ply

(8) Deflections to be limited to 1/270 of span of formwork member (Section 2.7)

Output column:
Timber SC3

concrete society

Ref	Calculations	Output.

LOADING

LOADING

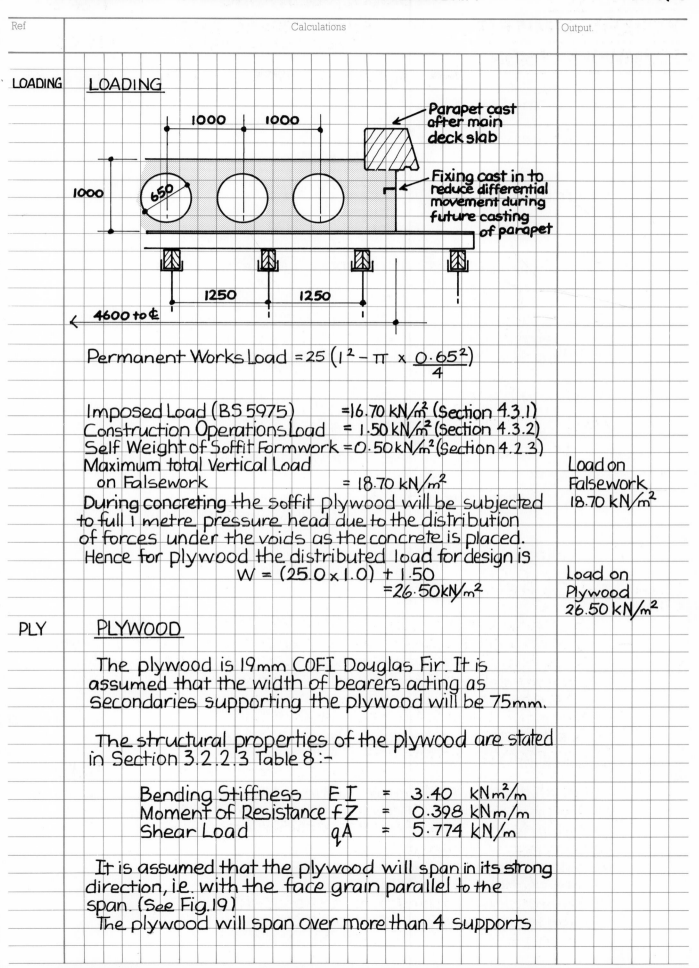

Permanent Works Load $= 25 \left(1^2 - \pi \times \dfrac{0.65^2}{4}\right)$

Imposed Load (BS 5975)	$= 16.70$ kN/m² (Section 4.3.1)
Construction Operations Load	$= 1.50$ kN/m² (Section 4.3.2)
Self Weight of Soffit Formwork	$= 0.50$ kN/m² (Section 4.2.3)
Maximum total Vertical Load on Falsework	$= 18.70$ kN/m²

Output: Load on Falsework 18.70 kN/m²

During concreting the soffit plywood will be subjected to full 1 metre pressure head due to the distribution of forces under the voids as the concrete is placed. Hence for plywood the distributed load for design is
$$W = (25.0 \times 1.0) + 1.50$$
$$= 26.50 \text{ kN/m}^2$$

Output: Load on Plywood 26.50 kN/m²

PLY

PLYWOOD

The plywood is 19mm COFI Douglas Fir. It is assumed that the width of bearers acting as secondaries supporting the plywood will be 75mm.

The structural properties of the plywood are stated in Section 3.2.2.3 Table 8 :-

Bending Stiffness	EI	$=$	3.40 kNm²/m
Moment of Resistance	fZ	$=$	0.398 kNm/m
Shear Load	qA	$=$	5.774 kN/m

It is assumed that the plywood will span in its strong direction, i.e. with the face grain parallel to the span. (See Fig. 19)
The plywood will span over more than 4 supports

Ref	Calculations	Output.

and B > 2t thus use Appendix B loading Case 5B formula :-

Maximum Moment in ply is 0.095 WL
where W = 26.5 x L

Hence   0.398 = 0.095 x 26.5 x L^2

Thus   L = 0.398m = 398 mm

Using 2440 mm sheets of plywood a suitable module is thus $\frac{2440}{6}$ = 406 mm

This represents only a 2% overstress on moment considerations. This in practice is reasonable provided the shear and deflection are not exceeded.

Checking the shear on the 406mm span gives :-

$$S = 0.525 \left(\frac{L-B-t}{L} \right) W$$

$$= 0.525 \left(\frac{406-75-19}{406} \right) 26.5 \times 0.406$$

$$= 4.34 \text{ kN/m}$$

Allowable is 5.774 kN/m
∴ O.K.

Output: Span 406mm

Checking the deflection gives

$$\delta = 0.0066 \times \frac{WL^3}{EI}$$

$$= 0.0066 \times \frac{26.5 \times 0.406 \times 0.406^3}{3.40}$$

$$= 0.000140 = 1.40 \text{ mm}$$

Output: $\delta_{ply} = 1.40$ mm

Permitted deflection is $\frac{406}{270}$ = 1.50 mm

∴ O.K.

Ref: SEC. TIMBERS

SECONDARY TIMBERS

Use 75 x 150 mm SC3 constructional timber at 406mm %c. Try primaries at 1250 mm centres so that the secondaries have to span 1.25 m. This dimension, in some cases, is preselected due to the choice of a modular support falsework system.

From section 3.2.1.3 Table 5

Moment of resistance	= 1.882 kN m.
Shear Load	= 10.08 kN
Bending Stiffness	= 139.14 kN m^2

concrete society

Ref	Calculations	Output.
	The distributed load on secondaries (max.) under voids will pick up the full design forces due to the method of restraint of voids, thus $(25+1.5+0.5) \times 0.406 = 10.96$ kN/m run. Thus load on one span of secondaries will be $W = 10.96 \times 1.25 = 13.70$ kN. Using loading Case 26 from Appendix B2 and assuming secondaries supplied in 3.95m min. length max. B.M. = 0.10 WL $= 0.10 \times 13.70 \times 1.25 = 1.71$ kNm < 1.88 kNm $\therefore$ OK	Max. B.M.= 1.71 kNm
	Max Shear = 0.6W $= 0.6 \times 13.7 = 8.22$ kN < 10.08 kN $\therefore$ OK	Max Shear = 8.22 kN
	Check max. deflection $= 0.00688 \dfrac{WL^3}{EI}$ $= 0.00688 \times \dfrac{13.7 \times 1.25^3}{139.14} = 0.00132$ m $= 1.32$ mm Limiting deflection to $\frac{1}{270} \times 1250$ mm $= 4.6$ mm $\therefore$ OK Thus centres of primaries at 1.25m is acceptable.	δ max = 1.32 mm
PRIMARY TIMBER	## PRIMARY TIMBER Use twin 75x225 Sc3 timbers at 1.25m %c spanning 1.50 m say. This may also be preselected due to the type of support falsework selected. The distributed load on primary timbers is only the actual load ie. $(16.70 + 1.50 + 0.5) \times 1.25 = 23.38$ kN/m run Thus load on one span of primaries is $W = 23.38 \times 1.50 = 35.07$ kN. Assume primaries fit over a min. of 3 spans: Hence use loading Case 26 Appendix B2. The structural properties of the primary timbers are stated in section 3.2.1.3 Table 4. Max. B.M. = 0.10 WL = $0.10 \times 35.07 \times 1.5$ = 5.26 kNm Allowable moment of resistance of twin 75 x 225 is 2×3.74 kNm = 7.48 kNm $\therefore$ O.K. Max. shear force = 0.60W = $0.6 \times 35.07 = 21.04$ kN Permissible shear load in two is = $2 \times 13.84 = 27.68$ kN $\therefore$ O.K.	Max. B.M.= 5.26 kNm Max Shear = 21.04 kN

Ref	Calculations	Output.
	Max. deflection $= 0.00688 \frac{WL^3}{EI}$ $= 0.00688 \times \frac{35.07 \times 1.5^3}{315.69 \times 2} = 0.00129\,m = 1.29\,mm$ Limiting deflection to $\frac{1}{270} \times 1500 = 5.5\,mm \therefore O.K.$ (Section 2.7) Thus centres of supporting falsework at 1.50 m is acceptable for the twin timbers.	$\delta\,max. = 1.29\,mm$
FALSE-WORK	## FALSEWORK The falsework grid will be $1.25 \times 1.50\,m$. From B.S.5975 the design vertical load per standard $= 1.25 \times 1.50 \times 18.70$ $= 35.06 + 10\%$ (B.S. 5975:1982 clause 43.3.1) $= 38.57\,kN$ This assumes the random placing of secondary and primary timbers which is good common practice in soffit formwork. Thus use a 40kN capacity falsework support system.	Leg load = 38.57 kN
WIND FORCES	## WIND FORCES From B.S. 5975, Clause 28.1 for the specified site Basic Wind Speed $V = 46\,m/sec$ (B.S. 5975 Fig.3) Factors $S_1 = 1.0$, $S_2 = 0.91$, $S_3 = 0.77$ Hence Design Wind Speed $V_s = 46 \times 1 \times 0.91 \times 0.77$ $= 32.2\,m/sec.$ From B.S. 5975, Table 12 the design wind pressure $q\,max. = 0.64\,kN/m^2$ (A) <u>WIND ON SOFFIT TIMBERS</u> : $W_m = q\,A_e\,c_f\,\eta$ Consider the wind blowing parallel to the secondary beams (B.S. 5975, Clause 28.1.12.2 (a)) $c_f = 2.0$, $\eta = 1.0$, $A_e = \left(\frac{19 + 150 + 225}{1000}\right) = 0.394\,m^2/m$ $\therefore \Sigma A_e\,c_f = 0.788\,m^2/m$ (B) <u>WIND ON SIDE FORMS</u> : Consider only the two edge forms (B.S. 5975, clause 28.1.12.2 (c).) $c_f = 1.8$, $A_e = 1.00$ Spacing of edge forms $l_w = 9200 > 8d$ (8000) Hence $\eta = 1$ $\Sigma A_e\,c_f = 1.0\,(1.8 \times 2.0) = 3.6\,m^2/m$ Maximum wind force on formwork $= (0.788 + 3.600) \times 0.64 = 2.81\,kN/m$ length of bridge. Vertical falsework standards are at 1.50m centres in the line of the bridge centre line. Thus wind force/row $= 2.81 \times 1.50 = 4.22\,kN/row$	

concrete society

Ref	Calculations	Output.
	This is the maximum wind force during the life of the falsework = W_m.	

This is the maximum wind force during the life of the falsework = W_m.

Considering the working wind W_W (Ref. B.S.5975, clause 42.1.3.1.)

$$W_W = \frac{4.22 \times 0.20}{0.64} = 1.32 \text{ kN/row}$$

Hence the supporting falsework will need to be designed to resist the above forces + wind loading on falsework at various stages of construction.

Minimum lateral stability design requirements to be the greater of (a) or (b) (B.S.5975, clause 43.4.1.):

(a) Identifiable horizontal loads + 1% vertical load.

(b) 2½% vertical load.

THE FALSEWORK DESIGN NOT COMPLETED IN THIS FORMWORK GUIDE

VOID FLOTATION

Assuming the voids are of circular shape and that the flotation is taken on full displacement of concrete. Thus flotation per void is :–

U = Volume × Density

$$= \frac{\pi \times 0.65^2}{4} \times 1 \times 25 = 8.31 \text{ kN/m}$$

Thus fitting restraints to alternate secondary bearers gives design load/fitting of

$U = 2 \times 0.406 \times 8.31 = 6.75 \text{ kN}$

Note: The fixings to the secondary timbers should be designed for this load as the design uplift load. There will be an inherent factor of safety in any bolts, banding etc., so it is not necessary to apply a factor on this value.

Ref column note: VOID FLOTATION

APPENDIX C4 WORKED EXAMPLE OF FORMWORK DESIGN	Project M25 UNDERBRIDGE			Sheet 1 of 14	
	Part of Structure INCLINED DOUBLE-FACED WALL FORMWORK			Drg Ref APP.C4	
	Job Ref A/C4	Calc by T.C.L.	Date 19.11.85	Check by P.F.P.	Date 15.12.85

Ref	Calculations	Output

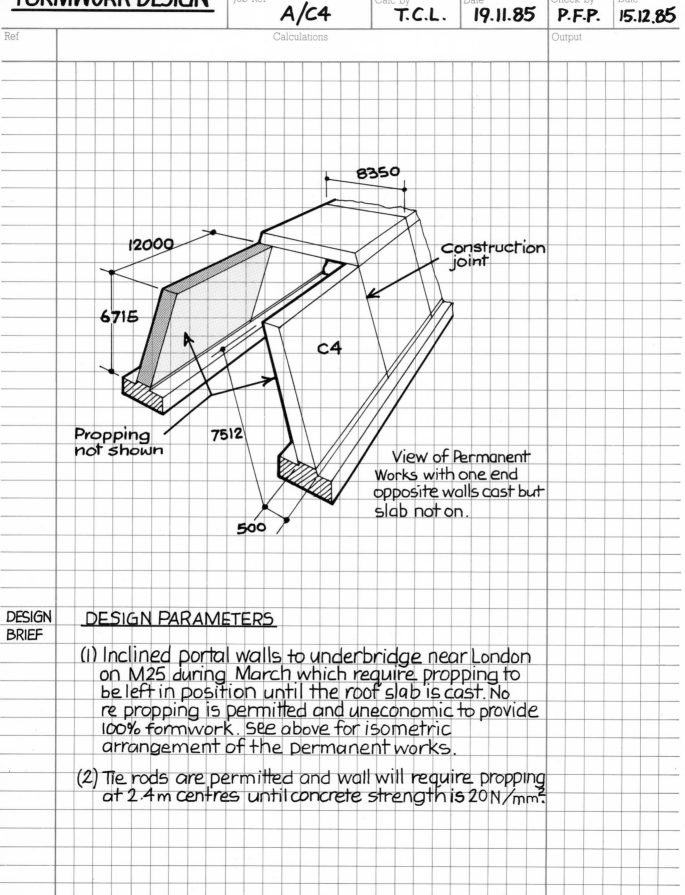

8350

12000

6715

Construction joint

C4

Propping not shown

7512

500

View of Permanent Works with one end opposite walls cast but slab not on.

DESIGN BRIEF

DESIGN PARAMETERS

(1) Inclined portal walls to underbridge near London on M25 during March which require propping to be left in position until the roof slab is cast. No re propping is permitted and uneconomic to provide 100% formwork. See above for isometric arrangement of the permanent works.

(2) Tie rods are permitted and wall will require propping at 2.4m centres until concrete strength is 20 N/mm².

concrete society

APPENDIX C4. INCLINED DOUBLE-FACED WALL FORMWORK

Ref	Calculations	Output

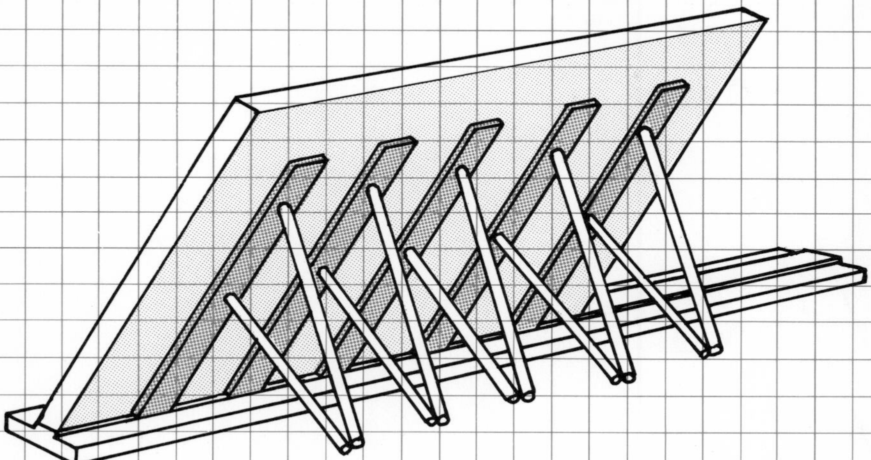

SCHEMATIC VIEW OF WALL PROPPING

(3) Panels of formwork between propping may be removed provided the props are not disturbed.

(4) All timberwork to be Strength Class SC4.

Timbers SC4

(5) Use Plywood Face of 19mm COFI Douglas Fir 7 ply Good One Side.

(6) Walls and underbridge are 48m long cast in four 12m long pours.

(7) Concrete will be Ordinary Portland Cement without admixtures. The method of placing gives a volume rate of 15 cubic metres per hour.

Concrete Group (1)

(8) Assume in March the concrete temperature is 10°C.

(9) Limit deflection of formwork members to 1/270 of span.

(10) Select a proprietary soldier system with tie rods limited to a safe working load of 95kN each.

Ref	Calculations	Output.
SHAPE		

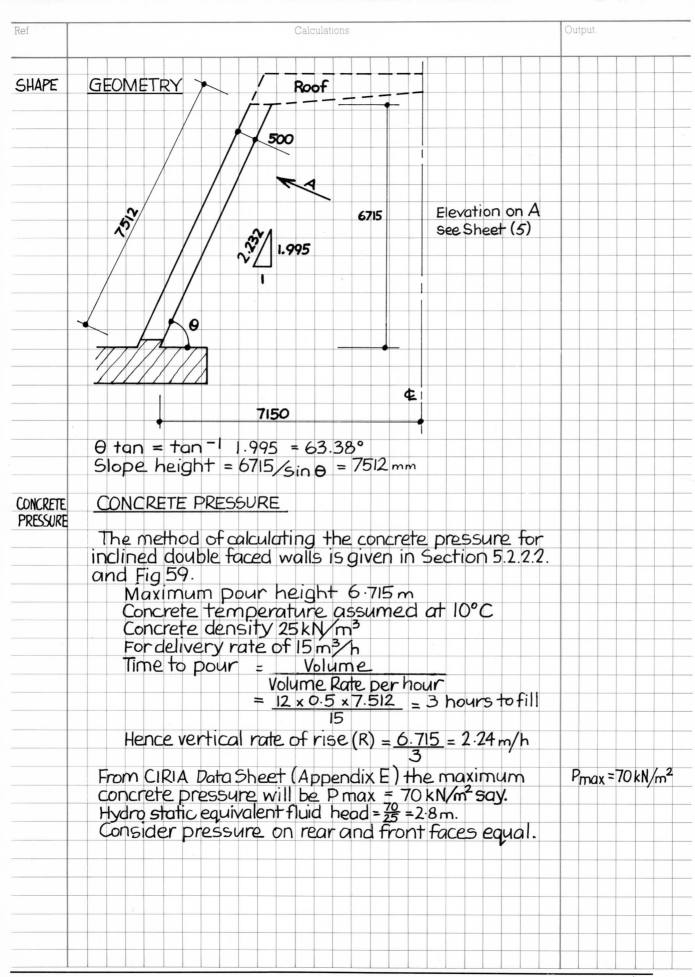

GEOMETRY

Roof

500

A

7512

2.232 1.995

6715

Elevation on A
see Sheet (5)

θ

7150

$\tan \theta = \tan^{-1} 1.995 = 63.38°$

Slope height $= 6715 / \sin \theta = 7512$ mm

CONCRETE PRESSURE

CONCRETE PRESSURE

The method of calculating the concrete pressure for inclined double faced walls is given in Section 5.2.2.2. and Fig 59.

Maximum pour height 6·715 m
Concrete temperature assumed at 10°C
Concrete density 25 kN/m³
For delivery rate of 15 m³/h

Time to pour $= \dfrac{\text{Volume}}{\text{Volume Rate per hour}}$

$= \dfrac{12 \times 0.5 \times 7.512}{15} = 3$ hours to fill

Hence vertical rate of rise (R) $= \dfrac{6.715}{3} = 2.24$ m/h

From CIRIA Data Sheet (Appendix E) the maximum concrete pressure will be P max $= 70$ kN/m² say.

Hydro static equivalent fluid head $= \frac{70}{25} = 2.8$ m.

Consider pressure on rear and front faces equal.

$P_{max} = 70$ kN/m²

Ref	Calculations	Output.

PLY — PLYWOOD

The structural properties of the 19mm COFI Douglas Fir plywood selected are given in Section 3.2.2.3 Table 9. Assume the plywood spans vertically with the face grain parallel to the span (See Fig.19) thus :-

Bending stiffness $EI = 3.40$ kNm^2/m
Moment of resistance $fZ = 0.426$ kNm/m
Shear load $qA = 6.186$ kN/m

Assume the walings are 75mm wide thus $B > 2t$ and formula from loading case 58 Appendix B can be used.

Maximum moment $= 0.095 \, WL$
where $W = 70 \times L$
Hence $0.426 = 0.095 \times 70 \times L^2$
$\therefore L = 0.253m = 253mm$

Assuming ply sheet size of 2440mm gives an ideal C/C of walings of 244mm

Output: Span of ply 244mm

Check shear of plywood gives :-
$S = 0.525 \left(\dfrac{244 - 75 - 19}{244}\right) 70 \times 0.244 = 5.51 \, kN$

Allowable shear load is 6.186kN $\therefore$ O.K.

Check plywood deflection gives :-
$\delta = 0.0066 \times \dfrac{70 \times 0.244 \times 0.244^3}{3.40} = 0.00048$

$= 0.48mm$
Allowable is $\dfrac{244}{170} = 0.90mm$ $\therefore$ O.K.

The reaction onto the walings from the plywood is thus
$R = 70 \times 0.244 \times 1.0 = 17.08 \, kN/m$

Ref	Calculations	Output.

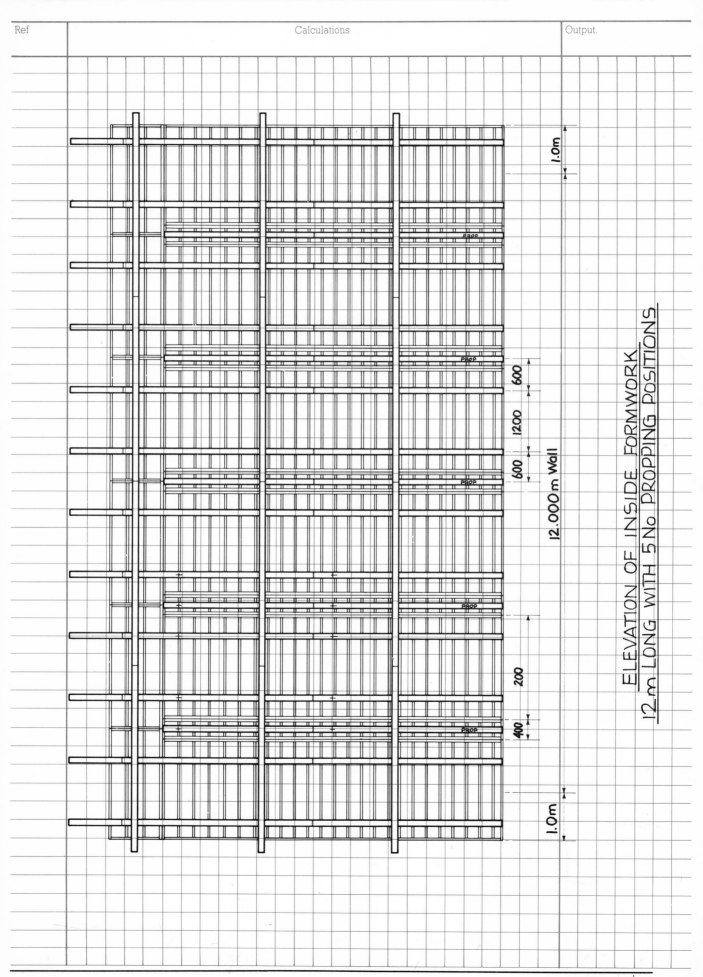

ELEVATION OF INSIDE FORMWORK
12 m LONG WITH 5 No PROPPING POSITIONS

Ref	Calculations	Output.

WALINGS

WALING TIMBERS

Try 75 x 150mm SC4 constructional timber walings at 244mm vertical centres. See elevation for layout of the members.

The concrete will span 2.4m horizontally between props at a strength of 20 N/mm², thus design props to be left undisturbed at 2.4 m C/C. Assume a 400mm section left in place gives a 2.0m panel width for reuse.

The load on the walings is 17.08 kN/m thus on 1.2 m span between soldiers gives
$$W = 17.08 \times 1.2 = 20.50 \, kN$$

It is necessary to check the inside forms and the outside forms.

Inside Forms: The layout will be as shown :–

Tie rods will be fitted through all soldier positions A, B, C and D etc.

For panel BC use loading case 6 from Appendix B.

Maximum moment is 0.0694 WL
$$= 0.0694 \times 20.50 \times 1.2$$
$$= 1.71 \, kN \, m$$

Shear load is 0.50 W = 10.25 kN

The structural properties of the 75 x 150mm SC4 timber are given in Section 3.2.2.3 Table 6 :–

Bending Stiffness = 156.54 kN m²
Moment of Resistance = 2.853 kN m
Shear Load = 11.45 kN

Thus <u>O.K.</u> for Moment and Shear capacity.

Ref	Calculations	Output.

Check deflection gives :–

$$\delta = 0.00608 \, \frac{WL^3}{EI} = \frac{0.00608 \times 20.50 \times 1.2^3}{156.54}$$

$$= 0.00138 \, m = 1.38 \, mm$$

Allowable is $\frac{1200}{270} = 4.44 \, mm$

∴ O.K.

Reaction on soldier at B is

$$R_B = 0.833 \times 20.50 = 17.08 \, kN \text{ per } 244 \, mm \text{ height.}$$

Outside Forms : On outside face there is no requirement for propping and the layout is :–

This splits the forms into three – the above is the two outer panels – the central one is slightly different.

$$M_E = 70 \times 0.244 \times 0.4 \times 0.50 \times 0.4 = 1.37 \, kN \, m$$

$$FEM_{FE} = 0.125 \times 70 \times 0.244 \times 1.2 \times 1.2 = 3.07$$

$$FEM_{FG} = FEM_{GH} = 0.0833 \times 70 \times 0.244 \times 0.6 \times 0.6$$
$$= 0.51$$

$$k_{FE} = \tfrac{3}{4} \, \tfrac{1}{1.2} = 0.625, \quad k_{FG} = \tfrac{1}{0.6} = 1.667$$

$$\therefore DF \quad FE/FG = 0.27/0.73 \quad GF = 0.5$$

concrete society

Ref	Calculations	Output.

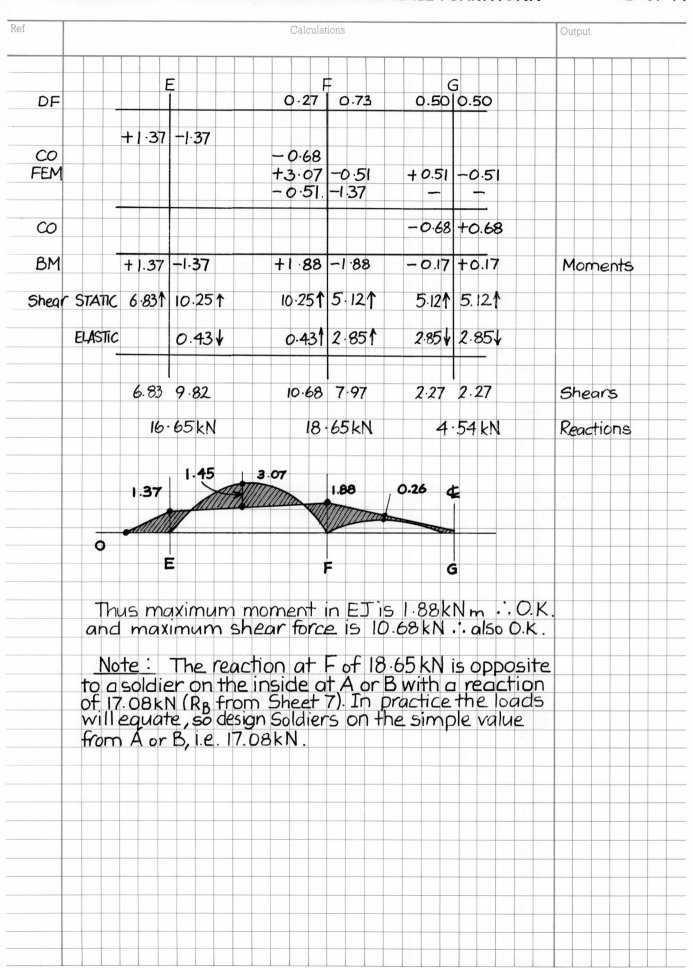

		E		F		G		
DF				0.27	0.73	0.50	0.50	
CO		+1.37	−1.37					
				−0.68				
FEM				+3.07	−0.51	+0.51	−0.51	
				−0.51	−1.37	−	−	
CO						−0.68	+0.68	
BM		+1.37	−1.37	+1.88	−1.88	−0.17	+0.17	Moments
Shear STATIC		6.83↑	10.25↑	10.25↑	5.12↑	5.12↑	5.12↑	
ELASTIC			0.43↓	0.43↑	2.85↑	2.85↓	2.85↓	
		6.83	9.82	10.68	7.97	2.27	2.27	Shears
		16.65 kN		18.65 kN		4.54 kN		Reactions

Thus maximum moment in EJ is 1.88kN m ∴ O.K. and maximum shear force is 10.68kN ∴ also O.K.

Note: The reaction at F of 18.65 kN is opposite to a soldier on the inside at A or B with a reaction of 17.08kN (R_B from Sheet 7). In practice the loads will equate, so design Soldiers on the simple value from A or B, i.e. 17.08kN.

Ref	Calculations	Output.
SOLDIERS		

SOLDIERS

Use proprietary steel soldiers and high tensile steel ties and 'she' bolts.

$$\text{Max. U.D.L. on soldier} = 70(0.4 + 0.6)$$
$$= 17.08/0.244 = 70 \text{ kN/m}$$

Note: The U.D.L. is NOT taken from the R_4 value given from the timber as this took account of the plywood continuity. In practice use overall value of load for the soldier.

From arrangement of tie positions max. B.M. and tie load will be in the lower section of wall.
Assume loading Case 38 (Appendix B)

With $W = 70 \times 1.2 = 84 \text{ kN}$

Max. B.M. at Tie $= -0.105 \times 84 \times 1.2$
$= -10.58 \text{ kNm}$

Max. Tie B.M. $= 0.078 \times 84 \times 1.2$
$= 7.86 \text{ kNm}$

Max. Tie Load $= 1.132 \times 84 = 95 \text{ kN}$

Select tie rod system with S.W.L 95 kN

The upper face of formwork and soldiers will have the forces applied as shown, but the lower face will have in addition a load arising from the propping of the sloping wall.

Output: Tie Load 95 kN

Ref	Calculations	Output.

PROPPING
CONDITION

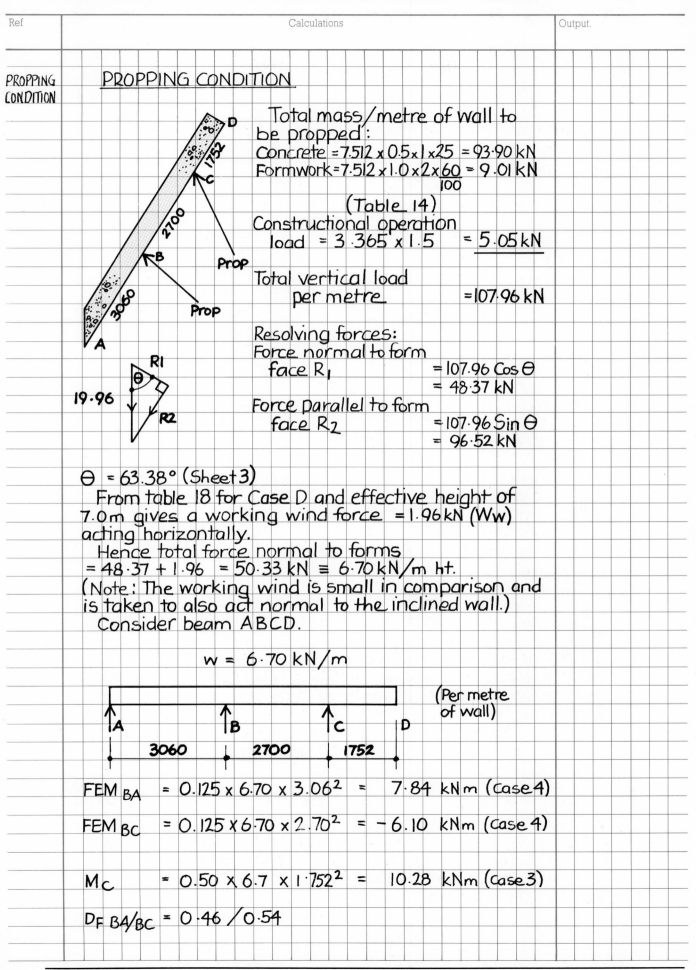

PROPPING CONDITION

Total mass/metre of wall to be propped:
Concrete = 7.512 × 0.5 × 1 × 25 = 93.90 kN
Formwork = 7.512 × 1.0 × 2 × $\frac{60}{100}$ = 9.01 kN

(Table 14)
Constructional operation
load = 3.365 × 1.5 = $\underline{5.05\,kN}$

Total vertical load
per metre = 107.96 kN

Resolving forces:
Force normal to form
face R_1 = 107.96 Cos θ
= 48.37 kN
Force parallel to form
face R_2 = 107.96 Sin θ
= 96.52 kN

θ = 63.38° (Sheet 3)
From table 18 for Case D and effective height of 7.0m gives a working wind force = 1.96 kN (W_w) acting horizontally.
Hence total force normal to forms
= 48.37 + 1.96 = 50.33 kN ≡ 6.70 kN/m ht.
(Note: The working wind is small in comparison and is taken to also act normal to the inclined wall.)
Consider beam ABCD.

w = 6.70 kN/m

(Per metre of wall)

A   3060   B   2700   C   1752   D

FEM_{BA} = 0.125 × 6.70 × 3.06² = 7.84 kNm (Case 4)

FEM_{BC} = 0.125 × 6.70 × 2.70² = −6.10 kNm (Case 4)

M_C = 0.50 × 6.7 × 1.752² = 10.28 kNm (Case 3)

$DF\ BA/BC$ = 0.46 / 0.54

APPENDIX C4. INCLINED DOUBLE-FACED WALL FORMWORK

Ref	Calculations	Output.

		B		C	
	0.46	0.54			
			+10.28	−10.28	
Moments		+5.14			
FEM	+7.84	−6.10			
Distribution	−3.16	−3.72			
Trial Moments	+4.68	−4.68	+10.28	−10.28	

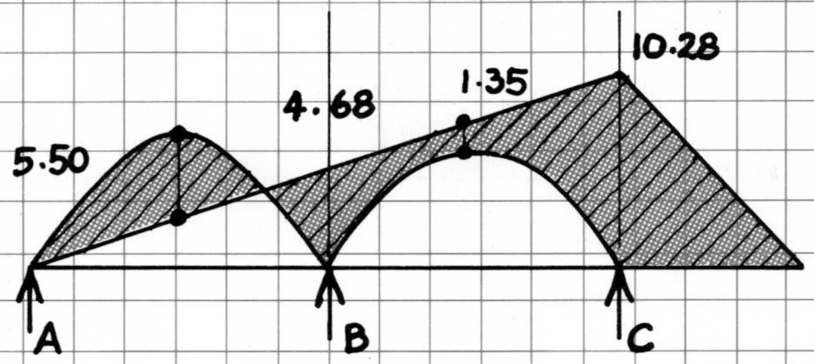

$R_A = \left(6.70 \times \frac{3.06}{2}\right) - \frac{4.68}{3.06} = 10.25 - 1.53 = 8.72\text{ kN}$

$R_B = 10.25 + 1.53 + (6.70 \times 1.35) - \left(\frac{10.28 - 4.68}{2.7}\right)$

$= 11.78 + 9.05 - 2.07 = 18.76\text{ kN}$

$R_C = 9.05 + 2.07 + (6.70 \times 1.752)$

$= 11.12 + 11.74 = 22.86\text{ kN}$

Checking the combined case for the inside soldiers will give an envelope for moment from initial inspection:

Max. Positive = 7.76 + 5.50 = 13.26 kN m

Max. Negative = 10.79 + 10.28 = 21.07 kN m

Both of these values exceed the permissible BM at a joint and a closer inspection is required.

Plotting B.M.s shows joint moments to be O.K. See Sheet (12)

Ref	Calculations	Output.

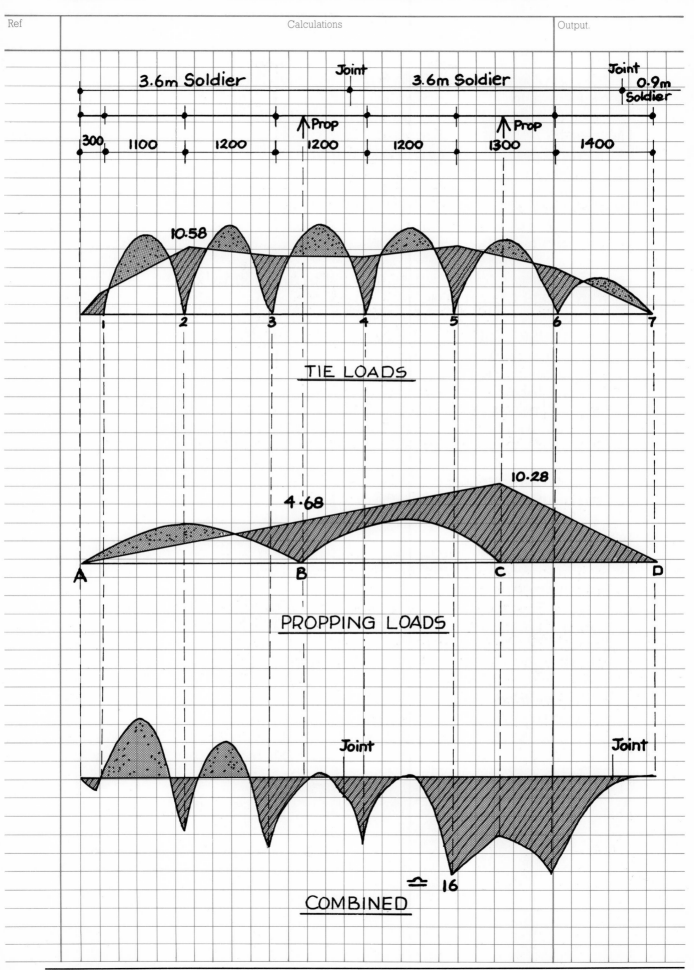

3.6m Soldier   Joint   3.6m Soldier   Joint
                                                           0.9m Soldier

300   1100   1200   ↑Prop   ↑Prop
                    1200   1200   1300   1400

10.58

1   2   3   4   5   6   7

TIE LOADS

10.28

4.68

A   B   C   D

PROPPING LOADS

Joint   Joint

16

COMBINED

Ref	Calculations	Output.

From Inspection: Select a soldier with a moment of resistance of minimum 16 kNm at tie rod position with tie load of 95 kN.

Resolve propping loads:

Prop at B at 82° gives axial load

$$= \frac{18.7}{Sin\ 82°} = 18.94\ kN$$

Prop at C at 60° gives axial load

$$= \frac{22.86}{Sin\ 60°} = 26.40\ kN$$

The prop on the soldier may not be fully loaded at this stage of construction.

CONSIDER MAIN PROPS LOADED AFTER STRIKING OF FORMWORK

Main props have to support 2.4m length of wall, and FULL wind overturning moment.

From Table 18 Case A the overturning moment is 10.25 kNm on force of 2.79 kN for maximum wind.

Hence increase in prop loads as ratio of values obtained above by $\frac{2.79 - 1.96}{50.33} = 2\%$ say increase

Apply further 2½% of concrete load to allow for lateral instability of falsework.

i.e. 2½% × 93.9 = 2.348 kN

$$\left(\frac{2.348 \times \frac{1}{2.232}}{50.33} \right) = 2\%\ Approx.$$

Hence total load per 2.4m is increased by factoring to the slope of the soldier and gives :-

$$\frac{1}{7.512} \times 50.33 \times 2.4 + 2\% + 2\% = 16.73\ kNm$$

per main prop

Pro-rata prop loads obtained by previous moment distribution by $\frac{16.73}{6.70} = 2.50$

Ref	Calculations	Output

Hence prop load B = 18·94 × 2·50 = 47·35 kN

prop load C = 26·40 × 2·50 = 66·00 kN

Check for forces on face of wall from prop loads:

Force F = 47·35 Cos 82° + 66·00 Cos 60°

= 39·59 kN

Equivalent force normal to face
= 47·35 Sin 82° + 66 Sin 60°

= 104·05 kN

θ_1 = 82°
θ_2 = 60°

Contact area of plywood = 7·51 × 0·40 = 3·00 m^2
from BS 5975 Table 18: Coeff. friction timber to concrete = 0·30

Hence frictional resistance = $\frac{104·05 \times 0·30}{2}$

= 15·61 kN
(F of S = 2)

Hence shear connectors are required.

Shear resistance required = 39·59 − 15·61
= 23·98 kN

Leaving 3 N° tie rods in position,

Shear/tie = $\frac{23·98}{3}$ = 8·00 kN

Note: Provide concrete base to foot of props to resist vertical and horizontal loads at this location.

concrete
society

<table>
<tr><td colspan="2">APPENDIX D1
WORKED EXAMPLE OF
BACKPROPPING</td><td>Project
FOUR STOREY CAR PARK</td><td>Sheet
1 of 1</td></tr>
</table>

APPENDIX D1 **WORKED EXAMPLE OF** **BACKPROPPING**	Project **FOUR STOREY CAR PARK** — Sheet **1 of 1**
	Part of Structure **SLAB BACKPROPPED THROUGH TO FOUNDATIONS** — Drg Ref **APP.D1**
	Job Ref **A/D1** — Calc by **T.C.L.** — Date **13.8.85** — Check by **P.F.P.** — Date **13.9.85**

Ref	Calculations	Output

Car Park – Total design load $= 8.00\,kN/m^2$
Self weight (slab) $= 4.50\,kN/m^2$
Live load $= 1.5 + 0.5\,kN/m^2$
(Construction operations load + form self weight)

Construction Load $= 6.5\,kN/m^2$

(4) ──────────────────────

(6.5)

(3) ──── SW 4.5 ──── 0.75 L.L.

(11.75)

$0.75\,kN/m^2$ is a live load allowance for incidental loads on floors

(2) ──── SW 4.5 ──── 0.75 L.L.

(17.00)

(1) ──── SW 4.5 ──── 0.75 L.L.

(22.25)

(0) ▨▨▨▨▨▨▨▨▨▨▨▨▨▨▨

This method assumes that props to levels 1, 2 and 3 are undisturbed. Thus loads are cumulative.

concrete society

APPENDIX D2 WORKED EXAMPLE OF BACKPROPPING	Project	MULTI-STOREY CAR PARK		Sheet	1 of 1
	Part of Structure	SLAB BACKPROPPED 3 STOREYS		Drg Ref	APP. D2
	Job Ref	Calc by	Date	Check by	Date
	A/D2	T.C.L.	6.9.85	P.F.P	10.10.85

Ref	Calculations	Output

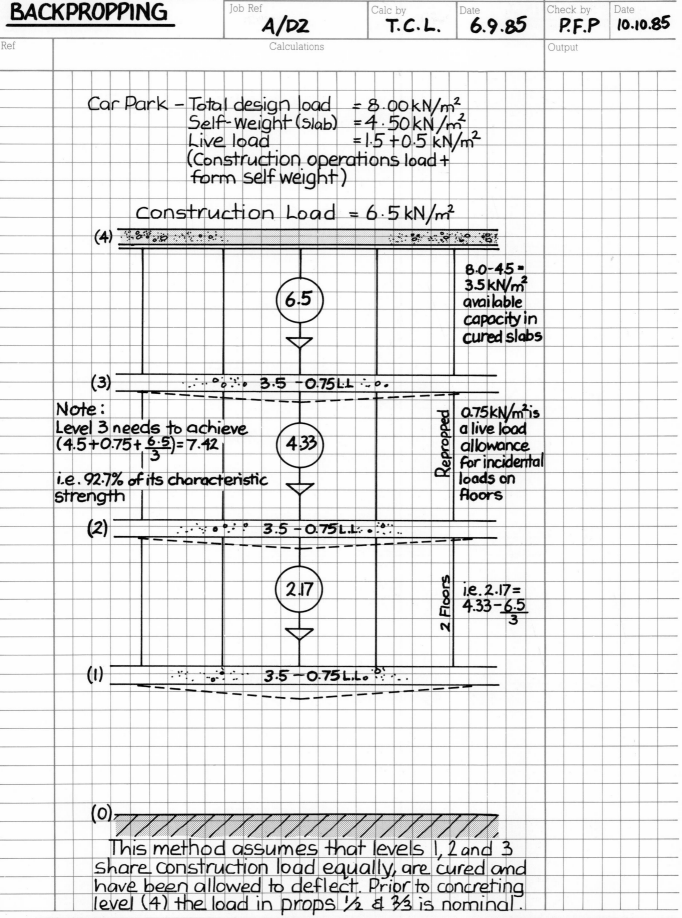

Car Park — Total design load $= 8.00\,kN/m^2$
Self-weight (slab) $= 4.50\,kN/m^2$
Live load $= 1.5 + 0.5\,kN/m^2$
(Construction operations load + form self weight)

Construction Load $= 6.5\,kN/m^2$

(4)

6.5

8.0 − 4.5 = 3.5 kN/m² available capacity in cured slabs

(3) 3.5 − 0.75 L.L.

Note:
Level 3 needs to achieve
$(4.5 + 0.75 + \frac{6.5}{3}) = 7.42$

i.e. 92.7% of its characteristic strength

4.33

Repropped

0.75 kN/m² is a live load allowance for incidental loads on floors

(2) 3.5 − 0.75 L.L.

2.17

2 Floors

i.e. 2.17 = $4.33 − \frac{6.5}{3}$

(1) 3.5 − 0.75 L.L.

(0)

This method assumes that levels 1, 2 and 3 share construction load equally, are cured and have been allowed to deflect. Prior to concreting level (4) the load in props ½ & ⅔ is nominal.

APPENDIX D3 WORKED EXAMPLE OF BACKPROPPING	Project OFFICE			Sheet 1 of 1
	Part of Structure SLAB BACKPROPPED 1 STOREY			Drg Ref APP. D3
	Job Ref A/D3	Calc by T.C.L.	Date 30.9.85	Check by P.F.P. Date 4.11.85

Ref	Calculations	Output

Office Block – Total load $= 11.5 \text{ kN/m}^2$
Self weight (Slab) $= 4.5 \text{ kN/m}^2$
Live load $= 1.5 + 0.5 \text{ kN/m}^2$
(Construction operations load + form self weight)

Construction Load $= 6.5 \text{ kN/m}^2$

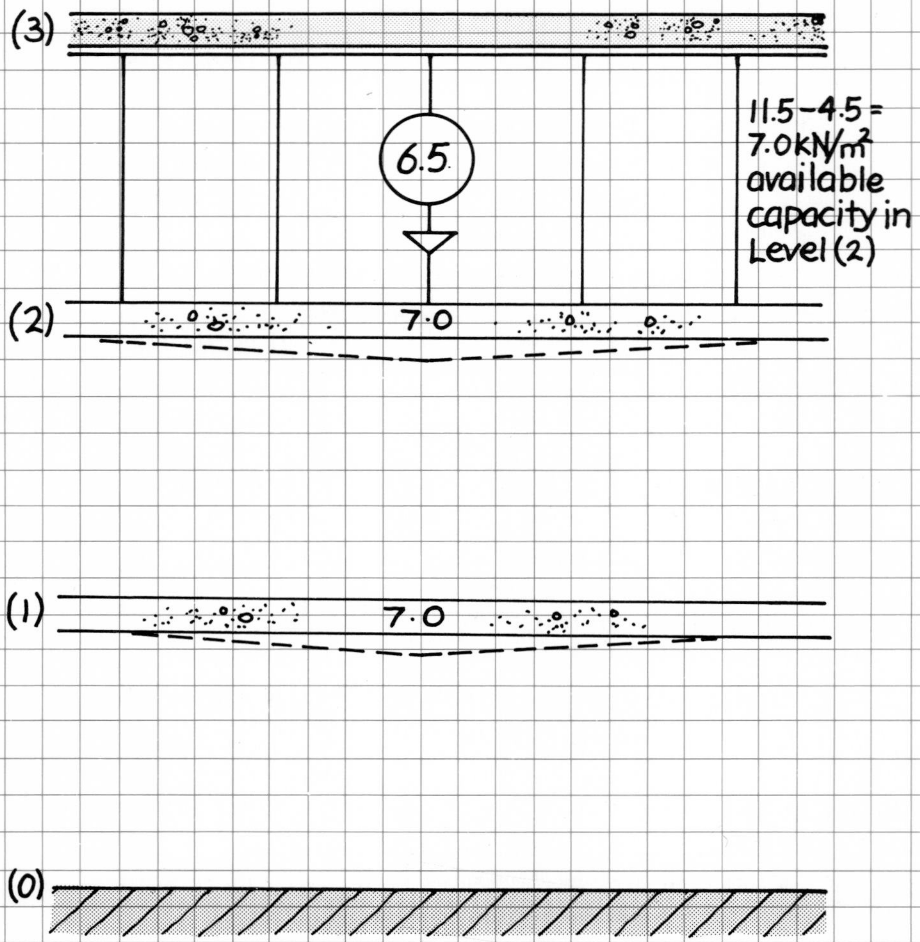

(3)

6.5

$11.5 - 4.5 = 7.0 \text{ kN/m}^2$ available capacity in Level (2)

(2)   7.0

(1)   7.0

(0)

APPENDIX D4 WORKED EXAMPLE OF BACKPROPPING	Project FLAT SLAB STRUCTURE		Sheet 1 of 3	
	Part of Structure FLYING FORM, BACKPROPPED 2 STOREYS		Drg Ref APP. D4	
	Job Ref A/D4	Calc by T.C.L.	Date 22.10.85	Check by P.F.P.	Date 5.11.85

Ref	Calculations	Output

Construction load (250 mm Slab)

Concrete $= 0.25 \times 25 = 6.25$

Live load $= 1.5 + 0.5 = 2.00$

(Construction operations load + form self weight)

$8.25\,kN/m^2$ Total

Total load
$8.25\,kN/m^2$

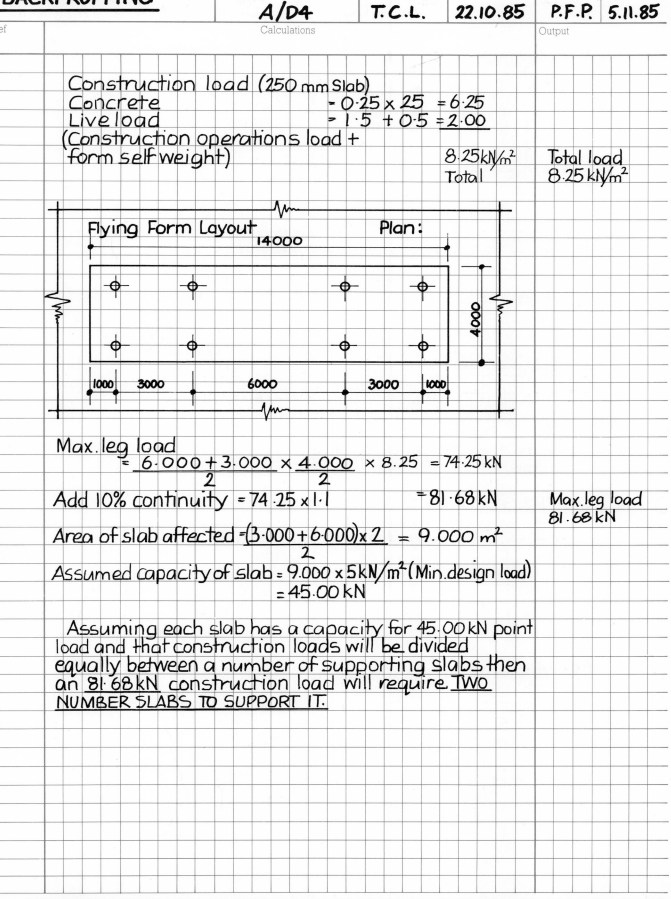

Flying Form Layout   Plan:

14000

4000

1000   3000   6000   3000   1000

Max. leg load

$$= \frac{6.000 + 3.000}{2} \times \frac{4.000}{2} \times 8.25 = 74.25\,kN$$

Add 10% continuity $= 74.25 \times 1.1 = 81.68\,kN$

Max. leg load
81.68 kN

Area of slab affected $= \frac{(3.000 + 6.000) \times 2}{2} = 9.000\,m^2$

Assumed capacity of slab $= 9.000 \times 5kN/m^2$ (Min. design load)
$= 45.00\,kN$

   Assuming each slab has a capacity for 45.00 kN point load and that construction loads will be divided equally between a number of supporting slabs then an 81.68 kN construction load will require TWO NUMBER SLABS TO SUPPORT IT.

Ref	Calculations	Output.

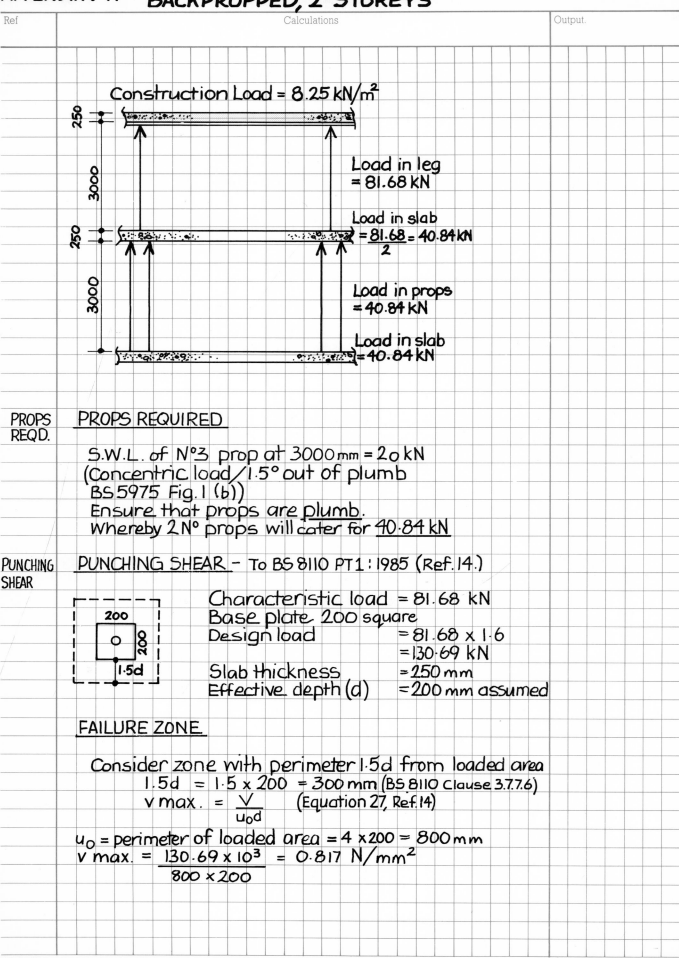

Construction Load = 8.25 kN/m²

250

3000

Load in leg = 81.68 kN

250

Load in slab = $\dfrac{81.68}{2}$ = 40.84 kN

3000

Load in props = 40.84 kN

Load in slab = 40.84 kN

PROPS REQD.

PROPS REQUIRED

S.W.L. of N°3 prop at 3000 mm = 2o kN
(Concentric load/1.5° out of plumb
BS 5975 Fig.1 (b))
Ensure that props are <u>plumb</u>.
Whereby 2 N° props will cater for <u>40.84 kN</u>

PUNCHING SHEAR

PUNCHING SHEAR − To BS 8110 PT1 : 1985 (Ref.14.)

Characteristic load = 81.68 kN
Base plate 200 square
Design load $= 81.68 \times 1.6$
$= 130.69$ kN
Slab thickness $= 250$ mm
Effective depth (d) $= 200$ mm assumed

FAILURE ZONE

Consider zone with perimeter 1.5d from loaded area
$1.5d = 1.5 \times 200 = 300$ mm (BS 8110 Clause 3.7.7.6)
$v\ max. = \dfrac{V}{u_o d}$ (Equation 27, Ref.14)

u_0 = perimeter of loaded area = $4 \times 200 = 800$ mm
$v\ max. = \dfrac{130.69 \times 10^3}{800 \times 200} = 0.817$ N/mm²

concrete
society

Ref	Calculations	Output.

Max. allowable $= 0.8\sqrt{f_u} = 0.8\sqrt{20} = 3.58 \text{ N/mm}^2$

perimeter $= u = 4 \times 800 = 3200 \text{ mm}$

Design shear stress $= v = \dfrac{V}{ud}$ (Equation 28, Ref 14)

$$= \dfrac{130.69 \times 10^3}{3200 \times 200} = 0.204 \text{ N/mm}^2$$

From Table 3.9, $v_C = 0.47 \text{ N/mm}^2$ $(d = 200, \dfrac{100 A_s}{b_v d} = 0.25)$

$\therefore v_C > v$ no shear reinforcement reqd. (clause 3.7.7.4, Ref. 14)

SUMMARY

Back propping to comprise 2 N°3 adjustable
props positioned at 300 centres under each
flying form leg. Through one floor only.

ASSUMPTIONS

(1) That permanent slab is capable of withstanding
point loads from table leg as previously
mentioned (and has attained 28 day strength).

(2) A continuity factor of 10% which it may be
argued is NOT APPLICABLE thereby reducing
leg loads (by 10%).

(3) That supporting floors have been allowed to
deflect and carry their own weight thus
eliminating the possibility of cumulative loads.

APPENDIX D5 WORKED EXAMPLE OF BACKPROPPING	Project FLAT SLAB STRUCTURE, AS D4	Sheet 1 of 2
	Part of Structure CONVENTIONAL BACKPROPPING, 2 STOREYS	Drg Ref APP. D5
	Job Ref A/D5 · Calc by T.C.L · Date 2.12.85	Check by P.F.P. · Date 8.1.86

Ref	Calculations	Output

CONSTRUCTION LOAD (250mm Slab)

Concrete 0.25×25 = 6.25

Live + forms $1.5 + 0.5$ = 2.00

$8.25 \ kN/m^2$

Support work generally comprises legs on 1.829 × 1.27 grid say

Leg load = $1.829 \times 1.27 \times 8.25$ = 19.16 kN

Add 10% for continuity = 21.10 kN

(BS 5975, Clause 43.3.1 Ref.2)

Area of slab affected = 1.829 × 1.27 (Worst case)

= 2.32 m²

ASSUMED DESIGN CAPACITY OF SLAB

= 2.32 × 5 kN/m² (min. design load from P.W.D)

= 11.60 kN.

Assuming each slab has a capacity for 11.60 kN point load and that construction loads will be divided equally between a number of supporting slabs then a 21.10 kN construction load will require TWO NUMBER SLABS TO SUPPORT IT.

Construction Load = 8.25 kN/m²

Load in leg = 21.10 kN

Load in slab = 10.55 kN

Loads in props = 10.55 kN/2.32 m²

Load in slab 6.55 kN

(250, 3000, 250, 3000 dimensions shown)

Ref	Calculations	Output.

<u>PROPS REQUIRED</u>

S.W.L. of N° 3 prop at 3000mm = <u>20 kN</u>
(See BS 5975 Fig 1 (b) Ref.2)
Allowable area on prop = $\dfrac{20 \times 2.32}{10.55}$ = $4.4\,m^2$

$\sqrt{4.4}$ = 2.09 m
Place back props on 2m x 2m max. grid or
the equivalent area.

<u>ASSUMPTIONS</u>

(1) <u>Supporting slabs have attained 28 day strength</u>

Note: The actual characteristic strength of the
middle slab will be
$\dfrac{10.55 + (6.25 \times 2.32)}{(5.0 + 6.25) \times 2.32}$ = 96%
of design 28 day strength at time
of loading.

(2) Supporting slabs have been allowed to deflect
and carry their own weight thus eliminating
the possibility of cumulative loads.

Appendix E – Concrete Pressure Data Sheet

This data sheet is applicable to concretes placed in nominally vertical, parallel-sided formwork and to compaction by internal vibration. Pressures for conditions other than those described in this data sheet, and further examples, are given in CIRIA Report 108.

Lateral pressures are at their greatest when there is continuous vertical concrete placing with constant vibration. These conditions are only applicable to columns, and a separate table is provided. For simplicity, a column is defined as a section where both plan dimensions are less than 2m. Other sections are called walls and bases. These designations are shown below.

The chart opposite can be used for concrete containing combinations of cements and admixtures as specified in each table. Caution is required because admixtures are classified by function at a stipulated dosage. Overdosing may well change the effect of an admixture. For example, a multiple dose of a normal water reducer may result in retardation. In this circumstance the table referring to concrete with a retarder should be used.

A major change from existing practice is the recommendation that superplasticised concrete should be included within the general grouping, and that it does not necessarily require design pressure equal to the fluid head.

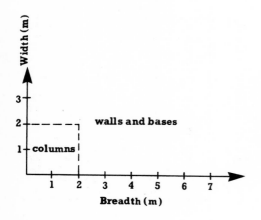

OPC	ordinary Portland cement
LHPBFC	low heat Portland-blastfurnace cement
PBFC	Portland-blastfurnace cement
PPFAC	Portland pulverised-fuel ash cement
RHPC	rapid-hardening Portland cement
SRPC	sulphate-resisting Portland cement
ggbfs	ground granulated blastfurnace slag
pfa	pulverised-fuel ash

Examples	**Design Pressure Distribution**

Wall: 0.5 x 10.0 x 6m high
OPC concrete with retarder
Concrete temperature at placing: 10°C
Rate of rise: 3 m/h
P_{max} = 90 kN/m²

*3.6 m = 90/25

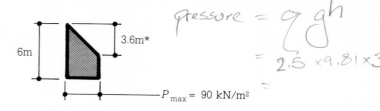

pressure = ρgh

= 2.5 ×9.81×3

=

Column: 0.5 x 1.75 x 10m high
OPC concrete
Concrete temperature at placing: 10°C
Rate of rise: 10 m/h
P_{max} = 150 kN/m²

*6 m = 150/25

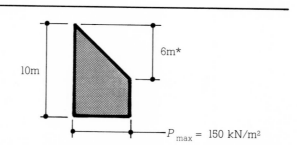

Wall: 0.2 x 2.5 x 3m high
OPC concrete
Concrete temperature at placing: 5°C
Rate of rise: 6 m/h
P_{max} = 75 kN/m²

*3 m = 75/25

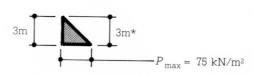

Design pressures

WALLS AND BASES — A wall or base is a section where at least one of the plan dimensions is greater than 2m

COLUMNS — A column is a section where both plan dimensions are less than 2m

P_{max} (kN/m²)

Walls and bases

Concrete Group	Conc. temp. (°C)	Form height (m)	0.5	1.0	1.5	2.0	3.0	5.0	10
1) OPC, RHPC or SRPC without admixtures 2) OPC, RHPC or SRPC with any admixture except a retarder	5	2	40	45	50	50	50	50	50
		3	50	55	60	65	70	75	75
		4	60	65	65	70	75	85	100
		6	70	75	80	80	90	100	115
		10	85	90	95	100	105	115	135
	10	2	35	40	45	45	50	50	50
		3	40	45	50	55	60	70	75
		4	45	50	55	60	65	75	90
		6	50	55	60	65	75	85	105
		10	60	70	75	80	85	95	115
	15	2	30	35	40	45	50	50	50
		3	35	40	45	50	55	65	75
		4	35	45	50	50	60	70	90
		6	40	50	55	60	65	75	95
		10	50	55	60	65	75	85	105
3) OPC, RHPC or SRPC with a retarder 4) LHPBFC, PBFC, PPFAC or a blend containing less than 70% ggbfs or 40% pfa without admixtures 5) LHPBFC, PBFC, PPFAC or a blend containing less than 70% ggbfs or 40% pfa with any admixture except a retarder (see Note)	5	2	50	50	50	50	50	50	50
		3	65	70	75	75	75	75	75
		4	75	80	85	90	95	100	100
		6	95	100	105	105	110	110	135
		10	120	125	130	130	140	150	165
	10	2	40	45	50	50	50	50	50
		3	50	55	60	65	70	75	75
		4	60	60	65	70	75	85	100
		6	70	75	80	80	90	100	115
		10	85	90	95	100	105	115	135
	15	2	35	40	45	45	50	50	50
		3	40	45	50	55	60	70	75
		4	45	50	55	60	65	75	90
		6	50	60	65	65	75	85	105
		10	65	70	75	80	85	100	120

Columns

Concrete Group	Conc. temp. (°C)	Form height (m)	2	4	6	10	15
1) & 2)	5	3	75	75	75	75	75
		4	85	100	100	100	100
		6	95	115	125	145	150
		10	115	135	145	170	190
		15	130	150	165	190	210
	10	3	65	75	75	75	75
		4	75	90	100	100	100
		6	80	100	115	130	150
		10	95	115	130	150	175
		15	105	125	140	165	190
	15	3	60	75	75	75	75
		4	65	85	95	100	100
		6	75	90	105	130	150
		10	80	100	115	140	165
		15	90	110	125	150	175
3), 4) & 5)	5	3	75	75	75	75	75
		4	100	100	100	100	100
		6	120	130	140	150	150
		10	145	160	175	195	215
		15	170	190	205	225	245
	10	3	75	75	75	75	75
		4	85	95	100	100	100
		6	95	110	125	145	150
		10	115	130	145	170	190
		15	130	150	165	190	210
	15	3	65	75	75	75	75
		4	75	90	100	100	100
		6	80	100	115	135	150
		10	95	115	130	155	175
		15	105	125	140	165	190

- The maximum pressures are in units of kN/m² to the nearest 5 kN/m². They were calculated assuming a concrete weight density of 25 kN/m³. Pressures for lightweight or heavyweight concretes should be calculated in a proportion to their densities.

- The pressures not in bold are outside recorded experience. The highest recorded pressures on site were 90 kN/m² for walls and 166 kN/m² for columns.

- The tables do not include the use of concretes which contain a retarder in combination with LHPBFC, PBFC, PPFAC or any cement blend. Guidance on these combinations is given in CIRIA Report 108.

Published by permission of the Director of CIRIA

concrete society

233

Appendix F – Organisations and Addresses (Current at June 1986)

Aluminium Federation,
Broadway House,
Calthorpe Road,
BIRMINGHAM B15 1TN.
Tel. No. 021-455-0311   Telex: 338024 BIRCOM G

American Plywood Association,
101 Wigmore Street,
LONDON W1H 9AB.
Tel. No. 01-629-3437   Telex: 296009 USAGOF G

British Plastics Federation,
5 Belgrave Square,
LONDON SW1X 8PH.
Tel. No. 01-235-9483   Telex: 8951528 LAFED G

British Standards Institution,
Publications Sales Department,
Linford Wood,
MILTON KEYNES, MK14 6LE.
Tel. No. 0908-320033   Telex: 825777 BSIMK G
Head Office
2 Park Street,
LONDON W1A 2BS.
Tel. No. 01-629-9000   Telex: 266933 BSILON G

Building Employers Confederation,
82 New Cavendish Street,
LONDON W1M 8AD.
Tel. No. 01-580-5588   Telex: 265763 BEC G

Building Research Establishment,
Bucknalls Lane,
Garston,
WATFORD,
Hertfordshire WD2 7JR.
Tel. No. 0923-674040   Telex: 923220 BRSBRE G

Cement and Concrete Association,
Wexham Springs,
SLOUGH,
Buckinghamshire SL3 6PL.
Tel. No. 02816-2727   Telex: 848352 CCA G

Central Electricity Generating Board,
Technical Documentation Branch,
Engineering Services,
Walden House,
24 Cathedral Place,
LONDON EC4P 4EB.
Tel. No. 01-634-5111   Telex: 883141 CEGBHQ G

Chain Testers' Association of Great Britain,
21-23 Woodgrange Road,
LONDON E7 8BA.
Tel. No. 01-519-3702

Chipboard Promotion Association,
50 Station Road,
MARLOW,
Buckinghamshire SL7 1NN.
Tel. No. 06284-3022

Concrete Society
Devon House,
12-15 Dartmouth Street,
LONDON SW1H 9BL.
Tel. No. 01-222-1822

Construction Industry Research and Information Association,
6 Storey's Gate,
LONDON SW1P 3AU.
Tel. No. 01-222-8891   Telex: 24224 MONREF G (reference 2063)

Construction Industry Training Board,
Training Headquarters,
Bircham Newton Training Centre,
KING'S LYNN,
Norfolk PE31 6RH.
Tel. No. 0553-776677   Telex: 81452 CITB G

Council of Forest Industries of British Columbia,
Tileman House,
131-135 Upper Richmond Road,
Putney,
LONDON SW15 2TR.
Tel. No. 01-788-4446   Telex: 25695 BCWOOD G

Department of the Environment,
2 Marsham Street,
LONDON SW1P 3EB.
Tel. No. 01-212-3434   Telex: 22221 DOEMAR G

Engineering Equipment and Material Users Association,
14 Belgrave Square,
LONDON SW1X 8PS.
Tel. No. 01-235-5316

Finnish Plywood International,
PO Box 99,
WELWYN GARDEN CITY,
Hertfordshire AL6 0HS.
Tel. No. 043-879-746

Glassfibre Reinforced Cement Association,
5 Upper Bar,
NEWPORT,
Shropshire TF10 7EH.
Tel. No. 0952-811397

Health & Safety Executive,
Library and Information Services,
Red Hill,
SHEFFIELD S3 7HQ.
Tel. No. 0742-78141   Telex: 54556 HSERLS G

Her Majesty's Stationery Office,
Publications Centre,
PO Box 276,
LONDON SW8 5DT.
Tel. No. 01-622-3316   Telex 297138 HMSOBK G

Institution of Civil Engineers,
Great George Street,
Westminster,
LONDON SW1P 3AA.
Tel. No. 01-222-7722   Telex: ICEAS 935637 G

Institution of Structural Engineers,
11 Upper Belgrave Street,
LONDON SW1X 8BH.
Tel. No. 01-235-4535

National Association of Formwork Contractors,
82 New Cavendish Street,
LONDON W1M 8AD.
Tel. No. 01-580-5588   Telex: 265763 BEC G

National Council of Building Material Producers (BMP),
10 Great George Street,
LONDON SW1P 3AE.
Tel. No. 01-222-5315
(Incorporates the Wood Wool Slab Manufacturers Association.)

Phenolic Foam Manufacturers Association,
45 Sheen Lane,
LONDON SW14 8AB.
Tel. No. 01-876-4415   Telex: 927298 ALLEN G

Plastics and Rubber Institute,
11 Hobart Place,
LONDON SW1W 0HL.
Tel. No. 01-245-9555   Telex: 915719 PRIUK G

Property Services Agency,
Whitgift Centre,
Wellesley Road,
CROYDON CR9 3LY.
Tel. No. 01-686-8710   Telex 917237 PSACRO G

Swedish and Finnish Timber Council,
21 Carolgate,
RETFORD,
Nottinghamshire, DN22 6BZ.
Tel. No. 0777-706616

Timber Research and Development Association,
Stocking Lane,
Hughenden Valley,
HIGH WYCOMBE,
Buckinghamshire HP14 4ND.
Tel. No. 0240-24-3091   Telex: 83292 TRADA G
Prestel 3511615

Water Byelaws Advisory Service,
660 Ajax Avenue,
SLOUGH,
Berkshire SL1 4BG.
Tel. No. 0753-372777   Telex: 449541 WRCENG G

Information on the above and other organisations may be found in CIRIA Special Publication 30, Guide to sources of construction information, 4th Edition, 1984.

concrete
society

Appendix G – Advertisements for Specialist Formwork Materials, Equipment and Services

BUILDING TOMORROWS WORLD

R·M·D
CONSTRUCTION EQUIPMENT

☐ STEEL FORMWORK ☐ RAPID PLY FORMWORK ☐ SPECIAL FORMWORK

☐ SUPER SLIM 2 SOLDIERS ☐ HEAVY DUTY PUSH PULL PROPS ☐ SLIMSHOR ☐ MINI-SLIM

☐ AL-FORM ☐ FLOOR CENTRES ☐ ROOM FORM ☐ FLYING FORMS ☐ SUSPENDED

SCAFFOLD ☐ ACCESS SCAFFOLD ☐ SUPPORT SCAFFOLD ☐ RAPID DECK ☐ PROPS

☐ TRENCH STRUTS ☐ ROAD FORMS ☐ TRESTLES ☐ FORMWORK TIE SYSTEMS

☐ REINFORCEMENT SPACERS ☐ TIESEAL ☐ STRONGSHOR ☐ LIGHT TRISHORE

☐ HEAVY TRISHORE ☐ R.M.D. 500 H33 HEAVY DUTY SUPPORT EQUIPMENT

Rapid Metal Developments Limited

Stubbers Green Road, Aldridge, Walsall WS9 8BW, England
Tel: Aldridge (0922) 743743 Use (0922) 53366 until Feb. 1987 International + (44922) 743743
Telex: 338514 RMDALD G Facsimile: (0922) 743400 (Group 3) Use 58726 until Feb. 1987

Aberdeen
Pitmedden Road Industrial Estate, Dyce,
Aberdeen AB2 0DP.
Tel: Aberdeen (0224) 723003

Belfast
Balmoral Road, Balmoral Industrial Estate,
Belfast BT12 6QA.
Tel: Belfast (0232) 669771

Bristol
North Road, Yate, Nr. Bristol BS17 5PA.
Tel: Chipping Sodbury (0454) 322820

Corby
Priors Haw Road, Weldon Industrial Estate, Corby,
Northants. NN17 1JG.
Tel: Corby (0536) 69819

Exeter
33 The Quay, Exeter, EX2 4AR.
Tel: Exeter (0392) 73595

Fareham
Bennet's Yard, Spurlings Lane, Wallington,
Fareham PO17 6AB.
Tel: Fareham (0329) 234197

Glasgow
1650A London Road, Glasgow G31 4QQ.
Tel: 041-554 7425

Liverpool
Woodward Road, Kirkby Trading Estate,
Liverpool L33 7UZ.
Tel: 051-546 2482

Newport
Ebbw Vale Wharf, River Bank, Newport,
Gwent NPT 2BS.
Tel: Newport (0633) 57944

Norfolk
Station Road Industrial Estate, Ayton Road,
Wymondham, Norfolk NR18 0QJ.
Tel: Wymondham (0953) 605470

Rainham
Chandler Works, Ferry Lane, Rainham,
Essex RM13 9DH.
Tel: Rainham (04027) 52975

Rickmansworth
134 Watford Road, Croxley Green, Rickmansworth,
Herts. WD3 3BZ.
Tel: Rickmansworth (0923) 776733

Scunthorpe
Brigg Road, Scunthorpe, DN16 1AP.
Tel: Scunthorpe (0724) 866116

Stockton-on-Tees
Ross Road, Stockton-on-Tees TS18 2NH.
Tel: Stockton (0642) 675915 Telex: 58221

Swansea
138 Heol-y-Gors, Cwmbwrla, Swansea SA5 8LU.
Tel: Swansea (0792) 464613 Telex: 48330

Wakefield
Hoist Yard, Thornes Lane, Wakefield WF1 5QJ.
Tel: Wakefield (0924) 375400

OVERSEAS
Republic of Ireland
Rapid Metal Developments Ireland Limited
Ballyboggan Road, Finglas, Dublin 11.
Tel: Dublin (0001) 302500/302164
Facsimile: (0001) 302741
Branches at:
Cork Tel: 966188 and Ballinasloe Tel: 42196

Australia
Rapid Metal Developments (Aust.) Pty. Limited
P.O. Box 169, St. Mary's, South Australia 5042.
Tel: (08) 277 1644 Telex: 82995
Branches at:
New South Wales: Sydney Tel: (02) 772 2144
Queensland: Brisbane Tel: (07) 266 3022
Victoria: Melbourne Tel: (03) 484 0527/8/9
Western Australia: Perth Tel: (09) 446 5900

New Zealand
Rapid Metal Developments (N.Z.) Limited
P.O. Box 22.316, Otahuhu, Auckland 6, New Zealand.
Tel: (09) 27 65955
Branches at
Wellington Tel: (04) 73 7663 and
Christchurch Tel: (03) 48 9621/9682

France
Réalisations Métalliques Développées S.A.R.L.
Port Fluvial, 2ème Avenue, 59000 Lille, France.
Tel: 20 92 85 36 Telex: 132934 RMDLIL F
Facsimile: 20 09 46 61
Branches at:
Rouen Tel: 35 36 00 50 Telex: 771929 RMDROUE F
and Paris Tel: (1) 39 88 14 66
Telex: 697968 RMDGOUS F

United Arab Emirates
Rapid Metal Developments (U.A.E.) Limited
P.O. Box 5801, Sharjah, U.A.E.
Tel: 357289 Telex: 68376 RMDEM
Facsimile: 010 9716 377260
Branches at:
Abu Dhabi Tel: 722039 Telex: 24101 RMD ADH
Also agents in countries throughout the world.

DOUGLAS

Who cares about Quality Assurance for Reinforcing Steels?

cares

CARES. The UK Certification Authority for Reinforcing Steels

For full information and comprehensive list of firms holding CARES Certificate Approval, please contact Evan Morgan, Executive Director, CARES, Oak House, Tubs Hill, Sevenoaks TN13 1BL. Tel: 0732 450000

Chart Formwork (Sales) Limited

Steel moulds and formwork, Fabrications, Precision and general engineers

Pivington Works,
Pluckley,
Nr. Ashford,
Kent TN27 0PG

Telephone: Pluckley (0233 84) 555
Telex No. 965555

concrete
society

Training Opportunities

FORMWORK APPRECIATION COURSE FOR GRADUATE ENGINEERS & TECHNICIANS

COURSE CONTENT

Appreciation of power tools, and woodworking machinery; formwork material and their characteristics, formwork anchors and fixing devices, types of formwork – timber and proprietary systems, their application and methods of erection for column walls, beams and soffits. Methods of obtaining special concrete finishes. Faults in formwork, release agents. Safety aspects appertaining to erection and striking formwork.

Other 'Engineers Appreciation Courses'

Timbering (Support to excavations)
Formwork
Scaffolding
Levelling and Setting Out
Steelfixing and Barbending
Cranes
Earthmoving

FORMWORKER (Craft Operative)
Apprenticeship Course. (Recognised by NJCBI) 3 Year Scheme –

Qualifications Attainable
Formwork (C & G 5821)
Advanced Craft (C & G 5822)

Age Requirement 16+

Pattern of Course Training
13 weeks 1st Training Period at Erith learning practical skills.
12 months Company related site experience
12 weeks 2nd Training Period at Erith
Remaining time up to 3 years is spent with your company gaining experience
Possibility for selection for Advanced Craft

CHILVER DAYS

All these courses are recognised by I.C.E. and qualify for credit as P.E.I.

The major part of all these courses is devoted to PRACTICAL work. It is assumed that the student will have already covered the theoretical knowledge required.

VENUE: Bircham Newton Training Centre. CITB., Bircham Newton, Kings Lynn, Norfolk. PE31 6RH

contact   Graham Boldero for Course Dates – Fees etc.

Telephone 0553 776677 Ext. 2249

Course – 5 weeks at Erith leading to Advanced Craft Certificate
Formwork Courses start on various dates during the year

For more information contact:

The Manager, Erith Training Centre, Manor Road, Erith, Kent. DA8 2AD
(Tel: 0322 349638)

CITB
CONSTRUCTION
Industry Training Board

It reigns
when you pour

No one type of formwork panel can meet all your needs. But one name can: Canadian COFI EXTERIOR plywood.

Whatever the project, whatever the finish, there's a purpose-designed, quality-certified COFI EXTERIOR plywood panel to meet your exact job specifications.

Sanded and Unsanded Douglas Fir panels give you tough, long-lasting, affordable quality and assured supply for all standard formwork; and every panel is backed by 30 years of project-proven and laboratory-tested reliability.

COFIFORM Douglas Fir panels feature extra strength and stiffness for demanding deflection criteria, even under wet service conditions. The sealed edges and oiled faces mean faster stripping and longer life.

Overlaid and Coated Formwork panels are available under a range of brand names; many incorporate chemical release agents for cost-cutting efficiency. You get smooth, blemish-free surfaces that require no rubbing down or filling.

Worldwide, the COFI EXTERIOR face stamp is the accepted hallmark of plywood excellence. So, before you pour your next concrete project, write, phone or use the Reader Service Card for *free technical data* and personal service support.

concrete society

concrete society

® Feb
Construction Chemicals

For accelerating, bonding, curing, damproofing, epoxy coating, formwork, grouting, hardening, insulating, jointing, 'K'rack filling/covering, levelling, moulding, nosings for expansion joints, oil proofing, plasticising, quick-setting, retarding, sealing, tiling, undersealing, varnishing, waterproofing, Xtra durability, 'Y'universal availability, 'Z'olving maintenance problems. Everything from A – Z

® Feb
the right choice

concrete society

four facts from Fosroc

Market leadership in construction chemicals

Unique international capability – With staff based in 26 countries, there is wide experience of many markets and products backed with a strong technical service capability in each operating company worldwide.

Comprehensive product range – With its high-performance products, Fosroc meets construction needs from concrete treatments, grouts, anchoring systems, and repair, to industrial adhesives and flooring, protective coatings, sealants and waterproofing systems, and timber treatment.

Efficient local supply – Serving the construction industry worldwide, Fosroc is geared to local supply through its network of 47 manufacturing plants in 22 countries.

World leader in product innovation – With the world's leading product development laboratory in the UK, Fosroc's international operations have local laboratory support in more than 20 countries.

flexible forms
in every way a tool for the innovative engineer

Conventionally, the method of casting in situ structures and shapes in concrete involves the use of formwork fabricated from rigid timber and steel. The essential requirement is that these forms provide an impermeable container holding the fluid concrete throughout the hydration period. The duration of this holding phase depends mainly on the desired concrete strength, the climatic conditions, safety of site personnel and the likely affect of the environmental conditions surrounding the finished structure. **Flexible Formwork** provides an alternative concreting method where the shutter can remain as a lost item or feature as part of the finished structure. These forms are constructed from permeable woven textiles having the ability to allow a controlled bleeding of the excess mixing water from the filling material, whilst restraining the loss of solids. This **Porous Wall** feature is fundamental to the whole concept of flexible forms in that the resulting rapid compaction of the filling material produces a concrete of higher strength and durability. Even underwater the compressive strengths are higher than those achieved by conventional methods in the dry.

Key advantages in this area of application are:

i The technical feasibility to produce consolidated masses underwater negating the need for cofferdams and dewatering. This is particularly beneficial when tidal or wave action would otherwise affect completion.

ii It possesses the ability to produce improved qualities in the filling material, therefore widening the choice of materials to be used.

Fast-Erosion Control

Grout filled fabric mattresses have achieved worldwide recognition in applications of erosion control for canals, rivers and sea defence. The reasons for adopting these dual layer flexible forms is simple – **ease and speed of installation** and **exceptional cost effectiveness**. Incorporating woven in filter strips it provides the finished slab with sand tight weep holes for relief of hydrostatic pressure in the embankment.

Dual layer flexible forms are available in thicknesses of 50mm up to 1000mm and a variety of styles to suit functional and aesthetic design requirements.

Geotextile Projects Ltd.
SPIRELLA BUILDINGS, BRIDGE RD, LETCHWORTH, HERTS. SG6 4ET   TEL (0462) 678448

concrete society

concrete society

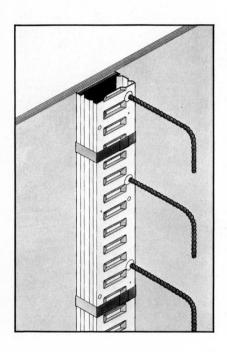 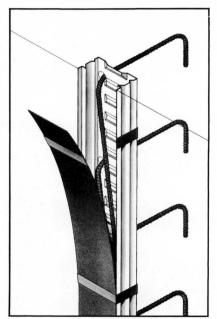 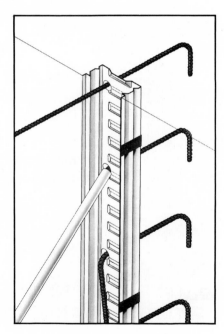

A MEMBER OF THE GLASSFIBRE REINFORCED CEMENT ASSOCIATION

SPECIALISTS IN GRC, GRG, MOULDINGS & REFURBISHMENT

LATTIS are the technical leaders in fibre reinforced cement and gypsum (plaster) components including textured or sculptured panels, columns, capitals and cornices, soffits and sunscreens.

We have extensive experience in prestige projects in the Middle and Far East where the highest quality is demanded.

LATTIS
LLANIDLOES, POWYS SY18 6DF
Telephone: 05512 2649/3161
Telex: 35579 LATTIS G

concrete society

CONCRETE RELEASE AGENTS YOU CAN DEPEND ON

Dependable Quality

Manufactured to the highest standards, the range of Logcote Chemical Release Agents and Logcreme Mould Oils have been specified on some of Britain's most prestigious projects including the Humber Bridge, G.P.O. Tower and major motorways. Grades suitable for all applications are available — from high quality versatile Logcote Super Release Agent to Logcreme — an economical dual purpose mould oil formulated for both wood and metal formwork. Both are UK WFBS Listed.

Dependable Delivery

Fast nationwide delivery free on quantities of 200 litres and over.

Dependable Prices

Very competitive prices on the full range —

RING LEEDS (0532) 452480 NOW

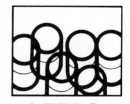

LEEDS OIL & GREASE CO. LIMITED

Chadwick Street, Leeds LS10 1LL.
Tel. (0532) 452480.
Established 1906.

Floral Mile,
Twyford,
Reading RG10 9SQ
Telephone - Wargrave (073 522) 3921
Telex - 848649 MABEYT G
Cables - Mabeyjon Reading
Fax - 073522 3941

1 Railway Street,
Scout Hill,
Ravensthorpe,
Nr. Dewsbury WF13 3EJ
Telephone - Dewsbury (0924) 460601
Telex - 557841
Fax - 0924 457932

STRONGFORM SYSTEM 160 - Soldier/Waling Equipment

160 kN Tie Load Capacity. 60kN Bending Capacity Soldier. 5.5 kN Shutter Beam Waling (equivalent to 9" x 3" timber). Full range of components and accessories. All components Hot Dip Galvanised for long life.

Shutter Detail

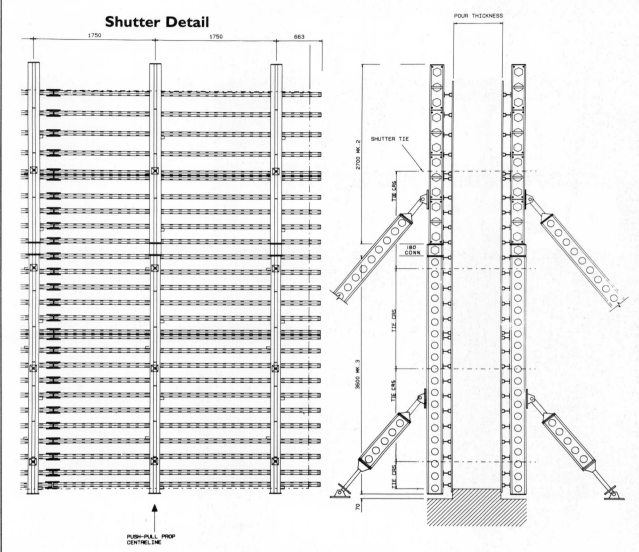

Special Detail

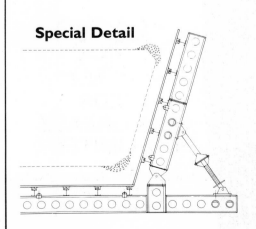

Shutter Beam Data

Properties
115 HD Waling Beam

2nd Movement of Area	122 cm^4
Section Modulus	19 cm^3
Cross Sectional Area	8.28 cm^2
Maximum resisting moment	5.5 kNm
Maximum permissible shear capacity	90kN

Standard Lengths

Mark	Length	Wt. Kg.
S3/2/1.55	1550	13.45
S3/2/3.1	3100	27.3
S3/2/3.8	3875	33.9
S3/2/4.6	4650	40.7
S3/2/6.2	6200	54.6

The shutter beam is equivalent to 9" × 3" SC4 timber waler

NOEplast Formliners
for beautiful surface textures,
the easy way!

Textured concrete is eminently suitable for all kinds of structures – in-situ or precast. At little cost NOEplast enables the modern architect or engineer to change an otherwise dull and uninspiring surface into a most attractive and interesting feature.

The wide variety of standard patterns gives choice between the bold, imaginative texture with a constantly interchanging play of light and shade, or the more sedate overall impression.

NOEplast textured formlinings offer a wide choice of natural and abstract patterns equally suitable for precast or in-situ concrete.

- tough flexible material
- often re-used 100 times or more
- faithfully reproduces the pattern each time
- wide architectural scope with over 50 standard patterns
- can also be made to your own design
- the economical way to get an attractive finish!

concrete society

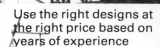
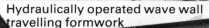

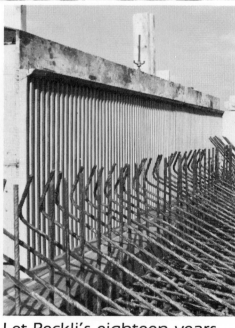

258

concrete society

Beat Clayheave Permanently...

The pressure exerted by clayheave can shift foundations and crack structures. Buildings may be protected against clayheave with CLAYBOARD, a void-former. CLAYBOARD is strong enough to support the weight of wet concrete during construction work, but is designed so that it will collapse under the force of ground heave without transmitting dangerous stresses to the building. CLAYBOARD effectively becomes a void in which any future expansion can take place.

Get the full technical details from:

Dufaylite Developments Ltd..
Cromwell Road,
St. Neots,
Cambs PE19 1QW
Tel: Huntingdon (0480) 215000
Telex: 32219

THE FORMWORK SPECIALISTS

Formwork is a specialist business and the National Association of Formwork Contractors is the only organisation representing specialist formwork contractors in the UK.

The Association strives to achieve the highest standards for the construction industry.

The NAFC is actively involved in the training of skilled operatives and has initiated a comprehensive training scheme for the industry.

The Association is also concerned with the development of technical standards through the British Standards Institution and liaison with manufacturers and suppliers.

NAFC members are reputable specialist contractors and applications for membership are vetted by the Council to ensure that the highest standards are maintained.

The Association is a member of the Building Employers Confederation and the Federation of Building Specialist Contractors.

For a list of members and further information please contact:
National Association of Formwork Contractors
82 New Cavendish Street
London W1M 8AD
Telephone: 01-580 5588 Telex: 265763

concrete society